Tamara K. Andrews

GRACE
SUFFICIENT

GRACE SUFFICIENT

A History of Women
in American Methodism
1760–1939

JEAN MILLER SCHMIDT

ABINGDON PRESS
Nashville

GRACE SUFFICIENT
A HISTORY OF WOMEN IN AMERICAN METHODISM, 1760–1939

Copyright © 1999 by Abingdon Press

This book is printed on acid-free, elemental chlorine-free paper.

Library of Congress Cataloging-in-Publication Data

Schmidt, Jean Miller.
    Grace sufficient: a history of women in American Methodism, 1760-1939 / Jean Miller Schmidt.
        p.   cm.
    Includes bibliographical references and index.
    ISBN 0-687-15675-0 (alk. paper)
    1. Women in the Methodist Church—United States—History.
2. Methodist women—United States—History.   I. Title.
BV8345.7.S35   1999
287'.082'0973—dc21   99-29271
                                                                                    CIP

Scripture quotations, unless otherwise noted, are from the Revised Standard Version of the Bible, copyright © 1946, 1952, 1971, by the Division of Christian Education of the National Council of the Churches of Christ in the USA. Used by permission.

Scripture quotations noted KJV are from the King James Version of the Bible.

99 00 01 02 03 04 05 06 07 08 — 10 9 8 7 6 5 4 3 2 1

MANUFACTURED IN THE UNITED STATES OF AMERICA

To Steve
For understanding and believing,

And to the women and men in my
Methodist extended family
For raising me in this rich tradition.

CONTENTS

ACKNOWLEDGMENTS

Over the course of the past decade, I have incurred many scholarly debts. Three very special colleagues, Kenneth E. Rowe at Drew and Russell E. Richey at Duke, my coauthors on another project, and Will Gravely at the University of Denver, have been companions on the pilgrimage toward this book. At various times they helped me think through its conceptualization, called my attention to or helped me locate key resources, read and commented on parts of the manuscript, and helped me celebrate large and small victories. I am deeply grateful for their thoughtfulness and support over many years. They are not, of course, responsible for remaining errors or omissions.

Other scholars also have contributed significantly to this work, especially Carolyn De Swarte Gifford, Rosemary Skinner Keller, Diane Lobody, Paul Chilcote, William Williams, Dee Andrews, Donald Mathews, Joanna Gillespie, Virginia Steinmetz, Greg Schneider, and Alice Knotts.

I am indebted to the Iliff School of Theology for the sabbatical leave in which I began this research and writing, and to my Iliff deans, Jane I. Smith and Delwin Brown, and Iliff faculty colleagues for supporting this project in important ways. Student assistants at Iliff have given me invaluable help with research and invigorated my spirits with their energy and enthusiasm. I am grateful to Dee Jaquet, Karen Hansen, Karen Lowe, Dorothy Rink, Becky Jo Thilges, Kama Hamilton Morton, and Kim Dickerson. A number of doctoral students in Religion and Social Change at Iliff and the University of Denver also helped: Jeanne Knepper with research on Methodist women and "holy dying," Gail Murphy-Geiss through several years of teaching United Methodist History with me as my GTA, and Maaraidzo Mutambara who read my manuscript through the eyes of a Methodist woman from Zimbabwe and gave me encouraging feedback. Margaret Manion provided skillful secretarial help and good humor early in the project.

I acknowledge with appreciation the helpful assistance of librarians and archivists at a number of United Methodist seminaries, especially Claremont, Drew, Duke, Garrett-Evangelical, Iliff, United, and Saint Paul. Special thanks go to Michael Boddy, Ken Rowe, Dale Patterson, William R. Erwin, Jr., David Himrod, Sara Myers, Paul Millette, Marshall Eidson, and Elmer J. O'Brien.

The seeds of this project were planted in the summer of 1980, when I was invited to give a course on women in the United Methodist tradition for the Yellowstone Conference Pastors' School at Flathead Lake, Montana. Since then I have also benefited significantly from the opportunity to present parts of my work in public lectures, including the J. Balmer Showers Lectures at United Theological Seminary in Dayton, the James A. Gray Lectures at Duke Divinity School, a conference on the Scholarly Writing of Denominational History sponsored by the Lilly Endowment, a lecture sponsored by the Institute for the Study of Methodism and Related Movements at Garrett-Evangelical Theological School, lectures for the annual seminar of the Virginia Conference Society for Wesleyan Studies, a lecture at the Montavilla United Methodist Church in Portland, Oregon, and the Wertsch Lectures at Saint Paul School of Theology.

I want to thank the wonderful women who were students in the course I taught on Women in Methodism in Iliff's 1998 summer school program. I wrote the Conclusion to the book and made important revisions to the manuscript after using it as a course text for the first time with them. The class members were: Debra Juarez, Jill Lane, Ruth Marsh, Karen McRae, Gwen Murphy, Peg Newell-Guazzo, Amy Stapleton, Janet Walsh, and Jane Zulauf. I appreciate both their many helpful responses and suggestions, and their own gifts and grace for ministry.

My family continued to believe in this project and understand its importance to me, even when it remained part of our lives far longer than any of us had anticipated. I thank especially my husband, Steve; my stepson, Erik, and stepdaughter, Jennifer; my mother-in-law, Ruth Schmidt; and my sister, Jan Brennan.

Finally, I will be forever grateful that I was baptized, confirmed, and in so many ways formed in this rich Methodist tradition. In a very real sense, this project began with my parents, Irene and Eugene Padberg, and with the women and men of my extended family who were so actively involved in the life of First Methodist Church of Hasbrouck Heights, New Jersey. Growing up there, I unfortunately heard little about the foremothers in the faith who fill the pages of this book. I learned more than I realized, however, at the knee of my maternal grandmother, Mae Emaline Moore Palmer, who cherished her life-service membership in the Woman's Society of Christian Service of The Methodist Church, and always wore her membership pin.

INTRODUCTION

In the fall of 1774 in Macclesfield, England, the eighteen-year-old daughter of an Anglican rector made a strange bargain with her mother: she would become a servant in her own house if her mother would permit her to attend Methodist meetings. Within weeks of negotiating this arrangement Hester Ann Roe had an evangelical conversion experience. She went on to become a member of the Methodist society and a leader of the small groups for spiritual oversight, called classes, into which the society was divided. She became a close friend of John Wesley, the founder of the Methodist movement, and eventually married one of his most trusted itinerant Methodist preachers. In 1774, however, Hester Ann Roe would have been the last person to foresee the extent to which she would become a model of Methodist piety and a spiritual guide for both women and men. Of all the early British Methodist women whose spiritual journals and letters were published, none had a greater impact on American Methodist women. Exploring her life will help us to understand her extraordinary spiritual influence.

HESTER ANN ROE ROGERS:
PATTERN OF PIETY FOR METHODIST WOMEN

Hester Ann Roe was born on January 31, 1756, in Macclesfield, a town south of Manchester in Cheshire, England, where her father was for many years a Church of England minister. She apparently showed religious inclinations from an early age. She remembered praying secretly and reading the Bible at the age of five, especially after viewing the lifeless body of her little brother who had died of smallpox. Her parents required her to give an account of the sermons she heard at church, to recite her catechism to them, and to say her prayers every morning and night. When Hester Ann was nine years old her beloved father died. On his deathbed he invoked a special blessing on his daughter, committing her to God's "gracious mercy and protection" and asking God to make her "his child and faithful servant" to her life's end.[1]

For some time after her father's death the young girl stayed at home grieving. Relatives and friends began to mock her for being so serious, and they convinced her mother to let her learn to dance, "to raise [her] spirits and improve [her] carriage." Soon Hester Ann began to delight in her proficiency at dancing and to aim to excel "not in piety, but in fashionable dress," in reading novels and attending plays; in "all the vain customs and pleasures of a delusive world." In spite of all these worldly temptations, she was confirmed at Macclesfield by the Bishop of Chester in 1769, at age thirteen, and formed strong resolutions to lead a new life.[2]

While visiting her godmother during the summer, she heard rumors that the new curate of Macclesfield, the Reverend David Simpson, was a "Methodist." For most of her family the name clearly carried negative connotations, summed up in the phrase that "to be a Methodist was to be all that was vile under a mask of piety." After returning home, young Hester Ann determined to go and hear him for herself, especially when she learned that he preached against dancing. She began to be affected by his sermons, but ridiculed them in front of her family so that no one would accuse her of becoming a Methodist.[3]

On the Sunday before Easter, April 1774, Simpson shared his own evangelical experience of conversion with the congregation and concluded his sermon by inquiring after the state of his parishioners' souls. Hester Ann felt herself "a lost, perishing, undone sinner," burst into tears, ran home and fell on her knees, and made a solemn vow "to renounce and forsake all my sinful pleasures and trifling companions." The next morning she ripped up her fine clothes, cut her hair short, and swore she would never dance again, all of which threw her relatives into confusion and dismay. She had been led to a clear sense of conviction of sin and desire for salvation, and Mr. Simpson's preaching had encouraged her to hope that God would make her "a new creature by grace."[4]

Hester Ann Roe went secretly to the Methodist service at five o'clock on Easter morning. On hearing the sermon by Samuel Bardsley, the Methodist preacher, she became convinced that these were the people of God and that they knew the way of salvation. Her mother threatened to disown her if she went again to hear the Methodists, and for eight weeks kept her closely confined at home. When other relatives tried to talk sense into the young woman, she became increasingly isolated and spent more and more of her time in private prayer. The usual summer holiday at her godmother's only made her feel keenly her separation from the "dear people of God." In October 1774 Hester Ann told her mother she was determined to leave home and take the job of a servant rather than be kept from the Methodists. At length Mrs. Roe agreed to the unusual bargain: if Hester Ann would become a servant in her own home she might attend the Methodist meetings. Family advisers assured the mother that the young woman would soon tire of this arrangement and that at least she would remain within the family circle.[5]

Hester Ann Roe began her new life as a servant on November 1. Only ten days later, on November 11, she had her own evangelical experience of (what the Methodists called) justification by faith and new birth. As she described it: "Again it came, 'Only believe.' 'Lord Jesus,' said I, 'I will, I do believe; I now venture my whole salvation upon thee.' . . . In that moment my fetters were broken; my bands were loosed; and my soul was set at liberty. . . . I was truly a new creature, and seemed to be in a new world! I could do nothing but love and praise my God."[6]

Mrs. Roe became very ill in the early summer of 1775. For about six weeks Hester Ann sat up with her at night until, she recalled, "at last my body began to fail. Indeed it was no wonder; for besides all my labour and fatigue, I used rigorous fasting."[7] The doctor attending her mother insisted that the daughter could not continue to sacrifice her life. He spoke to her godmother, and a "proper servant" was obtained to care for the household duties, including nursing her ill mother. This was in August 1775. "But it was then nearly too late; my health had received such a wound, as it did not recover in many years."[8]

Hester Ann Roe's spiritual struggles continued. In the language of Wesleyan theology, she was seeking Christian perfection or sanctification. She claimed that she retained her assurance of being a child of God, but that she felt the remains of "anger, self-will, and unbelief often rising, which occasioned a degree of heaviness and sorrow." Not knowing what to do, she resolved "to use more self-denial of all kinds, and whatever it cost me with respect to health or life, more fasting and prayer." Some told her that the Christian's warfare ends only with the death of the body. She began to believe them and to long to die in order to be free from sin. She could not be persuaded to take anything to restore her health, which was declining rapidly, and by the end of December she was so weak that she was confined to her bed.[9]

The turning point occurred on February 15, 1776. When a visiting cousin begged her to take medicine, she told him she would rather die than live. He rebuked her for setting up her own will above God's and asked her a crucial question, "Are you willing to live forty years, if the Lord please?" At first she felt "a shrinking at the thought," but after he left she fell on her knees in prayer and asked God's help. She summed up her struggle in this way: "I felt a thousand fears suggested, that if I lived, I might lose what I now enjoyed of the love of God; and perhaps be one day a dishonour to his cause. But I said, Lord, thy grace is ever sufficient; thou art as able to keep me a thousand years as one day!"[10] Still troubled by a sense of her own unworthiness, she was willing to live if her life would glorify God and be useful to other "immortal souls," but asked God not to let her "live a moment longer than I live wholly for thee."[11] She wrote in her journal, "The Lord brought me this day to an entire sacrifice of my will respecting life and death, and entered into a solemn covenant with my soul. . . . Now I can say with my whole heart in this respect, Thy will be done. Only perfect me in love, and let me live to thee, and spare me as long or as short a period as thou seest fit."[12] Not surprisingly, "from this day" she "speedily recovered strength."[13]

In a few weeks she was well enough to attend Methodist services again, and in listening to one of the Methodist preachers she came finally to understand what John Wesley and the Methodists believed about Christian perfection: that sin was destroyed not by death, but by "the power of the living God."[14] She was learning to trust not in her own heroic strivings, but in moment by moment dependence on the grace of God. On February 22, one week later, she finally realized her desire to be perfected in love.[15]

Hester Ann Roe now entered a period of great religious productivity. On April 1, 1776, she met John Wesley for the first time, and soon after became a Methodist class leader.[16] The twenty-year-old woman and the seventy-three-year-old Methodist leader began a correspondence that would last until he died in 1791. He addressed her fondly as "my dear Hetty." She spoke and wrote to him as "Dear Mr. Wesley," and looked forward to meeting with him on his annual visits to Macclesfield.[17] Hester Ann's religious influence grew as she led the classes, visited the sick, and prayed, testified, and exhorted in both private and public meetings.[18] She was still financially dependent on her mother and continued to live with her until 1784 (although her cousin Robert Roe named her as his heir when he died in 1782).

In 1782 the Methodist preacher James Rogers was appointed to Macclesfield, and he and his wife, Martha, became close friends to Hester Ann Roe. When Martha suddenly became gravely ill in 1783, Hester Ann cared for her like a sister. She was astonished, however, when Mrs. Rogers confided in her the strong desire that after her death her husband should marry Hester Ann. On August 19, 1784, with John Wesley's approval, Hester Ann Roe married the newly widowed Rogers and embarked with him on the strenuous life of a Methodist itinerant preacher's wife, first in Dublin and Cork, Ireland, and then in London. She not only became a stepmother to Rogers's two children, but the couple also had several children of their own in their ten years of marriage.[19]

In 1790 John Wesley appointed James Rogers to City Road Chapel. The couple resided in Wesley's house there and attended him in his last illness. In August 1792 the conference stationed James Rogers in Spitalfields (London), where Hester Ann Rogers died on October 10, 1794, at age thirty-eight, shortly after giving birth to a son. In his funeral sermon Bishop Thomas Coke said of her, "Almost everything that is good may be said of her, if she be viewed as a daughter, a wife, a mother, a friend, a private Christian, or as a public person, particularly as a leader of classes and bands in the Methodist society. Almighty grace, to which alone be ascribed all the glory, got to itself indeed a victory in this amiable woman."[20]

As Earl Kent Brown pointed out, Hester Ann Roe Rogers's life after her conversion experience was divided almost neatly in half, providing an outstanding example of both the piety and activities of an ordinary Methodist woman, and in her married years, the life of an itinerant Methodist preacher's wife.[21] Well versed in both the Bible and Methodist theology and an unusually gifted writer, particularly of spiritual letters, she was not only a pattern of piety for other Methodist women but a sensitive and skilled spiritual guide and counselor to both men and women. That she was her cousin Robert Roe's spiritual counselor is very clear in the series of letters between them from 1775 to 1780. The following letter from Hester Ann to her cousin, written in December 1778, is a good example:

> "My grace is sufficient for thee," saith the Lord; he who knows all your trials. Now, when by faith we embrace and rely on this promise, knowing he who is faithful will perform his word; we are strengthened by a sweet peace, and well-grounded confidence and hope, that shall never make us ashamed. And, while we continue to live by this faith, we more than conquer, whether our joy be little or great.[22]

Her advice seems to have been requested especially by those who were seeking sanctification. In May 1778 she responded to Robert's questions: "Yes, my dear friend, leave Christ to answer every temptation that besets you. He hath said, 'My grace is sufficient for thee.' This is enough: be not faithless, but believing. You ask if I am not in a delusion respecting my experience of perfect love? Blessed be God, I have not the shadow of doubt. . . . By looking constantly to Jesus, I receive fresh strength in every time of need. I know I am *now* right, and I trust him for all that is to come." A few months later she advised a Miss Bourn, of Newcastle: "It [sanctification] is retained, as well as received, by simple faith. We can have no stock of grace on hand, but live moment by moment, hanging and depending on the adorable Jesus. In him there is a full supply of all we want, or can want."[23]

In her spiritual journal Hester Ann Rogers quoted Scripture, verses of hymns (the pocket-size Methodist hymnbook having become for her, as for many early Methodists, a devotional book), and Wesley's sermons. She described the help she received from the typical Methodist means of grace, including band and class meetings, reading the Bible (on her knees), and attending the sacrament of the Lord's Supper. Her spiritual autobiography also demonstrates the importance of evangelical religion for young, single women as a source of identity and fulfillment apart from their families. Subsequent chapters will show how other young women followed her example, challenging parental authority in becoming Methodists and similarly adopting the countercultural lifestyle required of the early Methodist people (such as wearing simple dress and giving up dancing and other pleasures of fine society).

In concluding his funeral sermon, Dr. Coke summed up her influence in this way:

> For years before she married . . . a very considerable part of her time was daily spent in answering cases of conscience, spreading forth the loveliness and excellences of Christ to penitents, and in building up believers in their most holy faith. She then was a leader of classes and bands, and a mother in Israel to the young believers intrusted to her care. After her marriage, she still became more extensively useful.[24]

To this her husband added: "While speaking to, or praying with [those who attended her classes], many, very many, have been enabled to witness a clear sense of God's forgiving love; and others, at the same time, have obtained salvation from inbred sin—a doctrine this, of which she had the clearest views. And to its validity, her own conduct bore a constant testimony."[25] An example to others while she lived, Hester Ann Roe Rogers became a preeminent model of piety for American Methodist women through the publication of her spiritual journals and letters after her death.

RELIGIOUS LIVES OF ORDINARY WOMEN

Historians of women and American religion have tended to focus on women's religious activities rather than on women's religious lives. Studies of early American religion and spirituality have usually depended upon the journals and sermons of male preachers. In order to try to understand the religious lives of ordinary Methodist women, I have looked at their diaries, letters, spiritual autobiographies, and the accounts of their pious lives and holy deaths that appeared as obituaries in publications like the *Methodist Magazine.*

Exploration of women's religious lives can tell us much about the religious appeal of Methodism. In the pages that follow I have attempted to achieve a balance between the chronological description and thematic interpretation of Methodist women's history, and a more intimate portrait of individual women in this tradition. There are powerful stories of faith here that are part of the shared history of Methodist people, both women and men. I have also found that as contemporary women (especially, but not exclusively, in the United Methodist tradition) struggle with their own sense of call, they often resonate in powerful ways with the faith stories of these religious foremothers.

"GRACE SUFFICIENT"

In her spiritual writings Hester Ann Rogers referred frequently to the biblical promise in 2 Corinthians 12:9: "My grace is sufficient for you, for my power [*dynamis*] is made perfect in weakness." In this she was typical of eighteenth- and nineteenth-century Methodist women. This "grace sufficient" theme seems to have been central to their spirituality, particularly in relation to the Wesleyan doctrine of holiness or sanctification, but also as they tried to make sense of the struggles of their daily lives.

Grace was sufficient to keep them in the way of salvation. They understood what Albert Outler would later describe as the "heart of Wesley's gospel": that "lively sense of God's grace at work . . . sufficient grace in all, irresistible grace in none."[26] For these Methodist women, sanctification was not primarily a matter of virtue, but moment by moment dependence on divine grace. As one of them expressed it with simple eloquence and profound insight: "O that I may . . . be more and more assimilated to the image of God; possessing that inward and outward holiness without which the gates of Heaven will be closed to me.—Hence may I learn that as the present moment is all I can ensure; so constant and present living on Christ is my duty and privilege: and to depend on that grace which he has said shall be sufficient.—This is living by faith; this is the life I desire to live."[27]

Methodist women fundamentally affirmed the sufficiency of grace for all things, for living as well as for dying. Like Hester Ann Rogers they knew from experience that sometimes living is harder than dying. In the midst of their sufferings, griefs, illnesses, anxieties, and cares they relied on the assurance that God's grace would be sufficient for their day (Deuteronomy 33:25), for their need, as they needed it. Almost constantly reminded of the precariousness of life, they accepted it as a gift and attempted to live it a day at a time.

In their religious lives, as expressed in their journals, Methodist women trusted that grace would be sufficient to enable them to respond to God's call, even when they felt inadequate and unworthy. Contrary to our image of them, most of these women did not simply remain at home, but engaged, at considerable risk, in bridging private and public worlds as they endeavored to do what God required of them. Although they frequently asked, "Why me, Lord?" their ultimate trust in the sufficiency of grace freed them to share what they had. We will trace the variations on this "grace sufficient" theme throughout the book.

Women in American Methodism

Since the early 1980s, scholars have begun to recover and interpret the histories of women in a number of Protestant denominations.[28] Within The United Methodist Church, early efforts to encourage research and publication related to the history of women in this family of denominations resulted in the groundbreaking Women in New Worlds conference held in Cincinnati, Ohio, February 1–3, 1980. Attended by some four hundred registrants, it was the first national conference on church women's history of any major church tradition.[29]

Two volumes of papers from that conference were published under the same title, *Women in New Worlds*.[30] Until they went out of print in 1990, they helped to reshape the teaching and writing of United Methodist history and served as a catalyst for the recovery of women's history at the grassroots level.

When I began teaching United Methodist history at Iliff School of Theology in Denver in 1975, the only available book on the history of women in this tradition was Elaine Magalis's *Conduct Becoming to a Woman*, published through the Women's Division of the Board of Global Ministries of The United Methodist Church in 1973, and now out of print.[31] Lively and readable, it was an important pioneering effort. What is now greatly needed, and for the first time really possible, is a comprehensive narrative history of women in the American Methodist movement and family of denominations. This work attempts to meet that need.

A NARRATIVE HISTORY: OVER ONE HUNDRED SEVENTY-FIVE YEARS

As a narrative history, this is a work of synthesis, a beginning effort at describing and interpreting the larger picture into which the growing number of monographic and smaller studies fit. I have aimed to incorporate in this work the accumulated scholarship on the history of women in this tradition, and to supplement it with my own research where that has seemed fruitful or necessary.[32] My intention is to make this account as inclusive as possible in a number of ways: inclusive of the history of women in the predecessor bodies of The United Methodist Church as well as the broader American Methodist family of denominations, racially and ethnically inclusive, and representative of the rich diversity of women's experience across the nation and over nearly two centuries of Methodist history in this country.

It will be evident that this project builds upon and shares much with the new social history, the feminist movement and women's history since the late 1960s, African American history and other attempts to recover the histories of people of color, and efforts to map new denominational histories, including a new American

Methodist history. I hope this book will appeal not only to United Methodists and others in the Methodist family of denominations, but also more broadly to all who are interested in the religious history of American women,[33] denominational history, and U.S. religious history.

Actually this volume does not carry the history of women in American Methodism up to the present. In 1939 three bodies of Methodists, the Methodist Episcopal Church (1784), the Methodist Protestant Church (1830), and the Methodist Episcopal Church, South (1845), reunited to form The Methodist Church. In 1968 The Methodist Church joined with the Evangelical United Brethren Church, itself the result of the 1946 union of the Evangelical Church and the United Brethren Church, to form The United Methodist Church. With all of these mergers the history of women in the expanding tradition has grown richer and more complex.

To take just one example, anyone wishing to study the twentieth-century history of women organized for mission in this tradition would have to look at the histories of no fewer than twenty-one separate women's organizations. Similarly the story of the eventual success of women's struggle for ordination and full clergy rights in this tradition carries the reader to 1956 and beyond. Finally, contemporary attention to the status, role, and full participation of women in The United Methodist Church involves very recent history, with increasingly plentiful sources and the possibility of oral interviews with witnesses to and participants in this history. In my view, the trajectory of themes introduced in this volume comes to a natural culmination in 1939. An epilogue at the end of this work therefore looks ahead to a projected second volume that will give the full twentieth-century account of women united for mission, the continuing struggle for clergy rights, and subsequent issues of women's roles and participation in the church.

WOMEN'S ROLES IN THE AMERICAN METHODIST FAMILY OF DENOMINATIONS

In the countercultural and spiritually egalitarian atmosphere of the early American Methodist movement, women's voices were encouraged, and they played crucial roles in the establishment, expansion, and nurturing of Methodist societies. I have used the term "Mother in Israel" as a predominant image to describe women's roles in American Methodism in this first period, 1760s–1820s. Chapter 1 focuses on women's religious lives in these years; chapter 2 explores women's roles.

As the Methodist family of denominations became increasingly respectable and middle-class, the appropriate sphere for women was more clearly prescribed. I suggest that the primary image from the 1820s to the 1860s was that of the "True Methodist Woman." Chapter 3 illustrates Methodist versions of Victorian domestic ideology in advice books for women written by Methodist clergy in the middle years of the nineteenth century. Methodist women responded in a range of ways, some attempting to meet the ideal, others working within woman's sphere but testing the elasticity of its boundaries, a few protesting against the whole notion of separate spheres for women and men. This chapter explores prescription and reality in the lives of representative Methodist women from both the North and the South.

In spite of the prescription, women attempted to be faithful to God's claim on their lives. Chapter 4 looks at women who experienced a call to preach in these years, and how they responded to that call. Also in this period, women were becoming itinerant preachers' wives and holiness evangelists. Chapters 5 and 6 investigate their struggles to balance domestic and religious responsibilities.

In the 1880s, Frances Willard, Methodist laywoman and prominent leader of the Woman's Christian Temperance Union (WCTU), described the mission of the new ideal of womanhood as making "the whole world homelike." With this image of the "New Methodist Woman" we enter the much more familiar territory of woman's public work in the church and the world, beginning in the 1860s and continuing well into the twentieth century. Chapter 7 examines new spheres of usefulness for church women: the Ladies' and Pastors' Christian Union, the WCTU, and women's foreign and home missionary societies. Chapter 8 turns to the opening years of the struggle for women's ordination in the predecessor bodies of what is now The United Methodist Church.

In the 1880s the deaconess movement emerged as a new public ministry for women. Chapter 9 explores the possibilities for service opened by this movement. Chapter 10 demonstrates the difficulties women faced in gaining the right to participate fully as laypeople in the church. In chapter 11 we turn to racial-ethnic women in the Methodist family, examining how they made the Methodism brought to them by missionaries meaningful for themselves and their people and began to emerge into new positions of leadership. Chapter 12 explores Methodist women's roles as citizens and employed women, as licensed local preachers, and as social reformers in the first two decades after women finally achieved the right to vote in 1920. The Epilogue looks ahead to the culmination of all these struggles in the period from 1939 to 1968 and beyond.

WOMEN IN JOHN WESLEY'S METHODISM

The history of women in American Methodism can only be properly understood against the background of women's prominent leadership role in the eighteenth-century Methodist revival in Britain. Susanna Wesley, wife of the Reverend Samuel Wesley and mother of John and Charles Wesley, set the tone for such leadership by moving into a self-conscious pastoral ministry to her family and even to her husband's parish at Epworth after her childbearing years were ended.[34] Susanna's sense of pastoral vocation was reinforced in 1711 by reading an *Account* of Danish missionaries to the East Indies. "At last it came into my mind," she wrote in her journal, "though I am not a man, nor a minister of the gospel, . . . I might do somewhat more than I do. . . . I might pray more for *the people,* and speak with more warmth to those with whom I have an opportunity of conversing. However, I resolved to begin with my own children."[35]

Susanna began by setting aside an hour every evening for individual attention to the moral and spiritual development of her two sons and six daughters living at home. During her husband's lengthy winter absences to attend the Convocation of Clergy in London, she formed a Sunday evening society at the rectory. Here she gathered her household together to sing the Psalms, listen to her read printed sermons, and worship following the Order for Evening Prayer. During the winter of 1711–12, neighbors from the Epworth parish joined the family until the numbers attending the Sunday evening society were above two hundred. The Reverend Godfrey Inman, the curate in charge of performing parish duties in Samuel Wesley's absence, complained about these activities to the rector and Samuel Wesley wrote sharply about them to his wife. In a letter dated February 25, Susanna replied:

> I shall in as few words as possible tell you my thoughts. . . . There is not that I can hear of more than 3 or 4 that is against our meeting, of which Inman is the chief, for no other reason as I suppose but that he thinks the sermons I read better than his own. . . . This one thing has brought more people to Church than ever any thing did in so short a time. We used not to have above 20 or 25 at Evening Service, whereas now we have between 2 & 300 which is many more than ever came before to hear Inman in the morning. . . . Now I beseech you weigh all things in an impartial balance. On the one side, the honour of Almighty God, the doing much good to many souls, the friendship of the best among whom we live; on the other . . . the malicious senseless objections of a few scandalous persons. . . . I should add but a few words more. If you do after all think fit to dissolve this assembly, do not tell me any more that you desire me to do it; for that will not satisfy my conscience, but send me your positive command in such full and express terms as may absolve me from all guilt and punishment for neglecting this opportunity of doing good to souls, when you and I shall appear before the great and awful tribunal of our Lord Jesus Christ.[36]

Wisely, Samuel Wesley allowed the parsonage society to continue; the young John Wesley was a thoughtful member of it. His mother's example was a primary influence on John Wesley's attitude toward the leadership of women in the early Methodist societies.

For a full consideration of the role of women in early British Methodism, there are now a number of longer studies. Paul Wesley Chilcote's *John Wesley and the Women Preachers of Early Methodism* is the most thorough study of women's leadership, particularly public speaking, in the eighteenth-century Methodist revival and of John Wesley's gradual acceptance of women's call to preach within the early Methodist movement.[37] Throughout the eighteenth century, the ratio of female to male members of the Methodist societies was typically 2 to 1. Women were also "conspicuous as pioneers" in the establishment and expansion of Methodism.[38] Both facts profoundly affected the attitudes of the leaders toward the place of women in the movement.

BAND LEADERS, CLASS LEADERS, AND SICK VISITORS

Early Methodism offered substantial opportunities for lay leadership within the movement. The offices of band leader, class leader, and sick visitor were particularly significant areas of leadership for women. Wesley subdivided his early Methodist societies into small, homogeneous groups called "bands," according to sex and marital status. From 1742, all Methodist societies were also divided into "classes" of about twelve persons each, for the purpose of pastoral care and oversight of the membership and mutual accountability.[39] John Wesley himself appointed the men and women who were band and class leaders. Such leaders had to be persons of spiritual and emotional maturity. "Not only were they highly visible as representatives of the Methodist movement, but they were charged with the pastoral oversight of souls under their care." The most essential qualifications for this high responsibility were a clear understanding and experience of "God's saving grace and the way of salvation," the desire to assist and nurture others in this way of salvation, and personal qualities of integrity and trustworthiness.[40]

Because of the preponderance of women in the Methodist societies and the sexually segregated nature of the bands, there were large numbers of women band leaders. The more "family"-oriented classes were sexually mixed and these were more often led by men. However, where the classes were sexually segregated, women usually led the female classes and occasionally were even asked to lead men's classes. It was possible for women to exercise the role of class leader because of the expectation and encouragement that all members, women as well as men, would "speak freely" in these small groups.[41]

From the 1740s, Wesley also instituted the office of sick visitor—one who ministered to both the spiritual and temporal necessities of those who were sick. He saw this as related to the role of deacon or deaconess in the early church, and as a duty for women as well as men:

> Herein there is no difference; "there is neither male nor female in Christ Jesus." . . . You, as well as men, are rational creatures. You, like them, were made in the image of God; you are equally candidates for immortality; you too are called of God, as you have time, to "do good unto all men." Be "not disobedient to the heavenly calling." Whenever you have opportunity, do all the good you can, particularly to your poor, sick neighbour.[42]

Visiting the sick became another important training ground for women.

PRAYING, TESTIFYING, EXHORTING

Of greatest importance with regard to female preaching were three modes of public speaking that Chilcote aptly refers to as "communicating the Gospel in all but preaching": praying in public, testifying, and exhorting. All three were based on spiritual authority and empowerment and "grounded in the evangelical urge to save souls."[43] Public prayer was most accessible for women because it often took place initially in the home or in female prayer meetings. Yet it is clear from women's diaries that they often had to struggle to overcome their reticence and timidity about praying in public even in these more familiar settings. Some women, like Sarah Crosby and later Ann Cutler (known affectionately as "Praying Nanny"), became "highly gifted in the art of prayer."[44]

Other occasions for Christian fellowship, particularly the love feast, afforded opportunity for women as well as men to bear witness to God's transforming work in their lives. The love feast was patterned after the *agape* meals in the early church and contemporary Moravian services, and involved both the symbolic sharing of a simple meal and a more public spiritual sharing than that of the bands and classes. In the open fellowship and free expression of the love feasts, women gained important experience in communicating the gospel in public. John Wesley himself stressed the importance of women's speaking on these occasions: "The very design of the lovefeast is free and familiar conversation, in which every man, **yea, every woman,** [emphasis mine] has liberty to speak whatever may be to the glory of God."[45]

While preaching involved taking a text and interpreting it, exhorting consisted primarily of urging sinners to repent and turn to God. In the General Rules of the Methodist societies, members were enjoined to do good to the souls of others "by instructing, reproving, or exhorting all they have any intercourse with."[46] Exhortations were common in the classes and bands, but they also frequently followed the preaching of an itinerant. When there were no preachers available, an exhorter might speak in place of a sermon. The practice of exhorting was also an important feature of what Methodists regarded as "holy dying." Wesley encouraged women to "exhort their fellow Methodists in a variety of contexts, from the intimacy of casual conversation to the formality of public services of worship."[47] Considerable numbers of them felt this to be their duty and did function as exhorters.

FEMALE PREACHERS

In the years from 1761 to John Wesley's death in 1791, women's leadership in the Methodist revival was gradually expanded to include female preaching. It is only possible here to review briefly the steps by which this occurred. Sarah Crosby was almost certainly the first woman to receive John Wesley's informal authorization for her preaching activities. Converted in 1749 at the age of twenty, she experienced sanctification in 1760 and soon after began to experience a call to preach. At a Sunday evening class meeting in February 1761, nearly two hundred persons were present to hear Sarah Crosby's exhortation. Feeling she had come "perilously close to preaching"[48] she immediately wrote to John Wesley asking his guidance. Wesley's response deserves to be quoted in full; written from London February 14, 1761, it was addressed to "My Dear Sister":

Hitherto, I think you have not gone too far. You could not well do less. I apprehend all you can do more is, when you meet again, to tell them simply, "You lay me under a great difficulty. The Methodists do not allow of women preachers; neither do I take upon me any such character. But I will just nakedly tell you what is in my heart." This will in a great measure obviate the grand objection and prepare for [Methodist preacher] J[ohn] Hampson's coming. I do not see that you have broken any law. Go on calmly and steadily. If you have time, you may read to them the *Notes* on any chapter before you speak a few words, or one of the most awakening sermons, as other women have done long ago.[49]

The next crucial step in the transformation of John Wesley's attitude toward women preaching involved the activities of a remarkable woman, Mary Bosanquet. After experiencing an evangelical conversion in 1762, Mary Bosanquet (who came from a wealthy family in Essex) joined forces with Mary Ryan (a woman born of poor parents) to establish a Christian community in Leytonstone on the model of Wesley's Kingswood school and orphanage. This community took in some of the most destitute children and adults, a total of thirty-five children and thirty-four adults (chiefly widows) in five years. Eventually Sarah Crosby also became a part of the Leytonstone community. In 1768, the whole community moved to Yorkshire in order to expand its sphere of service. Known as Cross Hall, the new residence in the area of Leeds became "a vital center of Methodist worship and witness."[50]

In June of 1771, Mary Bosanquet wrote to John Wesley to ask his advice concerning the work in which she and Sarah Crosby were engaged at Cross Hall. Some of the Methodist preachers had begun to object to women's speaking, claiming it was "unscriptural." She explained her dilemma: "I believe I am called to do all I can for God, and in order thereto, when I am asked to go with Br. T. to a prayer meeting, I may both sing, pray and converse with them, either particularly, or in general, according to the numbers. Likewise when Br. T. goes to preach in little country places, after he has done, I believe I may speak a few words to the people, and pray with them."[51]

Mary Bosanquet's letter is probably the first defense of women's preaching in Methodism. On the basis of Scripture, she argues that women were occasionally called by God to preach and that the Pauline texts prohibiting women's speaking referred only to specific situations. She points to scriptural examples of women who could not be accused of immodesty but did publicly declare God's message. She concludes: "Ob[jection]:—But all these were extraordinary calls; sure you will not say yours is an extraordinary call? An[swer]:— If I did not believe so, I would not act in an extraordinary manner. I do not believe every woman is called to speak publicly, no more than every man to be a Methodist preacher, yet some have an extraordinary call to it, and woe be to them if they obey it not."[52]

In response to her letter, John Wesley first acknowledged that the "extraordinary call" allowed room for women preachers. In a letter from Londonderry to her on June 13, 1771, Wesley wrote:

> I think the strength of the cause rests there, on your having an *Extraordinary Call*. So, I am persuaded, has every one of our Lay Preachers: otherwise I could not countenance his preaching at all. It is plain to me that the whole work of God termed Methodism is an extraordinary dispensation of His Providence. Therefore I do not wonder if several things occur therein which do not fall under ordinary rules of discipline. St. Paul's ordinary rule was, "I permit not a woman to speak in the congregation." Yet in extraordinary cases he made a few exceptions; at Corinth, in particular.[53]

On September 17, 1776, Mary Bosanquet preached to several thousand people on the edge of a quarry at Goker and then standing on the steps of a horse block in the street at Huddersfield. Her journal account of this experience is perhaps the best-known description of the preaching of a woman in the Wesleyan revival. Even a brief quotation conveys something of its flavor. "While the people [in Huddersfield] were singing the hymn," she said, "I felt a renewed conviction to speak in the name of the Lord. My bodily strength seemed to return each moment. . . . So solemn a time I have seldom known; my voice was clear enough to reach them all; and when we concluded I felt stronger than when we began."[54] In November 1781, she married John Fletcher and embarked upon what was essentially a copastorate in his parish at Madeley until his death in 1785.

Between 1781 and his own death a decade later, John Wesley's changed attitude toward female preachers led to the official recognition of a number of women within the Methodist Connection. Sarah Mallet is perhaps the best known. Wesley first met her in early December 1786. Since 1781 she had experienced strange seizures, which only ceased when she finally conceded to God's call and began a public ministry of preaching. John Wesley not only gave her his advice and encouragement, he also made it possible for her to receive the formal authorization of the Methodist Conference meeting in Manchester in 1787. The "note" that was sent to her said: "We give the right hand of fellowship to Sarah Mallet, and have no objection to her being a preacher in our connexion, so long as she preaches the Methodist doctrines, and attends to our discipline."[55] Wesley continued to advise her on her preaching and support her ministry until his death.

Paul Chilcote identified forty-two women preachers among the Methodists prior to 1803.[56] After Wesley's death, a new generation of women preachers had to contend with the struggle between charismatic and authoritarian views of the ministry in a period of institutional consolidation. Under the leadership of Jabez Bunting, the Methodist Conference ruled in 1803 that any woman convinced that she had "an extraordinary call from God to speak in public" was advised to address "her **own sex,** and **those only.**"[57] After 1803, increasing numbers of aspiring women preachers left the Wesleyan Methodists to join groups like the Primitive Methodists or Bible Christians.[58]

Throughout the eighteenth century women gave prominent leadership to the Methodist movement in Britain. Constituting about two-thirds of the membership of the early Methodist societies, women took important initiative in the expansion of Methodism and held many of the crucially important lay leadership positions on the local level. All Methodists were expected to testify to their faith, grow in their Christian living, and exhort others to seek salvation. Women were encouraged, indeed required, to speak in Methodist meetings. Some of them were even accepted as preachers among the Methodist people.

In the 1760s, laypeople who had been Methodists in Britain began to immigrate to North America and organize Methodist societies here. When John Wesley's appointed missionaries arrived in 1769 and following, they found an already flourishing Methodist movement. Chapters 1 and 2 explore American Methodist women's religious lives and leadership roles in the founding era.

PART I

"MOTHERS IN ISRAEL"

1760s — 1820s

1

"GRACE SUFFICIENT"
Women's Religious Lives in the Founding Era

Early Methodist spirituality placed a high value on biography and spiritual narrative. For John Wesley, tradition was as much a matter of actual examples of Christian living or "genuine Christianity" as it was a repository of doctrine.[1] The religious experiences of the early Methodist people were encouraged, articulated, shared in a supportive community, and often recorded and published for their edifying and confirming impact on the lives of others. Relating one's conversion experience was a common characteristic of evangelical revival movements. In the class and band meetings and the larger love feast that were features of Methodist evangelicalism, women and men alike learned to tell the story of God's grace working in their lives and to experience that working in accord with the narratives they heard.[2] As Diane Lobody has argued, "The narrative structure of Wesleyan spirituality demanded that women tell their stories"; and, by so doing, it "opened a grammar of liberty" for them.[3]

PIOUS MEMOIRS

Fortunately this means that there are rich resources for studying the religious lives of ordinary Methodist women. One such source is the genre of religious writings of evangelical (not only Methodist) women described by Joanna Gillespie as "pious memoirs."[4] Women's pious memoirs, consisting of a short biography by the editor and extracts from the spiritual journals and letters of the subject, were usually compiled and published posthumously by relatives of the deceased or by clergy. Exploring one's spiritual development through diaries and letters was not only consistent with the practice of the Wesleys and the early Oxford Methodists, but became, for women, an important means of self-construction.[5] Not all women, of course, had the education or leisure to keep a spiritual journal.[6] Their voices were not, for that reason, lost to their own or future generations. Early Methodist publications like the *Arminian Magazine* and the *Methodist Magazine* regularly featured accounts of the holy lives and victorious deaths of both men and women (but more frequently women), including poor and illiterate women, that were submitted by Methodist preachers and others. We are also learning how to hear women's voices and their testimony about what the early Methodist experience meant for them, indirectly, through the journals and memoirs of the Methodist circuit riding preachers.[7] The early chapters draw heavily on these narrative materials.

Although (male) pastors had a considerable role in editing and interpreting women's published memoirs, female models were crucial for women's religious lives and also served as a pattern for their spiritual journals. The memoirs of both English and American women were part of "a functional pious memoir canon . . . , all reprinted and circulated among evangelical readers in America."[8] When Methodist itinerant preachers began carrying with them and selling to the Methodist people the publications of the Methodist Book Concern, one of the consistent best-sellers was "Hester Ann Rogers."[9]

A SPIRITUALITY OF "GRACE SUFFICIENT"

In their diaries and letters, Methodist women referred frequently to the scriptural promise in 2 Corinthians 12:9: "My grace is sufficient for you." Their pious memoirs offer convincing evidence that this "grace sufficient" theme was central to the spiritual lives and experience of ordinary Methodist women. As I suggested in the introduction, it was related both to women's understanding of the early Methodist theology of Christian perfection or holiness (as moment by moment dependence on the grace of God), and to their attempts to make sense of the struggles of their lives, especially regarding affliction and vocation.

After their American publication in 1804, the spiritual autobiography and letters of English Methodist Hester Ann Rogers were widely read by nineteenth-century American Methodist women. She became for them an important pattern of piety and spiritual guide. We saw how young Hester Ann Roe's coming to depend upon the sufficiency of divine grace was a critical turning point in her spiritual development and recovery from a near-fatal illness. From then on when she struggled with doubt and uncertainty, she was able to rely on that scriptural promise. As she explained, "Those precious words, 'My grace is sufficient for thee,' shall stand firm as the pillars of heaven: and when the enemy shall tell me— In such and such a trial thou wilt be entangled and overcome, I tell him, 'My Lord hath promised strength equal to my day,' and all his darts are instantly repelled."[10]

Women in the late-eighteenth and early-nineteenth centuries lived with the constant threat of illness and death, whether the ever-present possibility of their own death in childbirth, or the frequent loss of a child, or even a spouse. Referring to her "bodily distress," Mrs. Mary Mason wrote in her journal in 1822: "I found his grace, as heretofore, more than sufficient. I think the Lord does not bestow premature or unnecessary grace. All we can expect is grace equal to our day." Rejoicing at the safe birth of a daughter in 1828, she recorded in her diary, "Glory to his holy name for grace sufficient for our day."[11]

This spirituality of "grace sufficient" seems to have been a crucially important defining element in early American Methodism. In describing "the Methodist ideology," historian Donald Mathews claimed that a major difference between early Methodists and other evangelical Protestants was that the conversion event (justification, or forgiveness, and new birth) in Methodism was "no guarantee of final perseverance. The Methodist could not say 'I have been saved!' and leave it at that. The Methodist had to say: 'I have been saved, I am saved, I may be saved, I shall one day be saved.'"[12] In 1824 Elizabeth Lyon Roe, pioneer in Illinois Methodism, wrote in her journal, "I asked the Lord to take me to that better world, that I might sin no more, but I was reminded that I was a probationer, and that there were many duties and trials before me, but I felt assured that His grace would be sufficient for the day."[13]

Early Methodist women and men experienced the release and joy of forgiveness and a new relationship to God, but Wesleyan theology and practice urged them not to stop there. By actively cooperating with God's grace they were to press on toward sanctification and holy living. When Hester Ann Rogers longed to die in order to be free from the power of sin, she was led to trust not in her own prodigious efforts but in "grace sufficient." When she finally realized her desire to be perfected in love, she wanted to help others understand that experience and find it for themselves. She explained in a letter to her cousin: "You ask how I obtained this great salvation? I answer, Just as I obtained the pardon of my sin—*by simple faith.* . . . I knew the faithfulness of my God, and ventured on the promise . . . 'My grace is sufficient for thee.' O the preciousness of these words! I shall praise God in eternity that they are written in his book. This, and other such promises, have been proof for me against every opposition and trial I have met with."[14]

Catherine Livingston Garrettson was another early Methodist woman who longed for sanctification and submitted her daily life to rigorous scrutiny in order that no unknown sin might hinder her relationship with God. A member of the prominent Livingston family of New York State, Catherine was converted the day before her thirty-fifth birthday in 1787, and would later marry Methodist preacher Freeborn Garrettson.[15] In her study of Garrettson's manuscript diaries, Diane Lobody explained:

> Methodists were keenly aware that, however much grace was given to believers, they might very well backslide. Grace was not irresistible, and it took enormous effort for the believer to respond to grace affirmatively and energetically. The idea terrified Garrettson: "a disagreeable reflection on the falling off, of those who had once been favored children of the most high; sent me mourning to my room. Shocked at the fear that it might one day, be my melancoly case, I beged [sic] and prayed of the Blessed Jesus, to make his grace sufficient for me."[16]

As Lobody suggests, the fear so often expressed in Methodist women's diaries is not a fear of being damned; it is rather a fear of being separated from God or disappointing God that is rooted in a persisting sense of unworthiness. The diaries of Hester Ann

Rogers and Catherine Livingston Garrettson both point to the "wonderful paradox" of early Methodist spirituality: its recognition that life was an endless struggle, and its "soaring affirmation" that through God's grace "one could be more than a conqueror, that one could claim victory."[17]

There are other important common features in the diaries of these two women. Both demonstrated a "deep, profound, and intimate" familiarity with Scripture, finding in the biblical promises an "endless source of insight" into their own relationship with God at any given moment.[18] Each experienced a profound sense of union with God. As Rogers described it: "I dwell in God and God in me—I dwell in love, and love dwelleth in me—God is love, and he is all I want."[19] While all too conscious of their own unworthiness, both women knew the astonishing reality of being, as Lobody says of Garrettson, "loved by God into full humanness."[20] The diaries of these and other early Methodist women help us to understand their religious experience and appropriation of Methodist spirituality. Above all, through these diaries we are given a glimpse into the attractiveness of Methodism for women (again, in Lobody's words): "here women were not the alien and mysterious 'other,' but sisters and friends, and—at least in the eyes of God and themselves—inferior to none."[21]

Historian Donald Mathews interpreted the appeal of early Methodism to women and African Americans in terms of the "sense of release from prior constraints" and "entry into a new kind of life" that conversion created. Jo Gillespie argued that by attributing to Providence (I would say "grace," for Methodist women) a mandate for spiritual self-development, evangelical women in the early nineteenth century began to think new thoughts and examine new possibilities for their lives. If that meant they overflowed their "woman's place," they told themselves they were simply learning to live their commitment to the full as every Christian was called to do.[22]

Virginia Lieson Brereton's study of women's conversion narratives corroborates this interpretation. Brereton suggests that conversion narratives both affirmed women's roles in a patriarchal society and subverted some of the assumptions of that society. For many women, religious submission to God resulted in the loss of inhibiting self-consciousness and a new sense of inner authority. Through the experience of conversion, it was not unusual for them to find not only God, but also a worthy role in this world.[23]

PIOUS MEMOIRS AND EXEMPLARY LIVES

Brief illustrations from the genre of pious memoirs may give us a better understanding of the religious lives of ordinary Methodist women in early America, especially their use of the typical Methodist means of grace, their religious activities, and their spiritual networks of women. Hannah Syng Bunting, a Sunday school teacher in Philadelphia, kept a diary from January 5, 1818, the day she joined the church, until February 12, 1832, three months before she died. She wrote letters primarily to female cousins and friends. After her death the Reverend Timothy Merritt compiled her memoir, diary, and letters and published them in two volumes dedicated to Sunday school youth of the Methodist Episcopal Church.[24]

Why were these particular memoirs published? Timothy Merritt claimed that although Hannah Syng Bunting lived a life of "extraordinary piety," there was nothing in her life "but what all may aspire after, and attain to, under ordinary circumstances, and with ordinary means."[25] (When addressed to the Sunday school student, the message clearly was: "You can do it too!")

Hannah Syng Bunting's life story is fairly simple and easily told. She was born at Sharpsburg, Maryland, July 5, 1801. Her parents, Charles and Ann Bunting, soon returned to Philadelphia where they attended the Society of Friends. Her grandmother, Mrs. Esther Randolph, was one of the early Methodists in Philadelphia; according to the memoir, she was a member of Union Academy Church. Young Hannah's mother died when Hannah was still an infant, and her father raised her until she was twelve. She was then sent to school in New Jersey and became part of the Methodist household of a cousin. Eventually she returned to Philadelphia, becoming one of the first Methodist Sunday school teachers there in 1819. She was held up as a model and exemplar for Sunday school teachers and pupils alike. Colleagues recalled her deep sense of responsibility for the spiritual welfare of her pupils.

The major emphasis of the memoir, of course, is not on the details of Bunting's life, which was outwardly uneventful. It is rather on the richness of her spiritual life and her participation, in ways fairly typical for young Methodist women, in the means of grace afforded by the Methodist Episcopal Church in Philadelphia. Hannah Bunting's diary is full of accounts of love feasts, class and band meetings, sunrise meetings, female prayer meetings, camp meetings, and occasions for receiving the Lord's Supper. There is reference to the anxiety she (and other women) frequently felt regarding the duty to testify in public about their religious experience; she knew it was expected of her, but she did it "with much trembling."[26]

It was at a camp meeting in August 1824 that Hannah Bunting herself experienced the gift of sanctification. On Sunday afternoon one of the preachers had spoken from 1 Thessalonians 5:23, "And the very God of peace sanctify you wholly" (KJV). On Monday a love feast was held and the sacrament of the Lord's Supper administered, and Bunting began to long for "full redemption." Satan, she said, suggested many obstacles, such as, "If you obtain the blessing of sanctification, you will soon lose it, and thereby dishonour God." She resolved to *"believe,* and leave the event with God." On that occasion she experienced the witness of perfect love and went home to tell her class meeting about the great gift she had received.[27]

Her recollections of the Belleville (New Jersey) camp meeting she attended for nearly a week in June 1827 help us appreciate the importance of this aspect of the religious and social lives of Methodist women. She reflected on the beauty of the trip and the pleasure of meeting her female cousins at the campground. She kept a diary nearly every day of the meeting, always recording both the name of each preacher she heard and the text from which he preached. The last night she spent in "tent No. 10," first praying privately in a corner, then sitting near the entrance to the tent so she could exhort other young women as they came near. It is helpful to hear her own words:

> The severest cross was yet to be lifted: I was soon required to raise my feeble voice in prayer. The hundreds who surrounded me did not daunt me or prevent my trust in God. While I endeavoured to apply the promises to a sincere female, who for two nights and days

had been wrestling in an agony for full redemption, the answer came. Her soul was filled with pure seraphic joy. She rose on her feet, and, with feeling and clearness, declared what God had wrought. To my surprise the day dawned. So sweetly had the moments rolled, I had not even wished to close my eyes in sleep. The loud blast of the trumpet summoned us to the last meeting. . . . Why should any one dispute the utility of camp meetings?[28]

In February 1825 Bunting's sister Kitty married a Mr. H. DeHaven. Bunting's diary conveys her sense of loss; Kitty had been like a mother to her younger sister Hannah. From the letters in volume two we learn that Bunting continued to live with her sister and her husband. When Mr. DeHaven rented a house in the new Frankford section of the city, Hannah moved with them and found it difficult to leave the Sunday school in old-town Philadelphia. There was also no society of Methodists in Frankford. By August 1828, Bunting was writing about her sister's ill health. Kitty Bunting DeHaven died of consumption (tuberculosis) on November 30, 1830. Hannah's own death at the age of thirty would come barely a year and a half later.

Bunting's letters to female cousins, friends, and Sunday school students are almost entirely devoted to religious reflection and exhortation, with occasional reports of camp meetings and other edifying religious experiences. (These letters are another good example of Methodist women's exhorting through correspondence.) She reminds her cousin Hannah Bunting that the gospel nowhere promises exemption from trials and temptations, but only the assurance "that Divine grace shall be sufficient for all who put their trust under the shadow of the Almighty."[29] In 1826, she writes to answer her friend Mary Ann Walker's questions about the experience of perfect love: "I possess an evidence clear as the *sun*, that my *one aim* is to please God in *all things, small and great*. . . . I daily cast my infirmities into the abyss of God's mercy, and feel assured that he forgives me for Jesus' sake." She counsels her cousin Lydia Bunting not to look too much to her own unworthiness, but instead to rely "simply on the Saviour."[30] Clearly Hannah Syng Bunting allowed neither frail health nor her "timid nature" to keep her from being useful and from living a life perceived by others to be distinguished for its piety.

HOLY DYING

Pious memoirs give us rich detail about the religious lives of (usually) white, educated, middle-class women. We cannot claim, however, that they are representative of the diversity of early Methodist women's experience, and they are often fairly limited geographically. Here other sources are helpful. In the years from 1818 to 1828, the *Methodist Magazine* (New York) published the memoirs/obituaries of eighty-four American Methodist women.[31] Some appeared in a regular feature entitled "The Grace of God Manifested." Some were simpler obituary notices; others were listed as biography. These death memoirs were of women from all over the country: seventeen were of New England women, twenty-eight of women from the upper or Deep South, nineteen of women from the middle colonies of New York, New Jersey, and Pennsylvania, and three from the Midwest. (Some of the shorter notices did not indicate the woman's place of birth or later residence.)

The *Methodist Magazine* printed many more death memoirs of women than of men in these years. The obituaries of men were more likely to emphasize the accomplishments of their lives, while the women's stories focused primarily on the events leading up to and concluding in death. In a time without adequate pain medication, antibiotics, safe surgery, or hospitals, people died at home in deaths that were of long or short duration, but were generally painful and public. It was often the women who modeled a supreme benefit of religion, the ability to approach death unafraid. Women became the exemplars of the good, righteous, victorious Christian death for the community of faith; it was a final act of faithfulness.[32]

Many of these death memoirs were of young women. The possibility of death in childbirth was so real that women approaching childbirth regularly made up their burial clothes and exhibited concern about their own spiritual state. Of the eighty-four accounts of women's deaths printed in the *Methodist Magazine,* for example, thirty did not mention the woman's age at death. Among the remaining fifty-four, however, roughly half of the women (twenty-six) died in their twenties, six died between the ages of twelve and nineteen (two of whom, ages eighteen and nineteen, died in childbirth), and eight died in their thirties. That is, forty out of fifty-four died before age forty, the average age of the onset of menopause in the late eighteenth and early nineteenth centuries. Of the remaining fourteen, three died in their forties, three in their fifties, and eight lived to be sixty or older. (Three died in their seventies: Mrs. Mary Hawkins Carpenter of New York City, whose funeral was held in the John Street MEC; Mrs. Rebecca Pennington, one of the pioneer Methodists in western Pennsylvania; and Mrs. Drumgoole, born in Virginia, who was married for forty-nine years to the transplanted Irish Methodist preacher Edward Drumgoole.) Interestingly, the woman featured in these *Methodist Magazine* pages who lived the longest life was none other than Mrs. Sarah Wesley, wife of the Reverend Charles Wesley, who died on December 28, 1822, at the age of ninety-six!

The death accounts followed a general pattern: A woman was or was not raised in the faith (Methodist or other), experienced the need of salvation, usually in her early teens, sometimes fell away during the later teen years, but moved to a point of religious conviction, justification, and assurance of salvation sometime during her early adult life. An illness, either lingering or sudden, or some difficulty in pregnancy or childbirth, brought her to an awareness of the nearness of death. She struggled to regain health and then recognized the inevitability of her death. Friends and family sought assurances that she was secure in her faith. She made arrangements for the future care of her husband and children, if she had them. From her bed she exhorted friends, siblings, parents, children (also domestic servants, if there were any), perhaps even the doctor or her young pastor, urging them to see to their religious lives and duties, speaking perhaps more freely than she ever had before.

As the final stages of death came on, she testified to her joy in Christ's presence, sometimes describing a vision of Jesus or angels. As her limbs grew cold she asked those nearby to sing hymns with or for her. Even if she had grown delirious in an earlier stage, she regained clarity to assure those nearby that she rested secure, was ready for death and confident of her salvation. At the end she died praising God, or she slipped away in a peaceful sleep. Those who had been present felt their faith renewed and strengthened by her experience. Someone (family, friend, or the circuit preacher) then submitted an account of her exemplary life and death to the *Methodist Magazine* to be published for the wider edification of the Methodist people.[33]

The fullest memoir of an American woman in this sample was that of Miss Eliza Higgins, who died in 1821. Submitted by Joshua Soule (who thought it would be "profitable . . . as an inducement to early piety"), it was published in four parts in 1822.[34] Eliza Higgins was born in Connecticut. She was converted at a Methodist camp meeting at the age of twenty: "the Spirit of God bore witness with my spirit that I was a child of God, and at the same time I received a strong impression that I ought to make manifest what God had done for me."[35] It is clear that she continued to struggle with "taking up the cross" of testifying in public. On August 13, 1819, for example, she wrote in her diary, "The Saviour of mankind was many years travelling from the stable to the cross: and should I refuse to take up my cross, and follow my Lord fully, either in a small or large circle, I should be an ungrateful creature."[36]

In times of struggle or spiritual uncertainty, she found comfort in the promise of "grace sufficient." She wrote to her friend and "sister," Miss Almira Ostrander, in November 1818, "Many things have been said to wound my feelings; but the Saviour hath said, 'My grace is sufficient for thee.' . . . If the Redeemer has promised a sufficiency of grace, what have I to fear?"[37] Two years later she reflected in her journal on the "glorious plan of salvation preached by the Wesleyans": "I have feared lest I should fall; but my trust has been in the Lord, and I have found his grace sufficient for me."[38]

During the course of a long illness, "hundreds" had visited her sick room. As she neared the moment of death, this twenty-four-year-old woman testified to her faith: "The Lord is mine, and I am his; yes, yes, yes, I am going to heaven. Happy, happy, happy! Glory, glory to God. I have had a bright witness of my justification and sanctification." The writer of the account concluded, "She then took leave of all present, exhorting each individual to meet her in heaven."[39] She died on December 22, 1821.

Mrs. Harriet Donaldson Dusinbery (1802–1824) was a friend of

Eliza Higgins who died at age twenty-two, seventeen days after the death of her husband, Lancaster. (A funeral sermon was preached for both of them on February 19, 1824, at the John Street ME Church in New York City.) A letter from Harriet's friend, Mrs. Mary Mason, remembered with appreciation Harriet's service as secretary of the Female Missionary Society. She also recalled that Harriet had found it a great cross for one so young to converse and pray with the sick, but "she always endeavoured to take it up."[40]

Other death memoirs described how the woman who was its subject struggled with the "cross" of public speaking. Miss Margaret Anderson of Virginia, for example, was said to be "illiterate" and therefore had told her autobiography to a friend. She was enabled to "take up the cross" and pray in public. Reminiscent of Hester Ann Rogers, she also responded to the devil's torments by reaffirming her confidence that Christ was "as able to save me fifty years as one day."[41] Miss Lydia B. Leavitt (who died at age twenty-two) of Portsmouth, New Hampshire, wrote to a friend about the difficulty of speaking in class meetings: "I have too much of a man-fearing spirit, am too unwilling to take up my cross. When I can take it up, I feel so happy I think I shall never shun it again."[42] Mrs. Anna Matilda Moore (1803–1827) was from Chestertown, Maryland, where she died in childbirth at age twenty-four. Reflecting what must have been the experience particularly of *young* women, she was said to have been regular and diligent in attending class meetings, "though, as she often stated, it was a terrible cross to her to speak among those, whom she believed to have more experience in the deep things of God. But her tremors did not prevent her from discharging her duty."[43]

For many of these women, the experience of conversion or sanctification (or both) came at a camp meeting. Those who prayed for sanctification were often like Mrs. Theodocia Petherbridge (1793–1824) of New Jersey, who said that the fear of "venturing too far, of believing too much, or of deceiving myself, together with the suggestions of the adversary, would cause me to lose my hold."[44] She did finally experience "a clean heart." The stories of exemplary women were helpful. When Mrs. Matilda Porter from Georgia died in her twenty-ninth year, her memoir recalled that she had resolved to seek salvation after reading "the life of Hester

Ann Rogers."[45] On her deathbed Mrs. Hannah Howe (1783–1812), wife of an itinerant preacher in New England and New York State, gave one of her sisters "the experience of H. A. Rogers."[46] A pastor's wife comforted her dying friend Eliza M. Hyde (who was eighteen): "I endeavoured, in my feeble manner, to convince her that God would give her grace sufficient for that hour [death]."[47] When Mrs. Rachel Asbury, a minister's wife in Boston, knew she was dying, she told her husband, "It sometimes appears impossible for me to leave you; but God gives me the victory in these things, while I feel that his grace is quite sufficient for me even in this trying hour."[48]

What was it like when women exhorted from their deathbeds? When Mrs. Eliza S. Akers of Kentucky (1802–1821) died at age eighteen, she gave explicit instructions about clothes to be given to relatives and friends, described the plain style of coffin and shroud she wanted for herself, and gave her infant into her mother's care. She then exhorted, "Glory to God! I shall soon be done suffering—I shall soon be with Jesus—I shall soon be with my sister Matilda, who has been gone six years, and thus, will I embrace her—I want you all to recollect what I have told you, and not to forget it when I am dead and gone—O! that I had a voice that could be heard throughout the world; I would tell what my sweet Jesus has done for my soul."[49]

Miss Patty Brooks of New York (1795–1822) gave directions about her "pecuniary affairs" and how she wished to be laid out. She then specifically addressed her brother, "Benjamin! I am going to my Redeemer, and I want you to promise that by the grace of God you will prepare to meet me in heaven; and in token of this your resolution, give me your hand."[50] Miss Nancy Spears of South Carolina died in the home of H. Abbott, whose wife and daughter were members of the church to which Methodist preacher Reuben Tucker was stationed. (He had met Nancy Spears a few days before her death.) As she was dying, she exhorted Mr. Abbott to seek the salvation of his soul.[51] Mrs. Frances ("Fanny") Cook of New York City disposed of her temporal goods to all her relatives, gave orders for her grave clothes (insisting on having them made where she could observe the work), and gave specific directions for a plain coffin and for her funeral. Before she died, she said to her weeping family: "Why do you weep? This is no time for lamentation. I am just about to exchange a world of pain and sorrow, for a world of infinite and everlasting happiness; therefore, I beseech you, do not weep." She then said farewell to each member of the family separately, exhorting each one.[52]

When Mrs. Elizabeth Ruse died, she requested that, "for the benefit of others, an account of her death might be inserted in the *Methodist Magazine*, which she was in the habit of reading."[53] S. Mattison, who submitted an obituary notice for Mrs. Samantha Shepherd, said to the dying woman as she exhorted from her bed, "Sister, I am writing down some of your words. . . . What shall I tell them respecting the efficacy of religion on a deathbed?" He then recorded her reply.[54]

The eminent Methodist preacher Freeborn Garrettson submitted the memoir of Mrs. Prudence Williams Hudson of Delaware, daughter of one of the first families he met when he went to that region in 1779. "As the time of her confinement drew near, she had very solemn thoughts of eternity, and appeared to feel a presentiment that she should not long survive the approaching crisis; but she was athirst for holiness." Friends present prayed for her, and she gave birth to a son and also received "an evidence of perfect love." From her deathbed she exhorted her brothers and sister, then several classmates, but most important of all, her husband: "Now, my dear husband, there is one thing lays with weight upon my mind—your slaves. O my dear husband, break every yoke, and let the oppressed go free. You will find a blessing in performing such a duty." Freeborn Garrettson preached her funeral sermon; the memoir does not say whether Mr. Hudson subsequently freed his slaves.[55]

When Ellenor Everidge of Richmond, Virginia, died in her sixty-third year, her state of ecstasy continued for four or five days, and her sickroom was said to be continually crowded. She exhorted all who were present, telling church members to be attentive to their class meetings. The person sending in her death memoir testified, "I can truly say, as well as many others, that I never witnessed so victorious a death before."[56]

Although from a slightly later period, there are also comparable examples of holy dying in the death memoirs of United Brethren women, published in the *Religious Telescope*.[57] Mrs. Elizabeth Man-beck died in 1844 at the age of forty-nine, of consumption (tuber-culosis). The day before she died there was great weeping among those gathered at her bedside because "to all appearance her spirit had [already] taken its flight to the eternal world." However, she "came to," and said, " 'Don't cry for me, . . . for I am going happy'; and as long as she could speak, it was 'glory! glory!!' and when she could speak no more, she raised her hands in token of the victory she was about to gain, and then fell asleep in the arms of Jesus."[58] When Rebecca Kelley died in Ohio at age twenty-four, she exhorted her friends and family to "try to meet her in a better world." Then asking them to "tell the preachers and all the brethren that she was gone to glory," she "clapped her hands and shouted glory! glory! glory! hallelujah to God!! and then repeated the following beautiful lines: 'Farewell, vain world, I'm going home; my Saviour smiles and bids me come.' "[59] The night before thirty-eight-year-old Hannah Shoemaker died, she called her chil-dren to her bedside "to hear from a loving and pious mother her dying admonitions. She began with John, exhorting him to seek religion; Daniel she exhorted to be faithful to his trust; she called her little daughter Sophia, upon whom the duties of the family were soon to devolve, and gave her some instructions, commend-ing them all to God, and then told her husband not to grieve for her, that all was well."[60]

Although Frances Mary Harnes was only seven years old when she died, she told her friends "that they should not weep for her, and all to meet in heaven." Then, calling on the Lord to take her home, "she shouted glory as long as she had breath to be heard, then fell asleep and breathed her life away."[61]

It is one of the major arguments of this book that the spirituality of early Methodist women was characterized by a basic trust that God's grace would be sufficient for their day. However inadequate and unworthy they felt in the face of their afflictions, vocational decisions, struggles to grow in grace and love God wholeheart-edly, and eventual confrontations with death, Methodist women were able to live victorious Christian lives through constant dependence on divine grace. Perhaps it was easier for them than for most men to understand that holy living was, as David Watson aptly put it, "a relationship to be sustained rather than a state to be attained."[62]

In their faithful living and peaceful dying Methodist "Mothers in Israel" were models of piety for the early Methodist people. Chapter 2 will explore the crucial roles they played in early American Methodism.

2

"MOTHERS IN ISRAEL"
Evangelical Liberty and Public Domesticity

The picture of early American Methodism that is emerging from recent scholarship is striking.[1] Methodists and other evangelicals offered an alternative value system to that of the patriarchal world of the Anglican gentry in the upper South during the second half of the eighteenth century. Intensely spiritual community developed around social meetings like the weekly classes to which all Methodist members belonged, and the quarterly love feasts, those larger, ritualized gatherings where Methodists had "melting times" sharing their religious experiences with one another.

There was a radical spiritual egalitarianism in this early Methodism that tended to oppose the worldly hierarchies of race, gender, and class. As Donald Mathews put it, "In [Francis Asbury's] society, *poverty* and *weakness* [words often used in early Methodist preachers' journals to describe African Americans and women, respectively] were deplored, yet the worldly logic that demanded this attitude was confounded by the power of God, for those who were poor and weak in the world were rich and strong in the spirit."[2] Such liminal people were a means of grace within the Methodist meetings, conveying the love and salvation of God, and bringing that sense of communal bonding, individual esteem, and human equality that Victor Turner called *communitas*.[3]

What were the place and role of women in this picture? An understanding of the multiple meanings of "Mother in Israel," a phrase used frequently to refer to women who exercised influence and leadership among the early Methodists, is crucial for an assessment of women's roles. "Mother in Israel" was an affectionate title bestowed on early Methodist women as a sign of community regard for their spiritual leadership. Mothers in Israel were, like Deborah in Judges 5, spiritual mothers to their people. Typical death memoirs, like those explored in chapter 1, suggest a com-posite picture of a Mother in Israel: her house was for many years a home for the preachers and a regular preaching place, she led the class meeting, she held worship when the traveling preacher was not there, and she died a good, holy death, exhorting family members, friends, and neighbors to lead a more godly life.[4] Women were everywhere in this movement, and their functioning as Mothers in Israel often took them beyond the confines of traditional gender roles.

WOMEN—THE MAJORITY OF MEMBERS

Women significantly outnumbered men in the membership of the early Methodist societies. William H. Williams argued that women were "a clear majority" of the white membership of early Methodism on the Delmarva Peninsula, in spite of sexual segregation at Sunday worship (until the 1840s or later) and the exclusion of women from official duties such as voting for local church trustees. He stressed the importance of the supportive community of Methodist societies and class meetings for women. The Methodist Church was "the one institution on the Peninsula" that could meet women's needs for "intimate sociability." Daughters in many Peninsula homes were educated in spiritual values as well as trained to be good wives and mothers. Methodism, he suggested, "met the female need for independence, self-esteem, and power" that for men could be fulfilled in the commercial and political arenas.[5]

In her examination of the earliest membership records for the Middle Atlantic port societies of New York City, Philadelphia, and Baltimore, Doris E. Andrews found that women constituted close to two-thirds of the membership throughout the period from 1786 (the first membership records for Wesley Chapel in John Street, New York) to about 1800.[6]

Attempting to explain the attractiveness of early Methodism to women, Andrews emphasized that the hazards of the life cycle may have drawn women to a religious interpretation of the world, and that the Methodist societies supported women's development as caretakers of republican virtue and also as good housewives and evangelical mothers.[7] To young, single women in the port cities of Philadelphia, New York, and Baltimore, the Methodist churches offered important support both as "focal points for female association" and as a "source of economic last resort." Since the classes were for the most part segregated by gender and race, young women found in the Methodist class meetings a place for spiritual community with other women. The Methodist churches in New York City (Wesley Chapel in John Street and the Allen Street Chapel) not only gave financial help to those in need, but even organized a separate class meeting in the poorhouse. According to Andrews, the great majority of the recipients of aid from 1795 to 1801, and all the members of the poorhouse class, were women. While black women and widows were among those who received disbursements of cash or firewood (for fuel), most were white women, many of whom were young. For these women the "mutual aid" aspect of the Methodist church community was obviously of great significance.[8]

Methodist women were given a sense of their religious importance at an early age. Andrews found that the only children's class at New York in the 1780s–90s was a class of all girls. Bishop Francis Asbury paid attention to education for Methodist girls in 1791, urging that they be taught reading, writing, and sewing, but also that they be given religious instruction. That same year the list of works published by John Dickins for the Methodist societies in the United States included Elizabeth Singer Rowe's *Devout Exercises of the Heart*; it was the first book for women to be published by the Methodists in America. In it she taught women that the pursuit of holiness should be their highest concern.[9]

Finally, Diane H. Lobody has urged that women's experience within early Methodism was "not least a matter of women finding voice."[10] Both early Methodist spiritual discipline and Wesleyan theology "nurtured women's self-esteem by soliciting and celebrating their stories. . . . Women learned quickly that it was a responsible act to pay close attention and listen intently to themselves, and having done so then to speak with candor and courage. The very subversive spirituality of Methodism coaxed women into speech."[11]

METHODIST MEETINGS IN HOMES

Early Methodist preaching services were held in homes because there was often nowhere else to hold them. Women frequently initiated and promoted these meetings as well as the class meetings, those small groups for spiritual nurture and accountability that were so central to early Methodist organization and spirituality, and that were also held in homes. Methodist class meetings were crucial in encouraging women to speak in public, and women as well as men served as class leaders in the early years of the movement.

Methodism in America was begun by laypeople, acting on their own initiative, who had been Methodists in Ireland and immigrated to North America in the 1760s. The first Methodist society in North America was organized in the home of Robert and Elizabeth Piper Strawbridge in Maryland early in the 1760s. Likewise, Barbara Heck was instrumental in beginning the first Methodist society in New York City in the fall of 1766.[12]

Robert and Elizabeth Piper Strawbridge settled on Sam's Creek, in Frederick County, Maryland, in the early 1760s. Robert Strawbridge began preaching almost at once, first to his neighbors in his own log house and then traveling widely throughout the region (eventually as far as Maryland's Eastern Shore, north into Pennsylvania, and west into Virginia). As Frank Baker pointed out, this "fruitful itinerancy" might have been far less successful without his wife Elizabeth's "sympathetic encouragement during his brief intervals at home," and her "indomitable courage in tending their fields during his absences."[13] One neighbor who soon became a Methodist was John Evans, who helped Elizabeth Strawbridge with the plowing and experienced conversion after a "serious conversation" with her in her kitchen. She may therefore deserve the credit for "the first known Wesleyan Methodist convert in America."[14]

With the organization of a class meeting there as early as 1763, the Strawbridge home became the first center of organized Methodism in America. An African slave, "Aunt" Anne Sweitzer, is reported to have been a charter member of this early Methodist society.[15] Strawbridge later built a log meetinghouse about a mile from his home, probably in 1764. In 1768 John Evans was named class leader, and the class began meeting in the Evans home, where it became a center for Methodist preaching until 1809.[16]

Philip Embury and his wife, Mary Sweitzer, and Paul Heck and his new bride, Barbara Ruckle, were part of a group of Methodists that immigrated to North America in 1760, arriving in New York in August. Their families were Germans who had fled the French Catholic King Louis XIV's persecution of Protestants in the Palatinate, and settled in Ireland in the early eighteenth century. The Ruckles, Hecks, and Emburys were among the first Methodists in Ireland.[17]

Barbara Heck was long regarded as the "mother of American Methodism," for it was she who convinced her cousin Philip Embury to begin preaching and rounded up the little congregation that became the nucleus of the first Methodist society in New York in the fall of 1766. At the time of the 1866 centennial observance celebrating Methodist lay beginnings in America, women of the Methodist Episcopal Church raised money to build Heck Hall on the campus of Garrett Biblical Institute in honor of founding mother Barbara Heck. They also urged Methodist historian Abel Stevens to write a centenary volume on the women of Methodism.[18]

Barbara Ruckle Heck was born in 1734 and joined the Methodist society in Ireland in 1752, at the age of eighteen. According to Abel Stevens, her piety was "of the purest and profoundest character." Toward the end of her life she could say that "she had never lost the evidence of her acceptance with God, for twenty-four hours together, from the day of her conversion." She was recognized as a religious guide and counselor, a "Mother in Israel," before she had reached middle age.[19]

Philip Embury had been both a Methodist class leader and a local preacher while in Ireland, but he appears not to have asserted any religious leadership in New York until the fall of 1766, and then only at the insistent urgings of his cousin, Barbara Heck. As the well-known story goes, one evening while visiting family and friends she discovered a card game in progress. This devout Methodist woman indignantly threw the cards into the fire and, warning those present of "their danger and duty," went immediately to Embury and appealed to him to begin preaching. "Brother Embury, you *must* preach to us, or we shall all go to hell, and God will require our blood at your hands!" When her cousin replied, "How can I preach, for I have neither a house nor a congregation?" she was ready with an answer: "Preach in your own house and to your own company first." He agreed to preach, and she collected a congregation of four, including herself and her husband, Paul, John Lawrence, a fellow Methodist from Ireland who was working as her husband's hired man, and a slave woman named Betty. After the service Embury enrolled them in a class, which began to meet at his house. This was the beginning of the first Methodist society in New York.[20]

With the additional help of Captain Thomas Webb, a British army officer and Methodist lay preacher, the New York society grew steadily, renting a rigging loft in William Street for preaching services in 1767. The following year Barbara Heck helped instigate the leasing of a site for a Methodist preaching house to be erected on John Street. The site was later purchased, and the preaching house, named Wesley Chapel, was dedicated on October 30, 1768. Nearly two hundred and fifty "citizens of New York" of all classes subscribed to the building fund, including the mayor and two African female slaves known only as "Rachel" and "Margaret."[21]

When Wesley's first missionaries to America, Richard Boardman and Joseph Pilmore, arrived in October 1769, Philip Embury turned his pulpit over to them. In 1770 the Hecks and Emburys moved to the upper Hudson Valley, forming the first Methodist society north of Manhattan. Loyalist in their sympathies, the Hecks moved to Canada at the outbreak of the Revolutionary War and were instrumental in the organization of Canadian Methodism.[22]

PERSON-TO-PERSON EVANGELISM

Women often acted independently of their husbands in deciding to become Methodists. They were then particularly effective in evangelizing family members (sometimes including prominent husbands), friends, and neighbors.[23]

Judge Thomas White of Delaware is remembered in Methodist history books for having offered the refuge of his home to Francis Asbury for nearly two years during the American Revolution.[24] It was his wife, Mary White, who led her prominent husband to Methodism, and she must have had considerable spiritual gifts. Stevens says, "When the Methodists were met for worship, if there were none present more suitable, she took up the cross, led the religious exercises, and met the class; and she would have gone further and preached if Asbury had encouraged her."[25]

Elsewhere in Delaware and Maryland, major centers of Methodism developed around the homes of prominent friends of the movement. Ann Ennalls, from a planter family in Dorchester County, Maryland, married Richard Bassett, of Bohemia Manor, Maryland, and Dover, Delaware. A friend of Judge White's and later the governor of Delaware, Richard Bassett first met Francis Asbury at the White home while Asbury was in hiding there. Observing Asbury in conversation with some of the preachers, Bassett apparently was preparing to leave until Mary White assured him that the Methodist preachers were "some of the best men in the world." Lengthy conversation with Asbury over dinner at the Whites' allayed Bassett's misgivings sufficiently that he invited Asbury to visit his own home when he visited Dover. Asbury did visit the Bassett household, and both Ann and Richard became "zealous and exemplary Methodists." Richard Bassett founded Wesley Chapel in Dover, where he often served as a lay preacher, and their Bohemia Manor estate in Maryland became a much-frequented home for the preachers where Ann Bassett "delighted to minister to the way-worn itinerants."[26]

Prudence Ridgeley Gough was another devout woman who led her husband to Methodism. After Henry Dorsey Gough was converted, their country residence at Perry Hall, less than twelve miles from Baltimore, became a haven for the preachers, and the chapel there became a regular Methodist preaching place. (Francis Asbury, Thomas Coke, Richard Whatcoat, and Thomas Vasey stayed at Perry Hall while preparing for the Christmas Conference in 1784.) The large Gough household, including slaves, made up a congregation of a hundred. Like Richard Bassett, Henry Gough also preached at times. When there was no male present, Prudence

Gough led family devotions in the chapel. Asbury referred to her as his "faithful daughter," and Henry Gough credited her fidelity with restoring him to the Methodist fold after he had fallen away. "O," he said, "if my wife had ever given way to the world I should have been lost; but her uniformly good life inspired me with the hope that I should one day be restored to the favor of God."[27]

Sibling relationships were often important in spreading Methodism. For example, Ann, Catherine, Mary, and Henry Ennalls all became Methodists. Ann was converted to Methodism about 1799, while living in Dover, Delaware. She then converted her sister Catherine, who in turn converted their sister Mary. Through the efforts of Catherine and Mary, brother Henry (also called Harry) Ennalls was converted, along with a wealthy relative Henry Airey, who lived nearby. A letter to Ezekiel Cooper from Emory Pryor in 1790 reported: "Henry Ennalls and wife and sister have been converted to God since our quarterly meeting; yea, his housekeeper and all his Negroes down to those but eight years old."[28] On being converted, Henry Ennalls immediately freed his slaves.[29]

A HOME FOR THE PREACHERS

In addition to becoming Methodists (often independently), starting churches, and converting their families and friends, women frequently provided a "home for the preachers." Most of the early Methodist itinerant preachers were young, single men, dependent upon the hospitality of the Methodist people to whom they went. Methodist women not only offered these unmarried preachers the hospitality of their homes as the preachers traveled their circuits, but they also had considerable influence over them as spiritual mothers. Because Bishop Francis Asbury was also unmarried, historian Abel Stevens referred to these women, whose homes became centers for Asbury in each region and upon whose hospitality (and occasionally nursing skills) he came to depend, as the "female friends" of Francis Asbury.[30]

Mary White was one of these female friends of Asbury who encouraged and welcomed the itinerant preachers of the young

Methodist movement. Benjamin Abbott, about to leave the White home in 1782 for Barratt's Chapel, later recalled: "Mrs. White came to me as I sat on my horse, and took hold of my hand, exhorting me for some time. I felt very happy under her wholesome admonitions." Thomas Ware, another of the preachers, referred to her as a "mother in Israel in very deed."[31]

Henry Boehm testified to the crucial influence Sarah (Mrs. Henry) Ennalls had on his own ministry. "They had no children," he recalled, "and always made the preachers very welcome, and considered the younger as their children." Mrs. Ennalls, who was "a person of discernment," saw that he was suffering a deep spiritual depression about whether he had mistaken his call. When she found out that he was about to give up the work of the itinerant ministry and return home, she exhorted him "in the most earnest and emphatic manner" to keep on. "'My young brother,' she said, 'your eternal salvation may depend upon the course you are about to take. You may lose your soul by such an unwise, hasty step.'" Boehm resolved "in the strength of my Master to try again" and was still in the ministry over "threescore years" later. "Her wise counsel," for which he continued to be grateful, had "shaped [his] destiny for life."[32]

Other Early Mothers in Israel

Again and again, memoirs of early Methodist women pay tribute to their starting churches, offering a home for the preachers, and being Mothers in Israel to the early Methodist people. In western New York, Eleanor Dorsey, wife of Judge Dorsey, was "a heroine of the Church of those early times, and one of the friends of Asbury, her house being his home, and the shelter of many other itinerants." Three times the Genesee Annual Conference held its sessions at her house, according to Stevens, and during the sessions she would "entertain thirty preachers." Once in Lyons, New York, she was asked to accompany Thomas Smith, the circuit riding preacher, in house-to-house visitation, praying for the souls of the families in each house. By the end of the day, forty new converts had been added to Methodism.[33]

In 1794 a Mrs. Moore, who had become a Methodist, moved to Southold, Long Island, where there was as yet no Methodist ministry. She and two other women held a prayer meeting every Monday night to pray that God would send them a faithful minister. Meanwhile Methodist preacher Wilson Lee was at New London, Connecticut, intending to proceed to his appointment in New York. "Detained by contrary winds," he was led in prayer to cross the sound and visit Long Island. On his arrival in Southold he was directed to the house of Mrs. Moore who, recognizing him as a Methodist preacher, saluted him with the words "Thou blessed of the Lord, come in." A congregation was gathered, Lee preached, and a class was formed; that was the beginning of Methodist work in Southold.[34] Mary Wells, Ruth Hall, and a Mrs. Risley constituted the first Methodist class in New England, and Mrs. Peckett offered her home to the first Methodist itinerants in Vermont, who "found her to be a mother in Israel, and received from her much of their early religious guidance."[35]

In Virginia, Mrs. Sarah Roszel was a Mother in Israel whose house was a regular preaching place for more than half a century. She not only led the Methodist class but, in the absence of the traveling preachers, held regular public worship on Sundays, "which she opened by singing and prayer, after which she would read one of Mr. Wesley's sermons, and having enforced it upon the congregation by an appropriate exhortation, she would close the exercises by singing and prayer."[36] Sarah Low Norton's house in Kentucky was "ever . . . the preachers' home," and for more than twenty years she "visited, conversed, and corresponded," exhorting her friends "to seek the Lord." A woman of considerable intelligence, she wrote in a letter, "The world is not just toward our sex and mind; its customs are tyrannical, and calculated to keep us almost dunces. . . . I cannot believe the enlargement of our minds would make us masculine in our manners." She had her own burdens; being married to a man "who did not profess religion" was a heavy grief, and she suffered for many years with rheumatism. "Divine grace, nevertheless sustained her. That was sufficient."[37]

In Charleston, South Carolina, Mrs. Catherine McFarlane's house was not only the home of the preachers but also was regularly visited by Bishop Asbury when he stopped in Charleston, since she was "by special selection, the maker of the Bishop's knee-breeches. He used to say, 'No one can suit me as sister M.'"[38] In his history of Methodism in Charleston, the Reverend F. A. Mood also paid tribute to three African American women from this early period: Mary Ann Berry, a nurse of whom William Capers said, "I never knew a female, in any circumstances in life, who better deserved the appellation of Deaconess; . . . humble as was her position in common society, she was really a mother in Israel"; Rachel Wells, "remarkable for her humility and piety"; and Nanny Coates, who "also was a colored woman of marked piety and generosity."[39] Mood also mentioned the organization of a Methodist Female Friendly Association in Charleston in 1810, for the purpose of providing financial help to "any females of the Church in indigent circumstances."[40]

James B. Finley told the story, also repeated by Coles, of "two praying women of Georgia" whom God "raised up as pioneers in the glorious cause of Christ." Having settled six miles from each other in Georgia where there was as yet no Methodist society, these two pious Methodist women agreed to meet every Sunday, halfway between their cabins, to hold their own prayer and class meeting. There they testified to and exhorted each other. One Sunday they were overheard by a hunter who invited them to meet at his nearby cabin and said he would collect his neighbors. Believing it to be God's work, the women held their meeting that next Sunday. One read Scripture, led in singing the hymns, and prayed on behalf of the assembled congregation; the other told the story of her own conversion. "It was not long before several were happily and powerfully converted to God." After two weeks of this revival, the "two faithful heralds of the cross" had received "forty new recruits." Finally the news reached the itinerant preacher (laboring some forty or fifty miles away), who came and met the women and took over the work. Under his leadership the work spread farther, so that a "good large circuit" was formed where there had been none before.[41]

In the new West of Wheeling, Virginia (now West Virginia), Elizabeth McColloch Zane united with The Methodist Church in 1785. For many years Mother Zane's house was a home for the preachers, including Francis Asbury. The little society in Wheeling also worshiped in her house for several years, and "if at any time the preacher failed to fill his appointment, she was always ready to read a sermon, deliver an exhortation, lead class, or perform any other service the occasion might suggest."[42]

Madam Russell (as she was deferentially called) played a major role in the support and expansion of Methodism in the Holston River valley of southwestern Virginia. Elizabeth Henry Campbell Russell was the sister of Patrick Henry and the wife of two Revolutionary War heroes, William Campbell, who left her a widow in 1781, and William Russell. In 1788 General Russell and his family moved to a new log house in Salt Lick. In May of that year the Holston Conference, the first annual conference of the Methodist Episcopal Church to be held west of the Alleghenies, met only three miles from the Russell home. While awaiting the arrival of Bishop Francis Asbury, Methodist preachers Thomas Ware and John Tunnell held preaching services that the Russells attended and in which they were both converted. "The conversion of so prominent a family as the Russells drew many others to the infant Methodist movement." "General Russell's" (later "Sister Russell's") became a center of Methodism in the Holston River valley, and Bishop Asbury was a frequent visitor.[43]

After William Russell's death in 1793, his wife became even more active in the Methodist movement. In 1795 she relinquished her control of Russell's estate, turning it over to her daughter, and in accord with Methodist pronouncements against slavery, freed her slaves. In 1812 Madam Russell moved to a log house in Chilhowie, near another daughter. It contained a large room with a portable pulpit that could easily be converted to a place of worship. Elizabeth Russell's home became a "place of refuge" for the Methodist itinerant preachers. All were welcomed. "She gave freely fresh clothing, fresh horses, and money to any of these clergymen who were in need." She also prayed with them and encouraged them, often outlining courses of religious reading for them. Madam Russell gave generously of her own money to build Methodist chapels in southwestern Virginia and eastern Tennessee. The Madam Russell Memorial United Methodist Church in Saltville, Virginia, first dedicated in her name in 1824, stands as a monument to her.[44]

In an autobiography written in the 1820s, Julia A. Tevis described meeting Elizabeth Russell: "About this time I became acquainted with that excellent but eccentric old lady, Mrs. Russell. . . . 'Madam Russell,' as she was generally called, was a 'Mother in Israel,' and the Methodist preachers in those days esteemed her next to Bishop Asbury."[45]

Female Class Leaders

From about 1770 to 1815, women were appointed class leaders, the first position of authority in which women were officially sanctioned. Mary Evans Thorn was probably the first female class leader in American Methodism. A native of Bucks County, Pennsylvania, who had moved with her family to North Carolina and been active among the Baptists there, she returned to Philadelphia in the late 1760s after the death of her husband and became involved in the Methodist society. Joseph Pilmore appointed her a class leader perhaps as early as 1770. In the next few years she was put in charge of another class as well. A letter to her from Richard Boardman assures her that "a deep sense of insufficiency" is a necessary qualification for a class leader and that "it is better to ware [sic] out than to rust out."[46]

Because of her involvement with the Methodists, Mary Thorn was persecuted by the Baptists and disowned by her parents. "When a leader of three classes," she later remembered, "I was reproached with the name of 'Mother Confessor,' pelted through the streets, and stoned in effigy." Although a Methodist class leader, she apparently remained a member of the Baptist Church until tried before the Baptist Association and excommunicated from their fellowship for refusing to renounce the Methodists. At this point Francis Asbury was glad to say, "Now Sister, I will give you the right hand of fellowship."[47]

Mary Thorn taught school and made extra money by sewing for the preachers stationed in Philadelphia. During the Revolutionary War she served as a nurse in the city, coming down with smallpox herself, but making a full recovery. When St. George's was taken over by the British for a drill hall, her home became a Methodist chapel. She met and married Captain Samuel Parker, a prosperous ship owner, and returned with him to England. There, Boardman introduced her to John Wesley, and she and her husband both became active Methodists. Eventually the Parkers were "reduced to poverty" through a series of shipping disasters, and Captain Parker became an invalid. In 1813 Mary Thorn Parker was compelled to write to Bishop Thomas Coke and Dr. Adam Clarke seeking work for their son who was their only means of financial support.[48]

In about 1775 Mary Wilmer was appointed the second female class leader of the Philadelphia society. Soon after his arrival in America, Francis Asbury had found, in the home of Lambert and Mary Wilmer in Philadelphia, "one of those asylums that for years was among his choice resorts in the city, for Mary Wilmer loved and served him as Mary of Bethany did the Great Teacher." Asbury wrote in his journal as early as 1772 that "Sister Wilmer" had taken care of him when he was ill. He recalled that John Hood and Lambert Wilmer were among the first male members of the class in Philadelphia, before the arrival of Boardman and Pilmore. Both Mary and Lambert Wilmer served as class leaders in Philadelphia. Mary Wilmer still held a class in her home as late as 1794, but after her death in 1796, no women class leaders were appointed to take her place.[49]

Three women were class leaders in the New York society in the 1780s–90s: Sarah Day, Elizabeth Burnet, and Catharine Warner. As a result of a revival in 1790, the proportion of women who joined the Methodists increased in New York to 77 percent of the society membership by 1791. According to Doris Andrews there were sixteen classes in 1791 composed entirely of women—twelve white and four black classes. However, there were no women class leaders in the New York society by 1795.[50]

In Baltimore City Station, Francis Asbury had appointed three women as class leaders in 1792, two of them wives of local preachers. By 1800, however, all of the classes were run by men. Dee Andrews's work suggests that women fared more prominently in the smaller societies. In the less prosperous East Baltimore Station, for example, Elizabeth Shaffer, Martha Timms, Margaret Smith, Margaret Sampson, and Ellen Flanagan were class leaders between 1800 and 1815.[51]

Andrews claimed that women disappeared from the position of class leader at the same time the classes were beginning to be seen, as in the 1798 *Discipline,* as "universities for the ministry." The more institutionalized Methodism became, especially after its formal organization as a separate denomination in 1784, the less access women seemed to have to public roles or official capacities in the church.[52]

Praying, Testifying, and Exhorting

As in the Methodist movement in England, women's voices were heard praying, testifying, and exhorting in the prayer meetings, class meetings, and love feasts. Women exhorted in a variety of settings, from personal conversations or correspondence to exhorting on their deathbeds. Of particular interest is the practice of women's exhorting in public worship (after the formal preaching of an itinerant), since, in the case of men, "the post of exhorter was a common early entree to the ministry."[53] Benjamin Abbott told of a woman who exhorted on his Salem circuit in New Jersey about 1790: "One young woman rose and began to exhort the people; I stopped preaching, . . . and let God send by whom he will send; she went on for some time with great life and power." There were even a few women who traveled as exhorters during the 1790s. Richard Whatcoat's journal, for example, refers to Sarah Riker, Sister Mills, and Sister Henderson who "preached with freedom" in the summer months of 1792.[54]

There are similar examples from the Evangelical United Brethren side of the United Methodist family. An account in the spiritual journal of the Reverend Samuel Huber, a United Brethren minister, describes a religious revival among the United Brethren in 1815 in which "old women and young girls, when their souls were blest and made happy, would break forth into singing—shouting—praising—exhorting—prophesying—and talking about the Saviour in public congregations, to the utter consternation of old dry Pharisees."[55]

The phenomenon of female exhorting in the eighteenth century was not unique to Methodism. Catherine Anne Brekus argues that during the revivals of the "Great Awakening" (1740s in New England and the Middle Colonies, and 1760s in the South), the evangelical or New Light churches that supported the revivals also permitted female exhorting. Except for the Quakers (who permitted female preaching even in the Colonial era), these evangelical women were the first North American example of women's "speaking publicly in the churches."[56] Brekus includes the Methodists and African Methodists among these evangelical denominations, although she claims that, unlike the Separate Baptists, neither Presbyterians nor Methodists in the South allowed women to speak publicly during revivals. While not formally recognized as exhorters, the voices of Mary White, Prudence Gough, and others were certainly heard exhorting families, friends, and neighbors.

There is some evidence from this early national period that the issue of women's speaking in public became more controversial as the Methodist Episcopal Church became a more secure institution (and thus, in Doris Andrews's words, more of "a man's domain" than before). In the early 1780s, Anne Emlen, a Philadelphia Quaker, disputed with the minister of St. George's Methodist Episcopal Church, over the role of women in the church. Emlen chastised the congregation for not permitting a young woman to speak during the service. The minister explained that women were permitted to speak in private meetings but that the church members were divided about whether women should speak in public.[57]

CATHERINE LIVINGSTON GARRETTSON (1752–1849)

Catherine Livingston Garrettson must have felt keenly the growing conflict between (as Doris Andrews described it) "missionary zeal and the new domesticity."[58] In her analysis of Garrettson's spiritual diaries and dream journal, Diane Lobody found clear indications of Garrettson's evangelical urge to serve and her desire to exercise at least some of the offices of ministerial leadership. Particularly when comparing herself with the opportunities and abilities of her husband, Methodist itinerant preacher Freeborn Garrettson, Catherine expressed a strong sense of both frustration and insufficiency: "Ah! my dear Friend, if you knew how painfully I feel my own insignificance, you would pity me. No doubt you may have cares that I know nothing of; but have the consciousness that I have never felt, that of being useful."[59] In her resolution of this dilemma, Catherine Garrettson appears to have been representative of many white Methodist women of her day. Her ministry was centered in the home, but it was what Lobody aptly calls "a ministry of public domesticity."[60] When Catherine Livingston Garrettson died in 1849 at the age of ninety-six, she was widely revered as an example of holy living and dying, and praised as "in no trite, ordinary sense 'a mother in Israel.'"[61]

Catherine Livingston was born in 1752 into the "astonishingly wealthy and politically powerful" Livingston family of Rhinebeck, New York. All ten of the children of Judge Robert and Mrs. Margaret Beekman Livingston, including the six girls, were well educated. Nearly all the men in the family were involved in public office, and social life was a continuous round of "parties and balls and entertainments." Catherine's early years were lived in accord with her family's expectations, including attending her mother's Dutch Reformed Church in Rhinebeck in the summer and her father's Anglican congregation in New York City in the winter.[62] The Livingstons were all deeply committed to the American revolutionary cause, and experienced personal loss and suffering as a result, including the destruction of their home by the British in 1777. To the uncertainties of war were added a staggering series of personal losses: in 1776, the deaths within a three-week period of Catherine's grandfather, father, and brother-in-law; in 1785 the death of a sister-in-law; and in 1787 the sudden death of Catherine's closest friend, Mary Rutherford. This last death plunged Catherine into a period of solitude and prayer. On October 13, 1787, the day before her thirty-fifth birthday, Catherine Livingston was "irrevocably converted."[63]

The Livingstons were "wealthy, slaveholding, aristocratic, patriotic Calvinists." They were alarmed when Catherine was introduced to Methodism by one of the servants in her mother's household, and deeply distressed when she became a member. Her sense of self, her values, and her lifestyle had changed completely. (According to Lobody, this "Livingston peacock" had become a "Methodist wren.") In June 1789, the Reverend Freeborn

Garrettson, newly appointed to take charge of the entire area of New York, preached in Rhinebeck for the first time. He and Catherine Livingston fell deeply in love, and after five years of adamant opposition from her family, especially her mother, were finally married in June 1793.[64]

During the years from her conversion in 1787 to her marriage in 1793, Catherine Garrettson recorded her spiritual struggle in a remarkable journal. Wrestling with the demands of evangelical Christianity against the expectations of the world, Catherine literally built her life around prayer and meditation. Following the experience of what the mystics call "the dark night of the soul," Catherine came to know a profound mystical union with God. After her marriage to Freeborn, the focus of her spirituality shifted from a life of contemplation to a life of active service. She entered fully into the life of a Methodist itinerant preacher's wife, functioning as a spiritual director in a network of evangelical women and becoming deeply involved in the spiritual and temporal affairs of her community.[65]

In 1793 Freeborn was appointed presiding elder. Catherine traveled with him until the following spring when she settled in Rhinebeck to await the birth of their first child, a daughter named Mary Rutherford, in September 1794. In 1799 they built a larger home in Rhinebeck. First called "Traveler's Rest" by Francis Asbury, it became famous for its hospitality to Methodist itinerant preachers and others seeking rest. Diane Lobody describes Catherine Garrettson's ministry in this famous home:

> Within this home that was both public and private, Catherine constructed a ministry that was entirely acceptable as a feminine enterprise and yet as vibrantly pastoral as any man's ministry. She organized and presided over regular services of worship (barring only the celebration of the sacraments); she taught Bible and theology to children, young people, and adults; she mobilized and conducted prayer groups; she expounded the scriptures within the setting of home worship; she solicited testimonies of salvation and encouraged unbelievers to repent; and she functioned, both in person and in correspondence, as a pastoral counselor and spiritual director for a great variety of persons. She was in practice a preacher, teacher, evangelist, and pastor.[66]

Catherine Livingston Garrettson's ministry differed only in extent from that of many other Methodist Mothers in Israel of her day. Traveler's Rest became a center for the spread of Methodism throughout the Hudson River valley, beginning with Catherine's own prominent extended family and friends. "The only relevant concern for Catherine was her abiding responsibility to speak God's word and extend Christ's invitation to all the people of her world, just as every faithful Methodist woman rejoiced in doing."[67]

Elizabeth Lyon Roe (1805–1887)

As Methodism moved west into the Ohio valley from the 1780s on, its growth depended as much on "faithful Methodist families" who moved into the frontier from older Methodist settlements as it did on itinerant preachers.[68] One of the most remarkable autobiographies of Methodist women, in terms of what it tells us about early Methodism on the frontier and the religious lives of ordinary Methodist people, is *Recollections of Frontier Life* by Mrs. Elizabeth A. (Lyon) Roe.[69] Elizabeth Roe did not marry a Methodist preacher. She and her husband were active laypeople in early Illinois Methodism. Her account demonstrates the important role they, and other early Methodists like them, played in starting and supporting new churches on the frontier.

Elizabeth Ann Lyon was born in Kentucky in 1805. Her father was a prominent, "worldly-minded" businessman, absorbed in the early development of Kentucky. He supported religion because he thought it beneficial for society, but he had no time for it himself. Lyon's mother had been raised in a religious home, but became "a gay and fashionable woman" until she experienced "the pardon of her sins" and joined the Methodist Episcopal Church at nearly forty-seven years of age.[70]

From then on Mrs. Lyon was a strong religious influence in her daughter's life, having her baptized by the Reverend Peter Cartwright at age five and taking young Elizabeth with her to the Methodist class meeting that met at Father Reed's. Elizabeth's older brothers and sisters, who were still absorbed in the fashionable amusements of dancing and card playing, used to say to her, "I do believe mother will make a Methodist of you if you don't quit going out to old Mr. Reed's; we will not let you go out there any-more." Elizabeth's mother tried to explain to her daughter "the power of saving faith," and gave her "good books to read, such as the life of 'Hester Ann Rogers.'" Elizabeth remembered hearing her mother praying for her.[71]

While attending a grand ball at the urging of her older siblings, Elizabeth began to feel that she was "sinning against God" as well as her own "better judgment," and in the process grieving "one of the best of mothers." Returning home late and feeling very guilty, she went to the closet to put away her bonnet and stumbled on her mother, on her knees praying. Elizabeth went to her room, threw herself on her bed, cried out, "Lord, have mercy on me," and gave way to a flood of tears. The next morning she resolved, by the grace of God, to become a Christian.[72]

Soon after, the whole family attended a camp meeting being held by the Methodists and the Cumberland Presbyterians about twelve miles away. When Elizabeth Lyon went forward to the altar, her father made the family leave the camp meeting abruptly. Undeterred, on arriving home she took off her fancy dress and, retiring to a quiet place, found the conversion and assurance she had been seeking. "'Happy day that fixed my choice on thee, my Saviour, and my God. . . . I went home from camp-meeting a new creature," she recalled, "and everybody seemed to realize it."[73]

During the summer of 1820, Elizabeth Lyon met John Roe, "a very pious young man" who had formerly been a Quaker but had joined the Methodists after his conversion at a revival. They were married on November 11, 1821, although she was only sixteen and "not fit for a poor man's wife." On the day of their marriage they erected "the altar of prayer" in their house. John Roe was appointed class leader of the little class in their village.[74]

Within a few years of their marriage, Elizabeth Roe's faith was severely tested. In July of 1823 their first child, a son, died of croup at age ten months. That September her closest brother died; he was not quite twenty-one. In January her mother caught a bad cold, then pleurisy, and died within a month. Finally Elizabeth Roe could say, "This trial was sanctified to my good." As she explained,

"I felt assured that His grace would be sufficient for the day. And I have always found it so for nearly fifty years."[75]

In February 1827, the Roes left Kentucky for Illinois. Brother Charles Fowler had told them that Methodism was going to spread over the "Prairie State" and urged them to move there. They went first to Springfield, a small village where the class meeting met in a little log cabin. When they moved to Spring Creek, about seven miles away, there was no class formed in the immediate neighborhood. Brother and Sister Roe got the circuit preacher to make an appointment to preach at Sister Ferrell's, a large log house owned by a widow. They also organized a class. Again when they moved to Athens, their log cabin was scarcely completed when a preaching appointment and prayer meeting were scheduled there by the circuit preacher. Elizabeth Roe was involved in a female prayer meeting led by "dear old Mother Rogers," whose praying and exhorting were so powerful that it seemed "as though the Lord denied her nothing she asked for." The Roes remained in Athens about three years. "Truly it was a Methodist village," Elizabeth Roe recalled. "I have heard Brother Phelps say he had 'often stopped when he had been walking out in the morning or evening and listened and heard eight or ten families at prayer all at the same time.'"[76]

The Roes' lives were synonymous with Illinois Methodism until they moved to Nebraska in 1868. When John Roe died in 1871, Elizabeth Roe struggled to resign herself to his death, but it was difficult after nearly fifty years of sharing life—a frontier Methodist life—together. "I could not bear the idea that we should never unite our prayers at the family altar again; never again go together to the public worship, or social prayer or class meeting."[77] Roe closed her autobiography in 1885 with reflections on her eightieth birthday, recalling with joy the use that had been made of their little log cabin over the years: as a home for the preachers, as the place where a Conference missionary was sent (to preach and form a new circuit), as the Methodist meetinghouse (which, with a new addition, also served as a schoolhouse and a hospital), and as a regular preaching place where "many precious souls were converted."[78] Roe's account beautifully illustrates Gregory Schneider's point that in the early nineteenth century, the family became a "major nodal point" in the network of Methodist rituals.[79] Calling on her friends and readers to meet her in heaven, Elizabeth Lyon Roe concluded with the words of a favorite hymn, "' 'Twas Grace that brought me safe thus far, And Grace will lead me home.'" She died two years later.[80]

BIRACIAL CHARACTER OF EARLY METHODISM

This chapter ends where it began, with the radical spiritual egalitarianism of early American Methodism. As Will Gravely has reminded us, there were three powerfully interrelated themes in this Methodist biracialism: African presence, the organization from 1787 of independent black churches and denominations, and the ongoing struggle to establish and failure to maintain an antislavery norm. Both biracial and racially segregated classes and love feasts were common from the beginning, although segregating classes by race and, within racial differences, by gender increasingly became the pattern. From the 1790s until the denominational separations in 1813 to 1822, African Methodists constituted some 20 percent of the total membership of the Methodist Episcopal Church. Although the evidence we have is largely indirect for the early years, African Methodist converts (including women) responded in powerful ways to the good news of the early Wesleyan message, and their responses had a profound impact on other Methodists.[81]

Richard Boardman and Joseph Pilmore, the first English missionary preachers sent to America by John Wesley, wrote letters to him from New York in 1769 to 1771, describing how deeply affected they were by the response of African Americans to their preaching. Theirs and similar accounts by other preachers record not only the dramatic collective response of blacks to the message of salvation, but also individual cases, many of whom are black women. One African Methodist slave woman told Richard Boardman she could neither eat nor sleep because her master would not allow her to come to hear the Word. She "wept exceedingly," saying she had told her master she would work harder than ever if he would permit her to come.[82] An African Methodist woman in New York provided a fine example of holy dying:

I asked her, on the point of death, are you afraid to die? O no, said she, I know that he loves me; and I feel I love him with all my heart. She continued to declare the great things God had done for her soul, to the astonishment of many, till the Lord took her to himself. [83]

Joseph Pilmore wrote in 1770 of a class of about twenty black women: "I think upon the whole they are as happy as any Class we have got."[84] Freeborn Garrettson, in Maryland in 1783, described the spiritual journey of an African American woman: her soul had been set at liberty, she had received a clear witness of God's pardoning love, and had sought earnestly day and night until she received sanctification. She was a slave who was buying her freedom. "I have frequently seen her at five sermons running. In short, this is her experience; my trials are many, but every moment I'm happy in God, having an abiding witness."[85]

Doris Andrews described the existence of three black classes at St. George's Methodist Episcopal Church in Philadelphia in 1794, one of them led by Jonathan York, a black laborer. There were black women in all three classes, sixteen out of nineteen class members in one, three out of twelve in another, and ten women out of sixteen in Jonathan York's class. The majority of the African American Methodists in Philadelphia in the 1790s and early 1800s were women (with the exception of Bethel African Methodist Episcopal Church, having more men); most of the free African American women were domestic servants. Sarah Bass, a poor black widow, served as a nurse during the yellow fever epidemic of 1793. She was a member of the class at Bethel with Richard Allen. She and Allen were married by the white Methodist antislavery preacher Ezekiel Cooper in 1801.[86]

LIMINALITY AND COMMUNITAS

As we have seen, historian Donald G. Mathews suggested that women and African Americans, as persons of marginal social rank, powerfully conveyed the love and salvation of God to the rest of the Methodist assembly. In an attentive rereading of Francis Asbury's journal, Mathews found that when Asbury was under the stress of dealing with conflicts about the structure of

Methodism, he seemed unconsciously to seek out women and African Americans for spiritual reassurance. Mathews cites two brief examples from 1792: "We had a great love feast; the women led the way," and "I was comforted at the women's class meeting."[87]

Even a cursory examination of Bishop Asbury's letters to women does suggest the extent to which he found spiritual power in those whom the world regarded as "weak." In 1796 Asbury wrote to Mrs. Martha Haskins of Philadelphia, asking her with Sister Dickins (wife of John Dickins, Methodist book agent and preacher) to begin a weekly women's prayer meeting: "Oh my sister you have a suffering, dying life but the grace of God is sufficient for you. . . . Women are weak, but remember Eve, and Sarah, Miriam, Deborah, Hannah, Shebah's Queen, Elizabeth, Anna, Phebe and such like, bring the gifts to enrich the temple of God."[88] From New Hampshire, Asbury wrote in 1810 to Mrs. Mary Warfield in Maryland: "Grace and peace be multiplied to you and family and all the sisterhood that labor with those that labor in the word and doctrine. . . . Speak to all the sisters, aged and young, rich and poor. Pray with them, preach to them powerfully in companies."[89] To Mrs. Ann Willis (widow of Henry Willis, who at one time traveled with him) of Pipe Creek, Maryland, Asbury wrote in 1812 (my favorite example):

> Be a mother in Israel. . . . May you have souls not only justified, but sanctified in your house; . . . [W]atch on, pray and suffer on, believe on, fight on, like a *woman! Like a man for God.* [Emphasis in original.] . . . Be Frank's *sister* and his *mother* and prompter to all good.[90]

It is not surprising that Asbury encouraged the Baltimore society to meet together, once a week, not only in classes segregated by sex and race, but also as a whole, including both sexes and races apart from strangers, so that the whole society would be renewed. The importance of women, and also of blacks, in early Methodism lay not only in what they found for themselves, but also in what they meant to the collective life of the worshiping community. [91]

Evangelical Liberty and Patriarchal Sanction

The phrase "Mother in Israel," in its ambiguity, provided women with a useful image with which to ease their entry into more public ministry. As Mothers in Israel, women could have both evangelical liberty and patriarchal sanction.[92] Diane Lobody described the ministry of Catherine Livingston Garrettson as "public domesticity."[93] I would claim that "public domesticity" is a fitting description of the ministries of all these early Methodist Mothers in Israel. The functions of their ministries may have occurred in primarily domestic settings, but many of these were truly public households. These women were evangelists and spiritual mothers to their people.

PART II

"TRUE WOMEN"

1820s — 1860s

3

THE TRUE METHODIST WOMAN
Prescription and Reality

DOMESTICITY AND TRUE WOMANHOOD

What has been called by historians "the Methodist age of American church history" coincided with the domestic era in the history of white middle-class popular culture (roughly the 1820s to 1860s).[1] Basic to the domestic ideology of separate spheres was a heightened contrast between the home and the world, and the prescription of the former as (especially American-born, white, middle-class Protestant) "woman's sphere."[2] The shift from the subsistence farming and household production of the eighteenth century to modern industrial manufacture and work patterns meant that men's and women's lives began to diverge in new ways. Women in their domestic roles were to sustain traditional values and, by their selflessness, to compensate for and counteract the commercial and acquisitive values of the male world. Women began to be regarded as more "naturally religious" than men, and were taught to view their children's salvation and moral character as their primary responsibility (indeed, their major contribution to society).

Historian Barbara Welter suggested that "True Womanhood," the ideal by which a woman was to be judged (and to judge herself), was characterized by "four cardinal virtues—piety, purity, submissiveness, and domesticity."[3] The "true woman" was peculiarly susceptible to religion, which best suited her needs and also enabled her to lead men back to religion. She was urged to maintain her virtue, although men would try to assault it. What most distinguished her from men was submission. "Men were the movers, the doers, the actors. Women were the passive, submissive responders." This difference of the sexes did not, according to most of the advice givers, imply inferiority; it was simply part of the order of nature. Finally, the true woman's place was unquestionably in her own household, where she was expected to "dispense comfort and cheer."[4]

Books of advice on childrearing and household management were beginning to be written. Separate educational institutions for women were founded to prepare women adequately for their domestic influence and maternal duties. Women should be educated, said Emma Hart Willard, "in order that they [might] be of the greatest possible use to themselves and others." Ministers could, and did, use the concept of "woman's sphere" both to esteem the importance of women and to contain their influence.[5]

To be sure, prescription was not reality. It neither fit all women's experiences nor accurately reflected what women were already doing (although it may, in part, have reflected men's anxieties about what women were doing). For working-class women and most women of color, the cult of True Womanhood was not possible and perhaps not desired.[6] Even middle-class women did not uniformly follow its prescriptions, but functioned within a wide spectrum of responses. Many women in the nineteenth century did pay a high price for acquiescing to domesticity. Others worked within the ideology of woman's sphere to enhance their status, testing the elasticity of the boundaries sometimes beyond their own expectations. A small minority protested against the notion of separate spheres by appealing to *human* rights or equal God-given responsibilities.

ADVICE BOOKS BY METHODIST CLERGY

Methodist versions of this prescription were contained in advice books written by Methodist clergy in the middle years of the nineteenth century. Two of these books were written by the Reverend Daniel Wise, a New England Methodist minister who was appointed secretary of the Sunday School Union of the Methodist Episcopal Church and editor of Sunday school publications in 1856. *Bridal Greetings*, describing the "mutual duties" of husband

and wife, was published in 1854, and *The Young Lady's Counsellor,* on the "sphere, duties, and dangers of young women," the following year.[7]

The latter work makes it very clear that women and men are to live and act in different spheres—the home and the world. Man's sphere of trade, exchange, and artisan life is described with adjectives suggesting busyness, energy, and bustling activity. Woman's life, according to Reverend Wise, is more inward, contemplative, and comparatively solitary. It would be a lonely lot without the "supports of religion." Yet this exclusion of woman from "the stage of public life" does not imply the inferiority of her sex, but rather the difference of the sphere and duties to which God and nature have called her.

> What is the sphere of woman? Home. The social circle. What is her mission? To mold character,—to fashion herself and others after the model character of Christ. What are her chief instruments for the accomplishment of her great work? The affections. Love is the wand by which she is to work moral transformations within her fairy circle. Gentleness, sweetness, loveliness and purity are the elements of her power. Her place is not on life's great battlefields. Man belongs there. . . . But woman must abide in the peaceful sanctuaries of home, and walk in the noiseless vales of private life. . . . There, in a word, she must form the character of the world, and determine the destiny of her race. How awful is her mission![8]

The equivalent for southern Methodist women, written about the same time, was Bishop James O. Andrew's *Family Government* (1855).[9] There is no question that this bishop of the Methodist Episcopal Church, South, was a firm defender of woman's domesticity and submissiveness. Home was to be the "one spot on earth where all is peace"; the domain of the "one being whose gentleness shall soothe his [her husband's] troubles, and shall make her to him as the angel of God." Andrew's advice to the wife was: "In short keep a pure heart, bright eye, a kind look, loving words, a clean house, a well-managed pantry and kitchen: be neat and tidy in dress and person; love your Bible and your prayers, and you will likely have quite as much influence and power as any one good woman ought to be trusted with."[10]

Reinforcing the patriarchal image of the weak and dependent southern lady, Andrew was especially solicitous about the welfare of young women. He advised that their education be conducted, if possible, under the watchful eyes of their mothers because "young females are peculiarly exposed to injurious and fatal influences where a proper guard is not thrown around them; and this is especially the case if they have wealth in prospect." He also warned women who were ready for marriage to choose a mate carefully: "Man has strength and power, and these, if used legitimately, might be the strength and protection of the gentler sex; but if a base and corrupt heart give direction to such attributes, what may a feeble, helpless woman expect under the wing of such protection?"[11]

Above all, Andrew was concerned about religious duties, urging a new husband and wife to begin family worship the very first day of their life together; to give their children (especially their daughters) proper Christian instruction, by precept and example; and to provide the means of religious instruction for their slaves, if possible having them attend family worship. Again and again Bishop Andrew reminded young women that their principal calling was to be a "pious mother."[12]

METHODIST SUNDAY SCHOOL LITERATURE AND THE *LADIES' REPOSITORY*

In her studies of the literature of Methodist popular culture, Joanna Bowen Gillespie demonstrated how an eager female reader of this period could find "in her religious duties a new ground for her identity and self-development *within* her culturally-prescribed sphere."[13] The Methodist Sunday School Union was first organized in 1827 and was always closely connected with the Methodist Book Concern. In the 1840s and 1850s, as Gillespie indicates, the Methodist publishing house in New York City turned out "thousands" of four-by-six-inch Sunday school books. She studied 121 biographical narratives published in the 1850s by the Methodist Sunday School Union and found that "two principal female characteristics are visible: modesty and saintliness."[14] While these attributes of the ideal young woman would not seem to offer much room for self-empowerment, Gillespie came to a different conclusion. Modesty, according to her, "gave young women the authority to define, and pursue godly aspirations they set for themselves," and saintliness "gave them permission for innovating, or subverting, conventions or custom in the fulfillment of their own religious calling." These Sunday school narratives encouraged in young women a "modest sainthood" that would lead to a "vastly-expanded domesticity."[15]

The same thing occurred for their mothers, aunts, and older sisters who were readers of the *Ladies' Repository*. Published by the Western Book Concern in Cincinnati from 1841 to 1876, this first magazine specifically for Methodist women was intended to have as its central theme "religious domesticity."[16] Gillespie argues persuasively that "during its first two decades, the official public authoritative (male) voice" of its editors and writers "was perceptibly weakened, while the female reader's private, increasingly-independent agenda, religiously authorized and encouraged by her own 'in-house' print forum, became more and more audible."[17]

These readers' voices initially appeared in print on two main topics: "death and children" (remembering a dead friend, spouse, or child, or reporting on children's sayings). Increasingly, the women's own feelings were expressed in letters to the editor. Gillespie helps us recognize the emerging sense of self and spiritual independence that the Methodist woman was developing within her own subculture by the mid-nineteenth century. In this way, the *Ladies' Repository* provided a "literary bridge from the earlier genre of religious literature—pious memoirs—to the specialized women's religious journals of the post–Civil War era."[18]

Methodist women responded in a variety of ways to these prescriptions of True Womanhood. Mrs. Mary W. Mason of New York City was the epitome of the white, middle-class, urban Methodist mother and minister's wife in the 1820s to 1860s. But she was also the prime example of the Methodist woman organizer, beginning (to name just two) the first Methodist Sunday school in New York City (1815) and the Methodist Female Missionary Society (1819), of which she was the "Directress" for nearly forty years! Mrs. Ella Gertrude Clanton Thomas of Georgia struggled to reconcile the expectations of the image of the (white) "southern lady" with the stark realities of what it meant to preside over a slaveholding household. She would live long enough to move into a more public life after the Civil War. Fortunately both women left diaries that provide helpful access into their lives.

MARY MORGAN MASON (1791–1868)

Mary W. Morgan was born in Ireland on July 5, 1791. Her parents, William and Elizabeth, immigrated to America when she was three years old and settled in Philadelphia. Apparently they gave their young daughter little or no religious instruction. Her father had been a Wesleyan in Ireland but had lapsed from the faith, while her mother was said to have "imbibed the infidel sentiments of Thomas Paine and his contemporaries."[19]

Mary Morgan experienced conversion at age seventeen under the influence of her uncle John Morgan, a Methodist local preacher. From then on she resolved to live a new life, giving up "gay clothing" and "vain amusements." These religious convictions met with the strong opposition of her parents, who kept her from attending the Methodist class meeting (she would hide her class tickets in the linings of her shoes) and burned her spiritual journal. As Hester Ann Rogers had done before her, Mary Morgan bargained with her parents that she would do the work of a servant if they would allow her to attend the meetings. She did this for several months until she became ill. Although forbidden to see her, Mary's uncle wrote to her during this time to encourage her to trust in God's grace.[20]

The young woman was glad to move to New York City in 1810 to take a teaching position in a school for poor girls opened by the New York City Friends (Quakers). Finally free to affiliate openly with the Methodists, she joined the John Street Methodist Episcopal Church and soon after was able to live with her uncle and his family. Her journal during these years reveals her typical Wesleyan spirituality. She wrote on August 4, 1813: "Overcast in the morning, relieved in private devotion at noon, strengthened in class-meeting, instructed in religious company, and abundantly refreshed in the women's prayer-meeting in the evening. O! bless the Lord for the means of grace and religious privileges!"[21]

She had begun to search for Christian perfection and, "by the instructions of a mother in Israel," was praying for "a perfect submission to his will, a perfect confidence in his power, perfect faith, and perfect love, which casteth out all fear that hath torment." Later in August she attended a camp meeting up the East River. Never having been to one before, she took neither tent nor provisions with her, but found both provided by generous fellow Methodists. Friends were praying for sanctification, and she began to seek the blessing for herself. "While I was thus praising God for what I had already received, he imparted faith to believe on him for the blessing I so much desired. In a moment, O glory! . . . my idols were taken away . . . and my whole soul was sweetly lost in wonder, love, and praise." The next day she felt a steady peace and a more constant communion with God, and she returned to the city, she tells us, with deep regret.[22]

From this time on, Mary W. Morgan's life manifested a steadiness of purpose and a new zeal. Within a period of six years she was primarily responsible for founding four religious voluntary associations, two of which would have particularly long-lasting consequences. On November 8, 1813, she was instrumental in the formation of the New York Female Assistance Society, "for the relief of the sick poor of their sex."[23] In 1815 she began the first Methodist Sunday school in New York City, and the following year she helped to form the Asbury Female Mite Society for the relief of the wives, widows, and children of retired Methodist itinerant preachers.[24]

In July 1819 she persuaded a group of women to help her found an auxiliary society to the Missionary Society of the Methodist Episcopal Church, which was formed the previous April. The organizers of this Female Missionary Society affirmed their conviction that "*we* are not called to the more arduous employments of active life; we are exempted from the toils and cares of official stations in the Church; but God has, nevertheless, required of *us* that our all should be devoted to his service."[25]

In 1817 Mary Morgan married Thomas Mason, a young Methodist preacher from the South Carolina Conference who had been appointed to assist Joshua Soule in managing the New York City–based Methodist Book Room. Now she would have to juggle her benevolent activities and continuing spiritual pilgrimage with the demands of a rapidly growing family and marriage to an itinerant Methodist preacher. In August 1818, at the age of twenty-seven, Mary Mason gave birth to her first child, a daughter, Mary. In 1820 a second daughter, Elizabeth, was born, and a Miss Sarah Sickles came to live with the family and assist with child care. In twenty years Mason bore ten children, six girls and four boys. Not surprisingly, she found married life to be "fraught with more severe and numerous trials than are in general to be met in a single state," but expressed gratitude that God had given her a companion whose Christian life and godly conversation "provoke to love and good works."[26] Although often torn between spiritual concerns and family cares, she found strength and help in the female prayer meeting, which she attended regularly and frequently led.

After eight years at the Book Room, Thomas Mason was appointed in 1824 to Allen Street Church. From then on he was gone from home much more frequently, especially after being made presiding elder of the Troy District in upstate New York in 1828. Mrs. Mason now had to administer both home and benevolent activities during his repeated absences. She experienced the first death of a child, her daughter Anna, while her husband was away in February 1825.

Like the number of children, the list of benevolent societies initiated and led by Mary Mason increased steadily. She was one of the founders, in 1822, of the Asylum for Lying-in-Women, and remained one of its managers for more than thirty years. In 1833, she became female superintendent of the Greene Street Sunday school and, in 1838, directress of the Female Benevolent Society for the relief of poor women. That year her youngest child was born. The same year her eldest daughter, Mary, was married at age twenty to the Reverend John M. Howe. When that daughter died in childbirth in 1841, Mary Mason took the baby into her own household. Another daughter, Anna, married the Reverend John M. Reid in 1844 and died in July 1846. Now the grandmother had care of two grandchildren, both Mary's and Anna's babies. In addition, her husband, Thomas, had died of smallpox in 1844.[27]

That the New York Female Missionary Society lasted for more

than forty years was largely due to the efforts of Mrs. Mary Mason. She was its "directress" from the age of twenty-eight until her death in 1868 at age seventy-six. "When she died the society died."[28] From 1837 to 1857, the major commitment of the Female Missionary Society was to support Mrs. Ann Wilkins, who was a thirty-year-old widow at the time she volunteered for missionary service in Liberia. An indispensable source for understanding the relationship between Mrs. Wilkins and the faithful members of the Female Missionary Society is the correspondence over the years between Mrs. Wilkins and Mrs. Mason. Lengthy excerpts from this correspondence were preserved by Louise McCoy North in her book *The Story of the New York Branch of the Woman's Foreign Missionary Society of the Methodist Episcopal Church*, published in 1926. North captured the spirit of those early days: "In the writing desk of the First Directress, a bright, little chintz bag bears the label, 'Missionary Papers.' Among minutes of meetings, lists of subscribers, appeals in burning words, a little package of old letters is marked 'From Ann Wilkins.'"[29]

A letter from Mary Mason to "Sister Wilkins," dated October 26, 1845, reveals both the depth of the women's commitment and the limits of their perspective:

My Dear Sister Wilkins:
   My Heavenly Father is witness to my many prayers for your temporal and spiritual welfare, and my pleadings before both Missionary Boards in your behalf. . . .
   We are very much interested in all your movements. Do not fail to write to us at every opportunity. You can effect more by your letters than would many missionary addresses. . . . Give us all the interesting facts you can collect, especially to bring before the Sunday Schools.
   . . . Sometimes I visit you in imagination and see you surrounded by the poor, benighted African girls, listening with eager attention to the words of instruction from your lips, watching your every action in mute astonishment; and sometimes you see the tear start from the fixed eye or a sigh is heard from the penitent heart and your heart rejoices and you are inspired with fresh courage. Then again, you look for fruit, but where you expected to gather grapes, you find only thistles. The oppressive climate throws a languor over your physical powers and, your mental faculties sympathizing with

your languid body, you are ready to cry out, "Who is sufficient for these things?" Oh, my dear sister, in such times of oppression look to Jesus and, in the language of the Apostle, say rather, "I can do all things through Christ, which strengtheneth me." . . .

You may always look to our Female Missionary Board as to a family of sisters, who are ever ready to sympathize with you in all your afflictions and, as far as in their power, to lighten your burdens and to assist you in your labor of love. . . .[30]

Sister Wilkins soon established a school for girls in her own home. She developed the well-intentioned, but nonetheless dubious, practice of giving the children with whom she worked the names of famous Methodists. Thus there was a "little Mary Mason," and Wilkins never tired of sharing the young girl's progress in both knowledge and piety with the American woman for whom she was named. According to the missionary, Mary was "an extraordinary child for any country or color." When Wilkins was ill, the little girl cared for her, "ready to hear the lowest whisper, and attend with cheerfulness to my requests."[31]

Furloughed three times because of illness,[32] Ann Wilkins returned home to stay in 1857. On her arrival, she attended the communion service of the New York East Conference, then in session. Bishop Waugh announced that Sister Wilkins was present and invited her to come forward, which she did, leaning on the arm of Mrs. Mary W. Mason.[33] When Wilkins died a few months later at the age of fifty-one, Mary Mason was at her bedside. She said to her, "You have many friends. They will be asking the state of your mind at the last." The missionary replied, "All is peace—a holy calm!" The attendants who ministered to her last hours said of her, "It was like waiting upon an angel of God. We never saw such a person; such dying we never witnessed." What Ann Wilkins had called the "lovely sisterhood of missionary spirits in New York" did not long survive the death of this beloved missionary whom it had supported for twenty years.[34]

In 1852, Mary Mason finally retired from teaching after more than forty years. She took note of her sixty-fourth birthday on July 5, 1855: "This is my sixty-fourth birthday. What a monument of Divine mercy! A living miracle of grace!"[35] Her last diary entry was October 5, 1861; in it she recorded the death of her son William, noting with relief that he had left the world "in the triumphs of faith." Like all good Methodist mothers, she had been "groaning" all her life for "the redemption of my children."[36]

The last six years of her life, Mary Mason spent alternately with her daughters, Elizabeth Mason North and Jane Mason Curtis. The faithful Miss Sickles, her companion for forty-seven years, was "still beside her." She enjoyed the visits of ministers, friends, children, and grandchildren, but increasingly suffered from a "stealthy disease" that involved some memory impairment (perhaps what we would now call Alzheimer's disease), but never destroyed her spiritual discernment and ability to pray. She died at the home of her youngest daughter, Jane Curtis, on January 23, 1868; the funeral was held at the home of Elizabeth North.

Bishop Janes gave the principal eulogy at the funeral, and tributes and letters that poured in to the family also appeared in various Methodist periodicals. Her tombstone in the Sleepy Hollow Cemetery near Tarrytown bore the following inscription: "She labored more than fifty years for the aged, the young, and the poor. Well reported on for good works; she brought up children; she lodged strangers; she relieved the afflicted; she diligently followed every good work." She was almost universally referred to as a Mother in Israel. "Blessed are the dead which die in the Lord: . . . for they rest from their labors; and their works do follow them" seemed an especially appropriate summary of her life. The *Christian Advocate* called her "a central figure among Methodist women" and "a household word" for fifty years among New York Christians. Close acquaintants recalled that she "was ever crying out, 'Lord, what wilt thou have me to *do*?'" The secret of how she was able to accomplish so much was revealed by her son-in-law John M. Howe: "She was wont to remark, 'Let us attend to one thing at a time.'"[37]

Mary Morgan Mason's life offers an impressive illustration of how a woman regarded as the epitome of the (white, middle-class, urban, and northern) Methodist mother and minister's wife could, through her participation in women's religious voluntary societies, help to transform the boundaries of domesticity in the 1820s to 1860s.

SOUTHERN WOMEN

In the years before 1860, southern women were the subjects of a culturally defined image of the lady that would continue to shape their lives even beyond the experiences of the Civil War and Reconstruction. Although related to the image of True Womanhood that was part of the larger American culture in the nineteenth century, this image of the southern lady was "unusually confining" and the "sanctions used to enforce obedience [were] peculiarly effective."[38]

Barbara Welter had described the True Woman as pious, pure, domestic, and submissive.[39] The southern lady was all this, but more so. In a slaveholding society, the patriarchal family structure was regarded as divinely ordained. "Women, along with children and slaves, were expected to recognize their proper and subordinate place and to be obedient to the head of the family. Any tendency on the part of any of the members of the system to assert themselves against the master threatened the whole, and therefore slavery itself."[40] This helps to account for both the tenacity of the patriarchal system and the level of fear that lay below the surface of southern male consciousness and behavior.[41]

The image of the soft, submissive, weak, and dependent southern lady was perfectly complemented by the image of the strong, commanding, intelligent, and protective southern man. This antebellum southern woman was to be charming in her innocence, compassionate, long-suffering, pious, and devoted to God, her husband, her children, and her servants. There is every evidence that most southern women made heroic efforts to live up to what was expected of them. As Caroline Merrick of Louisiana wrote to a friend, "We owe it to our husbands, children, and friends to represent as nearly as possible the ideal which they hold so dear." Many women assumed that if they were discontented in the "sphere to which God had appointed them," it must be their fault and by renewed effort they could do better. In order to reconcile these expectations with the realities of their lives, they frequently developed "a steely self-control."[42]

Anne Firor Scott, Elizabeth Fox-Genovese, and others have argued convincingly for the importance of personal narratives—

diaries, journals, and letters—as a way for southern women to assess themselves, to "ground their consciences," and to gain a sense of control over their lives.[43] Unlike the pious memoirs of northern women, these southern women's diaries were not normally published as exemplary portraits for the edification of a public audience. Rather, they were private documents, frequently intended to be read by family members, especially daughters, but revealing considerable ambivalence even about the degree of self-disclosure permitted. These antebellum journals and letters have been preserved in manuscript collections throughout the South and are the best personal evidence of the importance of religion in the lives of these educated and wealthy women. In Scott's study of southern women before and after the Civil War, she found that these personal sources are much scarcer after 1865, when the available material has more to do with the creation of a public record. It may be that when life in the South broke apart during the Civil War and after, when women had to work out of economic necessity and began to act in the larger society in new ways, they no longer had the time or inclination to keep diaries and write personal letters as they had in the years before 1865.

Among the women whose diaries Scott and Fox-Genovese studied were four southern Methodist women: Frances (Fannie) Moore Webb Bumpas, Anne Turberville Beale Davis, Mary Jeffreys Bethell, and Ella Gertrude Clanton Thomas. The first three women lived in North Carolina; Fannie Webb Bumpas and Anne Beale Davis were both wives of North Carolina Methodist ministers. Ella Gertrude Clanton Thomas was a Georgia woman. Her diary is of particular interest for two reasons. Kept from 1848 to 1889, it spanned four decades (far longer than most comparable personal narratives). It also owes its survival to Clanton Thomas's female descendants: her daughter, who died in 1956, and after her death, Clanton Thomas's granddaughter and great-granddaughter. It has now been published and is therefore much more widely accessible.[44]

The diaries of these women reflect their intense preoccupation with personal piety and their self-assessment in light of both evangelical and cultural ideals. Fannie Moore Bumpas, for example, constantly worried about her "hard, cold heart," and prayed that

God would "revive thy work in this cold heart and make me entirely thine." As a preacher's wife, she was particularly conscious of the need for holy living. "Mr. B. [her husband] says we must try to live holier. Oh that I could. Spent some time today reading, weeping, and praying." A few months later she wrote, "I am not as much engaged in religion as I should be . . . too worldly." The responsibilities of children and slaves weighed heavily on slaveholding women. Elizabeth Fox-Genovese suggests that Fannie Bumpas spoke for many when she prayed for the "grace to enable me to govern my family aright."[45]

In their diaries, both Anne Beale Davis and Mary Jeffreys Bethell reflected on the importance of camp meetings. Davis wrote of having returned from a "glorious" camp meeting in October of 1838, which was "a time of outpouring of the Holy Spirit of our merciful God, in the awakening and conversion of sinners, and the sanctification of believers." In that meeting, "the fire of Divine love . . . rushed from heart to heart until each one in the tent was blessed with perfect love." Like Bumpas, Davis longed for more holiness in her life. On confessing her unfaithfulness to God, she recorded in her diary, "Thou knowest and I know, that without holiness of heart I cannot please Thee."[46]

Mary Jeffreys Bethell attended camp meetings almost every year. In 1856 she took her child and his thirteen-year-old nurse, Betty, with her to a camp meeting and was thankful when Betty experienced conversion. Bethell said a daily prayer that "*all* my children should become Christians, my *servants*, also." Accordingly, she made a commitment to "read the bible to them Sunday nights and instruct them, and sing and pray with them."[47]

Like northern women, southern women lived in terror of each successive childbirth and with a pervasive fear of death for beloved family members and especially children. For religious women there was consolation in believing that the frequent deaths of children were somehow a manifestation of God's will. Yet many women agonized over whether these deaths were a judgment on their own sinfulness or inadequacy. Mary Bethell, for example, kept reminding herself that these trials served to cut "the cords that bind us to earth."[48]

ELLA GERTRUDE CLANTON THOMAS (1834–1907)

Ella Gertrude Clanton was born on April 4, 1834, near Augusta, Georgia, into a large and very wealthy planter family. One of the most joyous times of religious involvement in her life came soon after her arrival at Wesleyan Female College in Macon, Georgia, in January 1849. Here she experienced conversion, attended prayer meeting every night with other young women who were also being converted, and participated in a "glorious revival."[49] The religious influences continued while she was there. She was reconciled with the "girl I most dislike in college," heard an exhortation given in the parlor by Bishop William Capers of Charleston, South Carolina (whose daughter was in Gertrude's class), and talked with others about their "spiritual welfare." Shortly after her seventeenth birthday on April 4, 1851, she wrote in her diary, "What a change a very great change has taken place in my every feeling. Yesterday I felt that although I had repented of my sins I was still unpardoned. . . . Now thank Heaven I feel certain of my acceptance with God. How delightful is the thought! . . . Can I ever doubt the goodness of my God, of my Saviour?"[50]

Clanton graduated from Wesleyan in 1851 at age seventeen. The next winter she made her debut in society, and wrote in her diary that, although she did not dance (being a good Methodist) and was "thus incapacitated from entering into all the excesses of gayety," she had spent a delightful winter as a fashionable young woman.[51] She soon began to be courted by James Jefferson Thomas, the brother of a school friend, who had completed his undergraduate work at Princeton and begun medical school in Augusta. Courtship was "the great and public moment in the life of the belle," and Clanton did her best to fulfill her role as expected. They were married in December 1852. Since Jeff Thomas also came from a Georgia plantation family, the couple were well off in spite of Jeff's abandoning his medical studies (a decision they both later came to regret).[52]

Gertrude Clanton Thomas usually attended St. John Methodist Church on Greene Street near the Clanton home. Now that she was a plantation mistress herself, she clearly demonstrated her desire for religious influences and her wish to share them with other family members. In that long, first journal entry since her marriage she wrote: "After church I partook of the Lord's Supper and was benefitted in an unusual degree. Oh! for an increased degree of Grace to know and do my redeemer's will. To live more as I should. More to the glory of God and the advancement of that holy cause of which I profess to be an unworthy disciple." She hoped to bring her sister and her husband to "the throne of grace" so that they, too, might "obtain pardon and redeeming love."[53]

Gertrude Thomas's feelings about her husband at this time reflect the cultural image of the southern lady. "I thank thee oh heavenly father for thy many mercys, but for none do I so sincerely thank thee as for *my husband.* Combining such moral qualitys [sic], such an affectionate heart, with just such a master will as suits my woman's nature, for true to my sex, I delight in *looking up* and love to feel my woman's weakness protected by man's superior strength."[54]

On several occasions, Thomas reflected on the purpose of her journal. She wanted it to be a book in which "one writes their thoughts and actions," but wondered if hers would ever accomplish that purpose. From the beginning she was torn between the "irresistible temptation" to write the feelings "which agitate my heart," and the fear of not knowing "by whose eye this page may be scanned."[55] Her first child was born in December 1853; it was a boy named Turner Clanton Thomas (after her father). She resolved to "persevere" in keeping her journal so that her children (especially the girls) might remember their mother's life, the "events unimportant in themselves yet they make up the sum of my life."[56]

Gertrude Thomas was in her late twenties when the Civil War broke out. She was active in the Augusta Ladies' Aid Society, sewing uniforms, making cartridges, and visiting the wounded in military hospitals. Her husband was at the front a total of about nine months in 1861–62. In mid-1862 he resigned his commission and joined a local militia in the Augusta area. By 1864 his wife was weary of the war, which came close to home when General William T. Sherman's army burned buildings on one of the Thomas plantations in Burke County.[57]

According to Nell Irvin Painter, there were three major religious crises in Gertrude Clanton Thomas's life: in 1864, when her beloved father died; in 1865, following emancipation; and in

1869–70, with "the first awful round of financial failures." Her father died in April 1864. In many ways he had been her strongest support, and she would miss his help at critical moments throughout the rest of her life. What made his dying particularly agonizing for her was anxiety about his spiritual state at the time of his death. Not only had he not been a member of any church, but he was also, like many other southern men, guilty of sexual relations with his female slaves, the offspring of which he then willed to his heirs.[58]

It is clear from her journal entries how much Gertrude Thomas was struggling to find religious consolation in those months after her father's death.

> I wish I had a book with a key to it in which I could write what I feel. . . . I find my thoughts recurring to the Catholic confessional (that great repository of secrets) with the longing checked by the idea that these priests are *men*. Again with a feeling of intense relief I think of Mary—Mother Mary! Christ's Mother! and shall I confess it, I almost find myself believing in the intercession of the saints. . . . I don't think Mr. Thomas understands or is interested in my struggles and trials. He listens sometimes when my "Heart unfolds its leaves" and I read to him some of its pages. Listens, but that is all.[59]

Or again the next month:

> People in olden times were "sore vexed with a devil" and mine is a want of faith—Tonight I was singing a song which I have heard twice lately, "How firm a foundation." Oh how consoling "As thy days may demand shall thy strength ever be." "That soul though all hell should endeavour to shake. I'll never, no never, no *never* forsake." Oh God, help me. I am very weak. . . .[60]

Most devastating of all was her loss of faith that came with the abolition of slavery. She had never realized how intimately her "faith in revelations and [her] faith in the institution of slavery" had been bound together. "True," she said,

> I had seen the evil of the latter but if the *Bible* was right then slavery *must be*—Slavery was done away with and my faith in God's Holy Book was terribly shaken. For a time I doubted God. The truth of

revelations, all—everything—I no longer took interest in the service of the church. . . . When I prayed my voice appeared to rise no higher than my head. When I opened the bible the numerous allusions to slavery mocked me. Our cause was lost. Good men had had faith in that cause. Earnest prayers had ascended from honest hearts—Was so much faith to be lost? I was bewildered—I felt all this and could not see God's hand.[61]

As Elizabeth Fox-Genovese explains, "The measure of Gertrude Thomas's despair reflects the measure of faith that she and other slaveholding women had had in the justice of their society."[62]

After the war Jefferson Thomas essentially "fell apart physically and emotionally." Their loss of the wealth and status that owning many slaves had symbolized was painful to them both, but Gertrude recovered fairly quickly once she had decided that slavery had been wrong.[63] By the summer of 1866 her health was good, but he still suffered from "immobilizing depressions." His "psychosomatic illnesses, his chronic mismanagement of his plantations and his business, his bitterness at the Confederate defeat and emancipation, and his habit (acquired during the war) of swearing before his pious Methodist wife severely strained the marriage."[64] Jeff Thomas also developed a drinking problem, and there are increasing references in Gertrude Thomas's journal to "skeletons" in the closet and to the pain caused by her husband's "habitual profanity."[65]

As many scholars have pointed out, war fundamentally altered relations between men and women in the South. Southern women began going out to work and speaking up in public. In this, Gertrude Thomas was typical. Between 1868 and the early 1890s, the Thomases lost much of their property. About 1875, Belmont burned, the home in which they had spent most of their married life. Although her husband had long opposed Gertrude Thomas's plan to work, he was finally converted by their desperate financial need, and she began teaching elementary school in 1878. She taught for six years, staying in the classroom until her mother's death in 1884. Then they moved to the Clanton mansion in Augusta and began to take in boarders.

Like most women, Gertrude Thomas had constantly feared the loss of loved ones. She had given birth to ten children, seven of whom survived past the age of five. She suffered one last devastating blow in 1879 when their seven-year-old son Clanton died. Her journal entry is worth quoting in full because she captures so eloquently the grief at the loss of a child that so many women had to experience, some experiencing it many times. After his death she had gone alone to his grave:

> Clanton is dead! . . . Clanton my bright, beautiful boy. . . . Oh Lord will I ever get used to this yearning, this craving to see my child, to put my arms around him and have him nestle to my side? . . . Oh, no, no! My God it is enough to make one cry out in utter despair. I stood and looked, then I knelt and tried to have communion with my child by prayer. All in vain. No gleam of comfort came. I walked around for a while and read inscriptions on other graves. I was trying to find some balm for my weary, hungry soul and thought, "Others have lost children. I know I am not the only mourning mother. . . ." [She went to funeral services in the afternoon and saw an inscription on a grave, "She is not here. She is risen."] *There* I found the message I had sought for all the morning. Clanton is not in that grave, his soul which left that body which we buried has been born into a new existence. But oh my boy, my boy what would I not give to see you now. Help me oh my God![66]

After the move to Augusta, Gertrude suffered a long illness. There was also a series of terrifying earthquakes in 1886–87. The last entry in Ella Gertrude Clanton Thomas's journal was August 30, 1889. She was fifty-five years old.

The editor of Gertrude Thomas's journal supplies a very helpful Epilogue. Virginia Ingraham Burr suggests that Thomas intended her scrapbooks to complement her journals and throw light on the public life she now began to lead. Although these activities are beyond the scope of this chapter, Thomas became active from the mid-1880s in the Woman's Home Missionary Society of the Methodist Episcopal Church, South; in the WCTU; and eventually even in the movement for woman suffrage. From the mid-1880s, Gertrude Thomas lived her dream of a useful life. In 1893, Jeff and Gertrude Thomas and their two unmarried daughters moved to Atlanta to live with their son, Julian Thomas, who had a successful medical practice there. Gertrude Thomas died in Atlanta on May 11, 1907.[67]

The "True Woman" of the 1820s–1860s was to be pious, pure, submissive, and domestic. She was to recognize the home as her proper sphere and being a pious mother as her major calling.

Mary Morgan Mason was by all accounts pious and pure. She may even have been submissive in the sense of trying to be a good helpmate to her minister husband, but she was anything but passive, weak, and dependent. On the contrary, she was an amazingly competent organizer and officer of numerous voluntary associations, and an effective public speaker. She had given birth to ten children, but she was in no way confined to her home.[68]

Outwardly submissive, Gertrude Clanton Thomas struggled inwardly with the values and lifestyles of both her father and her husband. As a southern woman and the mistress of a slaveholding household, Thomas had a domestic world that was not small, and its management took considerable skill. Her diary, unpublished until long after her death, reveals the depth of her struggles with the ideal of True Womanhood.

In spite of the prescription, some women like Fanny Butterfield Newell, a New England preacher's wife, and Jarena Lee, the first female preacher of the African Methodist Episcopal Church, experienced a call to preach and found ways to respond to that call as early as the 1810s and 1820s. Their stories will be explored in chapter 4.

4

"I DARE NOT REFUSE"
Women Called to Preach the Gospel

"I sometimes felt a longing desire, to go *'into all the world and preach the Gospel to every creature.'*" In these words Nancy Towle described the call to preach that came to her in 1818, when she was about twenty-two years of age. She continued:

> In imagination, I was there; and in dreams of the night, I was there, sounding salvation to the thoughtless thousands. But, nevertheless, I was not able to understand, how this could be consistently required of me. . . . I could find no person, to whom I dared disclose the secrets of my heart. But to the Lord alone, I made my supplication, day and night, that He would graciously reveal,—and bring me to submit, to all His holy will.
> . . . [I] thought, I would freely give [up] the whole world, . . . to be enabled to take up my cross, and discharge every duty incumbent upon me, in a public way.[1]

Women often described their being called to speak in public (and especially to preach) as taking up their cross. In 1821 Nancy Towle delivered her first public sermon and embarked upon the life of an itinerant preacher. By 1832, the year her autobiographical memoir was first published, she had traveled throughout Maine, Nova Scotia, Massachusetts, New York, Pennsylvania, Virginia, South Carolina, and even England and Ireland, preaching the gospel. Towle was one of the "over eighty" women Catherine Brekus discovered who were preaching between 1800 and 1845 among the Freewill Baptists, Christian Connection, Methodists, and African Methodists.[2]

Brekus has argued that (at least in these years) these denominations valued personal religious experience over theological education, favored revivals (and camp meetings) that overturned traditional constraints against women speaking in public, aspired to create "islands of holiness" that opposed nineteenth-century cultural values, and desperately needed new laborers in the field.[3] Brekus claimed that although "the Methodist hierarchy" encouraged women to speak in class meetings and love feasts, they "never officially recognized them as preachers."[4] Nevertheless, there were women in the Methodist denominations in this country who experienced a call to preach and became (unordained) traveling preachers as early as the 1810s and 1820s. Two of the earliest examples were Jarena Lee, a free black woman born in New Jersey and probably the first female preacher of the African Methodist Episcopal Church, and Fanny Butterfield Newell, wife of a circuit riding Methodist Episcopal preacher in the New England Conference. From the published spiritual memoirs of these two women, we know something about how they experienced and responded to their call.

JARENA LEE, AFRICAN METHODIST EPISCOPAL CHURCH (1783–1850?)

The Life and Religious Experience of Jarena Lee, published in 1836 and, in a longer version with a slightly revised title, in 1849, is one of the earliest examples of the genre of nineteenth-century autobiographical writings of African American women.[5] Published not by ministers but by the women themselves, they focused on the authentication of a black female self in a world that denied full humanity to that self through the combined forces of racism and sexism.[6]

Jarena Lee was born in Cape May, New Jersey, in 1783, to free but impoverished parents. She was converted at age twenty-one under the preaching of the Reverend Richard Allen, minister of Bethel African Methodist Episcopal Church in Philadelphia. About 1811, she apparently first felt a call to preach the gospel and went to see Richard Allen.[7] He told her he had no objection to women holding prayer meetings or exhorting the congregation after the sermon, but the rules of Methodism "did not call for women preachers."[8] In 1811, she married the Reverend Joseph Lee, pastor of a black church in Snow Hill, New Jersey, six miles from Philadelphia. Within six years, death took five members of her family, including her husband. She was left with two infant children, ages two years and six months. She moved to Philadelphia and Bethel Church after Reverend Lee's death. By this time, the African Methodist Episcopal (AME) Church was officially organized as an independent black denomination, and Richard Allen had been named its first bishop.

One day at a service in Bethel Church, a minister began preaching but seemed to have lost the spirit. Jarena Lee sprang to her feet "as by an altogether supernatural impulse"[9] and began exhorting. When she sat down and remembered the earlier conversation with Bishop Allen, she was afraid she might be expelled. Instead the bishop stood up and told the congregation how she had asked his permission to preach eight years earlier. Now he expressed the judgment that she was as called to preach as any of the preachers present. The Sunday after receiving this endorsement of her call to preach, Lee felt "moved to attempt to speak to the people in a public manner," but shying away from beginning in a church, she held a meeting in a woman's house nearby. For six months she stayed in the area and preached in homes; she was still keeping house with her young son who was "very sickly." However, a call came for her to preach among the Methodists at a place about thirty miles away. In spite of her son's illness, she accepted the call and remained there a week. Friends took care of her son while she was gone, and she returned home to find that no harm had come to him. As she recalls, "I now began to think seriously of breaking up housekeeping, and forsaking all to preach the everlasting Gospel."[10]

Soon after, Jarena Lee began her itinerant preaching career, first in the Philadelphia area; later from upper New York State to Maryland and as far west as Ohio. In one year in the 1820s, she claimed to have traveled more than two thousand miles and preached more than one hundred seventy-five sermons. She often traveled on foot, and spoke to large congregations, both black and white. When possible, she traveled with "a Sister," that is, another woman evangelist. She was completely dependent upon the hospitality of those to whom she went as a preacher. While on these journeys, she left her child with Bishop Allen and his family.

The 1849 edition of Lee's *Religious Experience and Journal* gives a vivid picture of the challenges she faced as an African American woman preacher. Often she encountered opposition to women preaching, but generally her confidence that God was with her was enough to carry her through the most difficult times. A close reading of her journal suggests that a sense of humor also helped. Her retort to an elder who was "averse to a woman's preaching" was forthright:

> And here let me tell that elder . . . that as far back as Adam Clarke's time, his objections to female preaching were met by the answer—"If an ass reproved Balaam, and a barn-door fowl reproved Peter, why should not a woman reprove sin?" [She went on:] "May be a speaking woman is like an ass—but I can tell you one thing, the ass seen the angel when Balaam didn't."[11]

When back in Philadelphia, Jarena Lee was invited by Bishop Allen to preach at Bethel Church. The bishop's support was important. In June 1823 she went with him and several elders to the AME General Conference in New York. While traveling in the Philadelphia area, in New Jersey, or in New York, Lee often mentioned preaching to mixed white and "colored" congregations. Her courage in confronting racial barriers was even more impressive as she moved farther south. In Maryland she was invited to address large congregations of "the old Methodist connexion," which she did "feeling thankful that the middle wall of partition had, thus far, been broken down." After another such occasion she recorded, "I preached in the Old Methodist Church to an immense congregation of both the slaves and the holders, and felt great liberty in word and doctrine; the power of God seemed without intermission." At a camp meeting of the AME Church she preached to slaves, some of whom, she was told, had walked up to seventy miles to worship God. It is remarkable how widely she traveled in both the South and the North as a free black woman during slavery.[12]

When confronted by a black male preacher in 1824 who told her it was something new for women to preach, Jarena Lee appealed to the example of earlier Methodist women preachers like Mary Bosanquet Fletcher. When he asked why she did not go to the

Quakers (since they had authorized women preachers), she replied simply that she was sent to the Methodists. Like the Hebrew prophets, she relied fundamentally on a God who says, "I will send by whom I will [send]." It was God's doing what instruments were used to call sinners to repentance.[13]

In what must have been early fall of 1827 on into the winter of 1828, Lee traveled by canal boat to Utica, New York, and from there to Rochester, Niagara, Buffalo, and other parts of New York State. She noted that some of her work there was in March, and it was cold and snowy; sometimes she was in a sleigh, the rest of the time she made her way on horseback or on foot. Having recently seen a book about John Stewart, the black Methodist missionary to the Wyandott Indians, Lee expressed a desire to meet the Indians near Buffalo. On arriving, she first asked the Indians to "pray for us," which they did in their own tongue. She then preached to them through an interpreter, and found them "endowed with a Christian spirit."[14]

During the 1830s there were increasing references in her journal to external events (particularly related to the struggle against slavery), such as the Nat Turner uprising in 1831 and various antislavery meetings, including a meeting of the American Antislavery Society in New York.[15] Finally in 1830 Lee was able once more to see her son, who had been with Bishop Allen and his family in Philadelphia. The bishop had sent her son to school, but after Allen's death on March 26, 1831, Jarena Lee placed the boy with a cabinetmaker so he could learn a trade. Some years later she rejoiced that this son had "embraced religion."[16]

By the 1830s Lee more frequently mentioned having traveled with or offered support to other women preachers or exhorters. For example, in 1839 she wrote of enjoying "good seasons together" in western Pennsylvania with Sister Zilpha Elaw, another early African Methodist preaching woman.[17] Reflecting that it is "better to wear out than to rust out," Jarena Lee finally drew to a close her narrative of "the first female preacher of the First African Methodist Episcopal Church."[18] Because she could not secure the support of the AME Church's Book Committee, Lee financed both editions of her *Life and Religious Experience* (1836 and 1849) herself. Nothing is known of her activities after 1949.[19]

By the time of the publication of Lee's *Journal* in 1849, a number of black women were actively preaching. Jualynne Dodson includes Sophie Murray, an evangelist at Bethel AME Church in Philadelphia; Elizabeth Cole, also of Philadelphia; Rachel Evans of New Jersey; and Harriet Felson Taylor, "the first female exhorter and local preacher" of Union Bethel AME Church in Washington, D.C.[20] In 1848, the Daughters of Zion, one of the women's societies in the AME Church, petitioned the General Conference that women be licensed to preach in the connection. In 1852, the AME General Conference defeated, by a large majority, a resolution to give women a license to preach; however, neither petitions for licensing and ordaining women nor women's preaching activities subsided with that vote.[21]

FANNY BUTTERFIELD NEWELL, METHODIST EPISCOPAL CHURCH (1793–1824)

Fanny Butterfield was born in Sidney, Maine, in 1793 and converted at age fifteen under the preaching of Methodist itinerant preacher Henry Martin. According to her account, her call to preach first came in 1809, when a messenger appeared to her in a dream and told her to take on the mantle of Brother Martin (who had recently died).[22] The following year she married the Reverend Ebenezer F. Newell and traveled with him around his circuits in Vermont and Maine. Her call to preach was reaffirmed in 1811 by a powerful religious experience. A few days after the birth of her first child, a son named Ebenezer, she had what we would now call a near-death experience, in which she was taken up into heaven where she met Christ. He greeted her with the words "Fanny, you must not come yet; thou shalt not die, but live, and declare the works of the Lord to the children of men."[23]

She had always been in frail health. In 1818, her husband volunteered to go to St. Croix, at the eastern edge of Maine, near the New Brunswick border. She was reluctant to go. As she wrote in her diary, "I have a comfortable place to live in, and my children are with me and tender; and to think of launching out again . . . to face the storms, and plunge through mud and snow in those wild regions. . . . I am ready to say, Have me excused, I cannot go." Her husband went off alone, but Fanny soon began to feel "the afflictions of my mind exceedingly heavy." She remembered Christ's words to her in the vision, "Fanny, go back." When her husband came back for her she went out to greet him with the words, "You have come back for help, have you not?" He answered, "Woman's help." She wrote in her diary, "He does not bid me stop travelling yet. Here am I, Lord, send me to the ends of the earth."[24] Fanny left her children with friends and accompanied her husband on the long, difficult trip by sailing vessel to frontier outposts that had been settled only eight years earlier. She died of tuberculosis several years later, at age thirty.

In many ways, Fanny Newell must have served as an example to early (white) American Methodist women who felt a call to preach. The first edition of her memoirs was printed within months of her death in 1824; it was in its fourth edition by 1848. That fourth edition, however, included something new: an introduction by an unnamed minister of the New England Conference who clearly understood Fanny Newell's call in terms of her willingness to assume the responsibilities of a Methodist itinerant preacher's wife, and wanted to stress that her public labors in the church had not caused her to neglect her domestic obligations. Her husband, Ebenezer, on the other hand, recognized his wife's own call. On proposing marriage to her, he wrote in his journal, "I viewed it my duty to bring her gift into the more public service of the church."[25]

Sometime in 1814 there was reference to a daughter as well as the son. Fanny still frequently traveled around her husband's circuit, although while the children were young she was more preoccupied with domestic duties. A diary entry for July 1817 is typical: "Our class and prayer meetings are attended with blessings from on high. . . . We maintain family devotion, and find a family blessing. O Lord, make me like Deborah of old, a mother in Israel."[26]

Fanny Newell's most rigorous preaching activities were related to the work in St. Croix, and in reference to these, she was more outspoken than ever about her public evangelical role. From Calais, she wrote in August 1818, "I arose, and spake to the people, and had great liberty. . . . Whatever may be said against a female speaking, or praying in public, I care not; for when I feel confident, that the Lord calls me to speak, I dare not refuse."[27] Later in the month, Fanny left her children, telling them she was going to "exhort poor sinners," and accompanied Ebenezer to even more remote regions that had to be reached by horseback and then by birch canoe. Here Fanny exhorted regularly after Ebenezer's sermons, her spirit "so stirred" within her that she was ready, she said, "to spend and be spent in the service of God; for it is better to wear out than to rust out."[28]

While visiting St. David's (New Brunswick), she reflected, "The enemy tried to disturb me with thoughts like these: Woman, you are not in the way of your duty—God has never called you to go to this and that place, or to speak in public—it is your own enthusiastic notion, and not from God. My mind replied, these thoughts are very congenial with my natural feelings, for I never sought, neither did I desire to be the wife of a preacher, much less an exhorter."[29] Fanny Newell served a full year with her husband in that frontier setting before they finally returned to Boston for the annual conference.

"Woe Is Me, If I Preach Not the Gospel"

Although their life circumstances were very different, Jarena Lee and Fanny Newell experienced their call in strikingly similar ways. In dreams, each woman saw herself preaching to large crowds; yet both felt their call as a heavy cross for a poor female to bear.[30] Neither woman had spiritual peace except in striving to do what she believed God required of her. As they expressed it, when they shrank from taking up the cross, they were pierced through with many sorrows.

Jarena Lee was fully persuaded that she was called by God to labor in God's vineyard. If not, she said, how could God consistently bear testimony in favor of the labors of "his poor coloured female instrument" in awakening and converting sinners?[31] After one of her preaching dreams, Fanny Newell wrote in her diary, "Could I preach as well awake as when asleep, I should think 'wo[e] is me, if I preach not the Gospel';—and even now, if I were a man I should be willing to go and preach Jesus. . . . My mind is led to view Jesus as the only Savior, and he is every way sufficient to save a helpless soul who trusts in him for grace, and receives power daily to conquer every foe."[32] After preaching in New Jersey on November 17, 1821, Jarena Lee reflected on her inadequacy for the task. "I felt my weakness and deficiency for the work, and thought 'who is able for these things,' and desired to get away from the task. . . . The Lord again cut loose the stammering tongue, . . . so that, glory to God's dear name, we had a most melting, sin-killing, and soul-reviving time."[33] Mrs. Zilpha Elaw said much the same thing, "Not that we are sufficient of ourselves . . . ; but our sufficiency is of God."[34] These women, and others like them, experienced empowerment and authorization from God to preach when the church still refused to grant them official acceptance. Although they struggled with a sense of unworthiness, God's grace was sufficient for them to overcome what they called a "man-fearing spirit."

HANNAH PEARCE REEVES, METHODIST PROTESTANT CHURCH (1800–1868)

At least one woman preached in church the smaller and more democratic Methodist Protestants from the 1830s. Hannah Pearce was born in England in 1800, converted at age eighteen, and shortly thereafter became one of the charter members of the Bible Christians. From the time of her conversion, she is said to have been zealous in exhorting her neighbors and convinced that she was called to preach the gospel. While only nineteen, she began an itinerant preaching ministry among the Bible Christians. Taking one year out to rest, she had traveled a total of nine years by 1831; her biography has a list of the circuits to which she was appointed.[35]

Probably in 1827, a Wesleyan Methodist lay preacher by the name of William Reeves was invited by a friend to go and hear Hannah Pearce preach. Being opposed to women preaching, he at first refused, but later reconsidered on the grounds that he might be wrong. When introduced to her after the service, as the story goes, he asked her how she could expound on a text for an hour without any notes, and she answered, "Throw away your crutches, and fight like a man!" To his credit he resolved to study the Word of God more faithfully, that he might improve his own performance.[36] Soon after their meeting he went to the United States, where he became an itinerant preacher of the newly organized Methodist Protestant Church in 1830.[37] For about a year he corresponded with Hannah Pearce in an effort to persuade her to come to America and marry him. Finally convinced that it was God's will, she sailed to America in April 1831. They were married in Zanesville, Ohio, in July, and from the day of their marriage "labored together in the gospel ministry" until her death in 1868.[38]

Hannah Reeves was apparently from the beginning an unusually effective and popular preacher. She traveled her husband's circuits with him, and there is evidence to suggest that her preaching was often preferred to his by the congregations they served. The following description of Hannah Reeves's preaching was published in the *Mount Vernon Gazette*, Ohio, October 1831, and reprinted in the *Methodist Protestant:*

> At length the female arose, evidently without the least embarrassment, and introduced herself to the congregation by a few brief remarks. She was apparently about twenty-five years of age, of a free, open, and pleasant countenance, and decently clad in the plain attire of the humble Quaker. . . . She manifested an unusual degree of zeal. Her voice was strong and clear, her manner easy and agreeable, her language chaste and eloquent, and her gestures few and unstudied. . . . During my journeyings, I have witnessed many displays of talent and eloquence in the pulpit, but never heard a sermon which left such an impression on my mind as that delivered by Mrs. Reeves.[39]

In further testimony to her reputation, she was asked to preach before the Ohio Annual Conference of the Methodist Protestant Church in October 1831, and a committee of key leaders of that denomination (including Nicholas Snethen and Asa Shinn) visited her to ascertain her wishes about accepting her own circuit appointment. She responded that all she wanted was the conference's concurrence in her labors with her husband.[40]

From then on they both traveled his circuit with the blessing of the church, Hannah sometimes taking separate appointments. When he was ill, especially for an extended period during 1832, she took his appointments; she was even invited to preach in meetings of the Methodist Episcopal Church and the African Methodist Episcopal Church. Hannah Reeves gave birth to three children between 1832 and 1842, all of whom died in infancy. She continued to preach during these years in spite of what was described as generally "feeble health." She died a good death on November 13, 1868, having preached for the last time earlier that year.

George Brown's biography of Hannah Reeves ended with a defense of female preaching. After describing her piety and character, he gave this simple summary of her life and accomplishments: "This pious lady lived long [sixty-eight years], preached much, and did a great deal of good in her day. God gave her many seals to her ministry. She never sought ordination, or any official position, in either an Annual or Quarterly Conference, for she had no higher ambition than to have liberty from the Church to preach the gospel of Christ to perishing sinners."[41]

LYDIA SEXTON, UNITED BRETHREN IN CHRIST (1799–1894)

In the 1840s several women applied to the United Brethren for permission to preach.[42] The 1845 General Conference ruled that the gospel did not authorize the introduction of females into the preaching ministry. In spite of that action, Charity Opheral applied to the White River Conference (Indiana) in 1847 for a license to preach and was given "a note of commendation."[43] Although the United Brethren General Conference of 1857 ruled against licensing women preachers, women of that church continued to be given letters of recommendation to preach. Lydia Sexton was granted a preacher's license by the Illinois Quarterly Conference in 1851, and continued to have it renewed annually, even after 1857.

Her story is of particular interest because it is in many ways so unlike that of the other pioneer preaching women. Born in 1799, Lydia Sexton was not converted at a young age, but rather as a mature woman of thirty-four who had recently married her third husband, Joseph Sexton. Her first two husbands had died tragically within a year or two of her marriage to them, in each case leaving a baby son behind. Not long after experiencing forgiveness and reconciliation to God, Lydia Sexton applied for membership among the United Brethren and, with her sister-in-law, became a member of the first United Brethren class meeting in Dayton.[44]

Soon the other members of the family were converted and joined the church as well, and Lydia and Joseph set up an altar for family devotions. At first Lydia Sexton would neither pray in prayer meeting nor speak in class, but she was reproved by the presiding elder for never having "a word to say for Jesus."[45] The conviction that she was called to preach grew steadily.

> All the day long and during the silent watches of the night, waking or dreaming, I seemed to have a large congregation before me, all in tears, as I told them the story of the cross. . . . I thought, if I were only a man it would be no hardship to me, nor even a cross, to preach, but rather a pleasure. But for me, a woman, to preach, even if I could; to make myself a subject of ridicule and comment among my friends and kindred, and thus also bring reproach upon our glorious cause![46]

When she searched the Bible, she found prophetesses, workers with Paul in the gospel, and many others. "I saw that in all ages of the world the good Lord raised up of his own choosing, men, women, and children." Year after year, Sexton recalls in her autobiography, she struggled on with all the common evasions: "I did believe firmly that it was my bounden duty to preach. But oh! that man-fearing spirit."[47]

In 1843 the Sextons moved to Jasper County, Indiana, where there was, as yet, no church. Methodist and United Brethren preachers began to labor there, and a union meeting was held, out of which a United Brethren class was organized. When Lydia Sexton's son became seriously ill, she finally covenanted with God that if her son's life were spared, "the remainder of my days should be devoted to his [God's] service, whatever might be the inconvenience or consequences." Within a week she agreed to preach, and an appointment was "given out" for her to preach in her own home. Her husband (who was the class leader) had misgivings at first, but consented when she told him there was no peace for her otherwise. After about a year of preaching, Lydia Sexton was urged to apply for a preacher's license. Her papers were presented to the next quarterly meeting, where she was examined by the presiding elder, and in 1851 she was granted a preacher's license by the Illinois Quarterly Conference.[48]

Her preaching labors naturally increased, and she began to travel. Here was a *married* woman preacher, but not married to a minister, who began to itinerate throughout the midwestern frontier. Her husband not only supported her preaching, but apparently traveled with her whenever possible. Sometimes she took another woman into the pulpit with her to exhort. She did all she could to encourage other women who felt called to preach. Moving ever westward, in 1865 the Sextons arrived in Kansas City, Missouri. In 1869, their children helped them celebrate their fortieth wedding anniversary. The following year this remarkable woman received notice that she had been appointed chaplain to the Kansas State Penitentiary. Accompanied by her husband, Lydia Sexton reported for duty on January 29, 1870. Although there was some initial opposition, she threw herself into the work. According to her own account, there were about one hundred seventy convicts. Her class book of November 17, 1870, listed eighty-two members, with "two exhorters and four class-leaders, and five are studying for the ministry."[49] She resigned her post in February 1871, for reasons of health.

Lydia Sexton's autobiography concluded in 1872 with one of her sermons. Her faithful husband, Joseph, died in October 1878; the *Autobiography* was published in 1882. She wrote in the introduction: "At this writing my mission is, 'relief to the destitute thousands of [African American] refugees who have fled for succor and safety' from Louisiana and Texas to southern Kansas. But as I go I preach the unsearchable riches of Christ. . . . Yours in the Lord. Lydia Sexton." Sexton moved to Seattle in 1890 with her youngest son and his family. She died there at the age of ninety-five on December 17, 1894.[50]

Jarena Lee, Fanny Newell, Hannah Reeves, and Lydia Sexton were pioneer women preachers in the African Methodist Episcopal and United Methodist traditions. Although Jarena Lee first experienced a call to preach in 1811, it was eight years before Richard Allen gave her permission to become an itinerant evangelist in the AME Church. She then traveled thousands of miles in the 1820s to 1840s, preaching to both African Methodist and Methodist Episcopal congregations. Fanny Newell was able to fulfill her call to preach by marrying a Methodist itinerant preacher in 1810, traveling his circuits with him, and exhorting regularly after his sermons. Although the editor of her published memoirs stressed that Fanny Newell's public labors had not caused her to neglect her domestic duties, she clearly was more than just a helpmate to her preacher husband. She always interpreted her experience of being restored to life in 1811 as God's giving *her* "a fresh commission to go and call sinners to repentance."[51]

In the smaller and more democratic Methodist Protestant Church, the gifts of Hannah Reeves were recognized and encouraged from the early 1830s. Although she was never ordained or even licensed to preach, she and her husband functioned very much like a clergy couple as they both traveled the circuits to which he had been appointed. Of these four pioneer women preachers, Lydia Sexton was the only one to be officially licensed to preach. After the Illinois Quarterly Conference of the United Brethren gave her a preacher's license in 1851, she continued to be an approved itinerant preacher until she retired in 1871.

While still under the sentence of domesticity, women found various ways to respond to God's claim on their lives. Chapter 5 explores the partnership in ministry of itinerant preachers' wives with their clergy husbands on the frontier, and in chapter 6 the "holy boldness" of female holiness evangelists, whose preaching exemplified "the promise of the Father" to pour out the Spirit on all flesh, so that both daughters and sons would prophesy.

5

PARTNERS IN MINISTRY
Itinerant Preachers' Wives

In spite of the prescription, as we have seen, some women like Fanny Butterfield Newell and Jarena Lee experienced a call to preach and found ways to respond to that call as early as the 1810s and 1820s. Also in these years, the role of minister's wife came to be seen as a new religious vocation for women.

ITINERANT PREACHERS' WIVES

In his wonderfully provocative book on the minister's wife, Leonard I. Sweet identified four distinct models of that role from the Protestant Reformation to the twentieth century: the Companion, who "held up her husband's hands in his sacred calling"; the Sacrificer, who "clasped her hands in pious resignation" and "'hindered him not in his work' by staying out of his way and raising the family on her own"; the Assistant, who "became her husband's right-arm, sharing many pastoral responsibilities and functioning as an extension of his ministry"; and the Partner, who "ministered with both her own hands," developing "a ministry alongside her husband."[1]

Sweet acknowledged that every minister's wife probably developed her own unique strategy, and emphasized that the different models did not represent paradigm shifts, but rather new roles that often coexisted and intermingled with older roles. Although Sweet's book is not specifically about Methodist women, it is significant that most of his examples of Methodist women are discussed under the rubrics of the Assistant and Partner models.[2] In order to explain the Assistant and the Partner models, which only began to emerge as possibilities in the late eighteenth and early nineteenth centuries, Sweet attempted to reconstruct "the diverse and complex historical experiences of this remarkable group of nineteenth-century women."[3] By the time he was finished, he had referred to much of the history of women in American religion in this period.

My approach to the minister's wife in this chapter is much more limited than Sweet's. A central theme of *Grace Sufficient* from the beginning has been the changing possibilities for women in the Methodist family of denominations to live out their own Christian vocation. Ministers' wives appear, therefore, in other places in this book; for example, as pioneer preaching women, as missionaries, or as founders of church women's organizations. Here I want to look at how and why becoming a minister's wife emerged in the 1830s to 1860s as a new, or perhaps redefined, area of religious activity for Methodist women.[4] For reasons that will become clearer as we proceed, I want to focus here primarily on itinerant preachers' wives on the moving frontier.

FROM CELIBATE TO MARRIED CLERGY

While Bishop Francis Asbury was alive, most Methodist itinerant preachers were young, poor, and single. Those who chose to marry were usually forced to "locate," that is, leave the itinerancy and become local preachers, in order to support their families. In their 1844 episcopal address, the bishops examined the problem of attrition from the itinerant ranks, "lamenting the easing of strictures against early clerical marriages and the growing number of preachers with 'local embarrassments' (that is, wives, children, and property)."[5] From Francis Asbury's perspective, the problem was not only that clergy marriages were a threat to the itinerancy, but also that itinerant marriages were unfair to the institution of marriage itself: "What right has any man to take advantage of the affections of a woman, make her his wife, and by a voluntary absence subvert the whole order and economy of the marriage state, by separating those whom neither God, nature, nor the requirement of civil society permit long to be put asunder?"[6]

Nevertheless, by the 1860s, most Methodist itinerants were married. What had happened to account for this transition from a largely celibate to a married ministry? The early-nineteenth-century idea that women were distinctively religious helped, as Julie Roy Jeffrey suggested, to establish a climate where "clerical marriage could be seen not as a necessary evil but, in fact, as a desirable goal."[7] Also, an increasing number of young Protestant women, "convinced that their duty to God required a commitment to evangelical work," saw marriage to a frontier itinerant preacher as promising "new and broad avenues of religious usefulness."[8]

ADVICE TO *The Itinerant's Wife*

In order to help women prepare for the vocation of minister's wife, and also to warn them of the difficulties of such a life, advice books began to be written by clergymen and clergy wives. A good example of this is *The Itinerant's Wife* by the Reverend Herrick M. Eaton, published in 1851.[9] Eaton recognized that the vocation of minister's wife was beginning to resemble a career, complete with educational requirements and more specialized skills. According to him, the Methodist itinerant's wife should be a person of good common sense, or "sound, practical judgment." She should have some basic knowledge of the Bible and church history, particularly the history of her own denomination. She should also read more widely, for example in contemporary magazines for women like the *Ladies' Repository*. She should be pious, and her piety should be steady, winsome, cheerful, and benevolent. Above all, the itinerant's wife must "love the itinerancy."[10]

Eaton acknowledged that foremost among the trials the itinerant's wife would face were the profound loneliness of separation from family and friends and continual partings. She could expect her life to be a series of good-byes, "from the time she leaves her paternal abode till she enters upon her final rest. The itinerancy allows no protracted respites; nor is there any escape from its demands, except by quitting its ranks. But to the faithful itinerant's wife no thought is so abhorrent as that of a *location*. She desires to *locate* only in the New Jerusalem."[11]

In his manual, Eaton described a particular model for clerical marriage in which, in spite of a woman's evangelical desire to serve, her primary duties were as wife and mother. Jeffrey argued convincingly that Eaton's insistent points suggested his worries. Because this new field of usefulness was ill defined, each itinerant preacher's wife would have to work out her own delicate balance between domestic and religious duties.[12]

Mary Orne (Mrs. Thomas) Tucker, New England, 1816–1840s

Mary Orne married the Reverend Thomas Wait Tucker in 1816 when she was twenty-two. She died on her seventy-first birthday, in October of 1865, and her husband followed her in death six years later. He was more than eighty years old and the oldest living member of the New England Conference. Her obituary in *Zion's Herald* gave fitting tribute to her nearly fifty years as an itinerant preacher's wife: "She greatly aided and cheered her companion in the peculiar trials of ministerial work."[13]

Mary Orne was born in Corinth, Vermont, in 1794. In her youth she witnessed a deathbed scene and heard Francis Asbury exhort every member of the household, including her, at the dying woman's bedside. She was not the first nor the last young woman in Methodism to be convicted of her sins at a dance. She experienced conversion in 1812 and soon after was baptized in the river by a Methodist local preacher from the neighboring town. She had no real religious instruction, although she did occasionally attend Methodist meetings to listen to the good preaching. After hearing one of these preachers, she was introduced to him the next day. He spoke to her about "the itinerancy of Methodist preachers" and asked her how she "should like travelling about." She replied that she "should like travelling for pleasure but not by necessity." Little did she know that she had been recommended to him as a suitable person for a minister's wife! Within six weeks she had agreed to become his wife, in spite of the opposition of friends who thought her foolish to unite her destiny "with that of a penniless Methodist preacher."[14]

Thomas Tucker was ordained an elder at conference in June 1816. While he was away at conference, Mary Tucker thought at length about the requirements for being an itinerant preacher's wife. She wished she knew more about the Bible, and that she were more accustomed to talking with people about their religion. She reflected, "I could hardly open my mouth in class, much less in the prayer-meeting. The thought that something was expected of a minister's wife greatly embarrassed me, and lessened my self-confidence. . . . Still I strove assiduously to do my duty according to my knowledge."[15]

Her husband's first appointment was to the Athens Circuit in Vermont, "a comparative wilderness." The circuit was one hundred and sixty miles in circumference, and it took its new preacher about three weeks to fulfill all his appointments. The roads being "exceedingly bad," Thomas Tucker was forced to travel them on horseback. At first his wife boarded with a family while he was away, but soon she decided to travel with him, riding "two upon one horse." The preaching places on this circuit were mostly log huts in dense forest. Their lodgings were usually uncomfortable, and Mary Tucker discovered that the life of a Methodist itinerant and his wife was often a "life of privation."[16]

The following year Thomas Tucker returned from conference to say that he had been appointed to the island of Martha's Vineyard. Mary Tucker confided in her journal, "What a change this was surely, from a wilderness of woods to a wilderness of water." They journeyed for three days to Boston, where they rested a few days, then on again to Falmouth, where they took a boat to the Vineyard. On one occasion, traveling back to Boston during a rough gale in an open sailboat, this young preacher's wife barely rescued her baby from falling overboard.[17]

In 1822 Tucker was sent to New London, Connecticut, a charge cut short by his severe illness, a "lung fever" that brought him close to death and necessitated his asking for a leave from the conference for three years. The next station, at Marblehead, Massachusetts, drew Mary Tucker's wrath. The society was small and the previous year had contributed only one hundred and fifty dollars for the support of its preacher. "Think of that, ye modern preachers," Tucker wrote in 1848, "one hundred and fifty dollars to support the preacher, wife, and four children!" In fact the family remained there only ten weeks because not enough money could even be raised to purchase their food. Mary Tucker could scarcely believe that the presiding elder had recommended this appointment for them. Some of their friends in Bristol, Rhode Island, heard of their circumstances and invited them to come and make their home with them until Mr. Tucker was well again. In the stage on the way to Bristol, a lady asked one of the children, "Where do you live, my little dear?" At a loss for an answer he replied, "I don't know," and then turning to his mother he said, "Ma, where is our home, haven't we *any home*?"[18]

When their daughter married in 1836, and their son found a position in Boston, Mary Tucker was anxious to remain as close to her children as possible until they were more experienced at being on their own. The conference met that year at Springfield, and she wisely attended with her husband in case her "presence might be of some use." When he was assigned somewhere in Rhode Island, she went to see Bishop Hedding and explained her reasons for wanting to be near her children, adding that she hoped he would not think her too officious. He smiled and said, "Not at all officious, Sister Tucker. Your request is reasonable, and should be granted." Their appointment was changed to Millbury, Massachusetts. However, it was the year of the financial crash of 1837, which had devastating consequences for this manufacturing town. At the quarterly meeting, the presiding elder, "seeing how precarious were our means of support," offered to move them to a more favorable situation, but they decided to stay with the people "and trust to Providence for our bread."[19]

And so it went from year to year, a new place every year or two, as often as not without provision for their accommodation. Mary Tucker wrote with ample justification in 1843: "It is one of the peculiar sins of omission on the part of our societies, that no provision is made to accommodate the preacher and his family upon their arrival at a station. Men hardly treat dumb animals so badly." Aside from the hardship and anxiety of providing for the family, the most difficult aspect for Mary Tucker of being an itinerant preacher's wife was clearly that of the incessant parting and moving to a new place. "Many a year of experience has hardly reconciled me to the trials of an itinerant life. It is a gypsy sort of life, yet it has its compensations."[20]

On their thirtieth wedding anniversary, Mary Orne Tucker mused about the signs of aging, concluding: "The romance of life has departed, and its sober realities succeed. How is it with thee, my soul, this evening? . . . Dear Lord, assist me to dedicate myself anew to the holy mission whereto thou hast called me!"[21]

In 1848, Thomas Tucker requested the conference to give him a "superannuated," or retired relationship, and it was granted. He had served thirty-six years in the itinerant ministry. Mary Tucker wrote, "A new era in our existence has commenced. Never before have we known freedom from the service of our friends or the Church, having always come and gone at others' bidding. Perhaps we shall soon tire of our liberty. . . ." They retired to a small home in North Quincy, Massachusetts, "purchased by our small savings and the assistance of our son." Suddenly stricken with a paralysis (very likely a small stroke) that left her unable to continue her writing, her account came to an abrupt end. It was a tribute to the early days of Methodism, in the hope that her church would "never discard the old fashioned means of grace, such as class-meetings, wide-awake prayer-meetings, camp-meetings, and other features which have in times past proved so efficient in the hands of our early preachers."[22] It was also a reminder of how little provision was made for the preacher's family in those days, and therefore unintentionally a tribute to the courage, strength, and evangelical calling of the early Methodist preacher's wife.

ANNA MARIA PITTMAN (MRS. JASON) LEE, OREGON MISSION, 1837–1838

In 1836 Anna Maria Pittman was chosen to be part of a reinforcement to the Oregon mission to the Flathead Indians. The Reverend Jason Lee, appointed by the Board of Missions of the Methodist Episcopal Church, along with his nephew Daniel Lee, and Cyrus Shepard, a schoolteacher, had arrived at Fort Vancouver on September 15, 1834, after an overland journey from New York that took eight months. They had set up a mission on the Willamette River, near present-day Salem, Oregon, and Jason Lee had asked the mission board for missionaries with practical skills, especially men with families, and for "pious, industrious, intelligent females."[23]

Accordingly, a group of thirteen set out for the mission on July 29, 1836, including Dr. Elijah White and his wife and two children; Alanson Beers, a blacksmith, with his wife and three children; William H. Willson, a carpenter; and the Misses Elvira Johnson, Susan Downing, and Anna Maria Pittman. They sailed from Boston around Cape Horn to Hawaii, arriving in Honolulu on December 24 after a trip of nearly five months. After remaining in Hawaii for the winter months, they set sail again on April 11, 1837, and arrived at Fort Vancouver on May 17.

Anna Maria Pittman was a member of the Allen Street Methodist Episcopal Church in New York City and had communicated to the Board of Missions her own wish to become a missionary to North American Indians. It seems that the board selected her not only for the contribution she could make to the mission as a teacher, but also as an appropriate wife for Jason Lee. As her letters to her parents reveal, Anna Maria was a "converted and committed"[24] young woman who, at the age of thirty-three, was eager to be useful, to "do something for God."[25]

Shortly before the group's departure from Boston, Pittman wrote her parents to let them know of her plans and to tell them it had been harder for her to say good-bye to them than they might have guessed. "Though I appeared so cheerful, you must not think I am void of that feeling, which nature has planted in the breast of Parent and child. Had I indulged in grief, I would have been unhappy, and made those so about me. But I find the grace of God is sufficient." She added, "I received the life of H[ester] A[nn] Rogers, and much obliged to you. May I copy her example."[26]

On June 5, 1837, Pittman wrote her parents from the Oregon mission. Their party had been welcomed warmly, and the female presence at the mission station was already making a difference. "We found things in old bachelor style; we females soon made a different appearance in the house. . . . Mr. Lee says he feels now as if he was home with so many females around them, the men seem much pleased." Later in the same letter she reported on a matter her family must have been eager to hear about:

You will be anxious to know if there is any prospect of my having a Protector. Let me tell you there is. Mr. J. Lee has broached the subject, it remains for me to say whether I shall be his helpmate in his important charge; I look unto the Lord who has thus far directed me in the path of duty. . . . I have thought much on the subject, and my own mind is fixed, relying on the grace of God which I have proved to be sufficient. I expect to give my heart and hand to J. Lee. When this union will take place I am not prepared to say, but probably soon.[27]

The wedding took place on July 16, a Sunday that had been chosen as the time for the first public communion service. There were actually three weddings on the same day: Jason Lee married Anna Maria Pittman, Cyrus Shepard married Susan Downing, and Charles Roe, a white settler, married an Indian woman called Miss Nancy. It must have been a full day of religious festivities, including also the celebration of the Lord's Supper, baptisms, and a love feast.

After some months it seemed advisable to enlarge the Indian missionary work in Oregon, so Jason Lee was pressed to go in person to request the Methodist Mission Board to send additional reinforcements and to acquaint the public with the Oregon country. He was reluctant to go, both because he felt he was needed at the mission and because his wife was expecting their first baby. He left on March 23, 1838, after a mere eight months of marriage; Anna Maria was six months pregnant. She gave birth to a baby boy on June 23, but both mother and baby died within a few days. Lee received the news early in September in Missouri, but continued his journey eastward although grief-stricken.

In a letter to her mother two days after Jason Lee left, Anna Maria explained how hard it was to let him go. Her words are a reminder that, at any time, ministers' wives may exhibit the features of more than one type of role. Surely this is an illustration of Sweet's Sacrificer model: "When I left home and kindred with all their endearments I felt it to be a sacrifice, but what is it in comparison with a separation from my *dearest half* especially in my present situation; it is through grace alone that I am enabled to submit. . . . If it is for the promotion of the cause of God, and duty calls my beloved companion from my embrace I cannot withhold him but bid him go in the name of the Lord."[28]

There are three very poignant letters from Anna Maria to Jason Lee, dated March 28, 1838, April 6, 1838, and April 14, 1838. In them her deep affection for her husband, physical difficulties in pregnancy, and effort to bear the separation with her characteristic courage and faith are all clearly revealed. He had obviously written to her as well, because she expresses gratitude to him for his letters in each of hers. The following excerpts are typical:

> I find my affections twining closer and closer about you; . . . I rejoice that our spirits can meet before the mercy seat [in prayer]; continue my dear to meet me there, morning and evening.[29]

> I still feel cheerful, sometimes lonely especially when obliged to lie down in pain, then I feel the loss of the dearest half, though weeping endures for a season joy returns again. . . . My mind seems to be gradually preparing for what I must pass through, and I feel to welcome whatever the Lord sees fit to call me to, even if it be unto death. . . . In the course of my religious experience, I have ever found that in the severest trials, the Lord seems to bestow the most grace.[30]

> Farewell my husband, God bless you, and return you to my embrace again, after a speedy journey—until then I shall endeavour patiently to wait. I remain your affectionate wife, in the strongest bonds of increasing love while life remains, Anna M. Lee.[31]

At a special meeting of the Methodist Board of Missions on November 14, 1838, Lee gave a detailed report of the Oregon mission. Favorably impressed, the board voted a large appropriation and agreed to send additional personnel. The so-called "Great Reinforcement" arrived in Oregon in 1840.[32] Although their purpose was to open branch missions to the Indians, it was clear to many that this would "expedite the settlement of the Oregon Territory." Among this number were Jason Lee and his second wife, Lucy Thompson Lee. On shipboard during the journey back to the mission, Jason Lee wrote to Anna Maria's mother to try to explain why he had been persuaded not to return to Oregon alone, but "to choose a suitable companion to accompany me."[33]

Although Anna Pittman Lee had experienced her own call to become a missionary to the Indians, her major contribution to the mission was through her marriage to Jason Lee and as a "helpmate" to him in his work. It is impossible to know how she might have shared in his ministry had she not died shortly after the birth of their first child. As difficult as it was for her to have him leave, she put his religious duty above her own needs and "hindered him not in his work."

ANNIE KIMBERLIN (MRS. WILLIAM) TAYLOR, CALIFORNIA, 1849

William Taylor was one of the two real founders of California Methodism. He was an ordained deacon serving appointments in the Baltimore Conference, and recently married to Anne Kimberlin Taylor, when he was asked by Bishop Beverly Waugh in 1849 to go as one of two missionaries to the California mission. Since the discovery of gold at Sutter's Mill the previous year, men had been pouring into California, and there was a great challenge to minister in the mining camps. The agreement to leave the East for California was very much a mutual decision. Returning from a meeting with the bishop, Taylor asked his wife, pregnant with their third child, if she was willing to go. Anne ran upstairs to her room, returning in a few minutes with her consent. She explained, "I went upstairs and kneeled down and said, 'Lord, Bishop Waugh wants to send us to California. Thou knowest, Lord, that I don't want to go . . . [but] if it is Thy will to send us to California, give me the desire to go.' In a second or two he filled and thrilled my whole being with a desire to go to California."[34]

William and Annie Taylor arrived in San Francisco in September 1849, after a journey of 155 days on a clipper ship around Cape Horn. Their daughter, whom they named Oceana, was born off Cape Horn. William Taylor gave a vivid picture of San Francisco in those days. "We stopped and took a view of the city of tents. Not a brick house in the place, and but a few wooden ones, and not a wharf or pier in the harbor. But for a few old adobe houses, it would have been easy to imagine that the whole city was pitched the evening before for the accommodation of a vast caravan for the night; for the city now contained a population of about twenty thousand."[35]

After some searching, the Taylors found Asa White and his family, whose rough board house covered with blue cotton cloth was the rallying point of Methodism in the city. The Methodist class there numbered about twenty. While at Brother White's, Taylor received a letter from William Roberts, the presiding elder, informing him that he had been appointed to San Francisco and that his fellow missionary, Isaac Owen (from the Indiana Conference), had been appointed to Sacramento and Stockton. Within six weeks, Taylor had built his own wooden house for a parsonage. He and his wife soon began a garden, bought some chickens, and even brought home a cow to provide milk for their baby daughter.

Taylor preached frequently in the open air to the miners, for example, at "the Plaza," surrounded by gambling and drinking houses and frequented on Sundays by many gamblers. Annie accompanied him on these preaching missions. William recalled, "When the appointed hour arrived I took with me my 'sweet singer in Israel,' the partner of my youth, who has stood by me in every battle; and down I went to the field of action." Taylor preached some six hundred sermons in San Francisco in the open air. As Jeffrey suggests, in the primarily male environment of San Francisco, Anne Taylor's "presence and hymn-singing" no doubt "helped gather crowds and reactivate forgotten faith by recalling pious mothers and early religious practices."[36]

REBECCA (MRS. ORCENETH) FISHER, CALIFORNIA AND OREGON, 1850s

Another pioneer preacher's wife who entered fully into her husband's ministry in early California was Rebecca Fisher, wife of Orceneth Fisher. Fisher had transferred in 1855 from the East Texas Conference to the Pacific Conference of the Methodist Episcopal Church, South. He was appointed to Stockton, California, where his wife's courage and evangelistic labors became legendary. On their arrival in Stockton, they found there was no bell on the church. "Sister Fisher determined to get one." Although the membership of the church was small and there was some prejudice against them, "through tears and prayers, hard work and persistent effort, she succeeded, and soon the silvery notes of a sweet-toned bell were calling worshipers to prayers."[37]

Brother Fisher is reputed to have been a powerful revivalist preacher, and he determined to hold a camp meeting about twelve miles above Stockton. Together he and his wife got together provisions and went out to the ground. Rebecca Fisher "cooked and washed dishes and fed the people until the revival began." Once the preaching began and "scores [of penitents] crowded the altar," Sister Fisher would work at the tent all day feeding the people and at night would "enter the altar" and "point the penitents to the world's Redeemer."[38] As a result of this successful revival a new circuit was formed and soon after, a church and parsonage.

The Fishers' efforts were not without opposition. One night during the revival when the altar was full of mourners and Rebecca Fisher was leading in prayer, someone threw "an explosive" among them. "The report was loud and distinct. Instead of confusing her, she became more earnest, the 'Amens' to her petitions were more hearty, the faith of the Church rose, and as a result they had very many conversions soon after."[39]

In 1858 when the prospect arose of establishing the ME Church, South, in Oregon, Orceneth Fisher volunteered and took his wife and two children with him. On one occasion at a camp meeting near Salem, troublemakers instigated a controversy about the flying of an American flag from the preacher's stand. "Several thousand persons were on the grounds," and mob violence seemed a very real possibility. Supported by a Mrs. Belt, a doctor's wife in Salem who stood with her and offered encouragement, Sister Fisher "stepped boldly up to the raging leader and ordered him to behave himself. . . . For a moment he looked into that calm, resolute face, and dropping his eyes and hanging his head, he became quiet." With order soon restored, most of the crowd took their seats, and Brother Fisher preached a powerful sermon.[40]

Both Annie Taylor and Rebecca Fisher shared fully in their husbands' ministries, each couple functioning effectively as a "missionary *pair*."[41] The rough mining frontier posed peculiar challenges. From assisting their husbands in pastoral visitation to playing highly visible roles in street revivals or camp meetings, these women helped to win the West for religious influences. No wonder J. C. Simmons could write, "The Church in California, in every period of its history, owes more to the women than to any other human agency."[42]

CATHERINE PAINE (MRS. DAVID E.) BLAINE, SEATTLE, 1850s

The earliest preachers in the Washington District of the Oregon Conference were John DeVore (originally from Lexington, Kentucky, but a member of the Rock River Conference), appointed to Steilacoom, and David E. Blaine (born in New York State and an ordained deacon in the Genesee Conference), appointed to Seattle in 1854. David Blaine was married in August of 1853 to Catherine Paine of Seneca Falls, New York. He and Catherine left New York on October 5, 1853, and sailed for Panama, crossing the Isthmus on the backs of mules, proceeding to San Francisco by steamer, from there by sailing vessel to Olympia, Washington, and from Olympia to Seattle by Indian canoe. They reached their destination on November 20, 1853.

Seattle was about a year and a half old, and had a population of less than one hundred persons when David Blaine held the first preaching service there on the first Sunday in December. The first Methodist church in Seattle had four members, including his wife. Catherine Blaine taught the first public school in Seattle, and also organized the first Sunday school. Both Blaines were good letter writers, and their frequent letters to family members back in New York State offer a vivid picture of frontier conditions in Seattle in the mid-nineteenth century, and of the life of a frontier preacher's wife.[43]

The Blaines' household goods had been sent to the wrong destination and therefore took ten months to arrive! Catherine's early letters are full of her descriptions of their efforts to build a home for themselves and to make their own simple furniture and household utensils. Like the Taylors in San Francisco, they planted a garden and bought a few chickens. Although the main part of the house was not yet finished and the Blaines were living in the wing, they had hosted Brother Devore and Brother Roberts, their presiding elder. Catherine explained, "Men always carry their blankets with them as they go from home, and we had some Indian mats to help make a bed for them on the floor at the foot of our bed. You would think it rather hard to be obliged to treat ministers so, but it is nothing after you get used to it."[44] In June of 1854, Catherine wrote to thank her father for giving her the advantage of a good education, so that she could be useful. "For without my education my sphere of action must be very limited, and my life would doubtless have been far less happy. Not that I find happiness in being separated from home and dear friends, but in following the manifest path of duty. Did I not think we were in that place for which Providence designed us . . . I should not live here contentedly."[45]

The physical and economic demands on women were heavy. Doing the washing, for example, was a challenge under the circumstances. There were no "pounding barrels" and a whole day had to be devoted to it, but Catherine wrote that she was getting "along so nicely with washing that if I were not the preacher[']s wife I should take in washing. It is very profitable." Again she described the difficulty of keeping house and taking charge of the school, as well as sewing and taking care of a sick neighbor.[46]

She proudly described the new church, but could not disguise her consternation that the people were so careless about keeping it "looking nicely." They could not afford to hire a sexton, so Catherine herself had cleaned the floor and had to clean it repeatedly to get rid of the effects of wet umbrellas and muddy shoes and juice squirted by the tobacco chewers. In July she wrote, "Tomorrow we design to go across the bay to be absent until Friday. We go in a canoe. On Saturday we expect to go up to Mr. Blaine's appointment, and Monday go on up some 40 miles. We shall walk, and so be absent most of the next week. I tell you, I am a capital walker."[47]

Catherine's report on the contents of the mail in July 1854 gives some indication of how frontier itinerant preachers and their wives kept in touch with family and church developments back home: "David got all he could bring home, in his arms at once. There were six numbers of *Ladies Repository*, four of the *National* [Repository]. . . . We now receive regularly the New York and Auburn *Advocates, Missionary* and S.S. [Sunday School] *Advocates*, [NY Herald] *Tribune, Seneca Falls Courier*, [the Methodist] *Quarterly Review, Repository and National*."[48]

When David had to be away four weeks to attend conference at Oregon City, Catherine admitted her loneliness. She was anxious that they might be moved to another appointment just as they had begun to make their new home comfortable. She was using homeopathic medicine to keep them in good health. Her first baby was born in January 1856; three days later they had to flee an Indian attack and were taken on board a warship for safety. They lost their house and garden, and because of the continued danger they were moved to Portland.

Moving to the next appointment was not a simple matter, as David tried to explain:

> We, that is, my wife and a month old baby . . . left Seattle in a little steamer, the first that plied these waters. We arrived in Olympia in a wagon drawn by mules and traveled to a point about 40 miles distant on the Chehalis River. The next day we had a canoe ride for some miles and another in a wagon drawn by three yoke of oxen. The mud was fearful. Our next conveyance was a canoe down the Cowlitz River and across the Columbia to St. Helens, where we boarded a steamer for Portland. This was not altogether a pleasure trip nor was it inexpensive. Our goods were sent round to Portland by sea. The freight on them and our own expenses were $100.00. Seattle was without a pastor the rest of the year.[49]

Catherine Blaine's evangelical work in the remote areas of the Pacific Northwest was multifaceted. She established a school and a Sunday school, but also frequently accompanied her husband on his appointments. By gardening and raising chickens she helped the family survive economically, and she was also the new church's only sexton. The benefits of a married clergy were especially clear on the frontier mission field.

FRANCES SAWYER (MRS. JOHN) MERRITT, COLORADO, 1870s–1880s

Not all frontier itinerant preachers' wives were able to lead physically active lives. Frances and John Merritt came to Colorado in 1871 not because of his vocation but rather because of her health. Recurring tuberculosis threatened her life, and they were told that a change in climate was her only hope. As Bishop Henry White Warren said in her funeral sermon twenty years later, "Who would have thought that under these circumstances she was coming to a great work? . . . Who would expect that that life, so feeble, would take upon itself the great matters of service—the great and sublime budding forth of its full love for the benefit of others?"[50]

Frances Helen Sawyer was born in a log cabin in upstate New York on November 18, 1839, to "godly and industrious" parents. Sent away to school in order to have better educational advantages, the sorrowing and homesick child returned home to spend the next two years as an invalid. It was probably during this time that she first contracted tuberculosis. At the age of sixteen she was converted at a Methodist revival in Canton, New York, where she had gone to live with her brother and his wife and attend the academy there. In 1861 she met the Reverend John Merritt at a camp meeting and they were married in August the following year, in the same church in Canton where she had experienced conversion. She was described as "peculiarly fitted, both by nature and grace, for the position and duties of a pastor's wife."[51] For several years they moved from appointment to appointment like most married itinerant Methodist preachers. When her health deteriorated seriously, John Merritt requested and received from Bishop Ames a transfer to the Colorado Conference.

The realities of life in the West were shocking at first. Stopping at the home of the Reverend George Adams, the Methodist preacher in Cheyenne, Wyoming Territory, Frances Merritt asked the preacher's wife why she had a revolver on the table. "She replied that the condition of society was such that she did not dare go to the door without it in her hand, or within easy reach. . . . The first night we were there a woman was shot, and we, accompanied by Mrs. Adams, visited her and told her of Jesus and his love. This was not an assuring outlook, and I feared my weak nerves could not endure such powerful tonics."[52] The Merritts traveled from Cheyenne to Denver, and then on to Pueblo to his appointment. At first Frances Merritt had great difficulty breathing in the high altitude.

Eventually, however, her health began to improve with frontier living in the dry Colorado climate. In 1872, the presiding elder of the Southern District was injured and John Merritt was asked to take over his duties. That summer the Merritts traveled with their adopted daughter, Ella, and Miss Ellen Merritt, John's sister, on his circuit in southern Colorado and New Mexico. The scenery was beautiful, but the experience was sometimes grueling: "One night, we camped on the banks of the Apishapa River, and what was our surprise in the morning to find a deep snow covering our tent and the ground! I could not see how this was to be a benefit to weak lungs."[53]

At Trinidad, Colorado, they found the Methodist church without a pastor, the Reverend Elial J. Rice having died several months before. The membership was composed entirely of women, who held all the official positions in the church. The Merritts reported that all the work of the church was "in excellent condition." The pastor's wife read sermons to the congregation on Sundays, and "kept up all the regular services of the Church until the next session of the Annual Conference."[54]

In 1876 John Merritt was made presiding elder of the Southern District and they moved to Colorado Springs. At this time, the Southern District included all of Colorado south of Denver, and the new presiding elder often had to be absent from home for eight to ten weeks at a time. In 1877 Frances Merritt was very ill, but by the summer she had recovered sufficiently to accompany him on an extended mountain trip, including Fairplay, Leadville, Salida, the San Luis Valley, and Ouray. She later recalled: "We traveled over eighteen hundred miles that summer in our carriage. . . . This out-of-door life bronzed my face, threw more iron into my blood, besides giving me the opportunity of seeing the grandest mountain scenery on the continent."[55]

In 1880 Frances Merritt's health began to deteriorate seriously. Fearing that she might not recover, her two sisters had come from the East to be with her in her last hours. Frances had a vision in which she was crossing a river in a boat. When she reached the shore, she heard a voice say, "No, it is forbidden you to even touch this shore now. You must return to the other side and continue to work for the Master. . . . There are years of great usefulness and joyful service for you on earth." Soon after, the presiding elder, Dr.

Earl Cranston, visited Mrs. Merritt, and after praying with her he said, "Sister Merritt, you are not going home just yet." She replied, confidently, "I know it; for the Lord has told me that he has more work for me to do."[56]

In 1884, John Merritt was appointed presiding elder of Colorado's Northern District, and in 1885 the Merritts moved to Denver. Although she could no longer travel with her husband, Frances Merritt worked from her home and her bedside. Driven by her own memories of difficult frontier appointments, Frances Merritt persuaded several other women at the annual conference in 1886 to help establish a Woman's Home Missionary Society. "When my husband came home from some of his frontier work, and told me how poorly the preachers had to live, and how brave they were, I could not rest. I felt that something had to be done, and I think the call came to me from God to organize the Woman's Home Missionary Society."[57]

In spite of her frail health, she was elected corresponding secretary, an office she held until her death. For the next three years, she hosted meetings, presiding when necessary, and she arranged for missionary speakers and wrote hundreds of letters—"facilitating shipments of barrels filled with supplies, furnishing rooms in schools, purchasing a pipe organ from an impoverished Texas church, bringing news from the East to the West."[58]

The duties of her office required that she speak in public, representing the work at annual conference and organizing local auxiliaries. Being naturally of a "retiring disposition," she did not welcome this public work. "But it seemed to be the path of duty marked out for her, and trusting Him who said, 'My grace is sufficient for thee,' she tremblingly went forward."[59] Amazingly, she even managed to travel thousands of miles.

Especially after the death of her only child, an adopted daughter, and upon taking up residence in Denver, Frances Merritt became "the Mother Confessor of the Conference." She called the younger preachers her "boys," and many of them, along with their wives, came to love her as a mother, and to look to her for spiritual advice and encouragement in their work. Her home was always open to all of the preachers. Her advice to a young pastor's wife seeking the blessing of perfect love is typical of the spirituality expressed in her memoir: "Do not look for feeling, but look for strength to carry you through every trial. . . . Walk by **faith**. Every moment you spend looking at anything but Christ makes you more wretched, and there is no salvation in it. . . . If you become impatient, do not give up, but ask forgiveness, and try again. Cling to the promise, 'My grace is sufficient for thee.'"[60]

In 1891 the WHMS decided to establish its own deaconess home in Denver. The board voted to name the home after Frances Merritt. Although she was too ill to attend the opening of the home bearing her name, Bishop Warren paid her the highest tribute in his address: "Well, what could a woman do who was always sick and poor herself? One does not have to be rich in order to be good, nor well in order to be great. Every one naturally recognized that that woman was an embodiment of the idea and spirit of this Home. So it was called the Frances Merritt Deaconess Home."[61]

Realizing that she would not recover from this episode of illness, Frances Merritt resigned her position with the WHMS at its anniversary meeting at the 1891 annual conference. There must have been few dry eyes when her letter was read. At the end she thanked the women who had sustained her in that work and concluded: "With my latest breath will I pray for the preachers of the Colorado Conference and their sacrificing families. Good-bye! I will meet you at the gate in the morning. Yours, nearing home, Frances H. Merritt."[62] This remarkable itinerant preacher's wife, who had been "a consumptive" for thirty years, died on December 8, 1891. In times of better health she had undertaken the responsibility of organizing a Woman's Home Missionary Society. When too ill to travel or continue active work, she was still able to be a spiritual guide to the preachers of the Colorado Conference and their wives.

Throughout the period when women were told their place was in the home, Methodist women found a meaningful religious vocation as itinerant preachers' wives. Given the near-primitive circumstances of daily life, the extent of their evangelical activities outside the home is truly remarkable.[63] Without their own profound sense of calling to the work it is hard to imagine how they could have endured the hardships entailed. It is equally difficult to imagine the success of Methodism on the frontier without them.

6

"A HOLY BOLDNESS"
Holiness Evangelists

The holiness movement was one of the ways in which the earlier Methodist tradition of religious leadership for women manifested itself after 1830. Nurtured in the Tuesday meetings of the 1830s and 1840s, the holiness revival in Methodism flowered in the holiness camp meetings of the 1850s–1860s. Female holiness evangelists, like Phoebe Worrall Palmer and Amanda Berry Smith, preached the beauty of holiness and modeled the obligation of women's speaking when the Spirit commands. Although Palmer and Smith became famous for their transatlantic preaching missions, they were not exempt from the familiar female struggle to reconcile religious with domestic responsibilities. Through their ministries they also helped to develop important female networks in the nineteenth century.[1]

PHOEBE WORRALL PALMER (1807–1874)

Phoebe Worrall was born December 18, 1807, the fourth of nine surviving children of Henry Worrall and his wife, Dorothea Wade. These pious parents had joined the Duane Street Methodist Episcopal Church in New York City and together established a devout Methodist home oriented around daily family worship. Although Phoebe felt she had given her heart to Christ at a young age and had become a member of her parents' church at age thirteen, she was sometimes troubled because she could not point to a definite conversion experience. Not long after her eighteenth birthday she wrote in her journal, "I long for the full assurance of faith."[2]

On September 28, 1827, at the age of nineteen, Phoebe married Walter Clarke Palmer, a young medical doctor who was busy establishing his own practice in New York City. He and Phoebe Worrall were kindred spirits. He had also been raised in a devout Methodist home, experiencing conversion at age thirteen. When they met he was active in the Allen Street Methodist Episcopal Church where he was superintendent of the Sunday school.

Their first child, Alexander, was born on September 27, 1828, and died nine months later. A second son, Samuel, born on April 29, 1830, lived only seven weeks. A grieving Phoebe tried to reconcile her faith with these losses. She reflected in her diary, "God takes our treasure to heaven, that our hearts may be there also. . . . After my loved ones were snatched away, I saw that I had concentrated my time and attentions far too exclusively, to the neglect of the religious activities demanded."[3]

In April of 1833, Phoebe gave birth to her first daughter, Sarah, and in August 1835, to a second daughter, Eliza. Both Eliza and her mother were critically ill that summer, and again Phoebe Palmer resolved to do more for God. After both mother and daughter recovered, the Palmers moved to a house at 54 Rivington Street, on New York's Lower East Side, and invited Phoebe's newly married elder sister, Sarah, and her husband, Thomas A. Lankford, to share it with them.[4]

The family's joy was short-lived when eleven-month-old Eliza died tragically in a nursery fire. As the anguished mother struggled to bring some meaning out of this tragedy, she experienced the unmistakable presence of God's love and grace as well as a new understanding of her vocation. From then on, Palmer resolved to spend the time she would have devoted to the care of her daughter to saving souls. She wrote: "If diligent and self-sacrificing in carrying out my resolve, the death of this child may result in the spiritual life of many." Her commitment to evangelism dated to this time of her daughter's death, and her evangelistic ministry can, at least in part, be seen as a memorial to her dead children.[5] The Palmers would have two more children, Phoebe and Walter Clarke Jr.

The house-sharing arrangement between the Palmers and the Lankfords had two important consequences for Phoebe Palmer's life. One was the successful resolution of her personal religious struggle under the influence of her older sister. The other was her involvement in a religious gathering, begun at her sister's initiative, which would become a major forum for Phoebe Palmer's leadership.

On May 21, 1835, Sarah Lankford received the blessing of entire sanctification she had been seeking. While reading *An Account of the Experience of Hester Ann Rogers,* Lankford came to the words, "'Reckon thyself dead unto sin'; and thou art alive unto God from this hour!" Following these instructions she fell on her knees and cried, "Yea, Lord from this hour . . . I dare reckon myself dead, indeed unto sin." From that moment she trusted that God had made her holy, although it was a week later before she felt the witness of the Spirit. Immediately she began to pray that her sister might also experience the blessing of holiness and urged her to seek it.[6]

By 1835 Sarah Lankford was leading women's prayer meetings at both the Allen Street and the Mulberry Street Methodist Episcopal Churches. The following February she decided to combine these two meetings into one, to be held at her own home on Tuesday afternoons. This was the gathering that became known as the Tuesday Meeting for the Promotion of Holiness. It would continue for nearly sixty years under the leadership of one or the other of these two sisters.[7]

SANCTIFICATION EXPERIENCE

Since her daughter Eliza's death, Phoebe Palmer had also been seeking a deeper spiritual experience. She began to teach the Young Ladies' Bible Class in the Allen Street Sunday School in April of 1837 and to study the New Testament for a deeper understanding of sanctification. In July she asked the members of the Tuesday Meeting to pray that she might receive full salvation. On July 26, 1837, a date she would always refer to as her "day of days," Phoebe Palmer made "an entire surrender" to God of everything in her life, her "body, soul, and spirit; time, talents and influence," as well as "the dearest ties of nature, [her] beloved husband and child." Receiving the assurance that her consecration was accepted by God, Phoebe Palmer knew this was the experience of sanctification she had been seeking.[8]

Although Palmer had earlier shied away from public speaking, she believed that she would lose the spiritual gift she had received if she did not testify publicly to it. At a camp meeting in early August she observed a number of people seeking salvation or "full redemption" and thought, "If there were only some one here to talk about the simple way of salvation by faith!" When an inner prompting suggested, "Why do you not do it?" she was quick to justify her reticence. "O, thought I, it would require a **special** commission to undertake a duty so formidable." That evening in prayer she felt "the gentle chidings" of the Spirit asking why her conduct had not corresponded with her faith. A short time later she spoke at a love feast but "felt no liberty" because she had only inferred that she enjoyed the blessing of full salvation. Continuing to struggle against her natural reticence to speak in public, Palmer increasingly, as the "duty of speaking was presented," felt "conscious assistance from on high" and was able to speak powerfully of the riches of grace she had experienced. The lesson in all this was clear to her: "A plain path seems marked out before me—the path of obedience."[9]

TUESDAY MEETINGS

In 1840 Phoebe Palmer assumed the leadership of the Tuesday Meeting when her sister and brother-in-law moved away from New York City. The meeting began to include men as well as women, after Professor Thomas C. Upham of Bowdoin College, a Congregational minister whose wife was a member, asked if he might also attend. He subsequently experienced entire sanctification under Phoebe Palmer's guidance. Many prominent Methodist figures became regular attenders of the Tuesday Meeting, including Nathan Bangs, a presiding elder (district superintendent) in New York City, Bishops Edmund S. Janes and Leonidas Hamline, and educators Stephen Olin and John Dempster. By the 1850s the meeting had become broadly evangelical, drawing ministers and laypeople from almost every Protestant denomination. The practices of the Tuesday Meeting became influential for the entire holiness movement.[10]

Although numbers of clergy were always present, laywomen and laymen were treated with equal respect as recipients of the gifts of the Holy Spirit. This theology, including the importance of public testimony, gave women a prominent leadership role in the holiness movement. Phoebe Palmer herself best described how the Tuesday Meeting was conducted:

> After the opening exercises, any one is at liberty to speak, sing, or propose united prayer. . . . Testimony follows testimony in quick succession, interspersed with occasional singing and prayer, as the circumstances may seem to demand. . . . In these meetings the utmost freedom prevails. The ministry does not wait for the laity, neither does the laity wait for the ministry. . . . How small do all merely earthly distinctions appear, when brought under the equalizing influences of pure, perfect love! And it is this equalizing process, that, to our mind, forms one of the most important characteristics of this meeting.[11]

Home meetings patterned after the Tuesday Meeting began to be organized in various parts of the Northeast and, later, throughout the country. By 1886 some two hundred such meetings were operating in the United States and abroad.

HOLINESS, EVANGELISM, AND PUBLISHING

The 1840s represented a watershed time in Phoebe Palmer's career. Along with the increasing invitations to travel beyond New York City to speak about Christian holiness came a clearer sense of her own vocation as a woman called to public witness. In the summer of 1840 she made her first evangelistic trip outside the city, visiting Rye, Williamsburg, and Caldwell's Landing, New York (the new home of Sarah and Thomas Lankford). From these small beginnings grew an evangelistic career unprecedented for a woman, especially one traveling alone. In addition to the Tuesday Meeting and her evangelistic efforts, Phoebe Palmer began to promote holiness through a vigorous publishing program. She became a regular contributor to the *Guide to Christian Perfection*, begun in Boston in 1839 and edited by the Reverend Timothy

Merritt.[12] The first issue of the *Guide* asked for responses from those who had experienced "the grace of sanctification." The editor addressed a special word to "the female members of the church," urging that, since "many of you have experienced the grace of sanctification, should you not then, as a thank-offering to God, give an account of his gracious dealing with your souls, that others may be partakers of this grace also?"[13] Women did respond to the editor's request, establishing through their writing important connections with other women.

Phoebe Palmer's first contribution was a description of her own spiritual journey toward holiness. It appeared serially in three parts, each entitled "Letter from a Lady to Her Friend" and signed simply, "P. P.," in December 1839 and January and March of 1840. Through this medium, Palmer advised other women that God's will was to make them "happy and useful," and therefore that they, too, should seek holiness. Summing up its importance in her own experience, Palmer wrote: "So conscious am I that all my sufficiency is of God, that for worlds I would not be left one hour without the *witness* that I have returned all my redeemed powers to Him, who has purchased them unto himself."[14]

The July 1841 issue of the *Guide* contained the holiness experience of Sarah Lankford, including her account of how the *Life* of Hester Ann Rogers had guided her to the experience. Other women wrote that they also had found "H. A. Rogers' Life" helpful in seeking sanctification.[15] Still others encouraged readers that God's "grace would be sufficient" to enable them to consecrate themselves to God, to "be wholly and for ever his, to live for him, to do his will," and to remain faithful to their covenant. "A Sister in the Fulness of Christ" testified, "I have found his yoke easy, and his burden light; the grace of God has been sufficient to keep me" for thirteen years.[16]

During this decade, Phoebe Palmer also published several books, including *The Way of Holiness* (1843), *Entire Devotion to God* (1845), and *Faith and Its Effects* (1848). In her first and probably most influential book, *The Way of Holiness*, Palmer described her own experience of sanctification. Addressing the question "Is there not a shorter way?" she outlined the holiness theology that would become so widely characteristic of the holiness movement as a whole. In Palmer's view, entire sanctification was presently available to all regenerate Christians who were ready to meet the scriptural requirements of consecrating all to God and believing God's promises. Employing what would be called her "altar terminology," Palmer explained that Christ was the altar that sanctified, or made acceptable, the Christian's total consecration of self. Once this consecration was complete, the seeker should exercise faith and lay claim to the scriptural promise of entire sanctification, with or without an accompanying emotional experience. This was what Phoebe Palmer meant by a "shorter way." As we have seen, another characteristic emphasis of her teaching was that public testimony to the experience of holiness was essential to the retention of it. These emphases gradually came to distinguish the holiness movement that ensued.[17]

THE ALTAR PRINCIPLE AND WOMEN

Scholars have variously interpreted the particular significance for women of Palmer's view of holiness. Theodore Hovet argued that the altar principle encouraged women's inner freedom *within* the domestic sphere. He suggested that the laying of one's all on the altar gave the (white, middle-class) mid-nineteenth-century wife and mother "a means of freeing her religious life from the chains of domestic responsibilities," especially from the "excessive emotional demands" of the domestic sphere.[18]

Palmer acknowledged that her own emotional dependence on her husband had significantly interfered with her spiritual development. She claimed that after offering "this last sacrifice" on the altar, she was able to see her husband "go with a contented heart about his Father's business in his own sphere, and I can go with a light heart to that assigned to me."[19] Other scholars thought that while Palmer's holiness doctrines served to reconcile some women to the confined domestic sphere, they could impel others (like Palmer herself) to move outside it.[20]

Hester Ann Rogers may well have been both the major source of Palmer's altar principle and her model of piety. In a letter to her cousin in 1776, Rogers professed feeling "very unworthy," yet convinced that God accepted "[my] offering up myself and my services on that *altar that sanctifieth the gift*."[21] Both Phoebe Palmer and her sister Sarah had been helped to experience holiness by reading Hester Ann Rogers. There are other similarities between the religious experience of Phoebe Palmer and that of Hester Ann Rogers, including the insistence on testimony for the retention of holiness, mention of interior warring with "the Tempter" (Satan), and frequent references to "venturing on the promise."[22] In *The Way of Holiness* Phoebe Palmer wrote:

> My faith in the reality of the work [of sanctification] grows stronger; I feel that, instead of its being presumptuous to believe, it would greatly grieve the Spirit of my condescending Saviour were I to doubt the all-sufficiency of his grace to sustain me in the full enjoyment of this blessing.[23]

Again, when Palmer was seriously ill, in "agonizing pain" and apparently close to death, she prayed that she might recover only if her living would glorify God. Like Hester Ann Rogers, her faith was strengthened through this experience: "And now, with all my heart, do I praise my covenant-keeping God for the lengthened trial through which I have passed. I used to say that 'grace is sufficient to sustain under all circumstances,' because I knew it. Now I can say, it is sufficient to sustain fully."[24]

A SPIRITUAL GUIDE FOR WOMEN

Through both the Tuesday Meeting and her published writing, Phoebe Palmer became a spiritual guide for many Methodist women. Letter writing was another means by which women provided mutual encouragement to one another in their spiritual journeys, and in this way Palmer both gave and received support. Among her closest friends were kindred spirits like Melinda Hamline, wife of Methodist Bishop Leonidas L. Hamline, and Mary D. Yard James, a Methodist woman exemplary for her piety and well known in Methodist circles in New York and New Jersey. Phoebe Palmer wrote often to both women beginning in the 1840s.

Mary James was thirty years of age when she first met Phoebe

Palmer on a visit to New York in late 1840. In the autumn of 1841 Palmer visited James in Mount Holly, New Jersey, and in May of the following year, James was invited to spend some weeks at the Palmers' home on Rivington Street. In the 1840s Mary James also began to write for publication. Her pastor, the Reverend George F. Brown, encouraged her to write the autobiographical *Mary; or, The Young Christian* (1841), because the majority of books for children showed pious children dying young. He wanted Sunday school literature to include examples of young Christians who grew to be vital and thriving adults.[25]

Phoebe Palmer, who well understood the struggle between domestic and spiritual responsibilities, had been instrumental in encouraging her friend Mary James to view her writing as a religious vocation. On a visit Palmer found the young mother engaged in making clothes for her children and learned that James made all her children's clothes and her own as well. Phoebe Palmer was clear in her reply: "The work required of you, writing for Jesus, is of vast importance. This no one can do for you, but making garments others can do in your place."[26] That the lesson was not lost on Mary James is clear from a subsequent letter to her husband:

> I know I have lost much by being engrossed with domestic cares and not doing what God required of me for His blessed cause. He has shown me that He desired me to be as Mary, sitting at His feet and listening to His teachings, ever ready to do His bidding, not as Martha, burdened with many cares. I see clearly that I must more frequently use my pen for Jesus.[27]

Like Phoebe Palmer herself, Mary James wrote poetry, hymns, and other pieces, but "Christian correspondence was the chief employment of this consecrated pen." The power of that pen as a spiritual guide is illustrated in the following, on spiritual weakness as a result of hurrying one's devotions:

> Then I saw that I had stepped aside, not because grace was insufficient to keep me, but because I had neglected to ask for that grace as I should have done. The grace of yesterday will not answer for today. I must have fresh supplies, daily, hourly, momentarily. It is only

by constantly looking to Jesus that I can resist the devil or keep myself unspotted from the world. Entire sanctification is retained only by the moment.[28]

A PUBLIC MINISTRY

In 1848 the Palmers transferred their membership from the Allen Street ME Church to a small, struggling mission congregation. In 1850 Phoebe Palmer also succeeded in persuading the Ladies' Home Missionary Society to begin a mission in the slum area of Five Points in New York City. Her work with both the Tract Society and the Female Assistance Society had brought her into contact with the poor in this area, and she was convinced that something more than evangelism was required. Consisting at first of a chapel, schoolrooms, baths, apartments for twenty needy families to be offered rent free, and facilities for a director, the Five Points Mission eventually included a House of Industry that employed five hundred people, a day school, and various other social programs.[29]

From 1850 on, Phoebe Palmer entered into the most active years of her public career. As new dimensions of her ministry unfolded, Walter Palmer began to travel with his wife and take an active part in her evangelistic meetings.[30] By 1857–58, Phoebe and Walter found themselves at the center of a remarkable evangelical revival that was interdenominational, largely urban, and primarily led by laypeople. Following the successes of these years, the Palmers accepted an invitation in 1859 to visit the British Isles. Walter gave up his medical practice altogether and never returned to it; he now became a full partner with his wife in the vocation of holiness evangelism.

In her public ministry as a holiness evangelist, Phoebe Palmer had encountered some resistance; other women told her stories of their being forbidden to speak in public. As a justification for herself and them, Palmer wrote *Promise of the Father* (1859), a defense of women's right to preach on the basis of the gift of the Spirit to both women and men at Pentecost. Claiming that the model of Pentecost should be normative in the church, Palmer presented some four hundred pages of well-reasoned argumentation: from exegesis of scriptural passages, especially the Pauline passages usually used to silence women; from historical precedent, beginning with the ministry of women in the early Christian church and culminating with women's leadership and even preaching in the eighteenth-century Wesleyan movement; from the inconsistent practice in so many churches of welcoming women's voices in some areas but silencing them in others; from the authority of various church leaders and scholars; and from the pragmatic needs of the church for women's gifts. Although Phoebe Palmer did not press for ordination for women, she insisted that women be permitted to pray and testify in the church and even to preach Christ for the conversion of sinners.[31]

Ten years later, Phoebe Palmer issued a slim volume entitled *Tongue of Fire on the Daughters of the Lord* (1869), a much shorter version of the arguments she had presented in *Promise of the Father*. Had not the Spirit of prophecy fallen upon God's daughters as well as God's sons on the day of Pentecost, when they all spoke in the midst of the assembled multitude as the Spirit gave utterance? "On what authority" then, Palmer asked church pastors, would they "restrain the use of that gift now?" Once more she reviewed the biblical and historical arguments in favor of women's preaching. Referring to the church in her own day, she powerfully described the "slowly crucifying process" to which "thousands of female disciples of every Christian land" have been subjected by "man-made restraints." Their "pent-up voices," she wrote, have long been "uttered in groanings before God." Palmer believed that the church had been "a Potter's Field where the gifts of women are buried!" She looked forward to the "resurrection of power" to be witnessed in the church "when women shall come forth, a very great army, engaging in all holy activities."[32]

In 1872, Phoebe Palmer became ill with kidney disease. By August 1874, her breathing had become labored, she suffered a heart attack, and she had become blind. She died a good death on November 2, 1874. Sixteen months later her widowed sister Sarah became the second Mrs. Walter Palmer. She continued the work of the Tuesday Meeting and the *Guide to Holiness* until her own death in 1896, at the age of ninety.[33]

Phoebe Palmer was an important transitional figure, both in her own effort to achieve an appropriate balance between domestic and religious duties, and in creating a holiness theology that would elevate (white, middle-class) women's domestic obligations to a higher spiritual level and even help to enlarge woman's proper sphere. For the black holiness evangelist Amanda Berry Smith, the struggle between domestic duties and religious calling had very different connotations.

AMANDA BERRY SMITH (1837–1915)

Amanda Berry Smith was a former slave and washerwoman who became one of the most powerful internationally known holiness evangelists of the nineteenth century.[34] Amanda Berry was born on a farm not far from Baltimore, Maryland, in 1837. Her father bought his own freedom and that of his wife and five children when Amanda was still young. Amanda's grandmother was "a woman of deep piety and great faith,"[35] and Amanda credited the power of her grandmother's prayers with the conversion of her mother's young mistress that led to the granting of their freedom. The Berry family moved to York County, Pennsylvania, "an abolitionist stronghold,"[36] and their house became a station on the Underground Railroad. Amanda had only a few months of formal schooling but was taught to read and write by her parents.

At the age of thirteen she began to work as a domestic in nearby homes and enjoyed the religious influences of revival meetings at "the Allbright Church" (Evangelical Association) and then the Methodist Church. At one of the Methodist meetings a young woman, Miss Mary Bloser, encouraged Amanda to go forward to the altar rail, and they knelt and prayed together. Amanda recalled that she "never knew a young person who knew how to so take hold of God for souls."[37] Amanda joined the church and began going to the Sunday morning class meeting, her parents going with her. However, these early religious yearnings were stifled by the insensitivity of her class leader, who made her "wait till the white ones were through," and her employer, Mrs. Latimer, who complained that she was late in serving Sunday dinner.[38] "From the beginning she had to struggle between nurturing her own spiritual life and conforming to the limits of a racially stratified society."[39]

In September 1854, seventeen-year-old Amanda married Calvin Devine. When the Civil War began he enlisted in the Union army and never came back. During the 1860s Amanda moved with her daughter, Mazie Devine, to Philadelphia. There she met James Smith, an ordained deacon in the African Methodist Episcopal Church. Amanda married him, thinking she was marrying a minister, but when the appointments were read out at the AME annual conference, his name was not on the list. James took a job in Brooklyn; Amanda found a tiny apartment in Greenwich Village where she lived with Mazie and took in washing to support them.

In 1855 Amanda was close to death when she had a dream or vision of a beautiful angel who told her three times to "go back." She then saw herself preaching to thousands of people at a camp meeting. When she awoke she was greatly improved and resolved to lead a Christian life, since she thought God had spared her for a purpose.[40] She finally experienced conversion on March 17, 1856. She was enabled to pray, "O, Lord, if Thou wilt help me I will believe Thee," and "in the act of telling God I would, I did." Peace and joy flooded her soul, and when she looked at herself she said, "Why, I am new, I am new all over." She prayed for and received the witness of God's Spirit to her conversion and never doubted it from that day on.[41]

SANCTIFICATION EXPERIENCE AND CALL TO PREACH

Central to her vocation as an evangelist was Amanda Smith's experience of sanctification, which occurred on a Sunday in September 1868. Although a member of Sullivan Street AME Church, Smith had gone to hear holiness preacher John Inskip at his Green Street Methodist Episcopal Church. There she found the experience she had been seeking: "The blessedness of the love and the peace and power I can never describe. O, what glory filled my soul! The great vacuum in my soul began to fill up; it was like a pleasant draught of cool water." She wanted to shout, but since she was the only black person in the church, she tried to restrain herself so they would not put her out. Finally, she shouted, "Glory to Jesus" and was greatly relieved when "Brother Inskip answered, 'Amen, Glory to God.'"[42]

Not long after, Amanda Smith experienced a clear call to preach. She began holding a regular prayer meeting in her apartment for a small group of women. All four of her sons had died in infancy, and in November 1869, her husband died of stomach cancer. "These family tragedies freed Amanda to pursue [her] religious vocation."[43] The very month her husband died, Smith felt led to leave New York, with the assurance that God would go with her. Up to that time she had preached primarily among her own people, in black churches in the New York area. She was grateful for the few ministers who would support a woman's preaching or speaking in public: "Thank God, there always were a few men that dared to stand by woman's liberty in this, if God called her." The following year the call to preach was even clearer and more insistent. While she was sitting in Fleet Street AME Church in Brooklyn, she suddenly saw the letters G and O being formed and heard a voice say to her, "Go preach." Again she was torn between "going to service" (as a domestic) and beginning evangelistic work, but she kept receiving the assurance, "My grace is sufficient for you. If you trust Me you shall never be confounded."[44]

In one of her first preaching experiences after this, she was called on to exhort after the preaching of Brother Holland, her former pastor in Lancaster, Pennsylvania. There was a large congregation, and when she stood up to speak she was frightened, trembling with cold chills, and a heart that seemed to stand still. But she looked to God, and God helped her. "The Lord gave me great liberty in speaking. After I had talked a little while the cold chills stopped, my heart began to beat naturally and all fear was gone, and I seemed to lose sight of everybody and everything but my responsibility to God and my duty to the people. The Holy Ghost fell on the people and we had a wonderful time."[45]

Like Jarena Lee, Zilpha Elaw, and Julia Foote, her free black Methodist preaching women forerunners, and like Phoebe Palmer and other holiness women, Amanda Smith preached in revivals, spoke in testimony meetings during camp meetings, sang, and prayed. She began to meet white holiness Methodists at camp meetings and occasionally attended the Tuesday Meeting. At the Sing Sing camp meeting in 1870, she went to Mrs. Butler's meeting for "ladies only," to hear her speak about the work in the zenanas (women's quarters) in India. She gave her last two dollars to the work of the Woman's Foreign Missionary Society of the Methodist Episcopal Church and received the *Heathen Woman's Friend*. While attending camp meetings at Ocean Grove in the early 1870s, she met local leaders of the WCTU and joined in 1875.[46] As a holiness evangelist she traveled to Britain, India, and Africa, returning home to the United States in 1890. She settled in the temperance community of Harvey, Illinois, and bought land for an orphanage. It was opened in 1899 and eventually became the Amanda Smith Industrial School for Girls. It was destroyed by fire in 1918, three years after Smith's death.[47]

Amanda Smith often suffered the hostility of both blacks and whites. When she attended the 1872 General Conference of the AME Church in Nashville, she was treated with disdain because of her "plain Quaker dress" and with suspicion as a woman preacher because the male clergy thought she was there to fight for the ordination of women. After describing this experience in her *Autobiography*, she wrote, "I give this little story in detail, to show that even with my own people, in this country, I have not always met with the pleasantest things. But still I have not backslidden, nor felt led to leave the church. His grace has ever been sufficient. And all we need to-day is to trust Him."[48]

Regardless of where they stood on the spectrum of responses to culturally defined prescriptions about their appropriate role, most Methodist women in this period engaged in considerable struggle to respond to God's call without neglecting their domestic duties. In the next several chapters we enter a different world, in which women were able (from the 1860s on) to move in various ways into the formerly proscribed "public sphere." At first they accomplished more public labors in the church and world through separate women's work, including the women's home and foreign missionary societies, the deaconess movement as a public ministry for women, and the participation of many Methodist women in the Woman's Christian Temperance Union. The long struggles for full clergy and laity rights for women would not reach a successful conclusion until well into our own century.

PART III

"NEW WOMEN"

1860s — TWENTIETH CENTURY

7

WOMAN'S WORK IN THE CHURCH
New Spheres of Usefulness

In 1886 Frances Willard, the well-known leader of the Woman's Christian Temperance Union, wrote an advice book entitled *How to Win: A Book for Girls.* In it she described the new ideal of womanhood: "If I were asked the mission of the ideal woman, I would reply: *It is to make the whole world homelike....* A true woman carries home with her everywhere.... But 'home's not merely four square walls.' ... Woman will make homelike every place she enters, and she will enter every place on this round earth."[1] With this image of the New Methodist Woman, we enter much more familiar territory, that of woman's public work in the church and the world, what women themselves regarded as "new spheres of usefulness."

In the midst of the rapid social and cultural changes of the post–Civil War era in the United States, the question of woman's appropriate work was being raised in every aspect of the life of Protestant churches. The contours of the debate in the Methodist family of denominations reflected the changing status of the churches themselves. In the 1860s to 1880s American Methodists moved, to use Kenneth E. Rowe's words, from outsiders to insiders socially, from side street to main street architecturally, from marginal to predominant denominationally. The vital partnership in ministry between laity and clergy—lay preachers and class leaders providing pastoral leadership at the local level while ordained traveling preachers made the rounds on their appointed circuits—changed dramatically when the circuit riders became professional, dismounted, and settled in the community.[2]

The movement of middle-class Protestant women into larger spheres of influence came primarily through their creation of organizations "for women only." The greatest impetus to women's activities came with the Civil War and the important role women played in nursing and relief efforts. After the war, Protestant women perceived other needs calling them from their homes into the world.[3] In the Methodist Episcopal Church, a new organization for women attempted to respond to this changing context.

LADIES' AND PASTORS' CHRISTIAN UNION

In March 1868 at a meeting in Philadelphia, the Ladies' and Pastors' Christian Union (L&PCU) was organized to employ the women of the Methodist Episcopal Church in a systematic program of home evangelistic work among the poor and neglected, under the supervision of the ordained clergy. Bishop Matthew Simpson, the resident bishop of Philadelphia, was a strong supporter. Its leading organizer and promoter was the corresponding secretary Mrs. Annie Wittenmyer (1827–1900), whose management skills were well known from her Civil War relief work, especially her supervision of army hospital kitchens under the auspices of the U.S. Christian Commission.

Claiming that "the entire system of religious activity in the church is undergoing a change,"[4] the officers of the L&PCU urged the organization of an auxiliary society in each church, with the pastor as president. Each parish would be subdivided into smaller districts and two or more women appointed to each for house-to-house visitation in order to appeal to the unconverted, invite strangers to church, help the sick and the poor, and bring the children into the Sunday school. By the time of the first Annual Report, local units of the L&PCU had been organized in some fifty local churches in ten states. According to the written reports submitted, some 23,000 families had been visited, nearly 11,000 "unconverted persons appealed to," 1,000 sick visited, 325 poor families helped, 419 children brought into the Sunday school, 233 meetings held in homes, and close to 100,000 pages of tracts distributed.[5]

At the first anniversary meeting of the L&PCU, held in the Green Street Methodist Episcopal Church in Philadelphia, addresses were given by the Reverend C. P. Masden, the Reverend C. H. Payne, and Bishop Simpson. Reverend Masden suggested that the new society was providentially devised to fit the character of the times (now that Methodism had become predominantly middle-class). He saw it as having a fourfold aim: (1) to do a needed work that the pastor did not have time to do, (2) to give laypeople a religious activity beyond attending church and listening to sermons, (3) to evangelize the masses—now that "the log cabin" had given place to "the Gothic chapel"—and (4) to develop the individuality and spirituality of the women of the church who composed "three-fourths of our members."[6]

The Reverend Payne claimed that women's influence in the apostolic church had been powerful, especially through the offices of prophetess and deaconess. The deaconess office, he thought, "was designed to be perpetual, and I would it were in the church today."[7] He encouraged the women present to enlarge and carry forward their work. In the closing address, Bishop Simpson rejoiced at the success of the society in its first year. "The object of this association is not that woman shall take the pulpit, or engage in any work that may be questionable, but simply to go forward in the discharge of those duties that woman has ever performed, *though not systematically and regularly* [emphasis mine]."[8]

All who promoted this new society seemed to agree on the need to organize women's work. In *Women's Work for Jesus*, Annie Wittenmyer argued that evangelizing the unchurched masses required home visitation, and that this work could best be done by *"the systematic, voluntary labors of Christian Women, under the direction of the regular pastorate* [emphasis in original]."[9] She believed that women, whose sphere was the home, were uniquely qualified to go into people's homes and "talk of Jesus, and duty and heaven," and that they would be welcomed where men would not.[10] In her book, Wittenmyer was addressing not only Methodist women, but all church women with sufficient leisure time to devote two or three hours a week to the work of visitation. She saw women's evangelizing work as a great undeveloped power that "might become a mighty enginery for good if properly combined and directed."[11] The Reverend I. W. Wiley, editor of the *Ladies' Repository*, agreed with Wittenmyer that women's nature made them well adapted to this work; he affirmed that home visitation was appropriate work for the "true woman."[12]

Begun in 1868, the new organization was authorized by the next General Conference of the Methodist Episcopal Church in 1872 as a "regularly constituted society" of the church. Its constitution was approved, a Board of Managers was set up, and pastors of all the churches were instructed to cooperate with the new society in its important work.[13] Of even greater significance, however, was the larger context in which this action took place.

WOMAN'S WORK IN THE CHURCH

The issue of woman's place and work in the church was hotly debated in the ME Church at every General Conference from 1872 through the 1920s. At the 1872 General Conference, a special Committee on Woman's Work in the Church was created to deal with the numerous resolutions pertaining to women's issues.[14] This committee reviewed papers on the "licensing and ordaining of women as preachers," "The Ladies' and Pastors' Christian Union," "The Woman's Foreign Missionary Society," and other propositions for the "enlargement of [women's] Christian and benevolent activity," noting that these recent developments were "a revival of the true spirit of Methodism." The final report of the committee endorsed the L&PCU and recommended the adoption of its constitution, supported the work of the Woman's Foreign Missionary Society (founded in 1869 and also officially authorized by this General Conference), and exhorted the women to "still greater zeal" in Sunday school, class meetings, prayer meetings, and love feasts. On the matter of licensing and ordaining women, however, it reported: "In regard to woman's preaching we must wait for further developments of Providence. We rejoice in the indications that women are called to be teachers of the Word of Life, and yet the instances are not sufficiently numerous to justify any new legislation in the Church on this subject."[15]

The same year an article appeared in the *Ladies' Repository* on the subject of "ancient and modern deaconesses" and "ancient and modern (Catholic) sisterhoods." Its author, Mrs. Susanna M. D. Fry, urged Methodists to consider the establishment of a deaconess order that would further the work already begun by the Ladies' and Pastors' Christian Union. She concluded:

> When will the women of America awake to a sense of their responsibility? And what great soul, filled with love to God and man, shall open the way and prepare the means whereby we may be enabled to compete successfully with our sisters of Rome, not only as general charity women, educators, and succorers of the unfortunate, but especially as nurses of the sick? . . . Earnest thinkers upon the subject of "Woman's work in the Church" are looking to the Quakers and Methodists to move forward in God's name, smiting the waters of blind prejudice, and leading their daughters into the full possibilities of an entirely devoted Christian womanhood.[16]

Bishop Simpson had become acquainted with Protestant deaconess work on a trip to Germany in the 1860s, and on his return to the United States began to advocate the founding of deaconess institutions. With his encouragement, Annie Wittenmyer and Susanna Fry traveled together in this country to urge the founding of benevolent institutions, including deaconess homes. In the fall of 1872 Wittenmyer herself visited the Lutheran deaconess centers at Kaiserswerth, Germany, with the thought that the L&PCU might introduce deaconess work into American Methodism.[17] However, her own energies soon became absorbed by the "Woman's Crusade" against alcohol and eventually the Woman's Christian Temperance Union, which she helped to found in 1874, becoming its first national president.

Meanwhile the work of the Ladies' and Pastors' Christian Union continued to be promoted in various ways. An article by J. H. Potts in the *Ladies' Repository* specifically related this organization to the long history of women's work in the church, reviewed its purposes and achievements, and assured all concerned that it was not intended to turn women away from their duties at home, but rather to occupy their leisure time. He urged that other societies be merged into "this general and regular Church organization" so that the work might be done "decently and in order."[18]

The Board of Managers of the L&PCU included Henry White Warren, Joseph B. Wakeley, and William Nast; for the women, Ellen Simpson, Annie Wittenmyer, Jennie Fowler Willing, Susanna

M. D. Fry, and Harriet B. Skidmore. In 1877 a new corresponding secretary was secured: twenty-three-year-old Mrs. Mary L. Griffith, wife of the Reverend T. M. Griffith (a minister in the Philadelphia Annual Conference). The minutes of the Philadelphia conference for 1880 included an appeal from the corresponding secretary, suggesting the opportunity the L&PCU afforded women to meet their "obligations to rescue the perishing," and recommending the formation of such an organization in every church.[19]

Mary Griffith also published a tract on *Women's Christian Work* in which she called on Christian women "to be saved from a spirit of pride and exclusiveness, and to be possessed of a burning love for souls, just because they are *souls*," to offer themselves utterly to God and go out into "the waste places of the earth with light and comfort." Revivals were even being attributed to the work of the L&PCU. "Dear sisters," she said, "come to this sweet work."[20] Many women did respond, but other organizations created by women for women only would have a wider appeal.

THE "NEW WOMAN" AND THE WCTU

As the national leader of the Woman's Christian Temperance Union (WCTU) from 1879 until her death in 1898, Frances E. Willard was a major influence in the redefinition of the image of True Christian Womanhood to include enfranchisement. The quotation from her that begins this chapter, in a slightly revised form, "Woman will bless and brighten every place she enters, and she will enter every place," became a favorite motto of the WCTU. As Carolyn De Swarte Gifford explained, this motto "boldly stated that women intended to move from the private, domestic sphere into the public world." That Willard was able to persuade vast numbers of WCTU women to accept this redefinition was part of the true measure of her genius.[21]

The Woman's Christian Temperance Union was formed in 1874 after the spontaneous church woman's crusade against saloons in Ohio and towns elsewhere in the East and Midwest. Annie Wittenmyer was its first president; Frances E. Willard was elected corresponding secretary. Many Methodist women became members of the new organization, and it received strong support from prominent clergy in the Methodist Episcopal Church, including Bishops Matthew Simpson and Randolph S. Foster.

The WCTU was initially organized with a single objective, to work for the prohibition of alcoholic beverages. Temperance was a woman's issue. By the 1870s the stark reality was that women and children were no longer safe in their homes as a result of male alcoholism, and the persuasive methods used in the woman's crusade had proved ineffective. Frances Willard was increasingly convinced that woman suffrage was essential for "home protection" if women were to move beyond "praying and pleading" to a more effective strategy for reform. She declared publicly for suffrage in 1876, and after her election as national president of the WCTU in 1879, demanded the Home Protection ballot for women so that they would have the political power to protect their homes from the curse of alcoholism and the liquor traffic.[22]

Willard claimed that God had called her (while "on her knees in prayer") to advocate woman suffrage. Like her, WCTU women typically experienced conversion to woman suffrage. As Christian women they were urged to develop themselves in order to become all that God was calling them to be. WCTU leaders "entreated, coaxed, commanded, and shamed" their members to persuade them to move into the public sphere. Willard told women they must be educated so that they would no longer shrink from acquiring power. Her vision of women's place in the public sphere was, as Gifford suggested, "limitless."[23]

Willard articulated that vision in 1895 as she attempted to prepare WCTU women to take their places in the coming century: "When that day comes, the nation shall no longer miss as now the influence of half its wisdom, more than half its purity, and nearly all its gentleness, in courts of justice and halls of legislation. Then shall one code of morals—and that the highest—govern both men and women; then shall the Sabbath be respected, the rights of the poor be recognized, the liquor traffic banished, and the home protected from all its foes."[24]

Under her "Do Everything Policy," thousands of Victorian "ladies" left the sanctuary of their homes and moved into active participation in a wide range of issues, including woman suffrage, social (sexual) purity, concerns of labor, peace and arbitration, welfare work, temperance education, and health. Classified under five major headings, "preventive, educational, evangelistic, social and legal, [and] organization," WCTU work was grouped into fifty different departments, each under the care of a superintendent. It was also organized at every level from the local to the national, with every level connected to the next. All "carefully mustered, officered, and drilled," the WCTU was "womanhood's Grand Army of the Home."[25] Through it women not only gained invaluable training and a new sense of their own power, they also moved beyond the church into social reform.

WOMEN ORGANIZED FOR MISSION

At the same time that Frances Willard was redefining the ideal of womanhood through the WCTU, women were organizing their own separate women's organizations in the church as well. The Woman's Foreign Missionary Society (WFMS) of the Methodist Episcopal Church was founded in Boston in 1869. It was the first of eight women's home and foreign missionary societies to be organized between 1869 and the 1890s in the Methodist, Evangelical, and United Brethren family of churches. The women who led these societies were committed to doing "woman's work for women." They were both intentional about strategies and aware of the benefits to themselves of being organized for mission. As the earliest of these societies, the WFMS of the Methodist Episcopal Church may serve as an illustration. However, all of the women's missionary societies faced essentially the same issues.[26]

BEGINNINGS: THE WOMAN'S FOREIGN MISSIONARY SOCIETY (MEC), 1869

The Woman's Foreign Missionary Society of the Methodist Episcopal Church had a rather inauspicious beginning: only six women braved a torrential rain in Boston on the afternoon of March 23, 1869, to listen to Mrs. Clementina Rowe Butler and Mrs.

Lois Stiles Parker, wives of Methodist missionaries to India, and to consider the possibility of organizing a Woman's Foreign Missionary Society. Those present became convinced that the gospel could only be brought to the women of India by women, resolved to organize, and appointed a committee to nominate officers. According to Clementina Butler's own account, when the others who had planned to come but were dissuaded by the weather heard what had been accomplished, they "forever regretted their lack of courage."[27]

Only twenty-six women came to the meeting the following week (the weather still not cooperating), but a constitution was adopted and national officers were elected. Mrs. Osmon C. Baker (wife of Bishop Baker) became the first president and the wives of the other bishops were made vice presidents.[28] There were initially three corresponding secretaries: Mrs. Harriet M. Warren, Mrs. Lois Parker, and Mrs. Jennie Fowler Willing. The membership fee was fixed at a modest sum, "two cents a week and a prayer," on the urging of Clementina Butler that no woman should have to say that she could not afford to join.[29]

It was decided to begin immediately the publication of a monthly magazine entitled *The Heathen Woman's Friend*; the first issue appeared in June of 1869. In the second issue Jennie Fowler Willing described the intention of the journal's founders:

> We need a constant enlightenment in regard to the world's claim upon our money and energy. . . . We need not so much . . . thundergusts of fervor, but showers of instruction. Just this lack the Woman's Missionary Society proposes to supply. Its auxiliaries in every city, village, and town will be associations for the diffusion of missionary intelligence. Its papers will glide into the homes of the land.[30]

The original title was changed in January 1896 to *The Woman's Missionary Friend,* as Clementina Butler acknowledged, "in recognition of the somewhat uncomplimentary implication of the title 'heathen,' but under either title the magazine has been a great force in extending information and inspiration regarding the work."[31] Although it took Mrs. Butler two hours of "most earnest pleading" to persuade Mrs. Harriet M. Warren to accept the editorship, she carried it on successfully for twenty-five years.

These things were not done without opposition from "the brethren." Dr. John P. Durbin, secretary of the Methodist Mission-ary Society (often referred to as the parent board), wrote to the women approving of their aim but advising them to "leave the administration of the work to the Board at home and the missions on the field." The women were invited to meet in Boston on May 7 with the secretaries of the parent board. Fearing that the women's success might interfere with regular church collections for missions, the board secretaries proposed that the women for-ward money raised to the parent board. In no uncertain terms the women insisted that they had organized an independent society and they would raise and disburse their own funds for the work they had undertaken. The women did, however, agree that they would "take no collections or subscriptions in any promiscuous [mixed] assembly," but would raise their funds in ways that would not interfere with the parent board and its work.[32]

The first public, or anniversary, meeting of the Woman's Foreign Missionary Society was held in Bromfield Street Church in Boston on May 26, 1869. As one historian described it, "The leaders of the Society observed the conventions of the day and sat demurely in the pews." The governor of Massachusetts, Methodist layman William Claflin, presided, and Drs. William F. Warren, president of Boston University, William Butler, and E. W. Parker spoke. At the end of this meeting, the women met to transact their own business, voting to send Miss Isabella Thoburn and Dr. Clara Swain to India as missionaries.[33]

Farewell meetings were held in Boston in October, and in New York in November 1869, to bid Godspeed to the first two mission-aries as they prepared to sail to India. The presiding officer at the Boston meetings was the Reverend Gilbert Haven, "always ready to champion the weak." One woman at the New York meeting recalled that a host of ministers were present "to see this strange thing that had come to pass, when two young women would leave their home and friends to sail thousands of miles away to a foreign shore, with no pledge of support save that of a handful of women!"[34]

As first organized in 1869 there were two basic units within the Woman's Foreign Missionary Society, the local church auxiliaries and the national body. Before the end of its first year, the society's officers had perfected a plan for regional units called branches to assist in organizing an auxiliary in each local church. The revised Constitution was adopted and six branches were organized. Thus, at the first Executive Committee meeting in Boston on April 20, 1870, the Philadelphia, New York, New England, Northwestern, Western, and Cincinnati Branches were represented by their corresponding secretaries and two delegates from each branch. The WFMS of the MEC was the first to organize in this way, with units at every level from the local to the national, and with each level strategically linked to the next. Because this decentralized structure allowed women in local societies to have a sense of direct connection to and ownership of the work, it was an important reason for Methodist women's success in enlisting support for their cause. Eventually eleven branches covered the entire country.[35]

"For Women Only"

The matter of women speaking in public was a major issue in these early years. Clementina Butler, newly elected corresponding secretary of the New York Branch, had agreed to speak in the interests of the new movement at the Sing Sing camp meeting in the summer of 1869, if a meeting could be called "for women only." Evidently curious about all this, five (male) ministers were seated in the rear of the tent when the meeting opened. According to accounts they refused to leave, in spite of Mrs. Butler's plea that she could not speak before men. Finally a "tall woman" in the audience summoned the policeman who was there to keep order in the camp, and he ordered the ministers to leave, "after which the meeting proceeded with great enthusiasm." The tall woman was Mrs. Harriet Skidmore, who became one of the foremost and best-loved leaders of the society.[36]

A significant milestone was achieved on the occasion of a farewell meeting in New York in September 1870, when the New York Branch sent out its own first missionary to India, Miss Fannie J. Sparkes. This time a "spirited motion" was adopted saying that this should be "a **woman's** meeting, addressed by women only."

Several women led the meeting in the reading of Scripture and prayer, in reminiscences of missionary life and appeals for support, and in the singing of the missionary hymn "From Greenland's Icy Mountains." Miss Sparkes made a few remarks, Mrs. Julia Olin presented her with a basket of flowers conveying the good wishes and prayers of all, a collection was taken up, Clementina Butler gave the closing address, and the meeting ended with the doxology.[37]

ORGANIZING LOCAL AUXILIARIES

Auxiliary societies multiplied quickly through the efforts of leaders like Clementina Butler. As a corresponding secretary of one of the newly formed auxiliary societies said, "There seems to be almost a charm in this Society to awaken the sympathies of our sex." Jennie Fowler Willing had few equals in her diligence to organize auxiliaries. "If you have no auxiliary society," she said, "get one up—or pray one down!"[38]

Methodist camp meetings afforded excellent opportunities to reach Methodist women on behalf of the new missionary society. The primary object of these gatherings was to spread "missionary intelligence." Women went home from camp meetings like Sing Sing and Round Lake, New York; Martha's Vineyard, Massachusetts; Ocean Grove, New Jersey; and Albion, Michigan, to become advocates for women's missionary work. Public anniversary meetings held at the camp meetings each year attracted large crowds.

The Heathen Woman's Friend was from the beginning an effective means of advancing the cause, as newly organized auxiliaries were reported in its pages. For example, in the August issue of 1870, a story entitled "Cheering Progress in New York" told readers that Clementina Butler, the corresponding secretary of the New York Branch, had just returned from an official tour in western New York "where she has not only organized a whole constellation of new auxiliaries (see Report in Business Department), but also brought about what may be called a 'missionary awakening' among the ladies of all that section."[39] Fourteen auxiliary societies had been organized in that region between May 16 and June 9!

The daughter of one of the early officers who traveled about organizing auxiliaries later reflected on the impact her mother's involvement had on her: "What a large part of my real education it has been to know the beginnings of the Woman's Foreign Missionary Society. Mother in her gentle, brave way doing what she had never done before and doing it calmly, sure it was right—and how it brought out the utterly unrevealed possibilities of so many quiet women in country churches—and how *one* was the spirit! Oh! wasn't it a blessed chance to begin one's life in such a group!"[40]

It is clear that family connections—mothers, daughters, sisters, cousins—were important in the leadership of these early societies. In the lists of members of the Passaic, New Jersey, auxiliary were the daughters of Mrs. Clementina Butler, "Miss J. Butler, Miss C. Butler." Similarly, when an auxiliary was formed at Sing Sing in October 1869, the records listed "Mrs. Charles Carter North" (Elizabeth Mason North) as president and "Mrs. Henry B. Curtis" (Jane Mason Curtis) as recording secretary. As Louise McCoy North wrote in her history of the New York Branch, "It is pleasant to think of these daughters of Mrs. Mary W. Mason, the first Directress of the Female Missionary Society of New York, whose life of eminent usefulness had closed in the preceding year, thus carrying forward into the new Society the service so dear to their mother's heart."[41]

THE REAL STRENGTH IS IN THE BRANCHES

The real strength of the Woman's Foreign Missionary Society was in the branches. The Executive Committee functioned only during the annual meeting, while the body of corresponding secretaries continued. The auxiliary societies related directly to the branches. Because of this structure, the corresponding secretaries had an enormous influence: they were the real contact between the central group and the workers on the local level. These corresponding secretaries, in the words of missionary historian Mary Isham, "assumed the labors of Hercules":

They were to foster organization of auxiliaries by tongue and pen, to secure the co-operation necessary to raise the needed funds, to promote missionary education in the churches and good relations with the Board, to guard the missionaries and seek knowledge of conditions, to wisely administer the treasure of life and gold entrusted to them.[42]

Pressed on one side by restrictions that hampered their raising money, and on the other by their perception of women's needs in other lands, these women looked to God for strength, wisdom, and empowerment.[43]

MARY CLARKE NIND

In addition to the ubiquitous Clementina Butler, Mary Clarke Nind and Jennie Fowler Willing well represent these early female missionary society leaders. When the officers of the Western Branch began to organize in Minnesota, they wisely enlisted the efforts of Mrs. Mary Clarke Nind of Winona. She traveled thousands of miles on behalf of that and other auxiliaries in Minnesota before being made president of the Western Branch in 1881. The following year she and Lucy Prescott, corresponding secretary of the Western Branch, itinerated in Colorado and Kansas. At the Annual Meeting of the Western Branch held in Topeka in 1883, Mary Nind proposed the division of the Western Branch into three branches, Des Moines, Minneapolis, and Topeka, giving as reasons the "vastness of the territory, the impossibility of advancing the work from one center, and a field manifestly beyond the possibility of proper care by the present officers."[44]

Mary Nind and Lucy Prescott became a familiar sight traveling by carriage throughout the Great Plains in every kind of weather and over inadequate roads. A local newspaper column from this period described them more accurately than the writer knew, perhaps, as "two traveling missionaries for the Methodist Episcopal Church." Indeed their accounts of the towns where they stopped to speak and the high-spirited stories of their attempts to find shelter for the night remind the reader of nothing so much as anecdotes about the early Methodist circuit riding preachers. The following description of Mary Nind's work as corresponding secretary of the new Minneapolis Branch was part of a funeral tribute to her upon her death in 1905:

> It was no easy task she set herself. Much of her "Branch" was wilderness. The towns were few and far apart, the churches weak and struggling, but these frontier pastors always had a warm welcome for one who brought such faith and hope and cheer and love of God with her. Her courage never faltered, as by faith she laid the foundations of this great organization in Minnesota, the Dakotas, Montana, Idaho, Washington and Oregon, traveling over the unbroken prairie and through the wilderness in wagon or cart or sleigh, in summer and winter, by day and by night, by freight train or day coach (never in a Pullman—the Lord's money was too precious for such luxuries), compassing as many as ten thousand miles in a single year, and counting it all joy to be engaged in her blessed work.[45]

To the women of the WFMS, she was "Mother Nind," or even "Our Little Bishop." It is not surprising that she was one of the five women elected by their annual conferences as lay delegates to the 1888 General Conference of the Methodist Episcopal Church. That conference voted against the eligibility of women to be lay delegates and the five women were unseated. (Female lay delegates were first admitted to the General Conference of the ME Church sixteen years later, in 1904.)[46]

JENNIE FOWLER WILLING

Jennie Fowler Willing (who seems always to have been referred to by this name rather than by her husband's name, as was the convention of the day) was born in Burford, in what is now called Ontario, Canada, in 1834. Her brother Charles became a prominent leader and eventually a bishop of the Methodist Episcopal Church. In 1853 she married William Crossgrove Willing, a Methodist itinerant preacher, and embarked on a genuine partnership with him in both marriage and vocation. William served charges in the Rock

River Conference in Illinois from 1860 to 1889, including four terms as presiding elder. In 1873 Jennie Willing was given a local preacher's license by the Joliet District (while her husband was presiding elder of that district) and put in charge of one of the mission churches.[47]

Jennie Fowler Willing dedicated her enormous energy and superb organizing skills to the Woman's Foreign Missionary Society as corresponding secretary for fourteen years, from 1869 to 1883. Initially, her job was to organize all the territory "from the state of Ohio to the Pacific Ocean."[48] She used the *Friend* as a regular forum for appealing to Methodist women on behalf of the society, constantly encouraging them to see themselves as capable workers and to see the society as their God-given task. While teaching English at Illinois Wesleyan University in Bloomington, Illinois, Willing became involved in the woman's temperance crusade. She helped to organize the national Woman's Christian Temperance Union and edited its newspaper for the first year. In 1884 she became the General Organizer for the Woman's Home Missionary Society of the ME Church.[49]

At the end of the first year, the subscription list of *The Heathen Woman's Friend* was 4,000; by 1895 it had increased to 22,000.[50] Other dimensions of the society's work from its earliest years are equally impressive. In the April 1870 issue of the *Friend*, Jennie Fowler Willing urged that there be "a missionary reading circle formed in every auxiliary society."[51] By October 1879, "Uniform Readings" for mission study were published monthly in the *Friend*. By 1894 these were published as a separate periodical called *The Study*; Mrs. Annie Gracey was chosen as its first editor. She was instrumental in a plan to awaken missionary enthusiasm across the country by distributing free leaflets. She chaired a committee of six, representing each branch, to prepare and send out this literature. The system of mite boxes (for the collection of small sums of money like the widow's two copper coins, or mite, of Luke 21:2) became almost a symbol of the society's ability to enlist the widespread support of women. Mite boxes were introduced by the New York Branch in April 1870 and soon adopted by the other branches.

WHAT "WOMAN'S WORK FOR WOMAN" DID FOR THE SENDERS

The early pioneers of the society saw its organizational apparatus as enabling spiritual purposes: "The many methods of service were and are but the channels of God's grace; the complex machinery, wheel within wheel, depends for its running upon the current of His mighty power. 'Two cents a week and a prayer' was made the seal of membership. The treasury has ever been close beside the altar."[52] An important manifestation of this spirit of gratitude to God was the annual Thank-Offering, a day of thanksgiving proclaimed each fall when women could bring special gifts as tokens of gratitude for the blessings the WFMS had brought to them and to women around the world. Of the benefits to Methodist women at home, one writer of Thank-Offering leaflets wrote that the society had taught Christian women to be "strong, confident, and happy in work they once thought they never could do." In the process of all this organizing, Methodist women gained invaluable administrative experience and established networks for support and action with women around the country. Jennie Fowler Willing once remarked, "Our paper ought to be called the 'Christian Woman's Friend,'—such blessed opportunity has it helped us find as co-workers with God; such growth and comfort and sweet fellowship as we have had in His work!"[53]

A WOMAN'S HOME MISSIONARY SOCIETY IN THE MEC

At its 1868 General Conference, the Methodist Episcopal Church gave official approval to the Freedmen's Aid Society (formed in Cincinnati in 1866) as an agency for the establishment of educational institutions for the freedpeople in the South. Dr. Richard S. Rust, corresponding secretary of the society, urged Methodist women to become involved, insisting that "the work of Christian women for their needy sisters in their own country is as indispensable as for the foreign field."[54]

Meanwhile Mrs. Jennie Culver Hartzell (whose husband, Dr. Joseph C. Hartzell, had been appointed pastor of Ames Chapel in

New Orleans, Louisiana, in 1869) had begun to minister to the needs of freedwomen in New Orleans. In 1877 Dr. Rust and his wife, Elizabeth, visited New Orleans and became convinced of the need for a woman's home missionary society that could take up the necessary work on behalf of "the poor black women and children of the Southland."[55]

At a meeting in Cincinnati on June 8, 1880, shortly after the close of the General Conference, about fifty Methodist Episcopal women resolved to form a Woman's Home Missionary Society (WHMS), "to enlist and organize the women of Methodism in behalf of the needy and destitute of all races and nationalities in this country," and with recommendation for special attention to "the Southern field."[56] Elizabeth Lownes Rust was named corresponding secretary; the new president was Mrs. Lucy Webb Hayes, a loyal Methodist and wife of U.S. President Rutherford B. Hayes. Lucy Webb Hayes served as national president of the society until her death in 1889, presiding at its annual meetings and presenting annual reports stressing the importance of the work.[57]

Within a few years, the aims of the WHMS had been significantly enlarged. There were bureaus, each headed by a secretary, to organize work with Indians, Mormons, blacks and "illiterate whites" in the South, Chinese immigrants, and peoples in the regions of "New Mexico and Arizona" and the "Western and North-western Frontiers." By the end of the first decade there were some seventy corresponding secretaries at the annual conference level, and the membership was reported to be "over 55,000 members in more than 1900 adult and juvenile societies. *Woman's Home Missions* had reached a circulation of 15,500."[58]

SOUTHERN METHODIST WOMEN

In these same years women of the Methodist Episcopal Church, South (MECS), were busy establishing their own women's missionary societies: a Woman's Missionary Society of the Board of Missions (later the Woman's Foreign Missionary Society), organized in 1878, and in 1886 the Woman's Department of the Board of Church Extension, subsequently the Woman's Parsonage and

Home Mission Society (still later the Woman's Home Mission Society).[59] Mrs. Margaret Campbell Kelley and Mrs. Willie Harding McGavock were instrumental in proposing the organization of a Woman's Foreign Missionary Society for the southern church and petitioning the General Conference for its approval. McGavock served as its first corresponding secretary from 1878 until her death in 1895, and Mrs. Juliana Gordon Hayes was president until her death, also in 1895. Southern Methodist women also had a woman's foreign missions journal, the *Woman's Missionary Advocate*, published from 1880 to 1910.[60]

Willie Elizabeth Harding McGavock (1832–1895) was born in Tennessee. She became a Christian at about ten years of age and united with McKendree Church in Nashville, where she retained her membership for the rest of her life. In 1850 she married David McGavock. They had two children, a son born in 1852 and a daughter, Bessie, who died at six years of age.

The "ruling passion" of Willie Harding McGavock's heart was the Woman's Foreign Missionary Society; her biographer said of her that she "was the pulse of the whole machine." She was credited with "great executive ability" and tenacious persistence in what she saw as her duty, while keeping herself "strictly within the bounds of ideal womanliness."[61] During the distress of "the war between the States" and the years of reconstruction, she was eager to give both private and public assistance wherever needed. In the summer of 1863, her church was taken by the federal authorities to be used as a hospital. When efforts at restoration began after the war, she led both a Pastor's Aid Society and a Woman's Bible Mission (employing women as Bible readers to visit the sick and minister to those who needed help).

For several summers, Willie McGavock sought relief from "relentless hay fever" by escaping to the White Mountains of New Hampshire. There she met women of the WFMS of the MEC and "a strong desire was kindled to do the same work" in her own church. In 1874 she petitioned the General Conference of the Methodist Episcopal Church, South, to organize a woman's foreign missionary society. Although unsuccessful then, her second appeal in 1878 won sufficient support and the society was organized. She was appointed corresponding secretary, and from 1878 until shortly before her death in 1895, her efforts were "unremitting" in appealing to every annual conference to organize the women into conference societies.[62]

In the 1880s she suffered from bouts of ill health. On one of these occasions she wrote, "And so when the time comes for another to take my place in this refreshing labor it will be well—well with me, well for the work. My prayer is that, whatever the issue, His grace will be sufficient."[63] There were joys as well as sorrows in these years. About 1884 her husband finally became a Christian, was baptized and received into her church. However, she was deeply grieved by the deaths of both their son's little daughter, her namesake, Willie, and their daughter-in-law, Lula Spence McGavock (their son and his family had lived with them). "I watched almost day and night by her bed of suffering," McGavock wrote of Lula's death, "and realized, 'As thy days, so shall thy strength be.'"[64]

In 1891 Willie McGavock seemed to be dying. After a powerful religious experience, a "gracious baptism of love" (very likely a sanctification experience), she reported being "called back to temporal life." Although confined to her bed for eleven weeks and "in an invalid's chair" for an entire year, she continued to "help forward the cause of missions." As she explained to a friend, "Do you marvel that, after 'sitting with Christ in heavenly places,' I came back reluctantly to life and its responsibilities? . . . I had found it far easier to die than to live; but if my Father has more work and suffering for me, he will give me grace sufficient. I am gradually recovering." On her death in 1895, Mary Helm paid her the following tribute: "One of the pioneers in woman's work for woman in her Church, she led the way bravely, nobly, yet most womanly, against much opposition and over many obstacles, for more than twenty years."[65]

As women of the Methodist Episcopal Church, South, sought to rebuild their lives after the end of the Civil War, they discovered that women could have a new role in southern society. As Sara Myers's study demonstrates, through their work in the Methodist women's missionary organizations, southern women began to move out of their homes and into the public arena, while at the same time managing to preserve their identity as "true women." They participated in activities that had previously been denied to southern women, such as speaking in worship services and lecturing during public meetings. Their schedules sometimes dictated that they must travel unaccompanied, which they managed to do without incurring social stigma. Although they tried to avoid open conflict with the men who controlled the church, they persisted in initiating their own plans and learned to maneuver around "denominational road blocks."[66]

Organized home mission work among women of the MECS was largely the result of the faith, vision, and genius for leadership of a frail woman from Kentucky, Miss Lucinda B. Helm. It was she who formulated the plan for a Woman's Department of Church Extension for Parsonage Building that was approved by the General Conference in 1886. As general secretary, she conducted all the correspondence of the department, provided the whole church with information about the new work through reports, leaflets, and articles for church papers, and communicated with the annual conference societies, visiting many of them. Within four years the work was represented in thirty-six conferences of the southern Methodist Church and involved more than seven thousand women working together to establish parsonages for the itinerant ministry in the South and the West. Helm's vision always was "nothing less than the fullest and completest organized effort for *home missions*." In 1890 the General Conference recognized the Woman's Parsonage and Home Mission Society as an official organization of the MECS. Lucinda Helm served as its general secretary until forced to retire in 1893 due to ill health, and continued to edit the society's journal, *Our Homes,* until her death in 1897.

Helm's work was carried on by another young woman from a prominent Kentucky family, Belle Harris Bennett (1852–1922). In 1884 Bennett was inspired by a summer conference at Lake Chautauqua, New York, to give her life wholly to God. Experiencing "the presence and power of God" and the "assurance of God-given leadership," she embarked on a life of remarkable significance for women in the Methodist Episcopal Church, South. She served for more than twenty-five years as president of the WHMS (1896–1910) and its successor, the Woman's Missionary Council (1910–22). Through her efforts, the Scarritt Bible and Training School was established in Kansas City in 1892, the Sue Bennett

School was opened for poor children in the mountains of Kentucky in 1897, the first church settlement house (judiciously called a "Wesley Community House") was begun in Nashville in 1901, the General Conference of her church was persuaded to authorize deaconesses in 1902, and the struggle for full laity rights for women in the MECS was launched in 1910 and successfully concluded in 1922.[67]

METHODIST PROTESTANT WOMEN

In 1879 Methodist Protestant women gathered in Pittsburgh to hear Miss Lizzie M. Guthrie, a missionary home on furlough from Japan, talk about the work to which they had contributed financially through the Interdenominational Woman's Union Missionary Society. Her inspiring stories were the catalyst they needed, and before the meeting ended the women present voted to organize the Woman's Foreign Missionary Society of the Methodist Protestant Church. They, too, went out to mobilize the organization of branches (conference organizations) and auxiliaries (local societies) across the church. Again, many of the first leaders of this society were married to prominent men in the denomination.[68]

The 1880 General Conference of the Methodist Protestant Church approved the organization, while also stipulating that methods for raising funds should in no way interfere with collections taken for the Board of Missions. As Ethel Born explains, the society's leaders "labored mightily under the principle of accommodation without capitulation."[69] At the next General Conference in 1884, the Board of Missions praised the work of the Woman's Foreign Missionary Society while attempting to make it an auxiliary to the Board. In 1888 the officers reported to the General Conference that in the nine years of their existence they had grown to three hundred auxiliary societies in seventeen conferences, that their publication, *The Woman's Missionary Record*, already had seventeen hundred subscribers, and that they had drawn up articles asking for the restoration to them of the power to raise and disburse funds, employ missionaries, and conduct their own business. Their request was granted, although they were placed under "advisory supervision."

Four years later, four women were elected by their annual conferences as delegates to General Conference (and seated), all of them deeply involved in the Woman's Foreign Missionary Society. The question of the relationship between the society and the parent board would, however, continue to be an issue.

UNITED BRETHREN AND EVANGELICAL
ASSOCIATION WOMEN

Donald K. Gorrell has written about the "new impulse" that prompted women of the United Brethren and the Evangelical Association to organize women's missionary societies after 1870. He claimed that by 1910 "the basic roles of leadership and service for laywomen had been determined and remained fixed until these two rather dissimilar churches of German background united in 1946."[70] Miss Lizzie Hoffman, a schoolteacher in Dayton, Ohio, sought the help of United Brethren minister John Kemp, and together they called a meeting of interested women and ministers in Dayton on May 9, 1872. Those at the meeting voted to organize the Woman's Missionary Association of the Miami Conference. The new organization received the commendation of the denomination's General Conference the following year. Delegates to a women's missionary convention drew up a constitution and elected officers for a church-wide Woman's Missionary Association in 1875, and in 1882 the women began publishing the *Woman's Evangel*. The first issue of this publication declared their intentions:

> The women are to send glad tidings of great joy through this medium. Not that they are to receive license to preach,—oh, no, we have plenty of poor preachers among the brethren,—but the women are to write, work, and talk in this special way for the salvation of their sisters who are in heathen blackness and darkness. What a blessed privilege! Oh, for a complete consecration to this important work.[71]

In contrast with the supportive relationship between women organized for mission and the United Brethren denomination, when Miss Emma Yost and others petitioned the Evangelical

Association in 1878, they were refused permission to organize. Two years later, Miss Minerva Strawman (later Spreng) raised the issue again. The General Conference of the Evangelical Association in 1883 authorized a Woman's Missionary Society, but stipulated that women's groups could exist only on the local level and then under the supervision of the preacher. Apparently a woman's missionary society was regarded by "the German element" of the denomination as "usurping too much authority."[72] In order to publish a periodical and support a special field of work, the women had to petition the Board of Missions. Both steps were finally approved in 1899, fourteen years after they had been requested!

Unfortunately the women of the Evangelical Association were directly affected by the division within their denomination in 1891, which led to the organization of the United Evangelical Church in 1894. In the mainstream Evangelical Association, the Woman's Missionary Society was slowly granted recognition and expanded opportunities. An editorial in the *Evangelical Messenger* in 1903 reported that "the Woman's Missionary Society of our Church . . . had some opposition and more distrust and disinterest to encounter. But it has clearly won the day. It has shown its fitness to survive and take its place in the family of the church."[73]

"THOSE WHO WERE SENT": THE WOMEN MISSIONARIES

Earlier in the nineteenth century, most women who went overseas as foreign missionaries were wives accompanying their missionary husbands or widows, like Ann Wilkins. Beginning in the 1860s women's foreign missionary societies were organized primarily to support the work of single female missionaries. The leaders of these societies were convinced that native women in countries like India and China could only be reached by female missionaries. Since missionary wives were already overburdened with family responsibilities and assisting their husbands, single women were urged to offer themselves for missionary service in order to evangelize and educate "their heathen sisters."[74]

Entire books could be (and have been) written about the lives and vocations of women missionaries. Here we simply take note of a few representative women missionaries who were sent out by the woman's foreign and home missionary societies of the Methodist family of denominations in the nineteenth century.

Miss Isabella Thoburn (1840–1901) dedicated her life to the education of Christian women in India after her missionary brother, James M. (later Bishop) Thoburn, invited her to join him in India and begin a boarding school for girls. When the Woman's Foreign Missionary Society (MEC) was founded in 1869, Isabella Thoburn and Dr. Clara Swain were sent to India as its first two missionaries. Within a year after her arrival in India, Thoburn began a school for girls in Lucknow, North India; by 1871 there were enough students to warrant the WFMS's purchase of Lal Bagh (Ruby Gardens) to house both a boarding and a day school for girls. In 1886 she founded Lucknow Woman's College, the first Christian college for women in Asia. She was its principal, chief fund-raiser, and one of its professors.

Isabella Thoburn labored tirelessly to establish the legitimacy of education for Indian women, believing that the great tragedy of their seclusion in zenanas (women's quarters) was the failure to develop their minds. Her vision was to educate native Christian girls to become teachers, doctors, and public leaders in India. She hoped that Indian girls trained at Lucknow would return home to shape the Christian family life of their homes and the spiritual life of their village churches, and to engage in evangelism. With these ends in mind, education at Lucknow was bilingual: English and one or more Indian languages. Thoburn's aim was to instill in her students a respect for India and commitment to serving its future. The spirit that motivated Thoburn's own service in India for more than thirty years is manifest in the conclusion to her address to the Indian missionaries in 1882: "To work for and with all classes of people, we must be one with all, and belong to no class ourselves, which will sometimes mean that we must become low-caste. Whatever it may cost, the result will repay the effort a thousand-fold."[75]

A major goal of the Woman's Missionary Society of the Methodist Episcopal Church, South, was to reach and convert adult women in China. While Bible women—indigenous women trained in the Scriptures—were helpful in visiting house to house, educational and medical work proved to be the most successful avenues of approach to Chinese women. The society sent Miss Lochie Rankin as its first missionary to China in 1878; she served as a teacher there for forty-nine years.

Miss Laura A. Haygood (1845–1900) from Georgia would coordinate the work in China from 1885 until her death. Haygood was principal of the Atlanta Girls' High School when she responded to Dr. Young J. Allen's appeal for an experienced educator to take leadership of women's work in China for the southern Methodist Church. In 1892 she founded McTyeire Home and School, a private high school for girls in Shanghai.[76] Although the intended goal of Christianizing the women of China was ultimately unsuccessful, women's educational and medical work in China touched many lives. The example of the individual missionaries represented a "revolutionary concept of womanhood" that profoundly impacted a new generation of Chinese women.[77]

It was Miss Lizzie M. Guthrie's inspiring account of her missionary work in Japan that led to the organization of the Woman's Foreign Missionary Society of the Methodist Protestant Church (MPC). In 1880 Miss Harriet G. Brittan was sent by the WFMS to Yokohama, Japan. At her instigation the women established a Brick Fund to raise money for a home and school in Yokohama. Although this caused tensions with the men on the Board of Foreign Missions, the ultimate result was the Eiwa Jo Gakko Girls' School in Yokohama. Miss Olive Hodges served with distinction as principal of the school for thirty-four years.[78]

The first field of work of the Woman's Missionary Association of the United Brethren Church (UB) was Sierra Leone, Africa. A UB woman who pioneered in home missions work was Miss Sarah A. Dickey of Dayton, Ohio. Dickey was one of three courageous young female teachers who went to Vicksburg, Mississippi, in 1863 as part of the United Brethren mission to the freedpeople. Ten years later she returned to Mississippi to found Mt. Hermon Seminary for black girls in Clinton; she would be its principal for thirty years.[79]

Women in the Methodist family of denominations were part of the much larger phenomenon of the women's missionary movement. By 1900, for example, there were forty-one female foreign missionary societies in the various Protestant denominations in the United States. Patricia Hill has estimated that the women's foreign mission movement enlisted more women than any of the other great women's movements of the nineteenth century. Its appeal can only be understood by appreciating that when middle-class (white) women began to reemerge into the public sphere in the second half of the century, the church provided the framework within which they could "test their wings" and develop the necessary skills.[80]

The benefits to American Protestant women of their being organized for mission should be clear enough from this chapter. The impact of their work on women of other lands is, of course, a much more complex issue. Thoroughly convinced of the emancipatory nature of Christianity and the degraded condition of non-Christian women, missionary women developed a critique of other religions and cultures on the basis of their treatment of women. Appalled by cultural practices like zenanas, footbinding, child marriage, polygamy, suttee (cremating a widow on the funeral pyre of her husband as an indication of her devotion), and female infanticide, they believed it their sacred responsibility as women to evangelize and uplift their "heathen sisters." They may well have exaggerated the incidence of these abuses against women while slighting indigenous reform efforts. With the best of intentions, but with the conviction of the absolute superiority of the Christian West, most missionary women had an unfortunate cultural blindness toward the sources of women's power in other cultures and religious traditions. Joan Jacobs Brumberg has argued that the popular ethnology developed by middle-class (white) evangelical women in the post–Civil War foreign mission crusade reinforced a sense of self-congratulation about the status of women in the United States, and ultimately influenced both American imperialism and the Progressive movement with its commitment to legislation for the protection of women and children.[81]

The women's missionary movement was also ambiguous with regard to the struggle in the United States for women's rights and suffrage. Protestant missionary women were not feminists in the sense of directly challenging the domestic ideology of woman's place. The very concept of women's work for women endorsed the message of women's pious, pure, and mothering or domestic nature. Yet missionary women preached another message by their own example, as they created new religious careers on the mission field for single women. The movement might well be credited, as historian Susan Hill Lindley has suggested, with "soft" feminism, "stepping out of women's roles by both accepting and enlarging them."[82]

As churches in the Methodist family of denominations (particularly the episcopal Methodist churches) sanctioned women's work in parish visitation and the Sunday school, and then in the 1880s as missionaries and deaconesses, it also denied women clergy and laity rights. That is, while women were denied access to roles of authority as clergy and laity within the church, opportunities increased in areas where need and gender stereotypes converged.[83] In the following three chapters, we will explore these struggles for clergy and laity rights for women as well as the deaconess movement that offered an alternative for women's public ministry.

8

"If God Calls, How Can the Church Refuse to Call?"
The Struggle for Ordination

In her appeal to the 1880 General Conference of the Methodist Episcopal Church, Mrs. Mary L. Griffith of Mauch Chunk, Pennsylvania, referred to women "rising up all over the land who feel moved by the Holy Ghost to preach" and who are "flocking into our theological schools as fast as the doors are opened." Her question to the members of the General Conference was, "If God calls, how can the Church refuse to call?"[1]

"What Shall Be Done with Them?"

The issue of licensing women as local preachers or exhorters refused to disappear after 1872. Resolutions and petitions variously asked the 1876 General Conference of the Methodist Episcopal Church: (1) to allow women to be licensed as preachers whose gifts, grace, and usefulness were evidence of their call; (2) to do away with gender distinctions in licensing to exhort; or (3) to permit women of religious character and gifts, who were not licensed to exhort or preach, to occupy a pulpit temporarily under the supervision and authority of the preacher in charge. In 1872 there had been considerable support for making the language of the *Discipline* gender-neutral so that women would clearly be eligible for all lay offices in the church, including stewards, Sunday school superintendents, and members of quarterly conferences. In 1876 some proposed to add exhorters and local preachers to that list.[2]

The Methodist press reflected the church's preoccupation with "the woman question." An article in the November 1869 issue of *Zion's Herald* (Boston) pointed to the "rapidly increasing" class of women "who have exercised the office of exhorters and local preachers, though without official authority." Admitting that these women had the necessary "gifts, graces, and usefulness," the author pressed the question, "What shall be done with them? Shall they continue their work outside of all recognition and authority?" The issue was not that these women had preached without authorization; clearly they had been invited by preachers to supply their pulpits, or allowed to preach at camp meetings, or given the support of individual presiding elders (district superintendents). However, Methodist usage required that such an important aspect of the church's work be placed "under some authority, if it is to be continued." The point was simple: "No layman is allowed to preach without license. Why should not woman be under the same responsibility? . . . Either the same rules ought to apply to male and female, or men alone be allowed to preach." The writer believed it would "save trouble if the matter be settled speedily."[3]

As we saw in chapter 7, church women in the United States had entered the public sphere in new ways to do relief work during the Civil War. At the war's end, they were ready to be involved in wider spheres of usefulness in the church as well. In "What Shall American Women Do Next?" Jennie Fowler Willing forcefully articulated what many Methodist women were feeling:

> He is an idiot who would ignore or deny woman's energy and capabilities, with the statistics of the Sanitary Commission staring him in the face. . . . No matter then about the women keeping silence in the churches. Their voices might be heard, the wide land over, reading, singing, talking, pleading for the soldiers. Now that the peril is past, it is not so easy to hush them down to parlor warblings and nursery lyrics.[4]

She went on to urge that women be given freedom to do whatever work in the church they could do best, even if that meant preaching. "Where God has endowed them with the dignity to command attention, the voice and language to embody their pity for the perishing, they certainly can speak to the starving masses about the great Salvation. There is enough Church and Scripture precedent for all this, to satisfy any who are fearful of innovation."[5]

In the postwar years, all branches of the Methodist family of churches were confronted in new ways with this issue. Already by

1866, Helenor M. Davison had been ordained a deacon by the Northern Indiana Conference of the Methodist Protestant Church, in all likelihood becoming the first woman ordained in the Methodist tradition.[6]

Licensing Women to Preach: Maggie Newton Van Cott (1830–1914)

In 1869 Maggie Newton Van Cott was granted a preacher's license in the Methodist Episcopal Church.[7] Born in New York City to Episcopalian parents of some prominence, Margaret Newton married Peter Van Cott in 1848. After their marriage, she joined the Dutch Reformed Church (of which he was a member) and helped him in his druggist business. They had two daughters, one of whom died in infancy. Following a powerful conversion experience in 1857 or 1858, Maggie began to attend prayer meetings at the Duane Street Methodist Episcopal Church and, after an experience of being "filled with the Spirit," was increasingly led to testify publicly there.[8] Like many women before her, she then experienced in a dream her call to preach. She dreamed that someone told her, "You must preach," and having ascended the pulpit and preached to a "dear old gentleman," she was amazed to be told that it was John Wesley. He rose from the congregation and reassured her, "Do not be alarmed, my child; you will speak before greater than I."[9] She read more and more Methodist literature and, shortly after her husband's death in 1866, joined the Methodist Episcopal Church.

Having a daughter to support, she at first planned to continue her husband's business. Gradually, and somewhat reluctantly, she began to teach Sunday school classes, then to do evangelistic work at the Five Points Mission in New York City, and eventually to lead Sunday evening prayer meetings there.[10]

She began to be sought after as an evangelist. In 1867, while attending the ordination service during the New York Annual Conference meetings at Bedford Street Methodist Episcopal Church, she poured out the yearnings of her own soul: "O God, why could I not have been a man, that I could be ordained for this great work of preaching the blessed gospel of my dear redeemer?"[11] In June of 1868 she gave up her husband's business to devote herself fully to evangelistic work.[12]

Some converts who had heard Maggie Van Cott preach during very successful revival meetings at Cornwallville, New York, invited her to preach in the church at neighboring Windham. The pastor, the Reverend Alonzo Church Morehouse, was initially "not in sympathy with women preaching, but submitted to it as cheerfully as possible."[13] Eventually convinced that God was blessing Van Cott's labors, Morehouse and the Prattsville presiding elder, the Reverend T. W. Chadwick, arranged for Van Cott to receive an exhorter's license from the Windham Circuit of the New York Conference. It was dated September 6, 1868, and signed by A. C. Morehouse, Pastor.[14]

While next engaged in evangelistic work at Stone Ridge, in Ulster County, New York, Maggie Van Cott was asked by A. H. Ferguson, the presiding elder, and Charles Palmer, the pastor at Stone Ridge, to appear before the quarterly conference for examination regarding her "gifts, graces, and usefulness." She satisfied her examiners and was awarded a local preacher's license on March 6, 1869, signed by the presiding elder.[15]

When the New York Conference met in Sing Sing, New York, for its 1869 session, the issue of licensing women to preach was raised and referred to a committee to report at the next conference. According to an article in the *New York Times* on April 25, 1869, a motion to disapprove the licensing of female preachers failed, as did a motion to censure Ferguson. But the *Times* quoted one clergyman as saying, "It is secretly understood that the 'Widow VAN COTT' will not have her license renewed."[16]

Mrs. Van Cott, meanwhile, continued to attract attention. A brief notice in *Zion's Herald* that fall reported on her "preaching acceptably to crowded houses" in the Revere Street Church in Boston, and noted appreciatively that "quite a number of conversions attended her efforts."[17] A week later a much longer piece, obviously written by editor Gilbert Haven, described her appearance, her preaching style, and her "great success" in winning souls to Christ. The author expressed gratitude to New York Methodism, especially to the presiding elder, the Reverend Ferguson, for having had the courage to give Van Cott a preacher's license. Haven's article is worth quoting at some length:

> Her personal appearance is prepossessing. She is large, well formed, with finely chiseled features, a soft, light eye, that under the excitement of discourse, flames with an unusual brilliancy; a voice of great volume for a lady, though not unlike Fanny Kemble's in strength and tone. She is dressed in plain black, wears a widow's hat of black, and in her costume, as well as manners, bespeaks the lady of breeding. She is as energetic and demonstrative as an actress, and has much dramatic power. This is her forte as a popular speaker. . . . Her words of rebuke ring out sharp and hot, while those of entreaty are soft and cooing as a mother's over a babe. . . .
>
> She will win, if possible, souls to Christ. Her success is great. One soon forgets whether she is a man or a woman. It is an earnest pleader for Christ with sinners, to whom he is listening. Men and women yield to her burning entreaties. . . . To all who object to her ministry, it is enough to say, that God evidently does not object to it. He has already honored her in the few years of her labor with hundreds of converts. . . .
>
> "Send by whom Thou wilt send," should be every honest Christian's cry. Let no one worry if God's ark does not rock as he may approve. . . . The Presiding Elder, Rev. Mr. Ferguson, who had the courage to change "his" to "her," in the certificate of a local preacher, and thus dare the frowns of his Conference, will yet receive their blessing for his courage to see and follow the will of God.[18]

During the spring of 1870, Maggie Van Cott supplied the pulpit of Trinity Methodist Episcopal Church in Springfield, Massachusetts, while the pastor was ill. Springfield was the site of the New England Conference session in April 1870, and many conference ministers heard her preach. An article in *The Methodist* (April 9, 1870) suggested that she might be proposed for admission as a probationer to the New England Conference, but no such action was taken.[19] The quarterly conference of Trinity Church did, however, vote to continue her license as a local preacher. Again the editor of *Zion's Herald* noted these developments with approbation. Referring to Trinity Church, he observed, "This church has crowned its history and good works by opening its house on its dedication to the Troy Praying Band, and Mrs. Van Cott. . . . Especially has it honored itself by giving Mrs. Van Cott a license as a local preacher. Her first license came from a country circuit in New York; her second, from the leading Methodist Church in Western Massachusetts, and in its leading city. It is a deed of which it will never be ashamed."[20]

In the (New York) *Christian Advocate* for the same date, editor Daniel Curry reported on these events from a somewhat different perspective. Summarizing news from the New England Conference, Curry mentioned that Mrs. Van Cott was "still in the city, holding crowded meetings." He then commented: "The chief actor in this work is now involuntarily, perhaps, a disturbing element in the Conference, it being understood that an application will be made for her admission into the body. For the accomplishment of this end our editorial *confrere* of *Zion's Herald* [Gilbert Haven], with characteristic zeal, is putting forth all his endeavors. Should he succeed, (as he probably will not,) he will undoubtedly feel that . . . he has not entirely 'lived in vain.'"[21] At the end of the same article, Curry noted with evident relief that "the application for the admission of Mrs. Van Cott was prudently withheld by the Presiding Elder of the district where she has labored."[22] Neither the New England nor the New York Conference was apparently willing to proceed further with this matter, although both David Sherman and Gilbert Haven had been outspoken in recommending Van Cott's ordination.[23]

Maggie Van Cott was twice invited by the Reverend Joseph Crane Hartzell to hold revival meetings at Ames Chapel in New Orleans, a biracial congregation where he was pastor. Hartzell gave her excellent press coverage in the *Southwestern Christian Advocate*, which he established in 1873, and in an editorial in 1874, he, too, supported her ordination.[24]

During 1874, Maggie Van Cott was in California for several months conducting revival meetings, and the issue of her ordination was also raised there. On September 2, 1874, the San Francisco District Conference recommended that she be ordained a deacon, but when the recommendation was brought before the California Conference it was refused by Bishop Stephen M. Merrill on the grounds that "the Board of Bishops did not recognize that any quarterly or district conference had a legal right to grant women licenses to preach."[25] Apparently most of the bishops agreed that the *Discipline* did not recognize the right of women to be licensed to preach, while numbers of presiding elders continued to give them local preacher's licenses. Noting that a local preacher is eligible for deacon's orders after holding a license for four years, the New York *Christian Advocate* contended in 1873 that Bishop Levi Scott's refusal to consider Van Cott for ordination in the New England Conference "must have been on the grounds that the candidate was not, because she could not be, a local preacher of the Methodist Episcopal Church."[26]

Both an appeal of Bishop Merrill's action and a report from the California Conference on the granting of local preacher's licenses to women were referred to the Committee on Revisals at the 1876 General Conference, but no definitive action was taken. During the 1870s, numerous women—perhaps seventy or more—had asked for and received local preacher's licenses in the Methodist Episcopal Church.[27] No wonder there was increasing pressure from both sides to obtain a ruling on the issue from the 1880 General Conference.

In 1880, two women, Anna Howard Shaw and Anna Oliver, applied to the Methodist Episcopal Church for ordination. Both women had obtained local preacher's licenses in the 1870s, had graduated from Boston University School of Theology, and had been approved by their conference examining committees as candidates for ordination. When it came time for the women to be presented for ordination at the appropriate session of the New England Annual Conference, the presiding bishop, Edward G. Andrews, refused to ordain them. They appealed to the General Conference, the major legislative body of the Methodist Episcopal Church, which met in Cincinnati on May 1, 1880.[28]

ANNA HOWARD SHAW (1847–1919)

Anna Howard Shaw was born in Newcastle-on-Tyne, England. Her family came to the United States when she was four years old and moved to the wilderness of the Michigan frontier when she was a young teenager. There she did the usual man's chores in the absence of her father and, in her spare time, "preached to a congregation of listening trees."[29] The Reverend Marianna Thompson, a Universalist minister, urged her to get an education if she wanted to become a minister. Mary Livermore, the famous temperance and later woman suffrage leader, told her, "My dear, if you want to preach, go on and preach. Don't let anybody stop you."[30]

She was soon brought to the attention of the Reverend H. C. Peck, presiding elder of the Big Rapids District, who proposed that she become a local preacher and helped her get her local preacher's license in 1873.[31] With the aid of Lucy Foot, the Methodist principal of Big Rapids High School where Shaw had enrolled at age twenty-four, Shaw was then admitted to Albion College in the autumn of 1873. After two years there, she enrolled in Boston University School of Theology, graduating in 1878 in a class composed, as she put it, of "forty-two young men and my unworthy self."[32]

Without a place in the dormitory and help with board (both of which were routinely given to male students), Shaw came very near to starvation while a student at Boston. At one point, when she was down to one box of crackers for food, with no heat in her apartment, her shoes "burst open at the sides," and no money for carfare, she accepted an invitation to do a week of revival work with a local church pastor. Discouraged and beginning to doubt her call to preach, she made a kind of wager with God. If the revival work brought her enough money to buy an inexpensive pair of shoes and food for a few days, she would continue her theological course; if it did not, she would give up. At the end of the week, in spite of a successful revival, the minister told her that she deserved fifty dollars for her work, but the collection had been low and there was not enough money to pay her anything. As Shaw stumbled out into the night, a woman came up to her and put five dollars in her hand, in gratitude for her having converted the woman's grandson. Shaw said, "I laughed, and in that exultant moment I seemed to hear life laughing with me."[33] She regarded that as a sign of God's approval of her ministry, and the turning point of her theological career. She never again lost hope.

After graduating from Boston, Shaw was invited to become the pastor of a Wesleyan Methodist Church in East Dennis, Cape Cod. Six months later the Congregational Church in Dennis, which was a few miles away, asked her to be their interim pastor. Shaw was pastor of these two churches for six and a half years. She had to struggle to establish discipline in the Wesleyan Church, but eventually won over the opposition, including a Captain Sears, whom she had earlier asked to leave the church. Several weeks later he came back to confess that in all the years he had been a member of that congregation, he had never seen the pulpit occupied by a minister with enough backbone to uphold the discipline of the church. "I've come here to say I'm with the gal," he ended. After that victory, the congregation was often heard to brag about the "spunk" of its young female pastor.[34] When Anna Howard Shaw applied to the New England Conference of the Methodist Episcopal Church for ordination in 1880, her story intersected with that of another young woman.

ANNA OLIVER (1840–1892)

Anna Oliver had assumed that name in order not to embarrass her distinguished Snowden family by her desire to become a minister.[35] She was born near New Brunswick, New Jersey, April 12, 1840, and baptized Vivianna Olivia Snowden. Her family moved to Brooklyn when she was growing up; she was well educated in Brooklyn's public schools and then completed both a college course and an M.A. degree (with honors) at Rutgers Female College in New York City. In 1868 Anna went to Georgia with the American Missionary Association (AMA) to teach black children. She left, however, after only a year, in protest over the AMA's discriminatory policy with regard to salaries for women teachers. In 1870 Oliver moved to Ohio. She studied art at the University of Cincinnati's McMicken School of Design from 1872 to 1873, became involved in the woman's temperance crusade, and (feeling called to the ordained ministry) enrolled in the theological school at Oberlin.[36]

Anna Oliver experienced Oberlin as a far less congenial place for women to engage in ministerial studies than she had expected. She then applied to a number of theological seminaries, finally enrolling in Boston University's School of Theology in the fall of 1874. When she graduated from Boston in 1876, she was one of four students chosen to give the graduation address. An article in the *Boston Globe* credited her with being the first woman in America to receive a B.D. degree.[37] Oliver had been given a local preacher's license earlier that year by the Jamaica Plain Quarterly Conference of the Boston District. It was dated January 23, 1876, and signed by D. Sherman, presiding elder.

In the fall of 1876, Anna Oliver began pastoral duties in a newly reorganized Methodist Episcopal Church in Passaic, New Jersey. For a time, she had as her assistant the black woman evangelist Amanda Smith. "Between them," a local newspaper reported, "Passaic is having a lively time; what with stirring up sinners and Christians on the one hand, and on the other, two women in the pulpit, and one black, the buzzing grows apace!"[38] Although she could report a 500 percent increase in membership in her first year there, the Newark Annual Conference replaced her with a regularly ordained male pastor for the next year.

When invited to preach at a weekly meeting of the New York Methodist preachers in 1877, Oliver was staunchly opposed by one of their number, the Reverend James M. Buckley, pastor of the large and prominent Hansen Place Methodist Episcopal Church in Brooklyn. Buckley said, in a convincing speech, "I am opposed to inviting any woman to preach before this meeting. If the mother of our Lord were on earth, I should oppose her preaching here. . . . There is no power in the Methodist Church by which a woman can be licensed to preach; this is history, this is the report made at the last General Conference. It is, therefore, not legal for any quarterly conference to license a woman to preach, nevertheless here is a woman who claims to have such a license, and we are asked to invite her to preach."[39] Needless to say, the invitation to Anna Oliver was withdrawn.

In 1879, Oliver took over another beleaguered Methodist congregation, this time in Brooklyn. The Willoughby Avenue Methodist Episcopal Church was sold at public auction under foreclosure and purchased by a group of men and women who asked Miss Oliver to be their pastor. To keep the New York East Annual Conference from claiming the property and appointing a male pastor, the group drew up the deed without the original Methodist trust clause.[40]

In March of 1880 Anna Oliver launched what she clearly saw as a test case on the ordination of women. The Jamaica Plain Quarterly Conference enthusiastically recommended her as a candidate for Deacon's Orders, and the alumni association of Boston University School of Theology sent a memorial to General Conference urging ordination of those women who felt called to the ministry, had received a theological education, and had the necessary gifts, grace, and usefulness.[41] At the New England Conference session on Saturday, April 10, 1880, when the names of the candidates for ministry were presented for vote of the conference and Bishop Andrews refused to submit Anna Oliver's name, Lorenzo R. Thayer, presiding elder of the Boston District, announced that he would appeal the bishop's decision to the General Conference. Someone proposed that Miss Oliver be permitted to address the annual conference on her reasons for seeking ordination, and for half an hour she spoke to them on the subject. At the end of her address, the following resolution was offered and adopted by a large majority: "*Resolved,* that our delegates to the next General Conference be and are hereby instructed to use their influence to remove all distinctions of sex in the office and ordination of our ministry."[42]

After Bishop Andrews refused to present the names of both Anna Oliver and Anna Howard Shaw for ordination, the two women called on him to ask for his advice. They were told bluntly that there was no place for women in the ministry of the Methodist Episcopal Church, and that they should leave the church if they persisted in their dream. At this point, they decided on different strategies. Anna Oliver said that she intended to stay in the church and fight for ordination. Anna Howard Shaw felt it would be better for her to leave. "I shall get out," she said. "I am called to preach the gospel; and if I cannot preach it in my own Church, I will certainly preach it in some other Church!"[43]

1880 General Conference

When the General Conference met in May 1880, Miss Oliver arrived in Cincinnati with her suitcase filled with copies of a pamphlet she had prepared for distribution to the (male) delegates. She was appealing the decision of Bishop Andrews, and asking for ordination to the pastorate.[44] The reasons she gave were essentially those she had given the New England Conference:

> I am sorry to trouble our dear mother Church with any perplexing questions, but it presses me also, and the Church and myself must decide something. I am so thoroughly convinced that the Lord has laid commands upon me in this direction that it becomes with me really a question of my soul's salvation. If the Lord commands me to just the course I am pursuing . . . I have no alternative. . . . Pastoral work is adapted to women, for it is motherly work. The mother has her little group, the pastor the flock. I recognize this field as suited to my natural qualifications.
>
> God sanctions my pastoral work. In proof of this I appeal to the record in Passaic, N.J., and Brooklyn, N.Y. But it may be said, notwithstanding the reasons just given, that I am *mistaken* in my call. Then it is a great pity *for myself* that I cannot be convinced that I am mistaken—a pity that I have lived in this delusion all these years. I have made every conceivable sacrifice to do what I believe God's will. Brought up in a conservative circle in New York City, that held it a disgrace for a woman to work, surrounded with the comforts and advantages of ample means, . . . I gave up home, friends, and support. . . . The things hardest for me to bear were laid upon me. For two months my own mother did not speak to me. When I entered the house she turned and walked away. I have passed through tortures to which the flames of martyrdom would be nothing, for *they* would end in a day. Is it possible that our Father would either lead or leave a child of His in such a delusion? In fact He has really given constant evidence that He sanctions my course. At every step He has met me.
>
> The Methodist Episcopal Church is the church of my choice. I have no one under God with whom to advise but the Bishops and Brethren of our Church. Therefore I do ask you, Fathers and Brethren, tell me, what would you do, were you in my place? Tell me, what would you wish the Church to do toward you were you in my place? Please only apply the Golden Rule, and vote in Conference accordingly. . . . If helped by you, my Brothers, then God bless you! If hindered by you, my Brothers, the Lord forgive you! But whether helped or hindered, with God's grace I will stand where He commands me to stand, because I can do no otherwise, and God takes all the responsibility.[45]

With regard to Anna Oliver in particular, there were two petitions. One was from the Willoughby Avenue ME Church of Brooklyn requesting that the General Conference make "such alteration or alterations in the Discipline as they may consider necessary to remove the disability or disabilities in the way of the *ordination*" of their pastor, Miss Anna Oliver.[46] It was signed by both female and male trustees, stewards, and class leaders of the church, and went to the Committee on the Itinerancy (ordained ministry), along with other petitions on licensing and ordination of women. The other was Lorenzo Thayer's appeal of Bishop Andrews's decision against the ordination of women. It was sent to the Judiciary Committee.

Under the direction of these two powerful committees, the 1880 General Conference decided against the ordination of women. In its first report, the Judiciary Committee ruled that Bishop Andrews's decision was "in accordance with the Discipline of the Church as it is," and therefore that Thayer's appeal should not be sustained.[47] The Committee on the Itinerancy rejected the petition of the Willoughby Avenue Church on the grounds that there was "no society in connection with the Methodist Episcopal Church known as 'Willoughby Avenue M.E. Church.'" In other words, the petition was dismissed on a technicality, without consideration of the subject matter.

On the issue of licensing and ordination of women, the Committee on Itinerancy was uncompromising. In its report, a majority of the committee declared: "They have considered the several papers referred to them in relation to the licensing of women as exhorters and local preachers, their ordination, admission to the traveling connection and eligibility to all offices in the church; and, inasmuch as women are by general consent of the Church accorded all the privileges which are necessary to their usefulness, the Committee recommends that in the respects named no change be made in the Discipline as it regards the status of women in our church."[48] The report was signed by Daniel A. Whedon, Chairman, and Isaac W. Joyce, Secretary. There was, however, a "Minority Report on the Status of Women in the Church." In it, nineteen dissenting committee members, both lay and clergy, affirmed "that this General Conference does hereby interpret the Discipline concerning all offices of the laity as applying to women in the same sense and to the same extent as to men."[49] The 1880 General Conference not only decided against the ordination of women but also declared that all local preacher's licenses issued to women from 1869 on were to be rescinded. The Methodist Episcopal Church would not grant women local preacher's licenses again until 1920.

A Severe Blow

There is every indication that increasing numbers of women were seeking licensing and ordination, and that women experienced the action of the Methodist Episcopal General Conference in 1880 as a severe blow. There is, for instance, the little-known story of Mary A. Phillips, whose father, the Reverend Dr. Jeremiah Phillips, was pastor of the Methodist Episcopal Church in Olney, Illinois, in the 1870s. Believing herself called to the ministry, Mary Phillips enrolled in Garrett Biblical Institute and, following her graduation, sought the endorsement of the Southern Illinois Conference. At its 1879 session, a motion was made to ordain her after a canvass of the members indicated that about two-thirds would favor admitting her to conference membership. The presiding bishop, Edward G. Andrews (the same bishop who refused to ordain Shaw and Oliver), would not entertain the motion. Since Mary Phillips had met Bishop Andrews while she was a student at Garrett and had been given no indication of his disapproval, she and others had assumed that he would support her candidacy.

Following the conference action rejecting his daughter, Jeremiah Phillips "went to work to vindicate the right of women to preach" and succeeded in obtaining a quarterly conference license to preach for a Mrs. Mary Longwood. In 1880, Bishop Andrews appointed to the Olney Church the Reverend William Wallis, known to be opposed to "the opening of the conference doors to women." Apparently he was subsequently "besieged" by advocates of the cause of women's right to preach. Mary Phillips died at her father's home on August 16, 1880, at the age of twenty-one. Her father believed she had never recovered from the shock of the bishop's refusal to admit her to the conference and blamed him for her death. "Why," he said, "did he not tell her at Evanston that she had mistaken the character of the Methodist Episcopal Church, and that she could not be received?" The headstone on her grave in the Haven Hill Cemetery in Olney bears the simple inscription: "Rev. Mary A. Phillips."[50]

Anna Oliver went back to her church in Brooklyn with determination to continue a faithful ministry in spite of the dim prospects for ordination and a regular appointment. The church published an impressive *Annual* for 1881, with "Rev. Miss Anna Oliver, Pastor" in bold type on its title page. She regularly welcomed women in the temperance and suffrage movements into her pulpit, as well as colaborers in the struggle for women's rights in the church (for example, Anna Howard Shaw, and Katherine A. Lent, an 1881 graduate of Boston University School of Theology). In spite of gifts from all over the country, including a "live buffalo from the plains of Kansas," the Willoughby Avenue Church finally had to be closed in March of 1883 because of financial difficulties. William F. Warren, president of Boston University, personally presented a memorial for Anna Oliver at the 1884 General Conference, but with James M. Buckley chairing the Committee on the Itinerancy, it was deemed "inexpedient to take any action on the subject proposed."[51]

Anna Oliver went to Europe in 1886 to try (unsuccessfully) to recover her health. She died at her brother's home in Maryland on November 21, 1892. Anna Howard Shaw helped the women gathered in Washington, D.C., for the National Woman's Suffrage Association convention in January 1893 to put her accomplishments in perspective. "Miss Oliver," Shaw recalled,

> was not only the minister and the minister's wife, but she started at least a dozen reforms and undertook to carry them all out. She was attacked by that influential Methodist paper, *The Christian Advocate*, edited by the Rev. Dr. James M. Buckley, who declared that he would destroy her influence in the church. . . . She had that to fight, the world to fight, and the devil to fight, and she broke down in health. She went abroad to recover, but came home only to die.[52]

AN 1880 ORDINATION

Not long after the 1880 General Conference, a minister in the Methodist Protestant Church (MPC) suggested to Anna Howard Shaw that she seek ordination in his denomination. In October 1880, her name was presented for ordination at the New York Annual Conference in Tarrytown, New York. After extended examination, in which she eventually silenced the opposition with her quick wit and debater's skill, she was approved for ordination and was ordained all by herself (the male candidates having already been ordained) on October 12, 1880. When Shaw returned to her East Dennis parish in time for church the following Sunday morning, she found the communion table set with a beautiful new communion service, purchased during her absence. In 1885, after seven years' ministry on Cape Cod, Shaw resigned as pastor of her two churches to devote herself full-time to the battles for temperance and woman suffrage.[53]

Although the Methodist Protestant General Conference voted in 1884 that Shaw's ordination had been unauthorized by the law of the church, the New York Annual Conference continued to recognize her ordination as valid. In 1889, the Kansas Conference of the MPC ordained Eugenia St. John, the wife of a Methodist Episcopal minister. The MPC had obviously begun to be known as a Methodist denomination in which women could be ordained. After 1892, full laity and clergy rights for women were virtually assured in the Methodist Protestant Church.[54]

On September 11, 1889, the United Brethren in Christ ordained their first woman minister, Ella Niswonger, who became a member of the Central Illinois Conference. Niswonger had been the first female graduate of the regular theological course at Bonebrake (later United) Seminary in Dayton, Ohio. In 1901 she also became the first woman to serve as a ministerial delegate to the United Brethren General Conference. Ella Niswonger was the first of many women to be ordained by the United Brethren (UB). By 1901, ninety-seven women were listed in the UB ministerial directory.[55]

WOMAN IN THE PULPIT

Frances E. Willard, president of the Woman's Christian Temperance Union, published *Woman in the Pulpit,* a strong defense of women's rights in the church, in 1889. Willard's book appeared the year after she and four other women had been refused seating as official, elected lay delegates to the 1888 General Conference. The "thoroughly exasperated" Willard now suggested that if men continued to refuse to share power with the women, perhaps women should "take this matter into their own hands" and form a new church in which they could receive full clergy and laity rights.[56]

In addition to presenting the "full range of arguments" for women's right to be ordained, Willard included in her book statements by prominent male ministers on the issue. One of them was Professor Luther T. Townsend, a Boston University faculty member, who urged that "these noble women should knock only once more at the doors of the Methodist General Conference, and if their signals and entreaties are again uncivilly disregarded, they should never knock again."[57] He warned that the church would be surprised at the number of Methodist clergy who would be glad to assist the women in an irregular ordination.

An article in the October 2, 1890, issue of the *Christian Advocate,* entitled "Letting in the Light," reported on the formation during the previous fall of a "New Century Club" in the Methodist Episcopal Church to be an advocate for women's rights in the church. In this article, editor James M. Buckley demonstrated how some of the church's "conservative sons" responded to Willard's threats. He blamed the WCTU (under Willard's leadership) for spearheading a general movement that not only favored lay representation for women to the General Conference of the MEC, but also "their admission to the ministry on the same terms and by the same methods as men . . . [and] Woman Suffrage in the State." He acknowledged the enormous influence that the organization, many of whose members were Methodist women, could bring to bear on the MEC by concluding that if the church in the first quarter of its second century wanted to become a mere adjunct to the WCTU, it had only to proceed in the direction Willard and others were urging.[58]

Quakers, Congregationalists, Unitarians and Universalists, and Freewill Baptists had been among the earliest religious groups in the United States to grant women the right to preach. All were characterized by either free church polity or a stress on empowerment by God's indwelling Spirit. In 1853 Antoinette Brown was ordained to a small Congregational church in South Butler, New York; she was probably the first ordained woman minister in America. The sermon at her ordination was preached by Luther Lee, a Wesleyan Methodist minister. The Reverend Olympia Brown was ordained a Univeralist minister in 1863. Disciples of Christ and Presbyterians, like the Methodist family of denominations, wrestled with the issue of women's ordination in the 1880s and 1890s.

Even limited clergy rights would not come in the Methodist Episcopal Church until 1924. In that year, the church decided to grant women "partial status," which meant that they could be ordained for a particular location in reponse to the emergency missional needs of the church; they were not members of the covenant body of clergy of annual conference and were not eligible for a regular conference appointment. At the Uniting Conference in 1939 that resulted in The Methodist Church, full conference membership for women was defeated by a narrow margin. Full clergy rights for women in The Methodist Church finally became a reality in 1956.[59]

9

METHODIST DEACONESSES
A Public Ministry for Women

On June 15, 1885, a young woman named Lucy Rider Meyer spoke to the Chicago Methodist Episcopal Preachers' Meeting on a subject of deep concern to her, "The Training of Christian Workers." Especially on her mind was the need for a training school to prepare women for religious leadership. Rider Meyer later remembered all the thought, hard work, and prayer that went into the preparation of that address. She always regarded it as "the entering wedge" that led to the opening of the Chicago Training School for City, Home, and Foreign Missions in October of that year and, less than two years later, to the founding of the Chicago Deaconess Home.[1]

LUCY JANE RIDER MEYER (1849–1922)

Looking back, Lucy Rider Meyer could see God at work in the circumstances of her early life preparing her to become a pioneer in training women for public ministry. Born in Vermont on September 9, 1849, to parents of Puritan ancestry, Lucy Jane Rider was raised in a strongly religious home where she "came to Jesus" at age thirteen in a Methodist revival and subsequently joined the church.[2] She credited her father, Richard Rider, with her lifelong love of the Bible, and her mother, Jane Child, with her thirst for knowledge. She graduated from Oberlin College with a B.A. degree in 1872 and attended Woman's Medical School in Philadelphia to prepare herself for marriage to a fellow Oberlin student who intended to become a medical missionary. All her plans were altered when he died suddenly in 1874. She later recalled, "There came a winter in my life, when all my plans were frustrated, and my future was blank." She returned to her parents' home in Vermont to grieve his death and try to discern what to do.[3]

After her father's death in 1876, Lucy Rider became the sole source of financial support for her mother and younger brother. Immediately she took a position as "Lady Principal" of Troy Conference Academy in Poultney, Vermont. After studying science at Boston School of Technology and teaching methods at Cook County Normal School, she became professor of chemistry at McKendree College in Lebanon, Illinois, in September 1879. A year later she resigned her professorship to accept the position of field secretary of the Illinois State Sunday School Association.[4]

A TRAINING SCHOOL FOR WOMEN

During her four years of service with the Sunday School Association, Rider met many young women whose lack of training kept them from lives of usefulness. The idea of a "school for the purpose of training young women for leadership in Christian work" gradually became the "dominant note" in her thinking.[5] During the winter of 1884–85, Rider taught Bible in Dwight L. Moody's School for Girls in Northfield, Massachusetts. Moody was unreceptive to her attempts to interest him in the idea of a Bible training school, perhaps because he already had his own ideas for such a school (Moody Bible Institute, founded in Chicago in 1886). In the spring of 1885 Rider visited New York to try to find support from Methodist women for a training school; they told her that the Methodist clergy there would not support it.

The financial issue was a very real concern. When Rider Meyer appealed to the Chicago Preachers' Meeting, the ministers gave her project their blessing, but made it clear that she would have to find the money on her own. She had no idea how to raise the money for a training school for women while her mother and brother were financially dependent on her salary from the Illinois State Sunday School Association. Her marriage on May 21, 1885, to Josiah Shelly Meyer, a secretary for the Chicago YMCA, enabled her to think seriously about becoming the principal of a training school for which she would take no salary at all.[6]

After a series of meetings in August, a committee composed of members of the preachers' meeting and representatives of both the Woman's Foreign and Woman's Home Missionary Societies (MEC) finally resolved to proceed with the establishment of a training school and to find an appropriate building to rent. The Meyers moved into a rented brownstone at 19 West Park Avenue in Chicago in early October and immediately began converting it into a school—the Chicago Training School for City, Home, and Foreign Missions (CTS).[7] J. Shelly Meyer became the business agent for the school while continuing in his job for the YMCA. To the Meyers' own funds that first year were added donations of both money and furnishings, largely contributed by Methodist women in the area. A systematic "Nickel Fund" campaign to support the school was launched among Methodist women and publicized in *The Message,* which began publication in January 1886. Eventually both Methodist women of wealth and Chicago businessmen, like William E. Blackstone and Norman Wait Harris, became major donors to the school.[8]

The first session of the school began with a lecture on October 20, 1885. There were only five pupils in that first class, but the number had increased to eleven by early November.[9] Among the members of this first CTS household were Lucy Rider Meyer's mother, Mrs. Jane Rider, and Elizabeth Holding, an old friend who had recently returned from missionary duty in South America. In addition to being principal, Rider Meyer regularly taught courses on the Bible. The resident teachers were few in the beginning, but ministers, teachers, and physicians from the Chicago area regularly donated their time to give lectures. The course of study was comprehensive, including Bible classes, but also studies in "hygiene, in citizenship, in social and family relationships, in everything that could help or hinder in the establishment of the Kingdom of Heaven on earth."[10] Since most of the students came from rural areas or small towns, an important aspect of the program from the beginning was the provision for fieldwork in the city (including house-to-house visitation).

When the lease on the rented building expired it was decided to buy a lot and build a new building for the school. J. Shelly Meyer selected a corner lot at Dearborn and Ohio Streets, and with major gifts from the Blackstone family and an anonymous young Chicago woman, the school opened in its new building on December 9, 1886. Fifteen students were part of the first graduating class on June 2, 1887.[11]

THE BEGINNING OF THE DEACONESS MOVEMENT

In the summer of 1887, Rider Meyer enlisted several of her trainees in a program of visiting and assisting the immigrant poor and needy in Chicago. A note appearing in the June *Message* announced this deaconess work with the modest claim, "We believe this thought . . . may be a seed with a life-germ in it which shall grow. We will plant it, and wait for the showers from Heaven and the shining of the sun."[12] It was the real beginning of the Methodist deaconess movement in the United States.

With the opening of a new school year, the principal decided to place the work on a permanent basis and asked two of her students, Isabelle Reeves and May Hilton, to become the nucleus of a deaconess home. They moved into a rented apartment within a few minutes' walk of CTS and were soon joined by Mary Jefferson and, a little later, by Miss Isabella Thoburn, principal of Lucknow Woman's College in India, who was home on furlough. The October issue of *The Message* announced the joyful news of the establishment of this first deaconess home in American Methodism.[13]

By March, a dozen deaconesses were living in the home. When the building next to the training school went on sale, a generous gift from a Mrs. A. M. Smith of Oak Park enabled its purchase, and an extension was built on the training school building connecting the two. The new quarters were ready for occupancy by mid-September.

The Methodist Episcopal General Conference met in New York City in May 1888. Two petitions were presented to that General Conference asking that deaconess work be recognized as an official ministry of the MEC; one from the Rock River Conference, and the other from the Bengal Conference in India. The latter cited the need for deaconesses with authority to administer the sacraments to the secluded zenana women of India. These petitions for the approval of the deaconess office were referred to the Committee on Missions, chaired by Bishop Thoburn. With his strong advocacy, the committee recommended endorsing the office of deaconess and provided a plan for organizing deaconess work in the ME Church. The duties of deaconesses were described as follows: "To minister to the poor, visit the sick, pray with the dying, care for the orphan, seek the wandering, comfort the sorrowing, save the sinning, and, relinquishing wholly all other pursuits, devote themselves in a general way to such forms of Christian labor as may be suited to their abilities."[14]

The committee's report was adopted and the office of deaconess received the official sanction of the Methodist Episcopal Church (although the General Conference declined to give deaconesses sacramental authority for the mission field in India or elsewhere). To regulate deaconess work, each annual conference was to appoint a Conference Board of Deaconesses, composed of nine members, at least three of whom must be women. This board would be empowered to license qualified candidates who were more than twenty-five years of age, had served a probationary period of at least two years, and had been recommended by a quarterly conference.

"MOTHERING NOT GOVERNING"

As Carolyn De Swarte Gifford astutely pointed out, the deaconess movement "occupied an ambiguous position in the struggle for church women's rights."[15] While sanctioning the office of deaconess, the 1888 General Conference simultaneously refused to grant laity rights to women (ruling ineligible the five women who had been elected lay delegates by their annual conferences).[16] From one perspective, the move to approve the public ministry of deaconess was a great gain for women. But from another perspective it "looked like a means to deflect women from their goal of equal rights in the church," since the 1880 and 1888 General Conferences had denied women both clergy and laity rights. The underlying message seemed to be that the church intended to define clearly the appropriate boundaries of woman's sphere in the church, "relegating her to mothering not governing, allowing her to be a pastor's helper but not a pastor."[17]

Lucy Rider Meyer herself interpreted the work of the deaconess as that of "the Mother in the Church," as part of the "characteristic ministry of women" to care for children and heal the sick. For her, the real origin of deaconess work in America lay in "the mother instinct of woman herself, and in that wider conception of woman's 'family duties' that compels her to include in her loving care the great needy world-family as well as the blessed little domestic circle."[18]

DEACONESSES AND NURSING

To prepare students to meet the needs of people they visited in the slum neighborhoods of Chicago, Rider Meyer included the basics of nursing in the course of study at CTS and called on Chicago physicians to teach them. Dr. Isaac Danforth, an early trustee of the school, helped Rider Meyer to establish a medical clinic at CTS for the dual purpose of offering better nursing training for the students and free medical care to Chicago's poor. Danforth himself was identified with "the cause of the urban poor and of women," being a pathologist at Rush College and Chicago Medical College, a staff physician at Saint Luke's Hospital, and dean of Woman's Medical College.[19] He taught the CTS students the course on human anatomy, and Dr. Eliza H. Root taught them hygiene and obstetrics. The direct successor to this medical clinic was Wesley Hospital, established with the guidance of Danforth in 1901. It was a "six story facility with modern operating room and 145 beds."[20] Although Rider Meyer never taught nursing at CTS, she completed her own medical training at Woman's Medical College of Northwestern University in 1887; she was listed in the CTS catalog as Lucy Rider Meyer, M.D.

Two types of deaconess work developed: there were nurse deaconesses and missionary deaconesses (also referred to as visitors or evangelists). The two-year training required for deaconesses was tailored to the needs of each type, nurses receiving both theoretical and practical preparation comparable to that of nursing schools, and all students being required to take courses in Bible, the *Discipline* of the ME Church, historical and doctrinal studies, and methods of social service.

ISABELLE A. REEVES: FIRST LICENSED DEACONESS

The first licensed deaconess of the ME Church was Isabelle A. Reeves, who had entered the Chicago Training School in January 1887 after reading Lucy Rider Meyer's call to young women to enter the school in order to train for Christian service. Reeves was consecrated and licensed as a deaconess on June 4, 1889, in Centenary Church, Chicago, along with two other young women, Fannie E. Canfield and Evelyn Keeler. She went to New York City in 1890 to become superintendent of the deaconess home there.[21]

Eight women, four of them trained nurses, were in the second class of CTS deaconesses, consecrated and licensed in June 1890. In his graduation address, Bishop William Xavier Ninde, former president of Garrett Biblical Institute, summed up the significance of the occasion: "A sphere has been opened to consecrated womanhood, worthy of her unshrinking devotion and tireless energies. To these wider and more absorbing activities the Church she loves so well calls and welcomes her. She has found her place. She takes it with every divine and human sanction."[22]

A "SISTERLY UNION": DEACONESSES AND THEIR WORK

From the early years of the movement, deaconesses were not only trained, they were also, as Lucy Rider Meyer explained, "costumed, and unsalaried, and they usually live in communities called Homes."[23] The deaconess uniform was a simple long black dress and a bonnet with white ties at the neck. Deaconesses wore it for the sake of economy, to eliminate the need for an expensive wardrobe, and for instant recognition and protection as they worked in dangerous urban neighborhoods. It also gave them greater accessibility to the poor, and a sense of "sisterly union." They received no salary, but only their board, uniform, and a monthly allowance. Most deaconesses lived in deaconess homes, which provided community for single women and enhanced their sense of being part of a sisterhood of service.[24]

Some issues related to supervision of deaconess work within the MEC had not been decided by the empowering legislation of 1888 and remained an unfortunate source of contention for years to come. They had to do primarily with whether the annual conferences or the Woman's Home Missionary Society could best protect deaconesses' goals and status within the church. Disagreeing with Lucy Rider Meyer on these matters was the other principal contender for the leadership of the deaconess movement, Miss Jane Bancroft.

Jane Marie Bancroft Robinson (1847–1932)

Jane Marie Bancroft was born in Massachusetts, the only surviving child of the Reverend George C. Bancroft, a Methodist Episcopal minister, and his second wife, Caroline. Jane Bancroft graduated from Troy Seminary and earned a Ph.D. degree from Syracuse University. From 1877 to 1885 she was dean of the Woman's College and a professor of French at Northwestern University in Evanston, Illinois. When Bryn Mawr College opened in 1885, she was awarded its first history fellowship and spent the next two years in Europe studying at the universities of Zurich and Paris.

Bancroft became interested in the Methodist deaconesses and their work while in Zurich in 1886. She wrote in glowing terms to Mrs. Elizabeth Lownes Rust, corresponding secretary of the WHMS of the MEC, who encouraged her to do a thorough study of the deaconess movement in Europe and present it to the WHMS on her return. Bancroft's study took her to deaconess institutions in Zurich, Paris, London, and Kaiserswerth, Germany. Her study of the European deaconess movement, *Deaconesses in Europe and Their Lessons for America,* was published in 1889.[25]

Speaking at the annual meeting of the WHMS in Boston shortly after her return to the United States in the fall of 1888, Bancroft inspired the women to action. They formed a committee to inaugurate deaconess work and named Bancroft chair. At its annual meeting the following year, the committee became a Bureau for Deaconess Work with Bancroft as general secretary. The resolution was adopted: "That the Woman's Home Missionary Society hereby expresses its willingness to assume the care of Deaconess Homes wherever such homes shall be intrusted to it, subject to the limitations of the *Discipline,* insofar and as rapidly as financial consideration will permit."[26] Bancroft began traveling across the country speaking about deaconess work and founding deaconess homes. In Cincinnati in the spring of 1891, Jane Bancroft married George O. Robinson, a Detroit lawyer and widower with four children. Robinson was an active Methodist Episcopal layman and founder of the Michigan *Christian Advocate.* He encouraged his new wife to continue her work with the Deaconess Bureau, which she did until 1904. She was elected president of the WHMS in 1908.[27]

INTEGRATION OR INDEPENDENCE?: CONFLICTING STRATEGIES

Lucy Rider Meyer and Jane Bancroft Robinson—these two gifted, extraordinarily well-educated, and dedicated Methodist women— vied with each other for the leadership of the deaconess movement in the Methodist Episcopal Church for nearly twenty-five years. One of Rider Meyer's supporters referred to this conflict as "the 'Thirty years' War' which . . . ended without victory and little glory to either side, and for a time threatened to wreck the cause for which it was waged."[28] Viewing the deaconess movement itself as an expression of religious feminism, Mary Agnes Dougherty interpreted the conflict between Rider Meyer and Bancroft Robinson as basically a disagreement over strategy: "Would integration or independence best serve their [the deaconesses'] feminist goals?"[29]

Rider Meyer wanted deaconess work to be directly under the supervision of the church through the annual conferences, to assure that deaconesses would have the same status as male officers of the church. Her model was referred to as the "Church Plan." Bancroft Robinson's view was rooted in a European model of deaconess work where the deaconesses worked under the supervision of a superior within the motherhouse. She believed that the Woman's Home Missionary Society, a separate women's organization in the Methodist Episcopal Church, ought to supervise deaconess work in order to protect its autonomy.[30]

There was much debate about both the "original intention" of the 1888 General Conference, which gave its approval to the deaconess office, and priority of origin. "Both sides took their arguments to the church for a solution. Each meeting of the General Conference between 1888 and 1922 saw the argument surface."[31] In 1908 there was hope for genuine reconciliation. Writing home from the General Conference in Baltimore, Rider Meyer expressed that hope:

> We have invited the other side to send a speaker to our meeting to present their point of view, and to join with us in a prayer meeting. We are making every effort for peace, and hoping and praying that this business may not come before the public on the Conference floor.[32]

The 1908 General Conference created a General Deaconess Board to guide all three forms of deaconess work: "the 'Church Plan,' the German Methodist, and the WHMS deaconesses." The new plan was recommended to all deaconesses in the opening Episcopal Address.[33] The solution, however, proved "illusory," both Rider Meyer and Bancroft Robinson being appointed to the newly organized board and continuing to maintain their own views.[34]

DEACONESSES AND THE SOCIAL GOSPEL

Mary Agnes Dougherty astutely argued that the significance of Methodist deaconesses could only be adequately understood in the context of the social gospel movement. Commenting on the strangeness of women's absence from the standard historical accounts of the social gospel, Dougherty wrote, "Is it possible that women did not participate in the movement for social Christianity? It is unlikely. What has happened is that women who were active in the social gospel movement behaved characteristically [as women], and in doing so have been overlooked."[35]

During the 1880s—generally agreed by historians to be the "seedtime" of social Christianity—Methodist churchwomen found in the ancient office of deaconess an appropriate model and institutional form for carrying out an active social gospel program. According to Romans 16:1-2, Phoebe was a *diakonos* (deaconess, a servant of the church) at Cenchreae, near Corinth. She responded to the hunger and disease she observed there with a ministry of service in the name of Christ.

So, too, late-nineteenth- and early-twentieth-century deaconesses were determined to transform the city. They began by "visiting," canvassing tenement neighborhoods to discover those in need of help. While ministering to people's basic needs and demonstrating neighborly concern, they also gathered important information on prevailing social conditions. As literature like the *Deaconess Advocate* reveals, they came increasingly to look for the underlying causes of the misery they found and then to attack the evil social structures responsible.

These women were activists rather than theorists. They saw what they were doing as "pure practical Christianity." They responded to Christ's call with the resolve to become *useful,* to further God's purpose for the world. Methodist deaconesses formed a new breed of church women. Trained for and consecrated to the order, they became experts in the field of Christian social service.[36]

ISABELLE HORTON AND THE BURDEN OF THE CITY

In 1894, at the age of forty-two, Isabelle Horton entered the Chicago Training School to become a deaconess. She was closely associated with Lucy Rider Meyer for many years, serving as associate editor of the *Deaconess Advocate,* becoming assistant principal of the school, and eventually writing the biography of her teacher and mentor. For ten years (1903–13) Horton also served on the staff of the Halsted Street Institutional Church in Chicago.[37]

While she was associate editor, the *Deaconess Advocate* ran regular columns on the social problems of the day. Horton's articles became increasingly characterized by a penetrating social analysis and clear willingness to call into question the existing social order. She advocated the use of the social sciences in addressing urban problems and urged readers to look for the root causes of poverty and human suffering.

In her 1904 book *The Burden of the City*, Horton made a persuasive case for the crucial role of the deaconess in urban home mission work. Trained, unsalaried, wearing distinctive garb to identify and protect her, and officially "set apart and consecrated" for her service, the deaconess was uniquely qualified for work in the cities. She might be a nurse deaconess or employed by a church or city mission, in charge of a kindergarten, day nursery, or old people's home, or employed as a Travelers' Aid to welcome and assist new immigrants. Whatever her particular service, Horton strongly believed that the deaconess should be especially committed to working with and for the poor.[38]

As Horton described it, being a deaconess was a demanding way of life, requiring, above all, the willingness to serve "for Jesus' sake":

> To be able to meet emergencies as they arise, and to live up to the requirements of her office, the deaconess must be kind, tender, sympathetic and yet decided. She should be fertile in resources and prompt in action, an expert in diplomacy, patient and tactful, and a shrewd judge of human nature. She must be able to turn nurse, cook, preacher or musician, in case of need, and to meet representatives of all classes of society with equal grace. To these advantages, she needs to add a constitution of steel and whalebone. All this without reference to the deep and strong religious life without which no woman should think of taking up this work.[39]

A prime example of the deaconess as representative of the Methodist social gospel, Isabelle Horton became a charter member of the Methodist Federation for Social Service in 1908. (Of the five women among the seventy-three founders, only one was not a deaconess and she was a settlement house worker. In addition to Isabelle Horton, the other four women were Mary McDowell and deaconesses Bertha Fowler, Grace Scribner, and Winifred Chappell.)[40]

"NOT I, BUT CHRIST": GROWTH OF THE MOVEMENT AND TRAINING SCHOOLS

In the MEC more than a thousand deaconesses had been consecrated for service in some ninety institutions by 1910. Other denominations in the Methodist family had also become part of the movement: the United Brethren in Christ beginning deaconess work in 1897, the Methodist Episcopal Church, South, in 1902, the Evangelical Association in 1903, and the Methodist Protestant Church in 1908.

Between 1880 and 1915, nearly sixty religious training schools were opened in the United States, "primarily for lay people and most of them for women." In addition to the Chicago Training School, two other pioneering Methodist institutions were the New England Deaconess Home and Training School, founded in Boston in 1889, and the Scarritt Bible and Training School, established in 1892 in Kansas City, Missouri, and moved to Nashville in 1924.[41]

In 1887 Belle Harris Bennett visited Lucy Rider Meyer in Chicago in order to confer with her about the possibility of establishing a training school for women of the Methodist Episcopal Church, South. Bennett had become convinced that southern women "longed to work in the Lord's vineyard," but did not "because they did not know how to work." Presenting her idea to the Woman's Board of Foreign Missions in 1889, Bennett was promptly appointed "agent" of the Board to raise funds and promote a training school. As a result of her efforts, Scarritt was able to open in 1892.[42]

Scarritt served initially to train women under the auspices of the Woman's Foreign Missionary Society. Increasingly its leaders became involved in home missions work and, after the establishment of the deaconess office in the MECS in 1902, in the training of deaconesses. An innovative part of Scarritt's program came with the hiring that same year of Mabel K. Howell "in the emerging field of sociology."[43]

Other training schools that came later were the Lucy Webb Hayes National Training School in Washington, D.C.; the Kansas City National Training School in Kansas City, Kansas; and the San Francisco National Training School in San Francisco. These were all under the authority of the Bureau of Training Schools of the WHMS (MEC). The first Training School for Colored Deaconesses was founded in Cincinnati in 1900. Two of the pioneering black deaconesses were Miss Anna Hall and Miss Martha Drummer, both graduates of the training school in Boston.

DEACONESSES IN THE METHODIST
EPISCOPAL CHURCH, SOUTH

In 1902 the General Conference of the Methodist Episcopal Church, South, voted to create the office of deaconess in the southern Methodist church. Belle Harris Bennett had sent a memorial to the General Conference describing the urgent need; she and Mary Helm had already spent two years laying the groundwork for its acceptance. Approval was not granted without "long and bitter debate" about whether such official recognition of women in the church would lead them to aspire to the ordained ministry or to compete with the work of the ordained minister. In granting the memorial, however, the General Conference made the Woman's Board of Home Missions entirely responsible for deaconess work.[44]

Mary Helm tried to allay some of the suspicions regarding the deaconess movement in an article in *Our Homes* entitled "What a Deaconess Is, and What She Is Not." As in the ME Church, Helm explained, deaconesses in the ME Church, South, were consecrated, trained, wore a uniform, lived in a Deaconess Home, and received no salary. A deaconess was *not* a preacher, ordained, or a "Protestant nun."[45] In 1903 Bishop Eugene Hendrix consecrated the first five deaconesses of the Methodist Episcopal Church, South: Mattie Wright (the first), Amy Rice, Annie Heath, Elizabeth Davis, and Anabel Weigle. Elizabeth Taylor, also a member of this first class of deaconesses, was consecrated several months later due to illness. These and other early deaconesses in the southern Methodist Church were said to be happy in their own work, "consummate homemakers," having a sense of humor, patient in facing difficulties, resourceful, working beyond the call of duty, adaptable, generous, persistent, and courageous.[46]

DEACONESS IDENTITY

Mary Agnes Dougherty suggested that the women who answered the call to deaconess life were part of the massive rural-urban shift in the United States in the last quarter of the nineteenth century, and that the deaconess movement itself helped to facilitate "their transformation from dependent daughters in rural families to semi-autonomous, independent women."[47] They were distinguished from the majority of women who flocked into the growing cities to find jobs because their entrance into deaconess work was the result of a religious experience or "call" to the full-time service of the deaconess. They relied on their faith to sustain them, and in their personal attention to human needs "they behaved toward strangers as they would have behaved toward friends back home." The deaconess, said Isabelle Horton, is "the maiden sister of the world."[48]

Methodist deaconesses sought to distinguish themselves from Catholic sisters on the one hand and secular social workers on the other. Like nuns, deaconesses were single women who lived together in a communal lifestyle and wore a distinctive costume. However, they took no vows and were free to leave the work at any time. As Dougherty suggests, Catholic sisterhoods did serve as "important models and inspiration for the movement," especially the hospitals, schools, and other institutions administered by nuns that were designed to meet the needs of the urban Catholic population. The attitude of deaconesses toward Catholic sisters was ambiguous: deaconesses both fought comparison with the Romish image and also emulated it.[49]

The secular model of the social workers was new, but for the most part deaconesses and social workers were friends. A good example is the relationship between Jane Addams of Hull House and Lucy Rider Meyer at CTS. Deaconesses often regretted the absence of a religious perspective in social settlements like Hull House, but they recognized kindred spirits in their mutual commitments to minister to the poor. In their advocacy of social justice as of equal or greater importance than evangelization, deaconesses were representative of the social gospel.[50]

Deaconesses were trained professionals who believed that a personal approach and sacrificial motivation were both important to their social service. As social work became more institutionalized in the twentieth century, keeping the appropriate balance in deaconess identity likewise grew more difficult. Deaconesses were sensitive to the criticism that professionalization meant renouncing woman's appropriate nature and sphere. The fear of some ordained ministers that deaconesses might have "pastoral ambitions" was another complicating factor. Lucy Rider Meyer was careful to reassure the church that recognition of the deaconess office would not mean that the "new woman" would crowd out the "true woman." The deaconess office, while offering a public ministry to women, was thus an interesting combination of traditional and modern images of Christian womanhood.[51]

DECLINE OF THE DEACONESS MOVEMENT

The deaconess movement seemed to be at its height in 1910, when 256 women came to study at CTS. In actuality, by 1910 the movement had already begun to decline. Changing attitudes toward the social gospel, new, secular career opportunities for women, and a growing conservatism in the churches all affected women's training schools, and with them, the deaconess movement. By 1914 Lucy Rider Meyer was alerting readers of the *Deaconess Advocate* to "our present crisis."[52] As a theological liberal, Rider Meyer began to have to defend her educational policy at CTS against conservative critics. She refused, however, to compromise on the matter of historical criticism of the Bible.[53] Troubled by ill health, Rider Meyer finally conceded to her husband's wishes and announced her intention to retire as principal of CTS. An even more painful concession for her was having to agree that its new head might be a man rather than a woman. In June of 1916, Louis Lesemann became the new president of CTS. Rider Meyer died on March 16, 1922. CTS would continue its independent existence until it merged with Garrett Biblical Institute in 1934. Dougherty summed up the impact of these changes: "Although CTS survived Rider Meyer's retirement, it was never the same institution. As a Bible school, it was too embarrassingly liberal by the 1920s, as a woman's training school it was too intensely religious to compete with secular professional schools, and as an institution of the social gospel it had outlived its usefulness."[54]

10

"BECAUSE THEY ARE WOMEN"
The Struggle for Laity Rights

The fundamental issue in the prolonged debate in the Methodist Episcopal Church about laity rights for women, as historian Carolyn De Swarte Gifford pointed out, was "whether or not women belonged in the political arena."[1] As Methodist women participated in increasing numbers in large and influential women's organizations like the Woman's Home and Foreign Missionary Societies and the Woman's Christian Temperance Union, men accurately perceived the threat to existing power relationships in the church and beyond. Some men supported the women's struggle for full participation in the church's governing bodies; others fought desperately to retain control, arguing that ruling was the proper sphere of man and expressly forbidden to woman in the Scriptures.

JAMES M. BUCKLEY

One of the foremost opponents of both clergy and laity rights for women in the church was the Reverend James Monroe Buckley, who served distinguished appointments in a number of prominent churches in Detroit, Brooklyn, and New York City, and was elected by the Methodist Episcopal General Conference of 1880 to the editorship of the New York *Christian Advocate*.[2] He held this powerful position continuously for thirty-two years, until 1912. Of his influence as editor it was said that when any important matter came to public attention, many people did not know what to think until "Dr. Buckley's editorial" came out in the *Advocate*.[3] It is also worth noting that Buckley was first elected as a General Conference delegate in 1872 and remained a delegate until 1912, serving eleven consecutive General Conferences spanning key decades of the debate concerning the rights of women in the church. A brilliant debater ("by common assent, acclaimed the greatest debater in Methodism, if not in the nation")[4] and witty and forceful writer, he was a formidable opponent. At the General Conferences of 1884 and 1888 he was chairman of the powerful Committee on Itinerancy (i.e., Ordained Ministry), and at the 1888 General Conference, a member of the special Committee on the Eligibility of Women (for laity rights). Conference was sometimes "facetiously reported as 'Dr. Buckley in Session,'" and he was said to have taken the floor seven hundred times in a single General Conference.[5]

LAY REPRESENTATION AND THE
1872 GENERAL CONFERENCE (MEC)

The struggle for laity rights for women should be set in the context of the preceding struggle for laity rights for men. The MEC admitted the principle of lay representation in 1872, to the General Conference only and not yet to the annual conferences, and only two lay delegates per conference.[6] At the 1868 General Conference, a plan had been formulated to submit the issue of lay delegates to General Conference to a churchwide referendum among male church members. Dr. David Sherman, a minister from Massachusetts, then moved to amend by striking out the word *male*, thus allowing women to vote in the referendum. He later recalled that he intended specifically to raise the issue of women's participation in the decision-making processes of the church. Sherman's motion was seconded by the elderly Dr. Henry Slicer, of the Baltimore Annual Conference, who did not miss Sherman's point. In his seconding speech he said, "And sir, if it were the last moment I should spend on earth, and the last articulate sound I should utter, I should speak for the wives, mothers, and daughters of the Methodist Episcopal Church. . . . I am for women's rights, sir, whenever Church privileges are concerned."[7] The report thus amended was adopted, "thereby submitting the question of admission of lay delegation to a vote of our *lay members without distinction of sex*."[8] Both laity and clergy voted in favor of the necessary change in the Constitution, and the General Conference of 1872 concurred, at which time the previously elected lay delegates were seated. Consequently, at the 1872 General Conference each annual conference delegation consisted of two laymen as well as the (ordained) ministerial delegates.

Where women were concerned, a principal issue in the debate would later be whether the 1868 General Conference *intended* to open the door to female delegates. David Sherman's account made it clear that that was indeed his intention.[9] When his motion to strike out the word *male* was pending, the question had been asked, "Will that make women eligible as delegates?" Apparently shouts of "no, no" and "yes, yes" came from the floor, but as was later suggested, these had only the weight of personal opinion and "no official force." (The opponents of women subsequently attempted to demonstrate that the intention had been to exclude women.)[10]

The General Conference of 1872, composed of ministerial and lay delegates, had raised the question of the meaning of the term "laymen," saying it must be understood to include all the members of the church who are not members of the annual conference (i.e., full-time ordained clergy). In harmony with this, the 1880 General Conference *"judicially interpreted"* the language of the Discipline by declaring that "the pronouns *he, his,* and *him,* when used in the Discipline with reference to stewards, class-leaders, and Sunday-school superintendents, shall not be construed as to exclude women from such offices." The Reverend Alpha J. Kynett summed up the significance of this:

> Under this authority of law many devout women were chosen to be stewards, class-leaders, trustees, and Sunday-school superintendents, and, as such, became members of Quarterly Conferences and duly-qualified electors of delegates to Electoral Conferences, and many of them were themselves chosen as delegates to Electoral Conferences, and continue to be chosen. Members of subsequent General Conferences held their seats by the suffrages of such *lay delegates* to Electoral Conferences.[11]

Two additional pieces of data are helpful here. The June 5, 1869, issue of *The Methodist* carried an "Address to the Female Members of the Methodist Episcopal Church," signed by a long list of prominent Methodist women. The address reviewed the action of the 1868 General Conference[12] and called on the church's female members "to take some pains to form a decided opinion, in order that we may so act as to promote in the highest degree the welfare of the Church." It was basically a call to women of the Methodist Episcopal Church to vote in favor of lay representation. It concluded, "It may be the felicity of the women of Methodism, upon the only occasion when they have been permitted to take part in the settlement of a great question, to bring to the Church healing and peace. And this, if we *can*, let us do. We could render our beloved Church no better service."[13]

Second, it is interesting to note that the most widely known and respected episcopal leader of the ME Church in the 1860s, Bishop Matthew Simpson, clearly saw and publicly articulated that asking women to vote was an important step in the full recognition of women as laity. At a meeting in favor of lay delegation held at the Smithfield ME Church in Pittsburgh in May 1869, Bishop Simpson said:

An additional interest has been excited by asking the vote of women also. We seem to be realizing the apostolic declaration: "There . . . is neither male nor female; for ye are all one in Christ Jesus." *Whatever may have been the design, this vote is opening a new era* [emphasis mine]. It may have been supposed that, as women had never been called upon to vote, they would naturally oppose a change. So, doubtless, the opponents reasoned. But they forgot that in woman's bosom there glows an instinct for liberty, and in every struggle for freedom she has been the friend of the lowly and suffering. Will she not read in this the dawning of a brighter day for herself? . . . You are training her for the ballot. A new day is coming. . . . I hope that, on this first ballot, she may speak wisely and well for the enlargement of our Zion and for the elevation of humanity.[14]

THE 1888 GENERAL CONFERENCE (MEC)

The 1880 ruling of General Conference that women who held local church offices could be members of a quarterly conference (the governing body of the local church) and, therefore, could vote for delegates from a local church to the electoral conference, which in turn chose delegates to the General Conference, meant that it was only a matter of time before women themselves would be elected as lay delegates to General Conference. In 1888 the issue of women's laity rights in the MEC was "put to the test" when five annual conferences elected women as lay delegates to General Conference: Angie F. Newman of the Nebraska Annual Conference; Mary Clarke Nind of the Minnesota Annual Conference; Amanda C. Rippey of the Kansas Annual Conference; Lizzie D. Van Kirk of the Pittsburgh (Pennsylvania) Annual Conference; and Frances E. Willard of the Rock River (Illinois) Annual Conference.[15] Seventeen women had also been elected reserve delegates. Most of these women were leaders in the women's missionary societies or the WCTU at either the national or the regional level.

Mrs. Angie F. Newman was the first to be elected, as the result of a movement led by the women of St. Paul's ME Church in Lincoln, Nebraska, to secure the election of a woman delegate; her election was unanimous.[16] When the lay electoral conference of Minnesota met in Minneapolis on October 14, 1887, Mrs. Mary C. Nind received 89 votes, and George H. Hazzard received 70 on the first ballot (61 being necessary for election). Their election was made unanimous. Interestingly, Angie Newman and Mary Clarke Nind were not present at the electoral conferences that selected them.

For months before the General Conference convened on May 1, 1888, at the Metropolitan Opera House in New York City, opposing sides on the issue of the legitimacy of women as lay delegates attempted to influence the delegates, and both the denominational and secular press were full of the subject. At the beginning of the General Conference, before the roll call and formal seating of delegates, the MEC bishops in their Episcopal Address gave their opinion that the five women could not be seated because their eligibility as delegates had not been properly determined according to the constitution of the MEC.[17] The question of eligibility was referred to a special committee, which was to report the following day. In the meantime the women were not to be seated.[18] A roll call of the unchallenged delegates was then taken, and the General Conference was organized for business.

On May 2, the report of the Committee on the Eligibility of Women was read and its adoption moved. A. J. Kynett, a ministerial delegate from Iowa, moved that it be laid on the table, printed in the *Daily Christian Advocate*, and made the order of the day for May 3. His motion passed. Although some delegates were in favor of giving the women seats on the conference floor while their eligibility was being decided, they did not prevail. The special committee of seventeen reported as follows:

> *Whereas*, after serious consideration and a free discussion for several hours they are convinced that, under the Second Restrictive Rule, which was altered by the constitutional process, the church contemplated the admission of men only as lay representatives; and that as it [the church] has never been consulted or expressed its desire upon the admission of women to the General Conference, they are compelled to report for adoption the following resolutions:
>
> 1. That under the Constitution and laws of the Church as they now are women are not eligible as lay delegates in the General Conference.
>
> 2. That the protest referred to this Committee against the seating of Amanda C. Rippey, Mary C. Nind, Angie F. Newman, Lizzie D. Vankirk [*sic*] and Frances E. Willard is sustained by the Discipline; and, therefore, they cannot legally be admitted to seats.
>
> 3. That the Secretary of the General Conference shall notify the legally elected reserve delegates from these Conferences that the seats herein referred to are vacant.[19]

After lengthy debate and much parliamentary maneuvering, the vote was finally taken on May 7, the sixth day of the General Conference, and the committee's decision sustained by a vote of 237 to 198.[20]

James M. Buckley argued that the intent of the lawmakers determined the meaning of the law, and believed "laymen" would never have been admitted to the General Conference in 1872 if the church had understood the term to include women. He favored the submission of the question to the church at large, "clinching his argument with the characteristic remark: 'He that cometh in by the door' the same hath a right to come in, but he that cometh in another way, is not as respectable as in the other case."[21] David H. Moore presented a series of resolutions providing for the seating of the women and for a reference of the question of constitutionality to the annual conferences and lay membership of the church, but they were not generally acceptable. Some thought "a good majority of the delegates" were prepared to vote for the admission of women if this could be done without a "cloud of illegality" hanging over the action.[22]

Only four of the women delegates-elect were at the conference. Frances E. Willard was called home at the beginning of the deliberations by the serious illness of her mother. The others remained throughout the debate ready to take their seats if the conference declared their admission constitutional. Mary Nind's diary entries during those momentous days are simple but revealing:

> Wednesday, May 2, Bishops' address and report on eligibility of women all against us, but if the Lord be for us, what matters? Friday, May 4. Another day of sharp debate, but no conclusions reached. Saturday, May 5. Still another day. Monday, May 7. Today we were ejected from our seats by a majority of 37 clerical and 2 lay votes, and the great debate is over, to come up again in 1892. All is serene in my soul.[23]

Frances Willard concluded her more extensive comments on the election to and dismissal by the General Conference with these prophetic words: "I confidently predict that we five women, whose election was thus disavowed, will have more enviable places in history than any who opposed us on those memorable days. Of them it will be written, while doubtless they did not so intend, that they committed an injustice; of us, only that in silence we endured it."[24]

"BECAUSE THEY ARE WOMEN"

The 1888 General Conference agreed to submit the question of women's eligibility as lay delegates to General Conference to a referendum by the entire church membership, requesting a report of the results in time for the 1892 General Conference. In 1891, opponents of women's laity rights distributed a pamphlet containing a series of editorials by James M. Buckley, which had first appeared in *The Christian Advocate.* Women's laity rights supporters countered by issuing a pamphlet by George W. Hughey, refuting Buckley's arguments point by point. (Hughey's pamphlet was published by the Woman's Temperance Publishing Association [WTPA], the publishing arm of the WCTU.)[25]

The first of Buckley's editorials dealt with what he called "abstract natural rights." He was willing to acknowledge that women had the right to "an influence equal to that of man," but not that this influence "should take the form of representation by delegates of her own sex and membership in the General Conference, and of ordination to the ministry, either or both."[26] Buckley cited statistics revealing what was really worrying him. He feared that proponents of abstract rights would prevail in the MEC, and that representation, whether lay or clergy, would eventually be based entirely on proportional representation. As Carolyn Gifford suggested, "Taken to its logical conclusion, he reckoned that this would mean that women would take control of the General Conference because they vastly outnumbered men in the denomination. . . . For Buckley and other conservatives within the MEC the specter of a GC ruled by women was even more horrifying than one ruled by the laity."[27]

Responding in part to Frances Willard's *Woman in the Pulpit* (1889), Buckley criticized "female suffragists" for "making void the law of God" by ignoring the "plain sense" of Scripture in encouraging women to transgress their appropriate sphere. According to both nature and divine revelation, he believed, man was to rule (at home, in the church, and in the nation). Thus it was fundamentally unscriptural to admit women to the General Conference as delegates because it would make them rulers.

As we saw in chapter 8, "Letting in the Light" was an attack on the WCTU, under Frances Willard's leadership, for interfering in the affairs of the Methodist Episcopal Church. Buckley had objected to the WCTU's advocacy of lay representation for women, their admission to the ordained ministry, and woman suffrage. He provided examples from the *Union Signal,* the "*official* organ" of the WCTU, to demonstrate his point about interference; for example, the attempt to connect the deaconess movement with the ordination of women, and the threat that the WCTU might "organize a church" if representation continued to be denied to women. He referred particularly to Miss Willard's address at the WCTU National Convention in 1889, in which she called for a resolution asking "the laymen of the Methodist Episcopal Church, who will in the fall of 1890 take action on the question of making women eligible as delegates to the General Conference, to 'do as they would be done by,' and the lay women to remember that 'there is neither male nor female in Christ Jesus,' and 'who would be free himself must strike the blow.'" Obviously he found threatening the enormous influence that this organization, many of whose members were Methodist women, could bring to bear on the ME Church.

Finally, Buckley summed up his main point: "All objections to the admission of women into the General Conference come at last to this—that they are *women* [emphasis in the original] and not men." Women should not be given legislative functions, according to Buckley, because they were already preoccupied with work of equal importance that, when they confined themselves to it, exerted a greater influence for good. Buckley's depiction of the dire consequences for women that would result from their participation in the "fray" of a General Conference prompted Hughey to reply:

> Those who have been to the General Conference a few times, and have witnessed the scenes here described, can not help but think that the admission of a few refined and cultured women to that body would have a very beneficial effect upon *some* of the members, and probably lessen the confusion very perceptibly. He [Buckley] says: "Since *masculine* mental and moral qualities can not be eradicated, to give women any opportunity in the General Conference, a plan must be devised to *feminize* the body." We think from an experience in three General Conferences with Dr. Buckley, that this would be a capital idea, and would be a great improvement in conducting its business!![28]

"Equal Rights in the Church"

Laity rights advocate Alpha Kynett's pamphlet *Our Laity: and Their Equal Rights in the Church* (1896) was a masterful summary of the long history of the question by an outspoken advocate of women's admission. Kynett and others like David H. Moore (who wrote the Introduction to Kynett's pamphlet) firmly believed that female Methodists were constitutionally eligible to membership in the General Conference, and had been eligible since the adoption of the amendment to the Restrictive Rules (that is, the Constitution) by which (in 1872) lay representation had been introduced.[29] Consequently they believed that the decision of the 1888 General Conference had been a mistake. As Kynett explained it, the assumption that women were ineligible rested on the *opinion* formulated by the Committee of Seventeen, on the basis of which the General Conference of 1888, "exercising its right to determine the qualifications of its own members, *decided* that the five women delegates, against whom some persons, to this day unknown to the General Conference or the Church at large, had lodged *with the bishops* a protest, were not entitled to seats as members of that body." The Neely Amendment was then offered and adopted as part of the report; it proposed that " 'upon concurrent recommendations of three-fourths of all the members of the several Annual Conferences,' a majority of two-thirds of the General Conference may add to the Second Restrictive Rule the explanation that lay delegates to the General Conference 'may be men or women.' " The result of the referendum was that a majority of 71,825 of the laity (including women) voted for the eligibility of women; on the question of changing the Restrictive Rule by adding the explanatory clause, a majority of the annual conferences voted in favor of the change, but the vote was 2,130 short of the required three-fourths.[30]

Because women had been chosen lay delegates to the Lay Electoral Conferences, and two women had been elected reserve delegates to the 1892 General Conference, the 1892 General Conference asked the Judiciary Committee to report on whether the terms "lay delegates," "laymen," and "members of the church in full connection," when used in the *Discipline,* implied distinction of sex. The committee proposed to reaffirm the action of 1888. The only dissenting member of the committee was Dr. David H. Moore, who immediately offered a substitute motion reaffirming (with slight amendment) the interpretation of 1872; that "in all matters connected with the election of lay delegates, the word laymen" must be understood "to include all the members of the Church who are not members nor presidents of the Annual Conferences (i.e. ordained clergy)." It was superseded by the Hamilton Amendment, which declared that if inserting the limiting word *male* did not receive three-fourths of the votes cast in annual conferences, and two-thirds of the votes cast in the General Conference, "*the rule shall be so construed that the words 'lay delegates' may include men and women.*"[31] The General Conference voted to substitute this for the report of the committee and it was adopted.

The key question then was the authority of the 1888 interpretation, as over against the "correction" of 1892. The conservatives claimed the authority of 1888; the progressives claimed that the 1892 decision had completely reversed the 1888 opinion. Kynett's pamphlet concluded by summarizing the case in this way:

> There is now no law against the eligibility of women. There is, therefore, no need of change. However, let the vote on the Hamilton Amendment and on the Baltimore-Neely Amendment be taken in all the Conferences. It may lead to the same result, and be more satisfactory to our conservative brethren. But whatever may be the issue of these votes, the General Conference of 1896 must pass upon the qualifications of its own members. Two "*elect ladies*" already hold credentials as delegates, and more are likely to follow. . . . Then let the General Conference so pass upon these new cases, as the Supreme Court of the Church, as to finally and forever settle the law on the firm foundations laid in 1872.[32]

In his Introduction to Kynett's pamphlet, David Moore aptly summed up the position of the progressives on the issue: "Its most determined opponents admit that the admission of women is inevitable. Apparently they hope only to delay it. But why delay? . . . A decided majority of those who have voted on the subject, both clergy and laity, has pronounced for the women. Hence there can be no doubt as to the judgment of the Church. A hearty and prompt acquiescence in this judgment by the General Conference would be the logical and democratic conclusion of this whole matter."[33]

Finally, in 1900 the General Conference ruled that women were eligible to be delegates, and in 1904 twenty-four women attended the General Conference of the MEC as lay delegates and another thirty as lay reserves.[34] These first women delegates were (their names as listed, followed by their annual conference and occupation, if given): Mrs. Ida T. Arms, Western South America (directress of college in Chile); Mrs. May C. Bliss, Detroit; Belle E. Bodkin, Southern California (assistant editor in Los Angeles); Alberta Crow, St. Louis; Mary A. Danforth, New Hampshire (returned missionary); Mrs. Gertrude Durrell, New England; Alice M. Hayman, Indiana (teacher); Mrs. Emeline A. Hypes, Southern Illinois; Mrs. Elizabeth S. Martin, Des Moines; Mattie Y. McMahan, Illinois; Lucy Rider Meyer, Rock River (principal of training school); Mrs. Emma L. Neeld, North India (missionary); Mrs. Medora D. Nickell, Nebraska; Juana Palacios, Mexico; Mrs. Lois S. Parker, North India (missionary); Mrs. Florence Richards, Central Ohio; Mrs. Minerva E. Roberts, Nebraska; Florence L. Snow, South Kansas; Agnes Snyder, Ohio; Annie T. Strickland, Little Rock (teacher); Viola A. Troutman, Kansas; Mrs. Lottie E. Valentine, Michigan; Mary S. Wilkinson, Northern New York (president of Folts Institute); and Mrs. Ada M. Wilson, North Indiana.

In gaining lay representation to the General Conference of the MEC, women had at last wrested one victory from their unremitting opponent James M. Buckley!

PIONEERS: METHODIST PROTESTANT CHURCH, 1892

The Methodist Protestant Church had left the MEC in 1830 in part over the issue of lay representation. The original constitution of this more democratic denomination gave equal representation in annual and General Conference to laymen, that is, to adult white male members. Both women and blacks were excluded. At the 1858 General Conference, when the issue of rights for blacks was about to divide the church, John J. Murray of Maryland proposed to amend the constitution to allow the annual conferences to determine who could vote and hold office. As William T. Noll pointed out, Murray's intention was to deal with the racial issue without splitting the church, but his proposal might also have benefited women. Murray's compromise was defeated in 1858, and the northern conferences formed a separate denomination that did include his proposal in their constitution of 1862. When the two branches of the church reunited in 1877, the constitution of the new church gave to the annual conferences the power to decide on matters of suffrage and eligibility to hold office.[35]

Although these actions had opened a door for the participation of women in the Methodist Protestant Church, Noll credits the Woman's Foreign Missionary Society for changing the mood of the denomination regarding women. As we saw in chapter 7, while the 1880 General Conference of the MPC gave its approval to the Woman's Foreign Missionary Society, the women had to struggle to preserve the autonomy of their organization. At the 1884 General Conference, the leaders of the WFMS were powerless to prevent the Committee on Foreign Missions from drafting a new set of rules that essentially made their society an auxiliary of the parent board. By 1888 the women had "explored and developed their political leverage" and were successful in persuading the General Conference to restore their former freedom. As the women's abilities were "increasingly recognized and appreciated by the men of the denomination," local churches began to elect women as lay delegates to annual conferences.[36]

Finally in 1892 four women were elected as delegates to the Methodist Protestant General Conference, three as lay delegates and one as a ministerial delegate. All of them had been leaders in the Woman's Foreign Missionary Society. Melissa M. Bonnett (West Virginia) was a returned missionary from Japan, Mrs. M. J. Morgan (Indiana) had been an organizer and officer of the Indiana Branch, A. E. Murphy (Iowa) was treasurer of her annual conference Board of Missions, and Mrs. Eugenia St. John (Kansas) had been a founder of the Kansas Branch of the WFMS. St. John, who had also been ordained an elder by the Kansas Annual Conference in 1889, was then elected by her annual conference as a ministerial delegate to General Conference in 1892.[37]

In the debate that occupied two full days of the General Conference, John J. Murray argued that the original intent of his 1858 proposal giving annual conferences the right to decide on matters of suffrage had never been to include women, and if that interpretation had been insisted upon, the union of 1877 would never have been consummated. Thomas Appleget, a pastor from New Jersey, countered that the same could be said of the rights of blacks in the MPC. Murray argued that the term "laymen" was intended to exclude women; Appleget asserted that there were many instances in the MP *Discipline* where "man" seemed to be used to include both sexes.

The crucial Credentials Committee, chaired by Murray's brother, J. T. Murray, submitted a majority report signed by four members and a minority report signed by three. The majority declared the election of women as lay and ministerial delegates to be in violation of the constitution. The minority affirmed that all the elected women delegates, both lay and ministerial, were entitled to their seats. Eugenia St. John called on the brethren of the MPC to give an example to all the churches and to the world of their church's "broad spirit of liberality to its representatives, of its progress in God's kingdom, of its willingness to live above prejudice." By a vote of 77 to 48, all four women delegates were seated.[38]

Even after the vote, the opponents of women's rights in the MPC attempted to introduce a constitutional amendment allowing women to be lay and clergy delegates to the General Conference, knowing that it would be difficult to secure the necessary two-thirds of the annual conferences to ratify the amendment. Supporters of women's rights replied with a substitute amendment permitting annual conferences to forbid women to be ordained or to serve as delegates to General Conference. This substitute passed overwhelmingly. Noll claimed that the mood of the 1892 General Conference had already been expressed when it voted, by a margin of two to one, to remove the word *obey* from the woman's marriage vow. He concluded: "The will of the church was clear: Those Methodist Protestant annual conferences that wished to ordain women or elect them to General Conference were free to do so."[39]

UNITED BRETHREN IN CHRIST, 1893

The following year, in 1893, the General Conference of the United Brethren in Christ included lay delegates for the first time.

Two of these were women: Mrs. Mattie A. Brewer (Lower Wabash) and Mrs. S. J. Staves (Des Moines). At its previous General Conference in 1889 the United Brethren had also approved the licensing and ordination of women.[40]

The United Brethren were clearly aware of the significance of their actions. In their quadrennial address to the General Conference, the bishops affirmed:

> Several conferences have chosen to send as delegates esteemed women from among them. These Christian women are here to-day accorded this highest representative trust in the Church, and are welcomed unchallenged to sit with us in the highest council of the denomination.... What a gathering is this to-day! It marks an epoch in our history. Fathers, young men of the shepherds of Israel; laymen, from all callings, who honor God with their substance; sisters, who represent the loving company at the early dawn of the resurrection morning, meeting first their risen Lord! May Jesus stand in our midst and breathe upon us these holy words, "Peace be unto you."[41]

A report on this 1893 General Conference commented on the presence of two women among the fifty-six lay delegates, describing Mrs. Brewer as "no foolishness about her—plain, matter-of-fact, attentive, earnest," and Mrs. Staves as "a typical Iowa lady, matronly, intelligent, refined, pious, missing nothing, intent on being faithful in her stewardship." The report ended with the pointed remark, "Well, well; will not some one kindly inform Dr. Buckley that now at least two respectable denominations admit women to participation in their highest lawmaking departments?"[42]

Laity Rights for Women in the Methodist Episcopal Church, South

In 1922 twenty women took their seats as lay delegates to the General Conference of the MECS. Eighteen women had been elected as lay delegates; one of them could not attend because of illness and three women lay alternates were called to replace elected delegates. The names of the eighteen women elected were: Belle Harris Bennett, Kentucky; Mrs. S. H. Bowman, Western Virginia; Mrs. H. A. Dunham, Western North Carolina; Mrs. J. LeGrande Everett, North Carolina; Mrs. R. L. Hobdy, Alabama; Mrs. R. P. Howell, Los Angeles; Carrie Parks (Mrs. Luke G.) Johnson, North Georgia; Althea Jones, Texas; Mrs. Fred A. Lamb, Southwest Missouri; Mrs. J. H. McCoy, Tennessee; Mrs. D. D. McGehee, North Alabama; Mrs. J. W. Mills, Texas; Mrs. W. L. Oliver, North Arkansas; Mrs. Nat G. Rollins, Northwest Texas; Mrs. F. F. Stephens, Missouri; Mrs. F. M. Tolleson, North Arkansas; Mrs. John S. Turner, North Texas; Mrs. L. B. Woodside, St. Louis. The three who were seated as alternates were: Mrs. J. H. Dickey, Louisville; Mrs. J. W. Perry, Holston; Mrs. J. H. Spillman, Kentucky.[43]

Belle Harris Bennett had for years led the struggle for women's rights in her church. Earlier chapters discussed her vital role in the opening of Scarritt Bible and Training School, the establishment of Wesley settlement houses throughout the South, and the authorization of deaconesses by the MECS General Conference.

At the 1906 General Conference, the General Board of Missions of the MECS recommended the unification of all the church's missionary work and, as a first step, urged the immediate merging of the woman's home and foreign missionary societies.[44] The bishops of the southern Methodist Church appointed a commission to study the issue and report to the next General Conference. Four women were named to this thirteen-member commission: Belle Harris Bennett and Tochie MacDonell from the home missionary society, and Maria Layng Gibson and Alice Culler Cobb from the foreign missionary society. Although opposed, these women were unable to prevent the commission from recommending the reorganization of all church missionary activity under one Board of Missions, on which women would have one-third representation, and merging the woman's home and foreign missionary boards into a single Woman's Missionary Council. These recommendations were accepted by the 1910 General Conference.[45]

Belle Harris Bennett had the difficult job of serving as president of the new Woman's Missionary Council. One of the major losses for southern Methodist women in the process of unification was that of *Our Homes*, the independent publication of the WHMS since 1892. As Virginia Shadron pointed out, in *The Missionary Voice*, the new paper of the Board of Missions, "The space allocated to women permitted little more than a straight reporting of Woman's Missionary Council business. While *Our Homes* had provided extensive coverage of the developing church-woman's rights movement, the editorial policy of *The Missionary Voice* precluded any discussion of the issue." Mary Helm, editor of *Our Homes*, immediately resigned her position and privately expressed the opinion that Belle Harris Bennett had exercised poor judgment in accepting the terms proposed by the commission on unification. (Bennett explained that she accepted the terms offered only because she feared "something worse.")[46]

The loss of autonomy for their women's missionary work made suffragists of southern Methodist women. On the challenging recommendation of Bennett, the WHMS board prepared a petition to the 1910 General Conference of the MECS requesting full laity rights for women. In all, the 1910 General Conference received 148 memorials, 637 petitions, and hundreds of telegrams in support of women's laity rights in the church. Belle Harris Bennett was invited to address the General Conference in behalf of the memorial from the WHMS; it was the first time a woman's voice had been heard in a General Conference of her church. It was a brilliant speech by an astute veteran. Bennett told the delegates that "the great Church" they represented needed "the womanhood of the Church" in its councils, and that it was "not a few" who believed that "the fulness of time" had come. She then issued this forthright challenge: "My brethren, this is not a matter of reason with you, [but] a matter of prejudice. . . . Put this act on its passage, and it will come back to another General Conference to be ratified, and [by then] a great many of us will be gone home to God. . . . After twenty centuries we stand knocking at the door of the Church of God, saying yet, 'My brothers, brothers, won't you take us in?'" In spite of her eloquent appeal, the memorial lost by a vote of 74 to 188.[47]

By the 1914 General Conference women were better organized. They had not only prepared for the General Conference with petitions and agitation in the church press, but they also appealed (although largely unsuccessfully) to the annual conferences to appoint a special committee to evaluate annual conference opinion on the matter. The bishops were adamant in their objection to granting women laity rights, and a majority of the committee to revise the constitution recommended against any changes. Again Bennett made a plea to the General Conference, this time claiming that laity rights for women were not radical and had been tried by other Methodist bodies without disruption of church harmony or government. Once more the motion to give women laity rights was defeated in the General Conference; the vote was 105 to 171.[48]

In the third quadrennium of the campaign, the cause of women's laity rights was organized primarily by the *Laity Rights Advocate*. According to Virginia Shadron, this paper began publication in 1912 or 1913, was financed entirely by private donations, and had no official church sponsorship. Although no copies appear to have survived, "extant fragments" suggest the existence of a more militant organization of missionary society women that provided the movement's major source of leadership and financial support. In one such fragment, Mary Helm claimed that an independent publication was necessary because "in the Methodist Episcopal Church, South, not only the women, but laymen and preachers are forbidden the right of free speech."[49]

At the 1918 General Conference the woman's memorial was adopted "after less than thirty minutes' discussion." In an attempt to forestall this action the bishops "declared the issue a constitutional question and vetoed the conference's action, but the conference reaffirmed its decision in a dramatic roll-call vote. On the morning of May 14, 1918, the delegates accepted the principle of woman's suffrage in the church by a vote of 270 to 50." This action on a constitutional question required ratification by three-fourths of the members of the annual conferences. It was achieved handily, only four conferences (including Bennett's Kentucky Conference) failing to affirm women's laity rights.[50]

Shadron astutely observed that the most decisive component in the success of woman's suffrage in the southern Methodist church had to do with the change in male leadership between 1910 and 1918. In 1918, 50 percent of the 320 General Conference delegates were in General Conference for the first time.[51] Although elected by the Kentucky Annual Conference as its first woman delegate to the 1922 General Conference, Belle Harris Bennett was too ill to attend; she died of cancer that July.

Evangelicals and "Laymen"

Lay delegates were admitted to the General Conference of the United Evangelical Church in 1898 and of the Evangelical Association in 1907, but in neither case were women included. In 1922 the two denominations united to form the Evangelical Church, which continued to exclude women from laity rights. Finally in 1946, anticipating the union with the United Brethren in Christ later that year to form the Evangelical United Brethren Church, the General Conference of the Evangelical Church included two women among its "laymen." They were Mrs. Edward Stukenberg (Illinois) and Irene Haumersen (Wisconsin).[52] These women were delegates both to the Evangelical Church's General Conference and to the EUB General Conference that followed it.

Once again, as in the struggle for ordination for women, the Methodist Protestant Church and the United Brethren Church were first among the predecessor bodies of the UMC to grant laity rights to women. In episcopal Methodism, gains were made more slowly. While women always had male supporters in their struggle for equality in the church, prominent leaders like James M. Buckley opposed women's exercising political power. Buckley was still convinced that women and men had their own appropriate and separate spheres of service in the church. He could be eloquent in summing up "what Methodism owes to women," but he feared and opposed women's seeking "a degree and kind of prominence" that he thought only men ought to hold.[53]

11

MISSIONS COMING HOME
Racial-Ethnic Women in American Methodism

Chapters 7 through 10 described women's emergence into public work in the church and the world from the 1860s to 1920, through women's missionary societies, the WCTU, deaconess work as a public ministry for women, and the long struggle of women for clergy and laity rights in the church. In this same period, Methodists were involved in missionary work with Native Americans, Hispanic Americans, and Asian Americans. At first the object of Christian missions, women of color by the end of this period were also emerging into the public as they assumed leadership roles in their own churches and women's organizations. This chapter will characterize briefly the history of each of these major racial-ethnic groups in the United States, summarize Methodist missionary activity among them, with particular attention to the work of Methodist women, and highlight the development of indigenous leadership, especially of women, in each of these communities of color.[1]

METHODIST MISSIONS AMONG NATIVE AMERICANS

In spite of John Wesley's (unsuccessful) efforts in 1736–37 to be a missionary to the Indians in Georgia, and his urgent expression of concern for the souls of Indian people in a letter to Francis Asbury fifty years later, American Methodists did not have an official mission to Native Americans until 1819.[2] In that year, the Ohio Annual Conference appointed James Montgomery missionary to the Wyandotts, with John Stewart as his assistant. Stewart, an African American, had initiated the work among the Wyandott people of northern Ohio in 1815, after being converted at a

Methodist camp meeting, joining the Methodists, and experiencing a powerful call to preach. He was assisted by Jonathan Pointer, also African American, who served as his interpreter. Through their efforts the principal leaders of the Wyandotts were converted, including Chiefs Between-the-Logs, Mononcue, John Hicks, and Squire Gray Eyes.[3]

Also in 1819 a Methodist Missionary Society was organized, following closely on the passage of the so-called "Civilization Bill" by the federal government that encouraged the establishment of Indian schools. Both the mission to the Wyandotts and the Missionary Society won the support of Bishop William McKendree and the official approval of the MEC General Conference in 1820. The new society was instructed to accept as its "first care" the institution of Indian schools "on the government plan, and under the government patronage." Having a special society within the Methodist Church responsible for mission represented a new departure for Methodists, who had previously seen their entire church as a missionary movement.[4]

From 1819 to the end of the Civil War, Methodist missionary activity among American Indian people might be summarized, as historian Bruce Forbes suggested, in four major clusters: (1) among the Wyandotts in Ohio (and later Kansas); (2) among the five major tribes in the Southeast and, following Indian removal, in Indian Territory (Oklahoma)—the Cherokee, Chickasaw, Choctaw, Creek, and Seminole peoples; (3) in the Great Lakes region; and (4) in the Pacific Northwest.[5]

The Wyandott Mission

After receiving a local preacher's license from the Ohio Annual Conference, John Stewart continued his work among the Wyandotts until forced to retire due to ill health. He lived with his wife, Polly Carter, in a small cabin adjacent to the Wyandotts, where he died of tuberculosis in 1823 at the age of thirty-seven. Several other missionaries followed, the most prominent of whom was James B. Finley. By 1826 the Wyandott mission "reported 300 church members, seventy Indian pupils in the school, fifteen Class Leaders, and four native preachers."[6]

A mission school was established under Finley's leadership with the agreement of the Wyandott chiefs, several of whom served as a committee to oversee the school. Finley engaged Harriet Stubbs as its first teacher. Two others, William Walker Jr. and Lydia Barstow, were added later. The school boarded students during the week, but most of them returned home on weekends. Although "as many as half of the Wyandott people were associated with Methodism, and many adapted considerably to white American culture," they were ultimately unsuccessful in resisting white pressures to remove them farther west. The Wyandotts were relocated to Kansas in 1843.[7]

The two acres of burial ground on which the meetinghouse stood were deeded to the Methodists. In 1899 a church was rebuilt on the same site, using the original stones. The only Wyandott present at the rededication was Margaret (Mother) Solomon. One of John Stewart's converts, Mrs. Solomon was the daughter of Chief Gray Eyes and had been in Harriet Stubbs's school in 1821 and 1822.[8] She had immigrated to Kansas with the tribe in 1843, but returned with her husband to Ohio in 1865 and died there in 1890.[9]

Missions Among the Five Major Southeastern Tribes

Methodist missions were begun among the Creeks in 1821, the Cherokees in 1822, the Choctaws in 1824, and the Chickasaws in 1835.[10] Richard Riley, himself part Cherokee, initiated the Cherokee mission by inviting a Methodist preacher from the Tennessee Conference, Richard Neely, to preach at his house. A Methodist society was formed and Riley was appointed class leader. By the end of 1822 a school had been established and a meetinghouse built by the Cherokees; in the summer, a well-attended camp meeting was held at Riley's. By 1827 William McMahon, superintendent of the Cherokee mission, reported "three Circuits, four schools, and 675 church members, with several of the Indians [men] serving as licensed Exhorters and Local Preachers."[11] Among those who became Methodists were John Ross, John F. Boot, and Turtle Fields.

In 1828 the state of Georgia began to pass laws designed to remove the Cherokees from their territory. Cherokee lands were declared confiscated and Cherokee laws null and void. The governor notified all missionaries working among the Cherokees that they would be arrested if they did not leave the state. Although the Cherokees resisted valiantly and many of the missionaries protested against removal, pressure was greatly increased with the passage by Congress of the Removal Bill in May 1830.

On September 25, eight Methodist missionaries, including James J. Trott and Dickson C. McLeod, met to draw up resolutions asking their denomination to support the Cherokee Nation. Declaring their "unanimous opinion" that removal would be "ruinous" to the Cherokees, they called upon American Christians to express their sympathy for the "aggrieved condition of the Cherokees" and oppose these policies of Georgia and of the federal government. The resolutions were printed in the New York *Christian Advocate* (October 26, 1830) and the *Cherokee Phoenix* (October 1, 1830). Cherokee Elias Boudinot added an editorial to the latter praising Methodists for being the first missionaries to speak out for his people's rights.[12] Unfortunately the Methodist missionaries were not supported by the Tennessee Conference, which refused to interfere with "political affairs." By the expiration date for removal in 1838, fewer than two thousand Cherokees had emigrated. Suddenly more than fourteen thousand Cherokee men, women, and children were forcibly herded into concentration camps and shamefully removed to Indian Territory west of the Mississippi on the "Trail of Tears."[13]

The Reverend Alexander Talley, M.D., was appointed to the Choctaw mission by the Mississippi Conference in 1827. Talley went from village to village preaching among the Choctaws; within three years he was able to report that four thousand Choctaws had been enrolled as church members. Apparently rationalizing removal as the best way to protect Indians from exploitation, Talley accompanied a band of Choctaws to Indian Territory during the winter of 1830–31.[14]

In 1821 William Capers of the South Carolina Conference was appointed missionary to the Creek Nation by Bishop McKendree. Although the Creeks were not yet open to having Christian preaching in their nation, they were willing to approve the establishment of an Asbury Mission School. Among its students were James McHenry, Samuel Checote, and George W. Steadham, all of whom later became prominent Methodists as well as leaders of the Creek Nation. The Creeks were forced to move to Indian Territory in 1836.[15]

West of the Mississippi the Cherokees, Choctaws, Creeks, Chickasaws, and Seminoles struggled to reconstruct their national lives. Although removal brought bitterness and distrust of whites and their religion, the Mississippi, Tennessee, and Missouri Conferences continued to send missionaries into Oklahoma.[16]

Missions in the Great Lakes Region

In the 1820s and 1830s a number of annual conferences began work with Indian people in the Great Lakes region. With the help of Mohawk evangelist Daniel Adams, John Clark of the New York Conference started a mission among the Oneida in Green Bay, Wisconsin, in 1832.[17] Soon a Methodist class was formed, a mission house was built and dedicated, and a school was organized. Miss Electa Quinney, a young Housatannuck (Stockbridge) woman, was hired as the first teacher. She and Daniel Adams married, and in 1837 went to the Seneca Mission in Indian Territory. After her husband's death Mrs. Adams "continued in service, highly esteemed for her intelligence and good work."[18]

Work among the Chippewa began as part of the Genesee Conference's mission to the Mohawks. In 1822 Peter Jones, a Chippewa living among the Mohawks, met Methodist preacher Seth Crawford. The following year Jones and his sister Mary were converted at a Methodist camp meeting. He became a Methodist preacher and was one of the founders of Methodism among the Chippewa at Sault Saint Marie.[19]

Other Native Americans were instrumental in the work among tribes in the Great Lakes region. Three young Ojibwa men—John Johnson, George Copway, and Peter Marksman—had been sent to Ebenezer Manual Labor School in Illinois with three non-Indian youth who were committed to missionary service. All of them became prominent church leaders. Peter Marksman was called by one historian "the outstanding Michigan Methodist Indian preacher of the nineteenth century."[20]

Pacific Northwest Missions

By the early 1830s the idea of a mission to the numerous Indian tribes in the Pacific Northwest (including the Chinook, Salish, and Nez Percé peoples) was being widely discussed back East. The "moving spirit" in the founding of the Oregon Mission was Wilbur Fisk, president of Wesleyan University in Middletown, Connecticut, who proposed to the Missionary Society (MEC) in 1833 that the Reverend Jason Lee be appointed "missionary to the Flathead Indians."[21] Fisk's original vision became formative for Lee upon his acceptance of the appointment: "Live with them—learn their language—preach Christ to them—and, as the way opens, introduce schools, agriculture, and the arts of civilized life."[22] When Lee and his group reached their destination, however, they did not find the Flathead tribe.

On April 28, 1833, Jason Lee and his nephew, the Reverend Daniel Lee, and Cyrus Shepard, a schoolteacher, left St. Louis as part of the overland expedition of Captain Nathaniel J. Wyeth. They arrived at Fort Walla Walla on the Columbia River on September 1, and at Fort Vancouver on September 15. There Dr. John McLoughlin of the Hudson Bay Company fed and housed them, and persuaded Jason Lee to set up his mission on the Willamette River. By his own account, Lee's motivation was to choose a location where a school could be supported by farming grain and vegetables. From the beginning, Lee had to struggle with the Indians' opposition to their children attending school, the deaths of several Indian children from diseases brought by the whites, and the ill health of Daniel Lee and Cyrus Shepard. In 1837 a sizable group of reinforcements arrived at the mission, having traveled by sea from Boston, around Cape Horn, and through the Hawaiian Islands. They included a medical doctor and his family and several white women, one of whom, Anna Maria Pittman, would become Jason Lee's wife. After 1837 the history of the Oregon Methodist Mission became inseparable from the settlement of Oregon Territory and its annexation to the United States; Homer Noley referred to this as "Lee's *other* mission."[23]

CREATION OF THE INDIAN MISSION CONFERENCE

At its 1844 General Conference the Methodist Episcopal Church created an Indian Mission Conference. At that same General

Conference the church divided over slavery. When the Methodist Episcopal Church, South, was organized in 1845 (its first General Conference meeting in 1846), the Indian Mission Conference became part of the southern church.

The Indian Mission Conference was convened by Bishop Thomas A. Morris on October 23, 1844, at Riley's Chapel, two miles east of Tahlequah in Indian Territory (Oklahoma). On his journey to the conference, Bishop Morris and three missionaries stayed at the home of Mrs. Electa Quinney Adams, Daniel Adams's widow. She welcomed the travelers and arranged Sunday services in her home, which were attended by Senecas, Stockbridges, Shawnees, Cherokees, blacks, and several white persons. Among the charter members of the Indian Mission Conference were three Native Americans: William McIntosh (Cherokee), John F. Boot (Cherokee), and William Okchiah (Choctaw). As Homer Noley suggests, the statistics for that conference "represented twelve years of reconstruction by Native American Christians since being exiled from their native homes": 27 local preachers, 85 white members, 133 black members, and 2,992 Indian members.[24]

Methodist missions in Kansas became part of the Kansas District of the Indian Mission Conference. The Shawnee Mission Manual Labor School opened in October 1839, with four teachers and seventy-two students from a number of Indian tribes (especially Shawnee and Delaware). In Arkansas two schools were established in the early 1840s: Fort Coffee Academy for the education of Choctaw boys and a school for girls at nearby New Hope.[25]

According to Wade Crawford Barclay, between 1819 and the division of the church north and south in 1844, the Methodist Episcopal Church established missions among some thirty-five Indian tribes. He summed up this mission activity as follows:

> Altogether, fifteen Annual Conferences sponsored missionary work among the Indians for longer or shorter periods of time, and not less than 214 preachers were given Indian mission appointments. This number does not include fifteen or more Indians who were received into Conference membership and given missionary assignments among their own people.[26]

In his book *Missionary Conquest*, George E. Tinker, an Osage-Cherokee, argues that from an American Indian point of view even the best-intentioned Christian missionaries were guilty of the cultural genocide of Indian people. As increasing numbers of white settlers moved into Indian lands, many were ready to justify Indian removal or even extermination. Most missionaries, including Methodists, probably were genuinely concerned about the well-being of Indian people. The fact that they saw "Christian civilization" as the best possible solution to "the Indian problem" indicates the degree to which they were people of their times. Because there was no clear distinction in their own minds between the Christian gospel and their own culture and its values, they (sometimes unwittingly) became complicit in the "destruction of Indian cultures and tribal social structures," with tragic consequences.[27]

CHANGING U.S. POLICY ON NATIVE AMERICANS

Expanding westward through Indian Territory from the 1840s through the 1860s and the dark days of the Civil War, the U.S. government waged war against the Plains Indians. A terrible blot on the record of Methodist-Indian relations was the massacre of several hundred Cheyenne women, children, and elderly men of Black Kettle's peaceful encampment at Sand Creek, Colorado, in November 1864. The attack was led by Colonel John M. Chivington, a Methodist preacher and presiding elder, and former missionary to the Wyandott people in Kansas.[28] Proposing that the "civilization" of Native people would be preferable to their extermination, an investigative commission in 1868 recommended a thorough reorganization of government bureaucracy dealing with American Indians.[29]

Three phases of U.S. policy on Native Americans can be identified after the Civil War. The first was President Ulysses S. Grant's Peace Policy, according to which Indian tribes were required to live within the bounds of reservations assigned to them, under the authority of the Indian agent. Instead of being controlled by the Bureau of Indian Affairs, all of the agencies dealing with Indian people (seventy-one in 1871) were now assigned to various Protestant denominations. Although at least three-fourths of Methodist Indian activity had been in southern hands prior to the Civil War, the northern Methodist church received all fourteen of the agencies allotted to Methodists in this post–Civil War period.[30]

The goal of Indian reform policy in the 1880s was to break up tribal relations and their reservation base and to encourage individualism, citizenship, education, and the assimilation of Indian people. The Dawes, or General Allotment, Act of 1887 provided for the allotment of reservation lands in severalty (that is, for private ownership of these lands). Finally in 1934, the Indian Reorganization Act accorded a measure of respect to Indian culture by allowing the Indian land base to be built up and by encouraging tribal governments.

This complicated history is the necessary background for examining Methodist women's work with Indian women. Home missions women, most of them white and middle-class, viewed Native American women through the lenses of their own cultural values, typically failing to comprehend the delicate balance of power in gender relationships among various Indian nations. From their perspective Indian women needed to be rescued from the "discomfort and degradation of heathen life" and converted to Christianity and civilization. Industrial schools where Indian girls would be trained in "all the duties of housekeeping" would, these home missions women thought, be a catalyst for Indian people's taking the "long step from the tepee and tent of nomadic life to the Christian home."[31]

WOMEN'S WORK FOR INDIAN WOMEN

Through their women's missionary societies, women of the Methodist Episcopal Church, South, participated in the effort to develop schools and academies among the transplanted Indian nations in Oklahoma. In 1853 the Reverend John H. Carr and his wife opened the Bloomfield Academy for Chickasaw girls. Four years later Elizabeth Fulton, the eighteen-year-old daughter of the Reverend DeFarr T. Fulton (a Methodist missionary to the Cherokee), became part of the academy's teaching staff. Although she married George B. Hester two years later, Elizabeth Fulton Hester continued her teaching. During the Civil War she "taught a class of twelve Indian boys, all of whom became chiefs, and she later became active in both foreign and home missionary societies."[32]

The Harrell Institute at Muskogee in Indian Territory was founded as a school for girls by the general mission board in 1881 and became a major project of the Woman's Missionary Society (MECS) in 1886. The Reverend Theodore F. Brewer was Harrell's first president. He and his wife, Mary Elizabeth, were from Mississippi and had served at the Asbury Manual Training School in Indian Territory before coming to Harrell Institute. Mrs. Brewer was instrumental in organizing a local Woman's Missionary Society at Harrell in 1884, and in the Indian Mission Conference in 1886.

When the Reverend J. J. Methvin was appointed missionary to the western tribes of Oklahoma toward the end of the 1880s, his wife insisted that the whole family (including herself and their five children) should go. They began the Anadarko mission, which eventually became a project of the WFMS. Miss Helen Brewster became a key figure in the camp work at Fort Sill with Kiowa and Comanche Indians. When Methvin could not secure a preacher who would stay at a second mission station near Mount Scott, he decided to send Helen Brewster there as well. "She, under God, I trust, will save that place to our Church," he said.[33]

It was lonely and difficult work, especially for a single woman. Brewster visited and lived with the Indians in their camps, gradually winning their trust and affection by reading, talking, praying, and eating with them. She attempted to learn their languages, although she used interpreters when available. Excerpts from her April 1896 report to Methvin demonstrate the demanding nature of her work:

> 7th, went out to Mt. Scott; 8th, quilting at Passouiders, and earnest Christian talks with them; 9th, visited Comanche camps, and had services in three; 10th, had services at Pooxocuts; 11th, such a pleasant service at Kiowa camp, and organized a woman's prayer meeting; 12th, Sunday, held the preaching service at Sankadota's house, as it was quite cold; 13th, at home, quite sick; 14th, better, able to be

about. . . . 26th, Sunday, held service here; no interpreter; did my own talking, praying, and singing, dividing it evenly between English and Comanche, with God's help; 28th, 29th, and 30th, at Mt. Scott, Virginia [Stumbling Bear] was gone, and I hardly knew how I would manage without her to interpret the Kiowa for me, but I didn't want to go away without giving them some of my time, so I went round to their camps, trusting in God to open a way. At the first house I found that white man who was raised among the Kiowas; he did my talking. At the next house I found three school Indians, so held the service and prayer in English; at another held it in Comanche, the Indian man interpreting. God greatly blessed my soul. The next day had some most precious times with the Comanches. Truly God is using my broken talk to his glory, just as you said he would. How your words of cheer help me![34]

It is difficult, of course, to measure the impact of Brewster's work. Methvin told the missionary women of the MECS that they had every reason to be encouraged. "Some one said recently," he reported, "that the woman's work was the only solid thing here. That may not exactly be the case, but it would hardly be possible for us to hold the work together were it not for the woman's work."[35] Helen Brewster no doubt shared many of the views of nineteenth-century white Methodists about the need for Indians to become "civilized." Yet her willingness to meet Kiowa and Comanche people where they lived, her attempts to learn their languages, and her genuine and growing affection for them are evident. Virginia Stumbling Bear, who interpreted regularly for "Sister Helen," would become part of a strong Methodist presence among the Kiowa people.[36]

Nine women's missionary societies had been organized in Indian Territory by the WFMS of the Southern Methodist Church by the late 1890s. Somewhat disrupted by the dissolution of the separate Indian Mission Conference in 1906, the work was reestablished in 1918. In 1938 Mary Beth Littlejohn worked in small churches in the Indian Mission Conference as a deaconess under appointment by the Woman's Missionary Council.

Systematic work among American Indians by Methodist Episcopal women began with the organization of the Woman's Home Missionary Society in 1880. From the beginning, Indian mission work was one of the five major "fields of need" identified by the WHMS, along with work among freedpeople in the South, Mexican Americans, Mormons, and the Chinese. By the time of the second Annual Meeting in November 1883, the various fields of work had been divided into bureaus with a secretary in charge of each. Harriet (Mrs. H. C.) McCabe was the first secretary of the Indian bureau. The rationale given by Methodist women for their work among Indian tribes (in both its positive and negative aspects) would remain constant throughout the existence of the WHMS: "The Indians in the Territories and in Alaska are the victims of our injustice and wrong, and have claims upon us for Christian civilization not to be surpassed by heathen of foreign lands."[37]

Native American mission work in the WHMS was divided into three geographical areas: Indian Territory (Oklahoma), work among the southwestern tribes in New Mexico and Arizona, and work among the Aleuts and Eskimos in Alaska. Miss Sarah Moore and Miss Maria Clegg opened a mission among the Jicarilla Apaches in New Mexico in 1887, living in a small log house, starting a day school, and visiting "from tent to tent."[38] Other projects were begun among the Navajos in New Mexico and among the Pawnees, Poncas, and Osages in Oklahoma. By the end of the 1880s work was begun among the natives of the Aleutian Islands.

In 1885 Frances L. Gaddis and her fourteen-year-old son Frank arrived on the Pawnee reservation. By 1887 Gaddis had begun a sewing class attended by some eighty women, a Sunday school, worship services, and recreation classes for the children. The mission was continued under WHMS sponsorship until 1907. Gaddis went on to begin a mission and school among the Osage in 1888. The project became the Adelaide Springer Osage Mission.

Also in 1888 a young woman named Miss Emma Clark began work among the Ponca at White Eagle (Indian Territory), another mission project initiated by Frances Gaddis. The February 1889 issue of *Woman's Home Missions* carried Clark's account of Thanksgiving and Christmas celebrations with the Ponca Indians. Assisted by an interpreter, Clark talked to them (at Thanksgiving) "of God's love in giving them good harvests, and caring for them," and said their attendance showed that "they were grateful to the Great Spirit for his love and care for them. I thanked them for all their kindness to me since I came among them, and invited them to attend my Sunday-school, and meetings on the Sabbath, and closed by inviting the Chiefs to come to my house after the feast was over." At the meeting with Chiefs White Eagle and Standing Bear and others, Emma Clark "explained to them about my coming here, that it was to do them good, and teach them the right way of living, etc." She went on to urge them "to take up farms and cultivate them as the white men do, and told them that the Missionary women were trying to help them." Standing Bear is reported to have replied that he had been East and that what Miss Clark said was true, "The Missionary women were their best friends."[39]

When Elizabeth Rust, corresponding secretary of the WHMS, traveled throughout Indian Territory in 1889, she and her husband, Dr. R. S. Rust, visited the mission home in Ponca. At the end of a Methodist service Chief Standing Bear reportedly told Mrs. Rust: "I do not know whether I want your religion or not. . . . I want something. My heart is sad. You have education. We have never had a chance to learn. I do know that I want my children to have a better chance than I have had." Elizabeth Rust also gave the women of the WHMS a brief report on the work of Emma Clark: "She teaches the women sewing and other house keeping duties, and visits them in their homes with helpful effect, and they come to the little chapel that has been erected in connection with the home for Sabbath School and religious exercises, but she feels that for great or permanent results a school for the children is necessary, and the pupils must largely be lodged in the [mission] home." She urged Methodist women to *"redouble"* their prayers, efforts, and sacrifices for these *"lonely* toilers in the field."[40]

Among the other Methodist Episcopal women who worked as missionaries with Native Americans were Flora York, with the Pottawatomie tribe in Kansas; Mary Eldridge and Mary Raymond among the Navajo in 1890 (at the turn of the century the whole mission was moved to Farmington, New Mexico); and Emily C. Miller among the Yakima Indians in central Washington. The Alaska bureau of the WHMS initiated Methodist missionary work in Alaska. The women's most significant project was the Jesse Lee Home at Unalaska, founded by John A. and Mary P. Tuck and carried on by Agnes Soule and her husband, Albert Newhall (later moved to Seward and finally to Anchorage, Alaska).[41]

Native American Women

American Indian women played an important role in bridging between home and church. Although she did not speak English, Mrs. Samuel Checote, wife of the Creek chief and Methodist pastor, "made her home a center for Methodist life for both Indians and missionaries" until her death in 1873.[42]

When J. J. Methvin, accompanied by his wife and children, began the Anadarko mission in western Oklahoma in the late 1880s, one of his first encounters was with the "notable female Indian religious leader" Virginia Stumbling Bear, daughter of the Kiowa chief. She had been raised under Christian influences and educated at the Indian School in Carlisle, Pennsylvania. Methvin described their meeting in this way:

> About 11 o'clock pulled up in Kiowa village. Interpreter not there. Found Virginia "Stumbling *Bear*," an old Carlisle student, rather averse to filling the office of an interpreter, finally consented, gathered a congregation together and in the smoke of a tepee sang and prayed and preached. Virginia Stumbling Bear nursed two children and interpreted at the same time.[43]

In a letter to missionary women in Nashville, Tennessee, requesting financial support for the work at Fort Sill, Helen Brewster enclosed a shorter letter from Virginia Stumbling Bear. "*My Dear Sisters,*" it read, "I interpret for Sister Helen, because I always love to tell my people about how I love Jesus, and that He is my Friend. . . . Luther, my husband, is a Christian, and we have prayer together: and we are going to have a blessing at our table when we get moved home to our new house. I wish you to know how glad I am that so many of my friends know about Jesus and go on *His* road. . . . Pray for me and all the Indians, and we will pray for you too. From your Sister, Virginia Stumbling Bear." Frederick Norwood suggests that her service as interpreter for the missionaries at Anadarko was "crucially important," both for the mission and for her, and that her marriage to Luther Sahmaunt established "a veritable dynasty of church leaders."[44]

In 1889 the U.S. government opened land in the central part of Indian Territory to white settlement, as a result of which Oklahoma Territory was created in 1890. The emergence of women's societies for home and foreign mission work came at about the same time as the increased white membership in the Indian conference. This meant that the early leadership of women's work, especially at the district and conference levels, was almost inevitably in the hands of white women. In local churches, especially all-Indian churches, Indian women had a better opportunity to fill leadership roles and "they exercised them faithfully and well."[45] These developments had their culmination in the dissolution in 1906 of a separate Indian Mission Conference. A "new day for leadership" by Indian women in district and annual conference enterprises came after 1918, when the Indians again had an "all-Indian agency" in the restored Oklahoma Indian Mission.[46]

The children of Virginia Stumbling Bear and Luther Sahmaunt became prominent church leaders in this post-1918 period. Their daughter Nannie was born in 1893, grew up in the Methodist church, and studied at Methvin Institute. In 1908 she married Guy Quoetone, a Kiowa educated at Methvin Institute and the son of Rekobeah and Jimmy Quoetone. Guy became a Methodist minister as well as a tribal leader and joined the Indian Mission Conference in 1921. Together Guy and Nannie kept the Methodist work going in Mount Scott after the Oklahoma Conference closed that mission, and persevered until it was revived. They had six children, two of whom, Allen and Charles, would be active (Charles as a minister) in The United Methodist Church.[47]

Nannie's brother, Joel Sahmaunt, married Guy's sister, Carrie Quoetone, in 1922. Carrie had attended Ft. Sill Indian School and Haskell Institute and held many positions of leadership in the Woman's Society of Christian Service and in United Methodist Women. She was honored in 1976 as Oklahoma Indian Mother of the Year. One of her ten children was Virginia (Mrs. Ray) McGilbray.[48]

Hazel Lonewolf Botone was the daughter of Delos Lonewolf, a Kiowa Methodist local preacher in the 1920s. She graduated from

Methvin Institute, married Matthew Botone, and helped him through the General Conference course of study for the ministry. One of the leaders of the Woman's Society of Christian Service in the Indian Mission Conference, she "encouraged the active participation by women in the life of the church and in society." When her husband died in 1961, Mrs. Botone continued his ministry as a local preacher until her retirement in 1971. She was ordained deacon by Bishop W. Angie Smith in the Oklahoma Indian Mission of The Methodist Church in 1966 and elder in The United Methodist Church in 1968.[49]

Indian people have struggled to preserve their spiritual traditions and cultural identity in the face of forced assimilation to white Christian culture and "civilization." At first accepted for the sake of survival, Christianity often provided a new organizing center for disrupted lives. Native American Methodist women have enriched the whole church as they have made the Methodist way of life their own and assumed positions of leadership. These few narratives are only illustrative of a rich history that deserves to be more widely known and celebrated. It is hoped they will encourage the preservers of memory in American Indian Methodist communities to share the stories of their illustrious women with the entire church.

Hispanic American Women and Methodism

Hispanic (or Latino), as Justo L. González has suggested, might be considered a shorthand description for "Hispanic-Indian-Black-Oriental-generally-Spanish-speaking people," including Mexican Americans, Puerto Ricans, Cubans, and others. After the Spanish conquest, the dominant facts in the history of Mexican Americans were the annexation of Texas by the United States in 1845, and the Mexican-American War of 1846–48, as a result of which more than half of what had been Mexican territory became part of the United States. Puerto Rico became a U.S. possession as a result of the Spanish-American War of 1898. Florida and Cuba were part of the same history until Spain ceded Florida to the United States in 1819. The immigration of Cubans to Florida has been affected by various political developments in their homeland, most recently by the Cuban revolution in 1959. The Census Bureau in 1988 projected that by 2080 there would be more than thirty million Hispanics in the United States, or close to 18 percent of the total population. Most Hispanics who converted to Methodism came with a long tradition of Christianity in their own cultures.[50]

As a result of the Treaty of Guadalupe Hidalgo, which ended the so-called Mexican War, "the native population became a conquered minority." Where Roman Catholicism had previously been the only legal religion, now freedom of religion came to Texas and New Mexico. Mainline Protestant denominations like the Baptists, Methodists, and Presbyterians "became interested in proclaiming their message to the Spanish-speaking population." By this time the Methodist Episcopal Church had divided into northern and southern branches. Most of the work of the Methodist Episcopal Church was in New Mexico, while the work of the Methodist Episcopal Church, South, was primarily in Texas. The stories of the work of each branch became one story after the reunification of the church (north and south and with the Methodist Protestants) in 1939.[51]

First Hispanic Methodists

Benigno Cárdenas was a Mexican priest in Santa Fe, New Mexico, when his territory suddenly came under the control of the United States and he was placed under the supervision of a French-born bishop. Cárdenas traveled to Rome to protest against this bishop, stopping in London on his return trip. There Methodist missionary William Rule encouraged Cárdenas to affiliate with the Methodists and work as a missionary among the Spanish-speaking population of New Mexico. Cárdenas agreed, joining the Reverend Enoch Nicholson, who was being sent to New Mexico by the Methodist Missionary Society. On November 20, 1853, on the plaza in Santa Fe in front of the governor's palace, Cárdenas preached "the first sermon in Spanish by a Methodist in the Southwest."[52]

In 1862 Alejo Hernández was in seminary in Mexico studying for the priesthood when he joined Benito Juárez's army of resistance against the French invaders. While on military duty Hernán-dez happened to read an anti-Catholic tract, *Nights with the Roman-ists,* left by another soldier during the Mexican-American War. Intrigued by the many references to Scripture in that book, he is said to have made his way to Brownsville, Texas, "in search of the Bible." In a small English-speaking church there he had a conversion experience. He later described that experience in a letter to a friend, "I felt that God's spirit was there; although I could not understand a word that was being said, I felt my heart strangely warmed. . . . I went away weeping with joy." Hernández went back to Mexico, but suffered persecution there for witnessing to his newfound faith and returned to the United States. There he met Methodists in Corpus Christi, Texas, and in 1871 was ordained deacon, becoming the first Mexican ordained to the Methodist ministry. He served only four years, in Corpus Christi and in Mexico City, before he died of a stroke at age thirty-three. He had been ordained elder in Mexico City in 1874.[53]

HISPANIC WORK BY SOUTHERN METHODISTS IN TEXAS

Laypeople were among the earliest to show interest in the Spanish-speaking population of Texas, especially David Ayres, who distributed Bibles in the Galveston area, and William Headen, from an Irish Methodist family, who learned Spanish well enough to teach Sunday school classes in Spanish in Corpus Christi.

In 1872 the Reverend Alexander Sutherland was appointed preacher in charge of the church in Corpus Christi and worked with William Headen. Two years later Sutherland was appointed presiding elder of the newly created Mexican Border Mission District. By 1878 Bishop Keener, the presiding bishop, wrote of the work in this district: "The Work is full of the vitality of the Spirit; conversions are general and every family has an altar and Methodism has been thoroughly Mexicanized. The only traveling deacons ordained at the Conference were Mexicans. . . ." In 1881 a Hispanic minister, the Reverend Santiago Tafolla, was appointed presiding elder. The culmination of all these efforts came in 1885, at a meeting of the West Texas Conference in San Antonio, when the

Mexican Border Mission Conference was organized to embrace all the Spanish-speaking work.[54]

Alexander Sutherland had insisted that everyone should be able to read the Bible, and that those who were literate had an obligation to teach others to read and write. The pastors and their wives were also encouraged to start schools. In 1881 the Woman's Missionary Society of the Methodist Episcopal Church, South, appropriated funds to send two missionaries, Miss Rebecca Toland and Miss Annie Williams, to Laredo, Texas, to begin a day school for girls on the Mexican border. The Laredo Seminary opened in spring of 1882 with Williams as principal and Toland as teacher. On October 20, 1883, Miss Nannie E. Holding of Kentucky became principal of Laredo Seminary. The school was chartered as a coeducational institution in 1890; Holding remained head of Laredo Seminary for nearly thirty years. In 1910 its name was changed to Holding Institute to honor her generous service. In a report Frank S. Onderdonk said of her, "[She] was in fact superintendent of all the woman's work in Mexico and made regular tours of visitation."[55]

When the Mexican Border Conference was organized in 1885, the work in Mexico, rather than that in the United States, was emphasized. All of that changed with the Mexican Revolution of 1910 that forced many people to come to the United States as refugees. The decision was made to separate the work in Texas from that in Mexico, and in 1914 the Texas Mexican Mission was organized, under the superintendency of the Reverend Frank S. Onderdonk. With his wife, Rowena Tyson Onderdonk, formerly a teacher at Laredo Seminary, Onderdonk addressed the problems of the thousands of immigrants from Mexico flooding into Texas. In 1917 he established Wesleyan Institute, a school for Mexican boys, in San Antonio, and in 1920, he opened Valley Institute, for Mexican girls, in Pharr, Texas. Miss Georgia Swanson was superintendent of Valley Institute from its founding until 1937. Beginning with only the first five grades, it eventually included a high school and a kindergarten developed by Miss Felicidad Méndez. In 1930 the General Conference of the MECS authorized the Texas Mexican Mission to become an annual conference.[56]

Hispanic Clergy Wives in Texas Methodism

Mrs. Clotilde Falcón Náñez has described the crucial role of Hispanic clergy wives in the growth of Methodism in the Southwest. The first, the wife of Alejo Hernández, whom he married in 1872, was apparently never mentioned by name in any of the church records. According to oral tradition, her family opposed her marrying Hernández because he was Protestant. Years later one of her daughters attended the new Laredo Seminary (Holding Institute). It was one of a number of schools for Hispanic girls where many young women were educated who later married Methodist ministers.[57]

Rosaura Garcia de Grado was born in Mexico in 1872 and married the Reverend Pedro Grado, a pioneer Methodist minister. Grado's early ministry was in Mexico, in Durango, and then in Cuencamé. In 1914 he was appointed to La Trinidad Church in Pharr, Texas, in the Rio Grande Valley. Anglo-Americans were settling in this region and refugees from Mexico were crossing the border in increasing numbers, which made for "great distrust and fear." One day Pedro Grado was warned that his life was in danger from vigilantes. He narrowly escaped to Mexico while his wife, Rosaura Grado, substituted for her husband as pastor of La Trinidad.[58]

Another pioneer Hispanic clergy wife was Isabel Hill de Verduzco, a native Texan and third-generation Methodist. Educated at Laredo Seminary and later in Mexico, Isabel was "completely bilingual." She married the Reverend Pablo G. Verduzco in 1900 and entered with great joy on the vocation of Christian service as a clergy wife. After her husband died in 1937 at Port Arthur, Texas, Mrs. Verduzco stayed on to help Mexican-Americans, teaching citizenship classes and assisting people with their various needs. She lived to be ninety-nine years old, dying at Hico, Texas, in 1972.[59]

As Mrs. Náñez explains, the influence of Hispanic clergy wives was heightened by Mexican culture's tradition of *machismo*, which "delegates the observance of religion to women." Protestants typically made their first converts among women, and congregations made up mostly of women and children were not uncommon— then or now. "As a result," Náñez continues, "a major concern for

Methodist ministers and their wives has continued to be the involvement of Spanish-speaking men in the congregations and the recruitment of men for the ordained ministry."[60] The crucial role of Hispanic women brings to mind the Mothers in Israel discussed much earlier in this book—those early American women who became Methodists, evangelized their family members and neighbors, and held Methodist meetings in their homes. Interestingly, Minerva N. Garza uses a similar term, "princess of Israel," to describe the Hispanic Methodist minister's wife.[61]

The tradition of *machismo* also allowed women to play an important leadership role in Spanish-speaking Methodism. Carolina A. Farias, for example, upon the unexpected death of her husband in 1920, was appointed to serve in his stead as pastor at Mission, Texas. The conference appointments listed her as "missionary" from 1920 to 1929, and for the next two years she served as assistant to the pastor.[62] Also in the 1920s, Elodia Guerra, a lay preacher, was named Conference Evangelist by Frank Onderdonk and preached in that capacity throughout the conference.[63]

METHODIST EPISCOPAL WORK AMONG HISPANICS IN NEW MEXICO

After the preaching efforts of Cárdenas and Nicholson in New Mexico, Nicholson went back East, and in 1855 the Reverend Dallas Lore went to New Mexico as superintendent of the mission. He visited Cárdenas, who was very ill; that is the last time Cárdenas appears in Methodist records. Interrupted because of the U.S. Civil War, the mission to Spanish-speaking people was reactivated in 1868 when the Reverend John Dyer was appointed presiding elder of the Rio Grande District of the Colorado Conference.

In the fall of 1869, the Reverend Thomas Harwood and his wife, Emily, went to New Mexico "to revive the Spanish-speaking mission." They began by organizing Sunday schools and holding religious services. Having studied Spanish intensively, Thomas Harwood gave his first sermon in Spanish in 1871. As a result of the Harwoods' efforts, the New Mexico Mission was established in 1872 as a mission separate from the Colorado Conference. Six native ministers were enlisted during the decade: Ambrosio C. González, Benito Garcia, Juan Garcia, Blas Gutiérrez, Marcos Barela, and J. Pablo Salazar. Finally in 1884 the Spanish-speaking work and English-speaking work became two separate missions, Harwood superintending the former.[64]

Schools were opened in Albuquerque for both girls and boys. In 1901 Emily Harwood said of the girls' school, "It had 70 of our brightest girls last year, who are being trained in all the arts of homemaking as well as in the usual studies taught in the schools. Some of these girls have become teachers, and others have become the wives of our young preachers, where they can make excellent use of their training."[65] The Mission Conference reached its peak in 1907, Harwood's last year as superintendent. There were 39 ministers, 6,000 Spanish-speaking Methodists, 45 Sunday schools, 34 church buildings, and 29 parsonages.[66]

RIO GRANDE CONFERENCE

A new chapter began for Hispanic Methodists with the unification of Methodism in 1939. That year a new conference was organized with the name Southwest Mexican Conference. There were mixed feelings about using the name "Mexican." That designation had been part of all the names referring to Spanish-speaking work in Texas, but it had never been used by the MEC for its work in New Mexico. At the annual meeting of the new conference in 1947, the issue of the name was hotly debated, resulting in a petition to the jurisdictional conference requesting that the name of the new conference be changed. The jurisdictional conference decided on the name Rio Grande Conference.[67]

Hispanic clergy wives first organized Hispanic Methodist women into Sociedades Femenil (women's societies) in the early 1930s. Clergy wives were also the presidents of these societies, including Carmen Lujan, 1933–35; Jovita O. Ramos, 1935–38; and Elodia A. Sada, 1938–44. When the Southwest Mexican Conference was formed in 1939, its Woman's Society established a ministerial education fund for the training of young, Spanish-speaking ministers. Sixty-seven ministers in the conference were helped to attend college through this fund.[68] In 1944 the Mission Program materials were first translated into Spanish for use by Spanish-speaking women's groups. The translator was Mrs. Elida G. Falcón (sister of Rosaura Grado and mother of Clotilde Falcón Náñez).[69]

UNITED BRETHREN WORK AMONG SPANISH-SPEAKING PEOPLE

United Brethren missionaries were also concerned about Spanish-speaking people in the Rio Grande Valley. Clarence Schlotterbeck's efforts resulted in the formation of "at least eight" congregations and the establishment of what became the North Texas Conference of the United Brethren Church. They also led to the establishment of the McCurdy Mission School at Velarde, New Mexico. Miss Mellie Perkins began the school in 1912, with the help of Susanita Martínez. Other helpers came, including Miss Kendig as "principal and pastor." From the first graduating class of six students in 1926, the school grew "to a 44-acre campus with an enrollment of over 500 students in grades one through twelve."[70]

HISPANIC METHODISM IN CALIFORNIA AND ARIZONA

The roots of organized Methodist work among Hispanics in California and Arizona were laid in the U.S. military occupation of this area in the war against Mexico in 1846. Before 1910 both the Methodist Episcopal Church and the Methodist Episcopal Church, South, established mission work among Spanish-speaking people in Arizona and California. For example, in 1879 the MEC began a Spanish-speaking mission in Los Angeles under the leadership of the Reverend Antonio Díaz. The MECS opened the Homer Toberman Deaconess Home in Los Angeles in 1904, under the supervision of the WHMS. This served as a base for city mission work, especially after 1913 when it was relocated in east Los Angeles. These efforts remained largely "scattered and uncoordinated,"[71] however, until increased immigration after the 1910 Mexican Revolution demanded a more comprehensive plan of outreach.

Vernon McCombs, a former missionary to Peru, served as super-intendent of Spanish work for the Southern California Annual Conference of the MEC from 1911 until he retired in 1946. At the time of the unification of the Methodist Church in 1939, there were thirty-seven Spanish-speaking churches with nearly three thousand members in the Latin American Mission of the MEC, and eleven churches with about one thousand members in the MECS. In 1941 the Latin American Provisional Conference was organized within the boundaries of the Southern California–Arizona and California-Nevada Conferences. Until the integration in 1956 of the various racial-ethnic conferences into the annual conferences in which they were located geographically, this was regarded as "the golden age of Hispanic Methodism" in terms of self-determination in the church. [72]

PUERTO RICAN METHODISM

In December 1898, the Treaty of Paris was signed, ending the Spanish-American War; under its provisions the United States assumed control over Puerto Rico. Roman Catholicism was disestablished, and under a comity agreement the island was divided into four regions, one of which was assigned to the Methodist Episcopal Church. In 1899 Bishop William X. Ninde and the Reverend A. B. Leonard visited Cuba and Puerto Rico. The following year a Methodist Episcopal mission was established with Dr. Charles W. Drees, who was fluent in Spanish, as superintendent. This became the Puerto Rico Mission in 1902 and the Missionary Conference of Puerto Rico in 1913, with the Reverend Manuel Andújar giving important leadership.[73]

Methodist women were involved in the work from its beginnings. Two deaconesses were sent to Puerto Rico in 1900: Miss Sarah E. White, a nurse, and Miss Isabel F. Horton, a recent graduate of Lucy Webb Hayes Training School. In 1901 the Woman's Home Missionary Society established a Bureau for Puerto Rico; Mrs. May Leonard Woodruff was bureau secretary. The George O. Robinson Orphanage (later School) was opened in 1902 under the leadership of Miss Sally Gill. By 1932 there were eighty-five pupils in the school and four Puerto Rican young women on the staff.[74]

In 1941, the Puerto Rico Provisional Annual Conference was established. Dr. Tomas Rico Soltero became the first Puerto Rican superintendent in 1949. The 1940s and 1950s saw "a new generation of pastors," including the Reverend Julia Torres Fernández, one of the first women pastors in Puerto Rico, and the Reverend Delores Lebrón Andújar. From early on, women had been active in Puerto Rican work, helping in visitation, as assistants to the pastors, and in Christian education. Among the first Puerto Rican women leaders were Mercedes Núñez, Fulgencia Constantino, and Carmen Velásquez. Mrs. Antonia M. Pereles was the first president of the WSCS.[75]

PUERTO RICAN METHODISTS IN THE NORTHEASTERN UNITED STATES

The first Hispanic Methodist congregation in the northeastern United States was most likely that organized at the Sands Street Church in Brooklyn (New York Conference) in 1893. The Reverend Alberto B. Báez and his wife, Thalia Valderrama, had an effective ministry among Hispanic Americans—most of them immigrants from Puerto Rico—from 1917 when they came to that congregation from Mexico until his retirement in 1961. Additional Hispanic Methodist congregations were organized in New York and other northeastern cities prior to World War II.[76]

CUBAN HISPANIC MISSION

In 1901, Miss Rebecca Toland went to Cuba to be in charge of a school for girls, Colegio Irene Toland, in Matanzas. It was named to commemorate her sister, Dr. Irene Toland, who had served as a nurse in Santiago in a yellow fever epidemic. Rebecca Toland would serve as head of the school for twenty-five years. Other girls' schools were established in Cienfuegos and Havana. Bible women and others were sponsored by the Woman's Missionary Council to do evangelistic work in Cuba.[77]

Cuban immigration to Florida increased considerably after the

Martínez-Ybor cigar factory moved to Tampa in 1886. Missionary work among Cubans in Tampa began in 1892, and within four years there were three Hispanic congregations. In 1914 the Latin District of Florida was created, including Key West, Tampa, and Cuba. Cubans also came to escape the oppressive Machado and Batista dictatorships from 1926 to 1940. When the center of Cuban population passed to Miami in the early 1930s, Methodist missionary work was begun there. The Evangelical United Brethren Church also opened a mission in Ybor City in 1942. The Latin District was dissolved in 1939 and its congregations incorporated geographically.[78]

Hispanic Methodist women were crucial in sustaining the faith in their homes and communities. Particularly where there was opportunity for Hispanic self-determination in church work, they exerted important leadership beyond the local church level.

ASIAN AMERICAN WOMEN AND METHODISM

The term "Asian American" encompasses a diversity of national groups that share some common cultural and sociopolitical experiences. These include Chinese, Japanese, Korean, and Filipino Americans whose forebears came to this country from the mid-nineteenth through the early twentieth centuries, and more recent immigrants from Asia, Southeast Asia, and the Pacific Islands.[79]

As Ronald Takaki explains, Asian immigrants were "'pushed' by hardships in the homelands and 'pulled' here by America's demand for their labor." They came to work on the sugarcane plantations of Hawaii, in gold mines, on railroad crews, as cannery and factory workers, and as farm laborers. Typically paid less than white workers, they were resented by those whose jobs they seemed to threaten. The ultimate outcome of this "ethnic antagonism" was the Chinese Exclusion Act of 1882 (barring the entry of "Chinese laborers") and the Oriental Exclusion Act of 1924 (aimed especially at the Japanese), which cut off immigration of Asians as "aliens ineligible to citizenship." Between 1849 and 1924 about one million Asian immigrants entered the United States[80]

The Chinese were the first to come to this country, most of them laboring men who came to work in the mines after the discovery of gold in 1849 and then in vast numbers on the railroads in the 1860s. Coming as sojourners hoping to save money and then return home, they typically found it impossible to save on their small wages and had to abandon that hope. The Chinese Exclusion Act of 1882 prevented most of these men from calling their wives to join them in this country. Students and merchant families did enter the country, and a number of Chinese women and young girls were forcibly brought here as prostitutes. The Exclusion Act was finally repealed in 1943.[81]

The second wave of immigrants, the Japanese, began to arrive in significant numbers in the Pacific Coast states, especially California, from the 1880s. Like the Chinese, these Issei, or "first generation," came seeking economic relief and found themselves subjected to new exploitation. They were predominantly young men, most of them from the farming class but comparatively well educated. Again the earliest Japanese women to arrive in any significant numbers were prostitutes. However, wives, children, and picture brides of Japanese shopkeepers and farmers arrived during the first twenty years of this century. Their children are referred to as Nisei, the "second generation." Further Japanese immigration was prohibited by the 1924 Exclusion Act.

In 1942 all people of Japanese descent living on the West Coast, two-thirds of them American citizens, were removed from their homes and incarcerated in internment camps like Amache in Colorado, Heart Mountain in Wyoming, and Manzanar and Tule Lake in California. The evacuees were allowed to take with them only what they could carry. Some died in the camps; some returned after the war to find their homes and farms ruined; some would try to build new lives in other parts of the country.[82]

In 1898 the United States annexed the Republic of Hawaii and took over the Philippines by defeating Spain. From 1903 Koreans from different walks of life came to the United States to escape Japanese imperialism. Most of them migrated to Hawaii and became laborers in the sugar and pineapple fields. Many Korean women came as well, either as wives or as picture brides.[83]

Filipinos also came after the annexation of the Philippines, first to Hawaii and then to the mainland in the 1920s. Ninety percent of the migrants were Catholic and many had been educated in schools established by the Americans; they were primarily farm laborers. The 1924 exclusion law did not apply to Filipinos because the Philippines was a territory of the United States[84]

CHINESE AMERICANS

Methodist work among the Chinese in America was done by the Methodist Episcopal Church. In 1866, three women of the Sixth Street Methodist Episcopal Church in Sacramento, California, started a class to help the Chinese in their city learn English and study the Bible. The following year the California Conference launched a mission to the Chinese by sending Dr. and Mrs. Otis Gibson, former missionaries to China, to begin work in San Francisco.

Gibson decided to use the Chinese Sabbath school in Sacramento as a model for efforts elsewhere. He believed that these schools would be the means of leading the Chinese to "adopt our higher form of civilization and our purer faith."[85] Within ten years, similar schools had been established in San Francisco, Los Angeles, Pasadena, and elsewhere in California, as well as in cities in Oregon and Washington. The WHMS was deeply involved in beginning and maintaining these schools.

After an energetic campaign to enlist support and raise funds, Gibson succeeded in opening a Chinese Mission in San Francisco. The mission house, including a chapel and classrooms, was dedicated on Christmas Day, 1870. There was also a "storefront" gospel hall located closer to the heart of Chinatown. Loke Chee Chow, probably both the first Chinese to be baptized at the mission and the first Chinese man in America to be given a Methodist exhorter's (and subsequently local preacher's) license, became Gibson's assistant preacher.[86]

Gibson had been superintendent of the Chinese Mission for seventeen years when ill health finally required him to retire from the work in 1885. He had not only started schools and missions and spoken tirelessly on behalf of the Chinese Mission, he had also fought courageously against anti-Chinese forces at the local, state, and national levels. He sometimes appeared in court to defend the human rights of Chinese women and was even burned in effigy by anti-Chinese mobs. He was esteemed as "the champion of the Chinese cause."[87]

Frederick J. Masters, also a former missionary to China, was appointed to succeed Gibson as superintendent of the Chinese Mission. During his superintendency, a number of Chinese converts were called to preach. In 1890 Hon Fan Chan came to San Francisco; he began to assist Masters in preaching at the gospel hall. Edwar Lee, who was a youth in the Chinese Church in San Francisco when Chan was pastor, recalled Chan's preaching to "overflowing crowds."[88]

In 1893 the different language ministries within the California Conference became organized as districts, the Chinese Mission becoming the Chinese District, with Dr. Frederick J. Masters as presiding elder. The mission house was destroyed by fire, along with much of San Francisco, during the 1906 earthquake, and funds had to be raised to build a new home for the mission. The Pacific Chinese (later the California Oriental) Mission Conference was organized in 1904. In 1945 this would become a Provisional Annual Conference with Dr. Edwar Lee as its superintendent. Lee was the first Chinese American to fill such a position and most likely the first American-born Chinese to become an ordained Methodist minister.[89]

The earliest Chinese immigrants were primarily males. A few women came as wives and daughters of merchants, but the majority of the women who came were imported as domestics or prostitutes. From the beginning of his ministry as superintendent of the Chinese Mission, Otis Gibson believed that something must be done for Chinese women. To neglect them "in the ministrations of the Gospel to the Chinese," he said, "would only tend to strengthen them in their heathen ideas that women have no souls and no personal rights in themselves, outside the will of their parents, husbands, or masters."[90]

In about 1870 several prostitutes sought refuge in a home operated by the San Francisco Ladies' Protective and Relief Society. A concerned church woman visiting some of these Chinese women reported that there were probably many more "trapped in this kind of slavery who would escape if they could find refuge somewhere."[91] The third floor of the Chinese Mission building had originally been planned as a "Female Department." After a Chinese woman named Jin Ho was rescued from drowning in San Francisco Bay in 1871 and came to stay at the mission house, the third floor became a dormitory and rescue home for Chinese women. Miss Laura Templeton of Sacramento was hired to work full-time with women at the mission. In 1877 Otis Gibson reported that of the forty-four Chinese he had baptized and received into the membership of the Methodist Episcopal Church, fifteen were women or girls from the rescue home. Six of these had married Christian Chinese men, "thus forming, in a small way," he said, "a pattern and nucleus of the *Christian home* among the Chinese."[92]

In response to Gibson's appeal, the Women's Mission Society of the Pacific Coast was formed in the summer of 1879 to "elevate and save heathen women on these shores." It merged with the WHMS in 1893. After the 1906 earthquake and fire destroyed the original building of the Chinese Mission, the society raised funds to construct a new home. Designed by a woman architect named Julia Morgan, the new Gum Moon Home was dedicated on January 27, 1912. In 1940 the decision was made to turn Gum Moon Home into a residence hall for "employed and student" Chinese girls.[93]

Peggy Pascoe has analyzed these "relations of rescue" between (white) home missions women and Chinese women. Methodist and other Protestant missionary women were fearless in entering brothels and hovels to rescue Chinese immigrant women from sexual exploitation, offering them refuge in the rescue homes, education, and training. Assuming that their female values of purity and piety applied to all women, these mission women hoped that isolating Chinese women in the rescue homes and surrounding them with Protestant influences would aid in their transformation to Christian women.[94]

In the role of Bible women, Chinese women themselves (many of them educated in Methodist missionary schools) were an important part of the missionary effort among their people. Being bilingual, they often served as interpreters. Bible women visited in homes teaching the Bible (and often the English language) to Chinese women and children. They also ministered to the needs of those who were lonely and sick. Among the Bible women in Los Angeles, for example, were Mrs. Lan Yui, who was converted by Mrs. T. F. Davis in 1896 and worked for a number of years as her assistant, and Mrs. Chan Kiu Sing, whose husband was pastor of the Chinese Church from 1908 until his death in 1923. Mrs. Chan continued to serve as a Bible woman after his death.[95]

JAPANESE AMERICANS

The first legal Japanese immigrant to become a Christian and a minister in America was Kanichi Miyama, who was converted in February 1877 through the ministry of Dr. Otis Gibson in San Francisco. Less than a year after his baptism, Miyama founded the Gospel Society, the "first organized group of Japanese in America." He then went on to lay the groundwork for "the first Japanese church in America, which was finally founded in 1879." Miyama was ordained elder and accepted into the California Conference of the Methodist Episcopal Church in 1884 and appointed to the Japanese church as Otis Gibson's assistant.[96]

In 1886 Merriman Colbert Harris and his wife, Flora Best Harris, (former missionaries to Japan) were sent to San Francisco, where he was appointed superintendent of what would become the Pacific Japanese Mission. Harris moved to Oakland and ministered to the Japanese there while making frequent visits to San Francisco to oversee Miyama's Japanese church. "From this small church," says Lester Suzuki, "M. C. Harris and Kanichi Miyama were to expand Methodism's outreach to Japanese in the entire West Coast and eventually into Canada and Hawaii."[97]

From 1886 to 1894, Japanese work was in the form of mission stations. By 1889 there were four: two in San Francisco, one in Oakland, and one in Los Angeles. In 1889 Terujiro Hasegawa, the second Japanese Methodist minister, was ordained. He was followed by increasing numbers of Japanese ministers in the 1890s. In 1894 Japanese work was organized into a district of the California Conference. In 1900 the General Conference granted the petition of Japanese preachers that the Japanese churches be given Mission Conference status. The following year the Japanese Mission Conference was divided into two districts, the Hawaii District and the Pacific Coast District.[98]

Taihei Takahashi was appointed to the Aiea-Waipahu charge in the Hawaii District. According to Suzuki, Mrs. Takahashi accompanied her husband to assist him in the work as he "visited the four camps regularly every week, looked after the sick, conducted a night school, and preached." She also taught a Japanese day school with twenty pupils and was superintendent of the Sunday school. Suzuki says of Brother Takahashi and his wife, "This shows the type of pioneer work that the early preachers undertook, and that the wife of the minister did just as much work or more."[99]

In 1904 another Japanese missionary, Dr. Herbert Buell Johnson, succeeded M. C. Harris as superintendent of the Pacific Japanese Mission. Johnson was especially zealous in opposing the Oriental Exclusion Act of 1924, speaking widely against it and leading the Methodist Episcopal General Conference to send a strong resolution to President Calvin Coolidge urging him to veto it; all to no avail. Suzuki described Dr. Johnson as "a voice in the wilderness crying out vigorously against injustice."[100]

The Woman's Home Missionary Society built a number of homes to minister to Japanese women and children. The Ellen Stark Ford Home opened in San Francisco in 1911. That same year the Catherine Blaine Home opened in Seattle as a home for women and girls. From the 1920s to the 1940s it was also a residence for youth ministers and women workers with youth. In 1915 Mrs. Kataoka, a deaconess, came to work with women and children at the Jane Couch Home in Los Angeles. As early as 1903 the Susanna Wesley Home was opened for women and children in Honolulu.

"One great result of the women's work," according to Lester Suzuki, "was the inspiration given to the American-born Nisei women." In 1926 Dr. Frank Herron Smith, successor to Herbert Buell Johnson, challenged Japanese youth at a huge Young People's Christian Conference, "We need 500 Nisei preachers and religious workers to minister to the entire Japanese population." The women were the first to respond, including Margaret Tann (Uyei), Edith Tsuruda (Furuki), Dorothy Funabiki, Yuki Kuwahara, Mary Oyama, Sumile Morishita, Rose Naka, Iseko Hayakaway, Grace Takahashi ("who served Wapato Church in 1933 and 1934"), Doris

Aiso, and Mariyo Okazaki ("who served Los Angeles in 1939 and Kingsburg in 1940"). Suzuki explains that most of these women served only a few years since "women were not accepted in the ministry."[101]

Among the well-known Japanese Bible women were Mrs. Kane Yajima who served in Seattle and San Francisco in the 1920s, and Mrs. Tokuji Komuro who assisted her pastor husband at the Japanese Church in New York City in the 1930s.[102]

KOREAN AMERICANS

The first Korean immigrants, 101 of them, arrived in Honolulu in January 1903. Methodism had been introduced into Korea by Henry Appenzeller in 1885, after an 1882 treaty between the United States and Korea opened that nation to Christian missionaries. (Prior to that, the Yi government had supported Confucianism and banned Christianity.) American Methodist missionaries not only preached the gospel but also emphasized education, medicine, and social welfare. In 1902 the Hawaii Sugar Planters Association had asked American Methodist missionaries in Korea to encourage their congregations to go to Hawaii. Twenty of the first 101 immigrants were members of the Naeri Methodist Church in Inchon and thirty-eight others were from neighboring churches.[103]

The Naeri Methodist Church sent the Reverend Hong Seung-ha to Hawaii. He was apparently the first Korean Methodist minister there and began the first Korean Methodist Church. The Koreans who went to Hawaii found a much harder life than they had expected. Many responded positively to the Christian faith. By 1916 there were thirty-one Korean-speaking churches in Hawaii and thirty-five mission stations with a total membership of more than two thousand.[104]

Besides seeking a better life in Hawaii, many Koreans sought to escape Japanese oppression in their country. Japan had annexed Korea in 1910 after defeating China in the Sino-Japanese War. Leaders of the Methodist Church in Hawaii often became involved in overtly political activities. For example, the Reverend Hong played a leading role in organizing the New People Society, a Korean political organization, in late 1903.[105]

Alice Chai has described the importance of the Methodist Church in the lives of Korean women who came to Hawaii between 1903 and 1924. Most of these women were wives or daughters of laborers, "attempting to free themselves from poverty, Confucian social and cultural constraints, and Japanese political and religious oppression."[106] Those of the "second wave" (1910–24) were the nearly one thousand young women who came as "picture brides" to marry Korean bachelor laborers after exchanging pictures with them. Plantation managers in Hawaii encouraged these marriages, believing that married males would be more reliable workers.[107]

The experience of arriving in Hawaii could be "shocking and frightening" for these young Korean women. Often the men had sent pictures of themselves taken ten to twenty years earlier, and the young picture brides, most of them ages eighteen to twenty-four, cried bitterly when they met their older prospective husbands for the first time. Some refused to marry and were sent back to Korea or they took refuge with church agencies. Many felt forced to go through with the marriage.[108]

In the sugar plantation camps, Korean immigrant women ran laundry services and cooked for the single men. Many women were widowed early and had to become businesswomen. The women gave each other financial help and moral support through associations called *kye* groups. Women were also responsible for teaching Korean language and culture to the second generation and for "preserving the cohesiveness of family and community."[109]

First-generation immigrant Korean women also played a key role in working for Korean independence. Chai credits American women missionaries with introducing "the concepts of political, religious, and personal freedom for women." Korean men in Hawaii participated in newly created social organizations for men only. Excluded from these, Korean immigrant women found Korean churches indispensable for perpetuating Korean culture and supporting the Korean national independence movement. The experience of Korean Christian women in church activities "provided them with the capability of organizing, implementing ideas, and working together for a common cause."[110]

One picture bride described the connection between her Christian faith and political work for Korean independence:

> When I look back now, the reason that I could come up with such independent ideas and could express my honest opinions even to strange men was that I had learned to express my thoughts in the church groups by having Bible study meetings and by visiting strangers' houses ... in the villages with ministers and Bible women to discuss the Bible. Because of my Christian faith I could endure the pain and suffering in my life.[111]

Korean Methodists came to the mainland United States after 1903, settling and organizing Korean churches in cities like Los Angeles, San Francisco, Chicago, and New York. In Los Angeles in 1904, Mrs. Frances Sherman, a retired Methodist missionary to Korea, started a mission school to teach English and the Bible to Korean immigrants. Shin Heung-wu served as local pastor until he returned to Korea. Later the Reverend Hwang Sa-yong became the pastor. Korean Methodist churches in the United States before 1945 helped members to cope with their harsh lives, as well as providing basic educational skills and raising the level of political consciousness after the Japanese annexation of Korea.[112]

Early Korean immigrant women served these churches in crucial ways. According to Ai Ra Kim, they taught Sunday school, managed Korean language schools, and raised money for scholarships for Korean children. "They also worked for the churches as deaconesses, stewardesses [female stewards], and choir members. Accordingly, their eyes and minds were opened through the churches."[113] There were also Korean Bible women. Kim and Chai agree that they were the "hands and legs" of the male clergy, "quasi-ministers" who combined the roles of evangelist, teacher, public health educator, and social worker.[114]

FILIPINO AMERICANS

For nearly four hundred years the Philippine Islands were ruled by Spain, and Roman Catholicism was the state religion. After the United States defeated Spain in the Spanish-American War of 1898, representatives of a number of Protestant churches began mission-ary activities in the Philippines. Methodist Episcopal Bishop James M. Thoburn delivered the first Protestant sermon in Manila on March 5, 1899. Among the early converts to the Methodist faith was Nicolas Zamora, who was ordained deacon by Bishop Thoburn in 1900.[115]

In 1906 Filipinos also began to come to the United States through Hawaii. A Filipino Mission was established, and Benito Ilustre became the first licensed Filipino minister in Hawaii. By 1921 there were eighteen preaching stations in the Hawaiian Islands, min-stered to by eleven exhorters and preachers, four nurses, and two Bible women.[116]

When Filipino immigrants arrived in San Francisco, Mr. and Mrs. W. P. Stanley were there to meet them and steer them to safe places to live and work. Stanley was pastor of the Howard Street Methodist Church and organized a Filipino Christian Fellowship there in 1920. Filipino work was begun in other places like Stock-ton, Oakland, and Fresno, California, and Seattle, Washington. In 1939, Filipino, Chinese, and Korean churches on the Pacific Coast were brought together to form the California Oriental Mission Conference. Artemio Guillermo also gave recognition to the "unselfish and devoted help of women" in the Filipino work. He mentioned Dionisia Castillo, Maria Dayoan Garcia, and Mrs. Helen Marquez in the WSCS, religious education, and young peo-ple's work in the 1940s to the early 1950s.[117]

Among Chinese, Japanese, Korean, and Filipino Methodists, the role of Bible woman was an important position of indigenous reli-gious leadership. Bible women were evangelists, teachers, and community workers, and served as a bridge between the church and the larger community. In many ways their work was similar to that of the deaconess although they typically had less formal train-ing. Christian faith obviously gave meaning, comfort, and hope to Asian American women. Asian ethnic local churches (which were often social centers for their communities) especially offered them opportunities to develop their personal and leadership skills.

Middle-class (white) women, in the Methodist family of denom-inations as in other mainline Protestant churches in the nineteenth century, assumed that their female values applied to all women.

They envisioned a universal sisterhood in which women would work together to overcome the oppression they all experienced from sexism, underestimating the differences among groups of women. To take a prominent example, Peggy Pascoe argued that while home mission women challenged racial biological determinism (in their conviction that race should be "no barrier to educational opportunity or to participation in religious activities"), they succumbed to a typically Victorian conception of a moral hierarchy of cultures. They equated the Christian gospel and women's emancipation with the adoption of middle-class Victorian family patterns, "as the first step upwards from heathenism to civilization."[118]

Fortunately, responding to white initiative is only part of the story of Native American, Hispanic American, and Asian American Methodist women's religious lives, roles, and impact. Although the terms of the acceptance of Christianity were defined by the normative white Christian culture to which people of color were required to assimilate, the grace is that Methodist women of color could, and did, make the Christian faith their own. In this process they have offered their own unique gifts, grace, traditions, and experience to the church, and the whole church has been enriched and transformed as a result.

12

NEW WOMEN AFTER THE VOTE
Citizens, Preachers, and Social Reformers
1920–1939

One of the most striking aspects of the change represented by the modern urban, industrial America that came of age between 1890 and 1920 was the emergence of the (middle-class) "college-educated, frequently unmarried, and self-supporting" New Woman. Through a host of newly created, female-dominated institutions, these women attempted to build a "maternal commonwealth" by demanding that female values shape the public world. As historian Sara Evans explained, these female values really represented the "politicized domesticity" of middle-class women. These New Women, who had chosen careers over marriage and motherhood, assured their critics that they would "unleash maternal skills and capacities on a needy world."[1]

By the 1920s the Victorian ideology of sharply polarized gender roles, in which women were perceived as moral guardians and convinced of a common female mission, was breaking down. In 1920 one in four women over the age of sixteen was part of the labor force. Images of the "flapper," with its expressive female sexuality, and the glamorized "working girl" were replacing older images of the pious and pure Victorian woman.[2]

On August 26, 1920, the long struggle for woman suffrage finally came to a successful conclusion with the ratification of the Nineteenth Amendment to the U.S. Constitution. The women's movement had been at the apex of its political power from 1900 to 1914. Curiously, the attainment of the right to vote (individually, as a citizen) seemed to undermine female solidarity, and women were increasingly incorporated into the individualistic ethos of a consumer economy.[3]

The earlier programs of separate women's organizations in the churches had been geared primarily to the needs and experience of middle-class married women. As increasing numbers of women entered the workforce in the 1920s, Methodist women were faced with the challenge of developing programs relevant to working women's needs for spiritual and intellectual growth and service.

A Women's Missionary Organization for Employed Women

A significant development among Methodist Episcopal women organized for mission was the founding in 1921 of the Wesleyan Service Guild as an employed women's auxiliary to the Woman's Foreign and Home Missionary Societies. Women in the MEC, MECS, and MPC had earlier encouraged the formation of evening circles for working women, but apparently nowhere had there been a self-conscious and intentional effort on a large scale to meet the needs of business- and professional women.

At the October 1920 meeting of the Northwestern Branch of the Woman's Foreign Missionary Society in Detroit, three women got together for the first time to talk about how employed women might be included in the mission program of the church. In the next few months, Mary Clapp, Helen A. Wesp, and Marion Lela Norris secured permission from the existing societies (WFMS and WHMS) to establish an experimental union society—including both foreign and home missionary work in one organization—for employed women in the Northwestern Branch. An expanded founding committee, including representatives from both the foreign and home missionary societies, met in December 1920 and February 1921 to recommend the establishment of the Wesleyan Service Guild as a "Business Women's Unit." By the fall of 1921 the geographical limitation was removed.[4]

In May 1923 the Wesleyan Service Guild (WSG) became an official auxiliary of the Woman's Home and Woman's Foreign Missionary Societies of the Methodist Episcopal Church. It now had a Central Committee, a constitution for local units, and a monthly newsletter called *World Service Greetings*. Marion Lela Norris served as its national secretary from its beginning to 1928, and also chaired its Central Committee.[5]

According to its constitution, the Wesleyan Service Guild offered working women a fourfold program: (1) development of spiritual life, (2) opportunities for world service, (3) promotion of Christian citizenship and personal service, and (4) provision for social and recreational activities.[6] The Guild existed both to meet the needs of its members and to encourage them to serve others. The spiritual part of the program was viewed as primary; "unlike so many organizational options available to women in the 1920s, [the WSG] was first and foremost a religious group" and its other purposes were understood to flow from this. Devotional guides were developed and distributed to the Spiritual Department chairs of the local units. By the end of the 1920s the Wesleyan Service Guild had an official hymn and a "Ceremony of Lights" for its basic worship ritual.[7]

Guild members pledged their financial support to mission projects. Special Guild projects included work with young businesswomen in Japan and with immigrant children at Campbell Settlement in Gary, Indiana. The members also met regularly to study and discuss foreign and home missionary work. A few were led to leave their regular jobs and enter the mission field themselves. Ada G. Townsend, Christian Citizenship chair of the Central Committee of the WSG in the 1920s, urged women to use their newly won political power for the betterment of their local communities and in support of women's and children's issues at the national level. Regarding the social and recreational purposes of the Guild, sharing an evening meal prior to the program became central from the beginning, and special social occasions like annual Guild banquets were encouraged.

Ann Fagan suggests that the wives and mothers in the older, established societies viewed the single, employed women of the Wesleyan Service Guild with some ambivalence in terms of their different understandings of woman's appropriate role. What both groups of women shared, however, was "the religious commitment to Christian service."[8]

During the depression years, WSG leaders admirably attempted to function as a support system for women facing unemployment or salary reductions and to keep them involved in Guild units regardless of their financial status. When the Methodist Episcopal

Church, the Methodist Episcopal Church, South, and the Methodist Protestant Church reunited in 1939 as The Methodist Church, the Wesleyan Service Guild became the only women's missionary organization to continue from the predecessor denominations into the new church. Representatives of the women's organizations had decided to press for one woman's organization for foreign and home missions. This became the Woman's Division of Christian Service, with the Wesleyan Service Guild as its auxiliary for employed women.

The new organization also adopted the threefold program division of the Guild: Spiritual Life, Missionary Service, and Christian Social Relations (Christian Citizenship). As secretary of the Guild, Marion Lela Norris became a full-time staff member of the Woman's Division and presided over the expansion of the Guild throughout The Methodist Church in the 1940s. When she retired in 1951 she could point with pride to its "phenomenal growth." Two significant additions to the earlier worship services developed for the Guild came in the 1940s: a Guild Pledge Service in 1945 and the final form of the Guild hymn, "This Is My Song" (to the tune of Jean Sibelius's "Finlandia"), with a third stanza written at Marion Lela Norris's request by Methodist theologian Dr. Georgia Harkness.[9]

"A WELCOME IN THE MINISTRY," 1920–1924

In 1920 women in the Methodist Episcopal Church finally regained the right to be licensed as local preachers that had been taken away by the General Conference of 1880. A number of factors contributed to the changing climate regarding women's rights in the church. The attainment of woman suffrage gave new urgency to women's struggles for access to positions of public religious leadership. An additional impetus for the renewed debate on the subject of women preachers was the founding of the International Association of Women Preachers (IAWP) in November 1919. The president of this ecumenical organization, and editor of its newsletter, *The Woman's Pulpit*, was a Methodist Episcopal woman named Madeline Southard. "As an elected lay delegate to the 1920 and 1924 General Conferences (from the Southwest Kansas Conference), Madeline Southard led the campaign to permit the ordination of women in the Methodist Episcopal Church."[10]

The IAWP sent a memorial (petition) to the 1920 General Conference requesting that women be licensed to preach, as did a number of annual conferences, district superintendents, and deans and presidents of colleges and universities, including Garrett, Drew, and Boston theological seminaries.[11] At that General Conference, Madeline Southard introduced a resolution calling for "ecclesiastical equality for women" with all appropriate changes to be made to the *Discipline.* Because it mandated disciplinary changes, the resolution was referred to the Committee on Itinerancy (Ordained Ministry). When the committee reported to General Conference several days later, it recommended that women be included as Local Preachers and that the issue of women's ordination be referred to a commission to report to the next General Conference. The report was adopted.[12] Although attempts were made to amend this report from the floor to include ordination as well as licensing of women, they were unsuccessful.

There were two claimants for the honor of first Methodist Episcopal woman to become a licensed Local Preacher in 1920: Winifred Willard (Trinity Church, Denver) and Witlia D. Caffray (First MEC of Wenatchee, Washington). Both were given local preacher's licenses by their local churches on Thursday, May 27, the same day the legislation was passed by the General Conference.[13]

Dr. James M. Buckley, long an opponent of women's laity and clergy rights in the church, was not present at the General Conference of 1920 to witness these developments. In 1912 he had served for the eleventh and final time as a delegate to the Methodist Episcopal General Conference. He also retired that year from the editorship of the New York *Christian Advocate,* to which he was first elected in 1880. He died on February 8, 1920, at the age of eighty-three.[14]

The first highly limited form of ordination for women was approved by the MEC at its 1924 General Conference. Just prior to the General Conference, Dr. Georgia Harkness, then associate professor of religious education at Elmira College, had written a powerful piece on "The Ministry as a Vocation for Women." Referring to the church as "probably our most conservative institution," Harkness lamented that the "wall of prejudice" was too strong for any but the most courageous of women to attempt to enter the ministry. "To put it baldly," she insisted,

> [the crux of the matter] is that women cannot enter a field where they are not welcome. Ordination is desirable, I believe, to put the stamp of the Church's approval upon the admission of women to its ministry. But what is needed even more is a general recognition by pulpit and pew of the legitimate place of trained women in this field. Women will never find a welcome in the ministry until the press and our present religious leadership have remoulded public sentiment. Ordination is a step in this direction, but it is a step—not the final goal.[15]

At its 1924 General Conference, the Methodist Episcopal Church granted women the right to be local elders. The Commission on the Licensing and Ordaining of Women affirmed "the validity of a woman's call to preach" and recommended to the General Conference "the ordination of women as local preachers" in order to give women sacramental authority in the local situation to which they had been appointed. The commission explained that it was not recommending full clergy rights for women because, in Methodism's connectional polity, admitting women to the annual conference would introduce the "peculiar and embarrassing difficulties" of having to guarantee "to every effective minister a church and to every self-supporting church a minister." The debate following the presentation of the report was heated, and a vote on the recommendation to ordain women as local deacons and elders was postponed to the following day. At that time Dr. Ray Allen, a clergy delegate from the Genesee Annual Conference, offered a substitute motion giving women all the clergy privileges granted to men. The General Conference defeated the substitute motion and then adopted the report of the commission giving women partial status: they could be ordained but not made members of the annual conference.[16]

Full clergy rights for women in the MEC would be delayed until

1956, and Georgia Harkness's "welcome in the ministry" remained for most women only a fond hope.

Southern Methodist Women and Racial Reform

Before the 1920s the Woman's Missionary Council of the MECS had initiated two forms of outreach to the African American community: financially supporting a women's program (1906) at Paine College in Augusta, Georgia, a Colored Methodist Episcopal college begun in 1883 as a cooperative venture with the MECS, and opening a number of social settlements called Bethlehem Centers, the first of which was begun in 1912 in Augusta, adjacent to the Paine College campus. Mary DeBardeleben was director of that first Bethlehem Center, and Louise Young, dean of students at Paine College, was supervisor of student volunteers at the center. A second Bethlehem Center was begun the following year in Nashville, near Fisk University, under the leadership of Sallie Hill Sawyer of the CME Church and with the financial backing of the Woman's Missionary Council.[17]

The lynchings, race riots, and Klan activities after the First World War spurred southerners to seek ways to bring about better relations between the races. In 1920 a young Methodist minister named Will Alexander led in the founding of the Commission on Interracial Cooperation, which would soon become the major interracial reform organization in the South. Alexander credited the Southern Methodist women involved with Bethlehem House in Nashville (on whose board he had served while a student at Vanderbilt) with teaching him to treat black people as human beings. "The women had that attitude," he said, "and I learned something from them. These women were in a sort of anteroom of the church, with freedom and liberty to think and act."[18] (It's a nice image to describe the relationship of the woman's missionary societies to the church!)

At the annual meeting of the Woman's Missionary Council in Kansas City in 1920, the women approved the establishment of a Commission on Race Relations with special concern for the needs of African American women and children. The unanimous choice of a woman to chair this new commission was Carrie Parks (Mrs. Luke) Johnson from Georgia, long active in women's home mission work and the daughter and wife of Southern Methodist clergy.

Uncertain as to how to begin, the women sought the advice of Will Alexander. He recommended that the commission accept the invitation to send delegates to the forthcoming meeting of the National Association of Colored Women in Tuskegee. Johnson and Sara Estelle Haskin were chosen to go. During the meeting they were simply given seats in the rear of the hall and invited to listen. At the conclusion of the sessions a gathering was arranged in the home of Margaret Murray Washington, widow of Booker T. Washington and organizer and president of the Tuskegee Women's Club, between the two white women and ten of the leading African American women in the South.

The atmosphere was initially one of uncertainty and mistrust. With good reason the black women suspected that the white women might be there to learn how to "better" their domestic help. Carrie Parks Johnson later reported on her feelings at that gathering. "I wanted to speak to them, but I didn't know how. I wanted to invite their frankness and confidence. Only after an hour spent in the reading of God's word and in prayer [was it possible to have] a discussion of those things which make for righteousness and for more Christian relations."[19] Led by Lugenia Burns Hope, wife of John Hope (president of Morehouse College in Atlanta) and founder and, for almost thirty years, head of the Atlanta Neighborhood Union, the black women spoke of their hopes and fears for their families and their race. Mrs. Hope concluded this eventful gathering by saying, "Women, we can achieve nothing today unless you . . . who have met us are willing to help us find a place in American life where we can be unashamed and unafraid." The impact on the two white women was considerable; as Carrie Johnson put it, "My heart broke, and I have been trying [ever since] to pass the story on to the women of my race."[20]

With the support of the Commission on Interracial Cooperation, Johnson began organizing a conference of white women leaders from various groups in the South. The meeting convened in the YWCA in Memphis, Tennessee, on October 6–7, 1920. About one hundred women were present. Carrie Parks Johnson and Estelle

Haskin told of their experience at Tuskegee and informed the group that they had been invited to hear the story these black women had to tell. When the afternoon meeting began and the four distinguished African American women guests—Margaret Washington, Elizabeth Ross Haynes, Jennie B. Moton, and Charlotte Hawkins Brown—entered the room, with no prompting every white woman in the room rose to her feet. Spontaneously Belle Harris Bennett began to sing "Blest Be the Tie That Binds," and the women, black and white, joined in, many of them crying openly.

Carrie Johnson encouraged candor from the black women. "We're here for some frank talk," she said. "In your own way tell us your story and try to enlighten us. You probably think we're pretty ignorant, and we are, but we're willing to learn."[21] Each of the four women spoke. Charlotte Hawkins Brown did not speak until the second day. Born in the South, she had been educated in New England, and had recently returned to North Carolina to open a preparatory school for blacks. She began her speech by sharing an emotional account of having been forcibly removed by a group of white men from her berth in the Pullman car on her way to the Memphis meeting.

"Friends," she said, "I came here with a feeling of humiliation, and I was glad that Mrs. Johnson didn't call on me yesterday. Last night I prayed, and I want to tell you it was a struggle. The thing that I have been praying for is that I may not lose hope in *you*." Brown's was a strong speech from start to finish. She spoke about lynching, telling the women that black women were convinced that white women could control their men. "So far as lynching is concerned, if the white women would take hold of the situation, lynching would be stopped." She talked about the oppressiveness of the myth of the promiscuous black woman. She concluded, "I know that if you are Christian women, that in the final analysis you are going to have to reach out for the same hand that I am reaching out for but I know that the dear Lord will not receive it if you are crushing me beneath your feet."[22] On the afternoon of the second day the white women said, "This has been a great experience. We are humiliated. We are ashamed. But we are determined that this is not the end."[23]

John McDowell's 1982 work entitled *The Social Gospel in the South* described this Memphis conference as a "conversion experience" for many of the women present. The Federal Council of Churches called it "the strongest force yet organized in the nation in behalf of the colored race." Charlotte Brown later said that the conference was "the greatest step forward since emancipation." Will Alexander claimed that after the Memphis meeting, southern white women were the most effective force in changing southern racial patterns.[24]

In spite of the emotional high of the Memphis conference, it was not so easy to build an interracial women's movement that would function from a genuine sense of mutuality and shared power. In preparation for the conference the black women had hastily drafted a position paper dealing with their most pressing issues. Without even consulting them, however, Carrie Parks Johnson made some significant alterations in their statement before reading it to the conference. She softened their condemnation of lynching, omitted their resolution on suffrage, and left out the preamble that demanded for black women "all the privileges and rights granted to American womanhood." The black women refused to allow the publication of this altered statement. After months of difficult negotiations, a compromise statement was worked out, but it was never published.[25]

Johnson died in 1929. Although she never openly questioned segregation, she had sought to educate white women about the inferior status imposed on their black sisters. Other southern Methodist women carried on the leadership role in improving race relations in the South. Bertha Newell succeeded Johnson in 1928 as superintendent of the Bureau of Social Service of the Woman's Missionary Council. (In a reorganization of the WMC structure in 1930, Newell became superintendent of the new Bureau of Christian Social Relations.) Alice Knotts credits Newell with pressing the woman's missionary societies "to engage in more local interaction between white women and African American women." Summer Christian Leadership Schools for members of the woman's missionary societies of the Colored Methodist Episcopal Church were one form of this increased interaction. Taught by leaders of the WMC, these events provided the opportunity for white and

African American women to live and study together for a week. Follow-up interracial contacts may have been even more significant, as sponsoring local white women's societies heard the reports afterward of black women delegates who had attended from their communities, and frequently continued to work together on local projects. Through the 1930s these summer leadership schools provided a crucial opportunity for African American and white Methodist women to experience enhanced mutual understanding and help.[26]

Jessie Daniel Ames, a Methodist woman from Palestine, Texas, was to lead one of the most important women's crusades in American history, the Association of Southern Women for the Prevention of Lynching (ASWPL), founded in 1930. She considered lynching a woman's issue, and called on women to repudiate the claim that lynching protected southern womanhood. By 1942 more than forty-three thousand southern women, many of them Methodists, had signed the antilynching pledge, which read: "Lynching is an indefensible crime destructive of all principles of government, hostile to every ideal of religion and humanity, debasing and degrading to every person involved. We pledge ourselves to create a new public opinion in the South which will not condone for any reason whatever acts of mobs or lynchers."[27]

Women opposed to lynching created an extremely effective network: they secured pledges from law enforcement officers not to tolerate lynchings in their counties, they headed off potential lynchings by immediate visits to officers demanding protection for the possible victim, and when a lynching was reported, the women in that vicinity who had signed the pledge investigated the crime and filed a report.

In 1949 Dorothy Rogers Tilly, a soft-spoken Methodist woman from Atlanta, would help to found the Fellowship of the Concerned, a successor to the ASWPL. The presence of its members at the trials of black people brought about significant changes in courtroom justice. As lynchings declined, the Fellowship became, in the 1950s, an advocate for desegregation of schools and public facilities. For her active role in this organization, Dorothy Tilly was shunned by former church friends, harassed by the Klan, accused of being a Communist, and subjected to threatening phone calls, but she was never dissuaded from her conviction that the church must promote racial justice.

As the northern and southern branches of episcopal Methodism (separated since 1844) worked in the 1930s toward reunion with each other and the Methodist Protestant Church (that had left in 1830), the most troublesome question was racial: What would become of the nearly 326,000 African American members of the MEC? A plan of union was proposed that would mean acquiescence to segregation in the church with the acceptance of a new jurisdictional structure. There would be six jurisdictions, five of them geographical and one, the Central Jurisdiction, racial. The black members of the new church would be gathered into a separate jurisdiction that overlapped geographical lines. While affording African American Methodists access to power in the election of their own clergy, district superintendents, and bishops, this structure would essentially keep them apart from other Methodists except at General Conference and as a result of special efforts at interracial fellowship.

In the report of its study group on Unification and Race Relations, the Woman's Missionary Council opposed this plan of union because of "its failure to provide for co-operation between white and colored Methodists in annual and jurisdictional conferences and in local communities." Southern Methodist women cited their own experiences of interracial fellowship with women of the CME Church as a model of what was possible.[28]

Women of the MECS finally won laity rights in 1922. From 1926 on, the Woman's Missionary Council petitioned every General Conference to grant women ordination and full conference membership. After the 1939 reunion, full clergy rights for women in The Methodist Church would become a reality only in 1956.

EPILOGUE
1939–1968

The years from 1939 to 1968 and beyond were of crucial importance for women in The Methodist Church. In these years Methodist women gained full clergy rights, merged their various women's missionary organizations into the Woman's Division of Christian Service of the Board of Missions, made major strides toward improving the status and role of women in the church, and contributed significantly to higher education. With the rest of their church Methodist women prepared for another church union, that with the Evangelical United Brethren in 1968 to form The United Methodist Church.

FULL CLERGY RIGHTS FOR WOMEN

Petitions for full clergy rights for women were before the General Conferences of both the Methodist Episcopal Church and the Methodist Episcopal Church, South, from 1928 (1926 for the MECS) until the formation of The Methodist Church in 1939. At the Uniting Conference in 1939, full conference membership for female clergy was defeated by a narrow margin (371–384).[1] In the Methodist Protestant Church women ministers were a problem at the time of union since in their own denomination they had already been granted appointment, pension, and annual conference rights equal to male clergy. Those who wished to continue in ministry after the merger had to concede the right of full conference membership.

By the time the General Conference of The Methodist Church met in 1956 in Minneapolis, it had received more than two thousand petitions asking for full clergy rights for women. Many of these came from Woman's Societies in local churches across the country, stimulated by the Woman's Division of Christian Service through its section on the status of women.

At the General Conference, the Committee on the Ministry, chaired by the Reverend James S. Chubb of Grand Island, Nebraska, came in with a compromise recommendation (narrowly approved by a vote of 40–32 in the committee) granting full clergy rights to women but with the stipulation that "only unmarried women and widows may apply." A minority report signed by seven members of the committee would have retained the previous rules, granting women local ordination but not conference membership. It was clear from the debate on the conference floor that the primary issue was still the same: whether the appointment of a woman minister would be unacceptable to some churches. Two attempts were made to get around the issue: one permitting a woman to be located when she could not be placed, the other giving the annual conferences the right to decide the extent to which they would implement the legislation. Both were defeated.[2]

The minority report lost by a vote of 310 to 425 and was not substituted for the majority report. By a vote of 389 to 297 the provision that married women could not apply was removed. "Then by an overwhelming show of hands" the delegates passed the historic motion putting into the Methodist *Discipline* the following simple but momentous words: "Women are included in all the provisions of the Discipline referring to the ministry."[3] Dr. Georgia Harkness commented (alluding to this action and a compromise worked out earlier to remove obstacles in the way of ending the Central Jurisdiction), "I think maybe we've had a miracle twice this week."[4] That same evening, May 4, the General Conference saluted Harkness for the "valiant fight" she had waged for this cause for many years and in recognition of "the peculiar satisfaction" she must feel.[5]

On May 18, 1956, Maud Keister Jensen was admitted on trial, in absentia, to the Central Pennsylvania Conference, becoming the first woman to receive full clergy rights in The Methodist Church. A graduate of Drew Theological Seminary, Jensen and her husband were on missionary service in Korea. Kris Jensen had been captured during the Korean War and interned for three years and was not able to be with his wife when she received her elder's orders on May 25, 1952. After his release in 1953 they went back to Korea. Maud Jensen's ordination had been recognized fully by the Korean Methodist Church (which admitted women to full conference membership after 1930 when it became an autonomous church).[6]

The second woman was Grace E. Huck, admitted on trial by the North Dakota Conference on May 22. While a child, Huck had practiced preaching to cattle and sheep on her father's ranch. She was ordained elder on June 4, 1949, and in 1956 was serving as director of Christian Education at First Methodist Church in Fargo, North Dakota. The third woman to be granted full clergy rights in The Methodist Church was Grace M. Weaver, received on trial and ordained elder by the Idaho Conference on May 23. A graduate of the Iliff School of Theology in Denver, Weaver was appointed pastor of the church at Emmett, Idaho, in 1955.[7]

According to the *Christian Advocate,* the "fourth, fifth, sixth and seventh" women ministers were received on trial as a class by unanimous vote of the Maine Annual Conference on May 27, 1956 (actually May 25, according to the conference *Journal*). They were: Gertrude G. Harris, Alice T. Hart, Esther A. Haskard, and Margaret K. Henrichsen.[8]

Emma P. Hill was admitted on trial by the Washington Conference of the Central Jurisdiction on May 26, 1956, apparently making her the first African American woman to receive full clergy rights in The Methodist Church. Mrs. Hill "came from a family of preachers." Her father, the Reverend W. G. Simms, had been pastor at Brandywine, Maryland, for seventeen years, and her mother had served the Ritchie, Maryland, church for fifteen years. Mrs. Hill was assigned to the St. Luke charge in Prince Georges County, Maryland.[9] On May 27, JoLorene I. Miller was received on trial by the Central New York Conference. Twenty-four women in all were admitted on trial by their annual conferences that spring, all but two of whom were received into full connection two years later in 1958.[10] (Although Georgia Harkness had been ordained elder in the Troy Annual Conference, she did not apply for annual conference membership in 1956.)

The struggle of women for full clergy rights, begun in the

Methodist Episcopal Church in 1880, was finally successful. It had taken seventy-six years and twenty General Conferences to achieve this victory of 1956!

ORDINATION OF WOMEN AND THE EVANGELICAL UNITED BRETHREN CHURCH

When the Evangelical United Brethren Church was formed in 1946 from the merger of the Evangelical Church and the Church of the United Brethren in Christ, the question of the ordination of women was a thorny one. The United Brethren had been ordaining women since Ella Niswonger's ordination on September 13, 1889, while the Evangelicals never ordained women. Once again (as in the case of The Methodist Church in 1939) women's ordination was sacrificed for unity. Although the status of those already ordained was not impaired, no provision was made for the licensing and ordination of women in the new church.[11]

Jonathan Cooney claimed that a number of annual conferences did ordain women between the years 1946 and 1968, despite pre-union agreements not to do so. His research found "at least twenty-three" women ordained elder in those years. Some of the women served churches in largely rural areas; others were part of a clergy couple and ministered with their husbands.[12] In terms of official church policy, however, the ordination of women would have to wait until the 1968 union that formed The United Methodist Church.

WOMEN ORGANIZED FOR MISSION

In 1940, six women's missionary organizations from three denominations—the Methodist Episcopal Church, the Methodist Episcopal Church, South, and the Methodist Protestant Church—came together to form the Woman's Division of Christian Service of the Board of Missions of The Methodist Church. Prior to the Uniting Conference of May 1939, the presidents of the national women's organizations called a series of meetings to plan for the unification of women's work in the new church. Two meetings were especially important: a retreat held in Cincinnati, December 10–12, 1938, for forty women of the three denominations, and a meeting in Chicago of an enlarged group of representatives of all the uniting women's organizations. "The task which these women faced was colossal. To take the best in a group of the divergent organizations and from it develop something better for a great new church was not a simple matter."[13] The presidents of these organizations in 1939 found that a major part of their task lay in preparing the members to take their separate histories into the future with a sense of common purpose and hope. In her final letter to the members of the Woman's Foreign Missionary Society of the MEC, for example, President Evelyn Riley Nicholson wrote:

> Graduation day is at hand. It is to be called Charter Day. Before September 15th [1940] every local church in . . . Methodism is to assemble its women to become charter members of the Woman's Society of Christian Service. We change our initials to indicate the widened sphere of our activities and the inclusive circle of our comradeship. . . . The Woman's Foreign Missionary Society is the oldest and largest of the uniting groups. It has had an extraordinary record, blessed of God. . . . Do not think of her as defunct. Her ideals and purposes live in the World Federation of Methodist Women and will be perpetuated in the W.S.C.S. She loses her life to find and enlarge it. In God's economy . . . there is change, but not loss. . . . [You] have come to the Kingdom for such a time as this.[14]

When the Uniting Conference of 1939 appointed a Joint Committee on Missions and Church Extension, the women who constituted the Woman's Section already "knew and respected and loved one another." Grace Warne Bragg became their chairperson. On May 4, 1940, the first General Conference of The Methodist Church, held in Atlantic City, approved the proposed plans without a dissenting vote. There were seventy-three women delegates to this General Conference, thirty of whom had been on the Joint Committee on Missions.[15]

The Board of Missions and Church Extension of The Methodist Church was organized in July 1940. This new agency had four divisions, one of which was the Woman's Division of Christian

Service.[16] Its official (monthly) magazine, *The Methodist Woman*, united the heritages of at least four women's missionary magazines.[17] "Nearly two million women became charter members of the new organization and started down the road together, seeking to become one in spirit and in mission."[18] There were three departments: Foreign, Home, and Christian Social Relations and Local Church Activities. In the third department, Louise Oldshue became the first chairperson and Thelma Stevens the executive secretary. Stevens would give distinguished leadership to this department for the next twenty-eight years.

In *Fellowship of Love: Methodist Women Changing American Racial Attitudes, 1920–1968*, Alice G. Knotts described the crucial role of the Woman's Division in leading Methodist women to reject segregation and work to break down racial barriers in both their church and American society.[19] "Discussion and disagreement within a framework of voluntary commitment and connection," Knotts explained, "provided a healthy environment that enabled persons to reevaluate their attitudes and uproot their prejudices."[20]

Leadership of the Woman's Division was shared at the highest level. Each of the three departments had an executive secretary who worked in a collegial relationship with the other two executive secretaries to recommend goals, initiate program ideals, draft resolutions, plan conferences, and then coordinate and implement the programs set by the approximately fifty elected officers. The position of chair of the Woman's Division staff meetings rotated on an annual basis among the executive secretaries.[21]

Nearly every local Methodist church had one or two women's missionary groups: a Woman's Society of Christian Service for full-time homemakers and a Wesleyan Service Guild (with evening meetings) for employed women. Local societies had close organizational ties with district, conference, jurisdictional, and national officers, including program officers who related to national staff. The Woman's Division staff required regular accountability from officers at every level, providing an effective connectional network and a strong sense of direction even in times of controversy. Most officers and many local Methodist women subscribed to *The Methodist Woman*, looking to it for information and guidance. Thus the Woman's Division was both a grassroots and a national organization.[22]

BLACK WOMEN ORGANIZED FOR MISSION IN THE METHODIST CHURCH

Prior to 1939, African American women in the black annual conferences within the Methodist Episcopal Church[23] had contributed their energies to the work of the church from the local to the national levels, particularly through the Woman's Home Missionary Society. Black women like Mrs. Hester Williams (Baton Rouge, Louisiana) had pioneered in establishing schools for black women and girls. Probably the first African American woman to serve the WHMS at the national level was Miss Bessie Garrison, who became a field-worker for the black conferences in 1907. The following year Mrs. M. C. B. Mason was named supervisor of the Bureau of Colored Deaconesses. Mrs. Hattie R. Hargis (Wilmington, Delaware, president of the Delaware Conference society), Mrs. Clara J. Wilson (South Carolina and later Cincinnati), and her daughter, Emma Wilson (Strother), exemplify the African American Methodist women whose leadership made possible institutions like the Friendship Homes that offered safe housing for young black women moving to northern cities, as well as kindergartens, clinics, and community centers.[24]

In June 1940, women from the nineteen black conferences (three delegates from each) met in St. Louis concurrent with the first meeting of the Central Jurisdiction. The women had two major concerns: "building fellowship among Central Jurisdiction women and electing black women to the Board of Missions and its Woman's Division of Christian Service." Elected for the 1940–44 quadrennium were Mrs. Hattie Hargis, Mrs. Irma Green Jackson (Shreveport, Louisiana), Mrs. Susie Jones (Greensboro, North Carolina), and Mrs. Ethel Clair, wife of Bishop Matthew W. Clair Sr., of the Baltimore (CJ) Area.[25]

The charter meeting of the Central Jurisdiction WSCS was in December 1940 in Cincinnati, Ohio. Mrs. Margaret Bowen was elected the first president.[26] She had grown up in Cincinnati and was educated at the University of Cincinnati. At the time of her election, Mrs. Bowen was principal of Gilbert Academy (a Methodist high school for girls) in New Orleans. In 1948 her husband was elected a bishop of The Methodist Church. Thelma

Stevens was speaker at that first meeting. A fellowship dinner was held that evening at Friendship House, where Mrs. W. H. C. Goode (the last national president of the WHMS) and Dr. Mary McLeod Bethune spoke. A member of the Methodist Episcopal Church since 1924, Dr. Bethune was president of Bethune-Cookman College in Daytona Beach, Florida. "Advisor to the White House, founder of the National Council of Negro Women and heroine to successive generations of black students, Dr. Bethune was one of the spiritual mothers of the Woman's Society of Christian Service."[27]

In 1941 the Department of Christian Social Relations (CSR) and Local Church Activities (LCA) hired an African American woman, Mrs. Charlotte R. French, as its office secretary. She would remain with the department until her retirement in 1959. Black women first joined the professional staff of the Woman's Division as field-workers assigned to the Central Jurisdiction. There were four who served during this 1940–68 period: Miss Lillian Warrick (later Pope), 1941–43; Miss Vivienne Newton (later Gray), 1945–46; Miss Theressa Hoover, 1948–58; and Miss Dorothy L. Barnette, 1958–64. "These workers itinerated, taught, interpreted, organized, trained, cultivated and, when called upon, handed out corsages. They were expected to be experts on everything related to Methodist women organized for mission, and they usually were."[28]

In her three years as field-worker, Miss Lillian Warrick visited all nineteen black conferences at least once and was instrumental in developing an awareness of what needed to be done to encourage WSCS success at the grassroots level. Miss Vivienne Newton, a graduate of Gammon Theological Seminary, worked with the Woman's Division as a field-worker for just a year. After her marriage to the Reverend Ulysses Gray, they would serve as missionaries in Liberia for twenty-five years.

Born in Fayetteville, Arkansas, and a graduate of Philander Smith College in Little Rock and New York University, Miss Theressa Hoover served as a field-worker for ten years. In 1958 she became a member of the staff of Christian Social Relations, and in 1965 she was named assistant general secretary for the newly created section of Program and Education for Christian Mission. In 1968 she was the natural choice for associate general secretary (chief executive officer) of the Women's Division of the General Board of Global Ministries of The United Methodist Church.[29]

When Miss Dorothy Barnette became a field-worker for the Woman's Division in 1958, she had been a social worker and assistant superintendent with the People's Community Center of New Orleans. She was moved to the Joint Commission on Education and Cultivation in 1964 and was tragically killed in an accident while in Nairobi, Kenya, in 1970.[30]

The first African American woman to be elected to a professional staff position other than field-worker was Miss Ethel Watkins (later Mrs. Harold Cost), who became an associate secretary for CSR/LCA in 1952.

Many of the black women who became leaders among Methodist women organized for mission were graduates of Gammon Theological Seminary, which opened a Woman's Department in 1934. Here African American women were trained to become "missionaries, deaconesses, directors of Christian education, local church workers, and pastors' wives." Miss Josephine Beckwith became the first black graduate of the National Training School for Christian Workers in Kansas City in 1942. She would serve for thirty-two years as a home missionary. Scarritt College for Christian Workers was not integrated until 1951.[31]

CHRISTIAN SOCIAL RELATIONS AND THE CAMPAIGN AGAINST RACISM

The history of women organized for mission in the Central Jurisdiction paid tribute to the Department of Christian Social Relations and Local Church Activities of the Woman's Division for having "mobilized Methodist women of all ethnic identities into one of the most sustained campaigns against racism ever witnessed in America."[32] In 1940 the department named an African American woman, Mrs. Susie (David D.) Jones of Greensboro, North Carolina, cochairperson (with Mrs. Paul Arrington of Jackson, Mississippi) of its standing Committee on Minority Groups and Interracial Cooperation.[33]

An early CSR/LCA slogan was "All Action Is Local," and much

of the significant work under the third department depended on grassroots initiatives. Dorothy Rogers (Mrs. Milton E.) Tilly of Atlanta, Georgia, was an outstanding example of a Methodist woman who brought together black and white women throughout the South to work on issues of racial justice. She was secretary of the Southeastern Jurisdiction CSR and, from 1949, head of the interracial and ecumenical church women's organization called the Fellowship of the Concerned.[34]

The First Assembly of the Woman's Division was scheduled to be held in St. Louis, Missouri, in May of 1942. Committed to a policy of refusing to meet in segregated settings, CSR/LCA secured the relocation of the assembly to Columbus, Ohio (only to find that hotels and restaurants in Columbus were less open than had been promised).[35]

The Woman's Division held schools of Christian mission at both the conference and jurisdictional levels. The Gulfside School (usually held at Waveland, Mississippi, in the 1940s and 1950s) became the school of mission for the Central Jurisdiction. There both black and white faculty offered "invaluable training experiences for black women assuming their proper leadership roles in the Methodist Church."[36]

THE WOMEN'S DIVISION AND UNITED METHODIST WOMEN

At the union in 1940, the model of Methodist women's missionary organization that prevailed was closest to that of the Woman's Missionary Council, MECS, in several respects. Foreign missionary work and home missionary work were unified in one organization; the women's work was separately incorporated but given a "coordinate administrative role" within the general board, and there was a distinctive Department of Christian Social Relations.[37]

In the unification of the Evangelical Church and the Church of the United Brethren in Christ in 1946 to become The Evangelical United Brethren Church, the model that prevailed was that of the Evangelical Church. The separate women's organizations of the two denominations became the Women's Society of World Service, which was governed at the national level by a twelve-member Women's Council. The United Brethren women's mission organization had been separately incorporated while the Evangelical women's missionary work had always been auxiliary to the general Missionary Society.[38] By 1946, however, both United Brethren and Evangelical women had developed unified women's organizations for foreign and home missions, and both were "accustomed to having their leaders sit as part of a general board."[39]

In 1964 a new organization was approved by the Board of Missions according to which the Woman's Division transferred the work of its home and foreign mission departments to other divisions of the board. In this restructuring, Mrs. Ann Porter Brown, the general secretary of the Woman's Division, became the first general secretary of the new unified board. This experience of integration was not, however, "as debilitating as that of women in other denominations" because organized Methodist women retained their "financial sovereignty—an essential ingredient of power and autonomy."[40] The Woman's Division in 1964 was organized in three sections: Christian Social Relations, Program and Education for Christian Mission, and Finance. Members of the Woman's Division also sat on the boards of the World and National Divisions. Theressa Hoover commented on the significance of 1964: "In retrospect, 1964 can be seen as our year of inoculation. A painful dose of integration insufficient to kill our separate women's organization was injected. This has helped protect us against further attacks of the disease."[41]

In 1968 The Evangelical United Brethren Church (EUB) united with The Methodist Church to form The United Methodist Church. Methodist and EUB women merged their work for mission "with no major upheavals." The name of the division became the Women's Division; auxiliaries at all levels were called the Women's Society of Christian Service and the Wesleyan Service Guild.[42] When the Board of Missions became the Board of Global Ministries in 1972, women were able both to protect the independence of their work and to renew their grassroots organization of women for mission by creating United Methodist Women (UMW). This new structure ended the separation of women into two groups, one primarily for homemakers, the other for employed women. It was also an effort to encourage the active participation and leadership of women of color and of younger women. UMW would have three program areas: Christian Personhood, Christian Social Relations, and Christian Global Concerns. The new organization for women in mission was ratified by the General Conference of 1972 and implemented at the local level by the end of 1973.[43]

In 1968 the Woman's Division successfully petitioned the Uniting Conference to create a Study Commission on the Participation of Women in The United Methodist Church. While the study commission proceeded with its work, the Woman's Division created its own Ad Hoc Committee on Churchwomen's Liberation. In 1972 this committee "gave primary support" to the first conference held at the Grailville center in Ohio on "Women's Consciousness and Theology." It also played a significant role in working for the establishment of the Commission on the Status and Role of Women (COSRW) by the 1972 General Conference and in contributing to the creation of United Methodist Women.[44]

Our story in this volume really ends in 1939, with the Epilogue affording a glimpse of what lay just beyond. Still ahead would be important firsts for women in the Methodist family: the first woman district superintendent (Margaret Henrichsen, Maine, 1967), the first woman bishop (Marjorie Matthews, 1980), the first black woman bishop (Leontine Kelly, 1984), for example. With additional gains for both clergy and laywomen would come both new dilemmas and new opportunities related to the second wave of feminism in the 1970s.

CONCLUSION
God's Call, Diversity of Women's Lives, and Grace Sufficient

In a provocative essay entitled "Women's History *Is* American Religious History," historian Ann Braude explores how the story of American religion would look if historians took as their point of departure "the fact that women constitute the majority of participants in religious activities and institutions."[1]

Women were consistently at least two-thirds of the church membership in the Methodist family of denominations throughout the almost two hundred years of this history. In the more fluid, early years of the American Methodist movement, before the founding of the Methodist Episcopal Church as a separate denomination in 1784, women's roles were primarily supportive (more presence than institutional power), but they were not narrowly and clearly prescribed. As in the English Methodist revival, women were pioneers in the establishment and expansion of the movement. They held important positions of lay leadership and were trained for those positions in the Methodist societies. Women's gifts were appreciated and needed in the movement, and there was considerable freedom to exercise them. The narrative structure of Methodist spirituality required that women share their spiritual experiences both privately and publicly, in the testimony, prayer, and exhortation of the bands, classes, love feasts, and occasions of Methodist worship. Among the people called Methodists, women felt valued and encouraged. Male authority may have controlled Methodism, but it did not control the movement of the Spirit!

With the increasing institutionalization of Methodism from 1784 through the 1860s, an increasing disparity between female presence and male authority occurred, and women's roles began to change. Just as there were no women preachers in Wesley Methodism in England after 1803, there were few if any women class leaders in American Methodism after 1800, when the classes were becoming "universities for the ministry."

The ideal of the True Woman reinforced gender stereotypes. Even more than in their role as Mothers in Israel, women struggled to define themselves and to find ways to fulfill God's call under male prescriptions of who they were. Women's journals and other writings became important means of self-construction and even group-construction in the woman's sphere. Women made choices across a wide spectrum of options in the context of domestic ideology. Some founded organizations to support other women, others married itinerant preachers, while still others felt called to preach and became exhorters or traveling evangelists. At least in these years the increased emphasis on "women's presumed natural piety" enabled women to use religion to assert moral authority.[2]

From the 1860s through the twentieth century, women not only moved into more public roles in both church and society, but became confronters of male institutional power as they tried to live out their dreams of ministry. Although those in leadership of Methodist women's missionary organizations appeared to work within the system (many were married to prominent church leaders), their nationally organized societies offered, in Braude's words, "a female alternative to the exclusively male hierarchies" of their denomination.[3]

The struggles launched in the 1880s for full clergy and laity rights for women were prolonged and difficult, especially in episcopal Methodism. The deaconess role offered women new options for public ministry, but probably deflected the pressure for ordination. As women continued to be excluded from roles of authority as clergy and laity within the church, they were offered increased opportunities in areas where need and gender stereotypes converged. For years, James M. Buckley served as the most visible spokesman for the male authorities of the church who opposed women's gaining and exercising political power as they feared their own loss of institutional religious authority. Buckley could be effusive in his praise of "what Methodism owes to women," but only when women remained in what he continued to regard as their appropriate and separate sphere.

In these years of struggle to gain access to clergy and laity rights in the church, women made choices to leave or stay that were fateful for them and also had a significant impact on other women. The power of choice was linked with privilege, and the choices for women of color were entwined with the double oppression of their gender and their race. White women and women of color did not make choices with the same resources or at the same level of risk. Sadly, white women had difficulty recognizing that their efforts to improve the lives of their sisters of color often perpetuated the very oppression they were committed to eradicating. Thus women's responses to God's call and their experiences of grace sufficient must be understood in relation to the diversity of women's lives and the uniqueness of their struggles.

Contemporary women in this faith tradition do not commonly speak of "grace sufficient," but they still resonate with its reality. They are more apt to talk about responding to God's grace, but they recognize, experience, and trust in its dynamic, regenerative power. Perhaps more than ever they recognize grace sufficient as having a communal quality involving accountability for how one's choices affect the lives of others. God's astonishing sufficient grace is seen as constant, but ever new; private, but also strength for the struggle. It is liberating, it is empowering, and it is available to all.

The story of Methodism in America is in many ways, as Ann Braude urges, the story of women's presence (Methodist women's history *is* American Methodist history!). I trust that these pages will contribute to the recovery and reclaiming of what has remained for too long a lost history. It is a story for women and men alike, for the sake of the wholeness and faithfulness of God's people, and the promise of a redeemed and just created order. If remembering is the basis of believing, the history of Methodist women may be a lesson in hope—that we are part of an ongoing journey, and that there is grace sufficient even for our day.[4]

NOTES

NOTES TO THE INTRODUCTION

1. The autobiographical *Account of the Experience of Mrs. Hester Ann Rogers* was written in 1792 when she was thirty-six and first published in England in 1796, two years after her death. Subsequent editions, of which there were many, included her funeral sermon preached by Dr. Thomas Coke, with an appendix written by her husband, and her spiritual letters. The first American edition was published in 1804 (New York: John C. Totten, for the Methodist Episcopal Church); see the typescript journal of the New York Conference, June 12, 1804: "Voted that the Tracts concerning Mrs. Hester Ann Rogers be printed." I used a slightly later edition of her *Account:* (Baltimore: J. Kingston, 1811), 3-6.

2. Ibid., 8-9.

3. Ibid., 15-16, 19. Although not associated with the Wesleys, Simpson was clearly an evangelical Anglican.

4. Ibid., 22-24.

5. Ibid., 25-26.

6. Ibid., 31. Hester Ann Roe kept a diary in which she recorded her spiritual self-examination during the twenty years between 1774 and 1794. Extracts from that private diary were edited by an unnamed British Methodist minister and published in London in 1818. See *The Life of Faith Exemplified; or Extracts from the Journal of Mrs. Hester Ann Rogers* (New York: Carlton & Porter, 1861). The date of her conversion experience is confirmed by the *Journal.* Her entry for November 11, 1775, begins: "This day it is twelve months since the Lord set my soul at liberty. O what a year of mercies!" (16).

7. In an article entitled "'Angel's Food'—A Case of Fasting in Eighteenth Century England," Joanna Gillespie argued that when Hester Ann Roe began fasting as well as keeping a journal in late 1774, fasting (living on "angel's food") became the "arena for, and symbol of, the battle of wills between Hester Ann and her mother." See *Disorderly Eaters: Texts in Self-Empowerment,* ed. Lilian Furst and Peter Graham (University Park, Pa.: Pennsylvania State University Press, 1992), 95-112.

8. Rogers, *Account,* 32-35.

9. Ibid., 35-36.

10. Ibid., 38.

11. Ibid., 38-39.

12. *Journal of Mrs. Hester Ann Rogers,* 23.

13. Rogers, *Account*, 39.

14. Ibid., 40. She was also reading John Wesley's *A Plain Account of Christian Perfection* (1766). The Christian perfection that Wesley taught was a limited perfection; it did not eliminate ignorance, error, infirmities, or temptation. It was sinless only in Wesley's sense of sin as a voluntary transgression of a known law of God. In other words, it was perfection of intention and motive; it was perfect love, or holiness. In Wesley's view, it was a way of life available to, and necessary for, all regenerate Christians.

15. Rogers, *Account*, 43-47.

16. She described this meeting in her *Account*: "On Monday, April 1st, Mr. Wesley came to Macclesfield, and I saw and conversed with him for the first time. He behaved to me with parental tenderness, and greatly rejoiced in the Lord's goodness to my soul; encouraged me to hold fast, and to declare what the Lord had wrought" (51).

17. See Paul Wesley Chilcote, "John Wesley as Revealed by the Journal of Hester Ann Rogers, July 1775–October 1784," in *Methodist History* 20:3 (April 1982): 111-23.

18. There are frequent references to her sick visiting throughout her journal for 1780. In his letter to her of December 9, 1781, John Wesley referred to her usefulness as a class leader: "My Hetty, you are . . . to watch over the new-born babes. Although they have much love, they have not yet either much light or much strength." JW *Letters*, 7:96; quoted in Earl Kent Brown, *Women of Mr. Wesley's Methodism* (New York: The Edwin Mellen Press, 1983), 208.

19. Her husband reported that in Dublin, "she met weekly three women's classes consisting of about thirty members in each," at Cork she met two large classes, and in London she was both housekeeper to John Wesley at City Road Chapel and in charge of two large classes. (Appendix to *Account*, 130.) Regarding the children, Earl Kent Brown says there were five; see *Women of Mr. Wesley's Methodism*, 217.

20. The sermon was preached at Spitalfields Chapel on Sunday, October 16, 1794. Ten years earlier the Reverend Thomas Coke had been ordained by John Wesley as one of the two superintendents (bishops) of the Methodist Episcopal Church in America. Funeral sermon, *Account*, 113.

21. Brown, *Women of Mr. Wesley's Methodism*, 199.

22. Rogers, *Account*, "Spiritual Letters," 216-17.

23. Ibid., 203-4, 210.

24. Funeral sermon, *Account*, 118.

25. Appendix to *Account*, 131.

26. Albert C. Outler, ed.,"Introduction to *Sermons*," in *The Works of John Wesley*, Bicentennial Edition (Nashville: Abingdon Press, 1984), 1:98.

27. *Memoirs of the Late Mrs. Mary Cooper, of London; Who Departed This Life June 22, 1812, in the Twenty-Sixth Year of Her Age, extracted from her diary and epistolary correspondence*, ed. Adam Clarke, 2nd Am. ed. (New York: J. Soule and T. Mason for the MEC, 1818), 99-100 (January 7, 1810).

28. See, for example, Lois A. Boyd and R. Douglas Brackenridge, *Presbyterian Women in America: Two Centuries of a Quest for Status* (Westport, Conn.: Greenwood Press, 1983); Margaret Hope Bacon, *Mothers of Feminism: The Story of Quaker Women in America* (San Francisco: Harper & Row, 1986); Mary Sudman Donovan, *A Different Call: Women's Ministries in the Episcopal Church, 1850–1920* (Wilton, Conn.: Morehouse-Barlow, 1986); L. DeAne Lagerquist, *From Our Mother's Arms:*

A History of Women in the American Lutheran Church (Minneapolis: Augsburg Publishing, 1987); and Catherine M. Prelinger, ed., *Episcopal Women: Gender, Spirituality and Commitment in an American Mainline Denomination* (New York: Oxford University Press, 1992).

29. The major impetus for the conference and related efforts came from the Women's History Project of the UM Commission on Archives and History; additional funding was provided by the Women's Division of the General Board of Global Ministries. Successive Women's History Project coordinators from 1977 to 1991 were Hilah F. Thomas, Carolyn De Swarte Gifford, and Susan M. Eltscher. For some of the early history of the Women's History Project, see Theressa Hoover, *With Unveiled Face: Centennial Reflections on Women and Men in the Community of the Church* (New York: Women's Division, General Board of Global Ministries, UMC, 1983), 57-60.

30. Rosemary Skinner Keller, Hilah F. Thomas, and Louise L. Queen, eds., *Women in New Worlds: Historical Perspectives on the Wesleyan Tradition*, 2 vols. (Nashville: Abingdon Press, 1981-82).

31. Elaine Magalis, *Conduct Becoming to a Woman: Bolted Doors and Burgeoning Missions* (Cincinnati: Women's Division, Board of Global Ministries, UMC, 1973).

32. For other examples of narrative histories motivated, in part, by the desire to "draw together and reflect upon" the fruits of the past twenty years of scholarship in American women's history, see Barbara J. MacHaffie, *Her Story: Women in Christian Tradition* (Philadelphia: Fortress Press, 1986); Sara M. Evans, *Born for Liberty: A History of Women in America* (New York: The Free Press, 1989); and Susan Hill Lindley, *"You Have Stept Out of Your Place": A History of Women and Religion in America* (Louisville: Westminster John Knox Press, 1996).

33. In an important review article, Elizabeth Fox-Genovese challenged scholars of women and religion to "take American women's spiritual and intellectual lives with the seriousness they deserve," and thus help us to understand how "the religious experience of American women illuminates the specific and changing role of religion in American society." ("Two Steps Forward, One Step Back: New Questions and Old Models in the Religious History of American Women," *Journal of the Academy of Religion* 53:3 [1985]: 465-71.)

34. See, for example, Frank Baker, "Susanna Wesley: Puritan, Parent, Pastor, Protagonist, Pattern," in Keller, Thomas, and Queen, eds., *Women in New Worlds*, 2:112-31.

35. Quoted in ibid., 121.

36. Transcribed from her manuscript letter in the Wesley family papers of the Methodist Archives at the John Rylands University Library, Manchester, England. (With thanks to Will B. Gravely.)

37. Paul Wesley Chilcote, *John Wesley and the Women Preachers of Early Methodism* (Metuchen, N.J.: Scarecrow Press, 1991). See also his shorter work, *She Offered Them Christ: The Legacy of Women Preachers in Early Methodism* (Nashville: Abingdon Press, 1993), and Brown, *Women of Mr. Wesley's Methodism*. Brown analyzes the various roles women played in Wesleyan Methodism, including their modeling of the Christian life, and presents biographical chapters on six English Methodist women, including Hester Ann Rogers.

38. Chilcote, *John Wesley and the Women Preachers*, 49.

39. Ibid., 67-72; see also David Lowes Watson, *The Early Methodist Class Meeting: Its Origins and Significance* (Nashville: Discipleship Resources, 1987).

40. Chilcote, *John Wesley and the Women Preachers*, 69-70. Among the most prominent female class leaders in early British Methodism were Grace Murray, Elizabeth Ritchie Mortimer, and Hester Ann Roe Rogers.

41. Ibid., 70-71, 85-86. Chilcote quotes from a letter John Wesley wrote to Mrs. Dorothy Downes, assuring her that there could be "no objection to your meeting a class even of men. This is not properly assuming or exercising any authority over them. You do not act as a superior, but an equal; and it is an act of friendship and brotherly love." (John Wesley, *Letters*, 6:233, quoted in Chilcote, *Women Preachers* , 71.) A man who had enrolled himself in a man's class led by a woman felt that he had acted wisely because she "stood spiritually and intellectually head and shoulders above every other member of the Society." (From William Jessop, *An Account of Methodism in Rossendale and the Neighbourhood* [Manchester: Tubbs, Brook, and Chrystal, 1880], quoted in Chilcote, 86.)

42. John Wesley, Sermon 98: "On Visiting the Sick," *Sermons* 3:396.

43. Chilcote, *Women Preachers*, 92.

44. Ibid., 94.

45. From John Wesley's *Journal* (July 19, 1761) 4:471; quoted in ibid., 98.

46. The General Rules of Methodism are reprinted unchanged, along with doctrinal standards, in every edition of the *Book of Discipline* of The United Methodist Church. See, for example, the 1996 *Discipline*, 71.

47. Chilcote, *Women Preachers*, 101. Chilcote compared exhorting after preaching to the earlier "prophesying" in the Puritan tradition; see ibid., 91, 103.

48. Ibid., 121.

49. John Wesley, *Letters*, 4:133. To the end of his life Wesley would claim that, unlike the Quakers, the Methodists did not allow women preachers in principle, but only in exceptional cases. John Hampson was one of Wesley's authorized lay preachers. The *Notes* to which Wesley refers are his own biblical commentary, *Explanatory Notes Upon the New Testament* (1755); the reference to other women would certainly include his own mother in her parsonage society in 1711–12.

50. Ibid., 129.

51. Bosanquet's letter is quoted in full in ibid., 299-304.

52. Ibid.

53. John Wesley, *Letters*, 5:257.

54. Chilcote quotes the description in full, ibid., 166-68, as well as her sermon in Appendix I, ibid., 321-27.

55. Quoted in Chilcote, *Women Preachers*, 195. On the original document, see also Chilcote, 213, n. 59.

56. The most famous was Mary Barritt Taft, whose husband, Zechariah, became an outspoken advocate of female preaching. See helpful biographical outlines and related bibliographical information in Appendix A, ibid., 253-87.

57. Ibid., 236; quoting from Conference *Minutes*, 2:188-89. The Dublin Conference for Irish Methodism had ruled in July 1802 that women who continued to preach or exhort in public should be excluded from the society (Ibid., 232-33). This change in sentiment about women's preaching also had a marked effect on the way Methodist women were remembered. For example, the account of the life of Elizabeth Tonkin Collett, the first woman preacher in Cornwall, was never published in the *Methodist Magazine* because its editor, Jabez Bunting, did not want to encourage young women to follow her example! (Taft, *Holy Women*, 2:116; quoted in ibid., 188.)

58. There are important new studies of women preachers in these movements; for example, Deborah M. Valenze, *Prophetic Sons and Daughters: Female Preaching and Popular Religion in Industrial England* (Princeton: Princeton University Press, 1985), and E. Dorothy Graham, "Chosen by God: The Female Itinerants of Early Primitive Methodism" (Ph.D. thesis, University of Birmingham, 1986). Graham's careful study has identified nearly one hundred women itinerants (that is, traveling women preachers who were given regular appointments) among the early Primitive Methodists. She gives a group biography of twenty of them whose diaries and autobiographies are available.

NOTES TO CHAPTER 1

1. John Wesley, "A Plain Account of Genuine Christianity" (originally a letter written in 1749 to the English deist, Dr. Conyers Middleton) in Albert C. Outler, ed., *John Wesley* (New York: Oxford University Press, 1964), 181-96; see especially 195-96.

2. A. Gregory Schneider suggests that the narrative pattern of "the way of the cross" was basic to what it meant to be Methodist in early America and that personal testimony was crucial for inducing and modeling this spiritual experience. See *The Way of the Cross Leads Home: The Domestication of American Methodism* (Bloomington: Indiana University Press, 1993).

3. Diane H. Lobody, " 'That Language Might Be Given Me': Women's Experience in Early Methodism," in *Perspectives on American Methodism: Interpretive Essays*, ed. Russell E. Richey, Kenneth E. Rowe, and Jean Miller Schmidt (Nashville: Kingswood Books, 1993), 127-44; quotes on 136-37. Lobody's work has done much to illuminate the narrative structure of Wesleyan spirituality.

4. Joanna Bowen Gillespie, " 'The Clear Leadings of Providence': Pious Memoirs and the Problems of Self-Realization for Women in the Early Nineteenth Century," *Journal of the Early Republic* 5 (Summer 1985): 197-221.

5. Ibid. Gillespie discusses autobiographical writing as a mode of self-construction "*within* the 'woman's sphere.' " Under John Wesley's guidance, the early Oxford Methodists used the diary as a means of promoting and charting their progress in holy living. See Richard P. Heitzenrater, "The Meditative Piety of the Oxford Methodists," in his *Mirror and Memory: Reflections on Early Methodism* (Nashville: Kingswood Books, 1989), 78-105.

6. Some women with little education and even less leisure did manage to keep a journal; see the discussion of the religious journals of African American women in chapter 4.

7. The work of Will Gravely, Diane Lobody, and Donald G. Mathews has been particularly important in this regard. Gravely has been attentive to the experiential testimonies of early African Methodists; Lobody has listened primarily for women's voices. In working on the journals of Francis Asbury, Don Mathews has discovered the impact on Asbury of the religious responses of liminal people (persons of "low estate"), especially women and Africans. For further discussion of the roles of women and African Americans in early American Methodism, see chapter 2.

8. Gillespie, "Clear Leadings," 197, and Appendix, 220-21.

9. The transcription of the manuscript book accounts (c. 1812–14) of Methodist circuit riding preacher Benjamin Lakin variously lists sales of "Mrs. Rogers," "N. Rogers," "Nester A. Rogers," and "N A Rogers." The transcriber was obviously

unfamiliar with the *Account of the Experience of Hester Ann Rogers,* published in its first American edition in 1804 (New York: John C. Totten, for the Methodist Episcopal Church). It went through numerous editions, including an 1832 printing for use in Sunday schools (New York: B. Waugh and T. Mason, for the Methodist Episcopal Church, 1832) and one edited by the Reverend Thomas O. Summers and published for the Methodist Episcopal Church, South, in 1854. See *Life and Correspondence of Mrs. Hester Ann Rogers,* with Corrections, Additions, and Introduction by Thos. A. Summers (Nashville: Published by E. Stevenson & F. A. Owen for the MECS, 1854). For the Benjamin Lakin transcription, see William Warren Sweet, *Religion on the American Frontier: 1783–1840,* vol. 4 of *The Methodists* (Chicago: University of Chicago Press, 1946), 700-706.

The publishing house of the Methodist Episcopal Church (MEC) was set up in Philadelphia in 1789 by the official Book Steward, John Dickins. Under Ezekiel Cooper's leadership the Book Concern moved to New York in 1804; this was the era of expansion when circuit riders regularly sold Methodist publications. For a history of Methodist publishing in this early period, see James Penn Pilkington, *The Methodist Publishing House: A History,* vol. 1 (Nashville: Abingdon Press, 1968).

10. Rogers, *Account,* 190. Methodist women typically combined the scriptural promises of 2 Corinthians 12:9 and Deuteronomy 33:25 ("As your days, so shall your strength be") and spoke of "grace sufficient for our day." In interpreting doubt and uncertainty as the work of the devil, Hester Ann Roe Rogers was typical of many early Methodist women. Lobody makes this point in her work on Catherine Livingston Garrettson (see #15 below).

11. Elizabeth Mason North, *Consecrated Talents: or, The Life of Mrs. Mary W. Mason* (New York: Carlton & Lanahan, 1870; Garland Reprint, 1987), 93-94, 122.

12. Donald G. Mathews, "Evangelical America—The Methodist Ideology," in Richey, Rowe, and Schmidt, eds., *Perspectives on American Methodism,* 17-30. (Quote is on 21.)

13. Mrs. Elizabeth A. (Lyon) Roe, *Recollections of Frontier Life* (Rockford, Ill.: Gazette Publishing House, 1885; Arno Press Reprint, 1980), 614. This idea of being subject to a period of testing and trial was basic to Methodism; for example, in "probationary" church membership or "probationary" membership in the ranks of the ordained ministry.

14. Rogers, *Account,* 204-5. Methodist women's understanding of this promise is consistent with the apostle Paul's in this Corinthian passage. Forced to compete with the "super-apostles" in Corinth, Paul claims that "under the cross of Christ, divine power is 'made perfect in weakness.'" The presence of divine grace does not assure that afflictions will be removed, but that they can be borne. On the Corinthian correspondence see Robert Jewett's article in *Encyclopedia of Early Christianity,* ed. Everett Ferguson (New York: Garland Publishing, 1990), 234-36.

15. The definitive study of Garrettson's previously unexplored manuscript writings is Diane Lobody, "Lost in the Ocean of Love: The Mystical Writings of Catherine Livingston Garrettson" (Ph.D. diss., Drew University, 1990). Garrettson kept a spiritual diary from her conversion in October 1787 until her marriage in June 1793.

16. Ibid., 89. Lobody is quoting from the manuscript diaries Bk. 2, February 24, 1788.

17. Ibid.

18. Ibid., 100.

19. Rogers, *Account*, "Spiritual Letters," 203-4. Garrettson actually used very similar language to describe her relationship with God; see Lobody diss., 131.

20. Lobody diss., 134. A. Gregory Schneider makes much the same point about the impact on women of the doctrine and spiritual practice of perfect love: "It was confidence in a self that was no longer a woman's own self, but God's, and that, nevertheless, felt freer and more authentic than she had ever felt simply on her own." *The Way of the Cross Leads Home*, 182.

21. Lobody, " 'That Language Might Be Given Me,' " 144. For a discussion of women's *roles* in early American Methodism, see chapter 2.

22. Donald G. Mathews, *Religion in the Old South* (Chicago: University of Chicago Press, 1977), 104-5. (Cf. "Evangelical America—The Methodist Ideology," in which Mathews describes the subversive possibilities of Methodist "liberty," the power of self-determination conveyed by the liminal event of new birth. See 23-26.) Gillespie, "Clear Leadings," 210.

23. Virginia Lieson Brereton, *From Sin to Salvation: Stories of Women's Conversions, 1800 to the Present* (Bloomington: Indiana University Press, 1991). See especially 28-40. In her analysis of the rhetoric used by evangelical women to characterize their new relationship to God and Christ as a result of their conversion, Brereton found that the women often spoke of the "sufficiency" of grace (21). This suggests that while the centrality of the "grace sufficient" theme was characteristic of the spirituality of Methodist women, it was not unique to them.

24. *Memoir, Diary, and Letters of Miss Hannah Syng Bunting, of Philadelphia, Who Departed This Life May 25, 1832, in the Thirty-First Year of Her Age*, compiled by the Reverend T. Merritt, 2 vols. (New York: T. Mason and G. Lane, for the Sunday School Union of the Methodist Episcopal Church, 1837).

25. Bunting Memoir, I:14-15.

26. Ibid., 98.

27. Ibid., 62-64.

28. Ibid., 125-27.

29. Bunting Memoir, II:35.

30. Ibid., 59, 91.

31. I want to express appreciation here to my research assistant, now the Reverend Dr. Jeanne Knepper.

32. A. Gregory Schneider described the ritual of "happy dying" among Methodists as an instance of social religion that, like the class meeting and love feast, created a "community of intense feeling," an experience of themselves as the "family of God" in opposition to the world. As we suggest here, these deathbed rituals had a "quasi-public character," with considerable power to move those who witnessed them. See "The Ritual of Happy Dying Among Early American Methodists," *Church History* 56:3 (September 1987): 348-63. For a fuller treatment of these issues, refer to Schneider's *The Way of the Cross Leads Home*.

33. After I wrote this section I happened to look again at Earl Kent Brown's *Women of Mr. Wesley's Methodism*. He surveyed the sixty-seven obituaries of women in the *Arminian Magazine* (London) from 1778 to 1790 and found, as I did, that the women in these obituaries were all exemplary for their good deaths. He quotes Wesley's explanation for including obituaries in the magazine, "Nothing is more animating to serious people than the dying Words and Behaviour of the Children of God" (*Arminian Magazine* 5:4 [1781]: 153). He also unexpectedly confirms the point I have been making: "Discussions with husbands and friends contain the repeated affirmation that the grace of God is sufficient to bear the burden

of death, as it has been to bear the burdens of life." See Brown, *Women of Mr. Wesley's Methodism,* 107-13.

34. *Methodist Magazine,* vol. 5 (1822): 5-8 (May–August). Quote from Soule is 5:5 (May 1822), 167.

35. Ibid., 170.

36. *Methodist Magazine,* 5:7 (July 1822): 258.

37. Ibid., 5:6 (June 1822): 216.

38. Ibid., 5:7 (July 1822): 258.

39. Ibid., 5:8 (August 1822): 294.

40. Ibid., 7:5 (May 1824): 171.

41. Ibid., 3:8 (August 1820): 417.

42. Ibid., 5:2 (February 1822): 60.

43. Ibid., 11:4 (April 1828): 136.

44. Ibid., 7:12 (December 1824): 448.

45. Ibid., 10:2 (February 1827): 85.

46. Ibid., 1:1 (January 1818): 25.

47. Ibid., 2:7 (July 1819): 267.

48. Ibid., 8:9 (September 1825): 341.

49. Ibid., 4:12 (December 1821): 465.

50. Ibid., 5:11 (November 1822): 417.

51. Ibid., 6:8 (August 1828): 302.

52. Ibid., 7:2 (February 1824): 105.

53. Ibid., 6:11 (November 1823): 489.

54. Ibid., 8:11 (November 1825): 446.

55. Ibid., 9:11 (November 1826): 409-13.

56. Ibid., 6:10 (October 1823): 381-83.

57. This official denominational magazine of the United Brethren began publication in 1834. Initially materials were available in both English and German. (The counterpart for the Evangelical Association was *Der Christliche Botschafter,* 1836. The first EA English language newspaper was the *Evangelical Messenger,* published in 1848.)

58. *Religious Telescope,* 4:1 (July 31, 1844): 8.

59. Ibid., 4:4 (Sept. 25, 1844): 39.

60. Ibid., 4:7 (Oct. 23, 1844): 55.

61. Ibid., 4:2 (Aug. 14, 1844): 13.

62. David Lowes Watson, "Methodist Spirituality," in *Protestant Spiritual Traditions,* ed. Frank C. Senn (New York: Paulist Press, 1986), 225.

NOTES TO CHAPTER 2

1. Some of the major contributors to this new scholarship are: Donald G. Mathews, *Religion in the Old South* (Chicago: University of Chicago Press, 1977), and "Evangelical America—The Methodist Ideology," in *Perspectives in American Methodism,* ed. Richey, Rowe, and Schmidt (Nashville: Kingswood Books, 1993); William H. Williams, *The Garden of American Methodism: The Delmarva Peninsula, 1769-1820* (Wilmington, Del.: Scholarly Resources, Inc., 1984); Rhys Isaac, *The Transformation of Virginia, 1740–1790* (Williamsburg, Va.: The Institute of Early American History and Culture; Chapel Hill: University of North Carolina Press, 1982); Russell E. Richey, *Early American Methodism* (Bloomington: Indiana University Press, 1991); A. Gregory Schneider, *The Way of the Cross Leads Home: The*

Domestication of American Methodism (Bloomington: Indiana University Press, 1993); and the authors of essays (for example, Will B. Gravely, Doris Andrews, and Diane H. Lobody) in Richey, Rowe, and Schmidt, eds., *Perspectives on American Methodism* (Nashville: Kingswood Books, 1993).

2. Donald G. Mathews, from an unpublished paper entitled "Francis Asbury in Conference," 27.

3. Ibid., 27, 4.

4. Many of the women whose death memoirs were published in the *Methodist Magazine* and the *Religious Telescope* were described as "Mothers in Israel."

5. Williams, *Garden of American Methodism*, 107-9.

6. Doris E. Andrews, "Popular Religion and the Revolution in the Middle Atlantic Ports: The Rise of the Methodists, 1770-1800" (Ph.D. diss., University of Pennsylvania, 1986). That women significantly outnumbered men in church membership was not unique to the Methodists. As early as the mid-seventeenth century women outnumbered men in the New England churches, and during the years of the Second Great Awakening (1795–1830), women typically comprised about two-thirds of those joining evangelical churches. Mark Schantz discovered that women also joined churches in Providence, Rhode Island, in greater numbers than men. Although women outnumbered men by significant margins at both Congregational and Baptist churches, "the most lopsided margin in town" was among the Methodists, where the dominance of women over men was two to one. See Mark Schantz, "Piety in Providence: The Class Dimensions of Religious Experience in Providence, Rhode Island, 1790–1860" (Ph.D. diss., Emory University, 1991), 177.

7. Andrews, "Popular Religion," 164-80. Among the factors accounting for women's greater attachment to the church, historians have noted particularly the theological transformation toward a "heart-centered" religion or a religion of the "affections." On women and evangelical religion see, for example, Nancy F. Cott, *The Bonds of Womanhood: 'Woman's Sphere' in New England, 1780–1835* (New Haven: Yale University Press, 1977), 126-59; Martha Tomhave Blauvelt, "Women and Revivalism," in *Women and Religion in America,* ed. Rosemary Radford Ruether and Rosemary Skinner Keller, vol. 1, *The Nineteenth Century* (San Francisco: Harper & Row, 1981), 1-9; and Schneider, *The Way of the Cross Leads Home,* 42-48.

8. Andrews, "Popular Religion," 185-92. Andrews's claims about poor relief are based on her analysis of the New York society's financial records.

9. Isaac Watts's collection of Elizabeth Rowe's meditations and prayers was first published in England in 1738 and soon became a religious classic. See Andrews,"Popular Religion," 175-76, 187. Kenneth E. Rowe also called my attention to the significance of Elizabeth Rowe's work.

10. Lobody, "That Language Might Be Given Me," 129.

11. Ibid., 140.

12. Both Maryland and New York have claimed priority in the founding of American Methodism. For example, John Lednum's *A History of the Rise of Methodism in America* (Philadelphia: published by the author, 1859) argued for the priority of Maryland, while Joseph B. Wakeley in *Lost Chapters Recovered from the Early History of American Methodism* (New York: Carlton & Porter, 1858) defended the priority of New York. Among more recent historians there has been a clear consensus in favor of Maryland's priority. Frank Baker and Russell E. Richey have also sought to press the larger issues in the question of Methodist origins, Baker

emphasizing the importance of lay initiative and Richey arguing that American Methodism was decisively molded by its development in the upper South. See Frank Baker, *From Wesley to Asbury: Studies in Early American Methodism* (Durham, N.C.: Duke University Press, 1976), 28-50, and Richey, *Early American Methodism*, 47-64.

13. Baker, *From Wesley to Asbury*, 39.

14. Frederick E. Maser, *Robert Strawbridge: First American Methodist Circuit Rider* (Strawbridge Shrine Association, Inc., in cooperation with Academy Books, Rutland, Vermont, 1983), 19. Also Edwin Schell, "Beginnings in Maryland and America," *Those Incredible Methodists: A History of the Baltimore Conference of the United Methodist Church,* ed. Gordon Pratt Baker (Baltimore: Commission on Archives and History, The Baltimore Conference, 1972), 5. Elizabeth Strawbridge's role in the conversion of John Evans was confirmed by his daughter, Sarah Porter, who (at the age of eighty-four) recalled it for John Bowen. See John Bowen, *Robert Strawbridge and the Rise and Progress of Methodism on Sam's and Pipe Creeks, Md., From the Year 1764* (Baltimore: Baltimore Methodist Print, 1856).

15. See Lewis Baldwin, "Early African American Methodism: Founders and Foundations," in *Heritage and Hope: The African American Presence in United Methodism,* ed. Grant S. Shockley (Nashville: Abingdon Press, 1991), 24, and William B. McClain, *Black People in the Methodist Church: Whither Thou Goest?* (Cambridge, Mass.: Schenkman Publishing Co., 1984), 16.

16. Baker, *From Wesley to Asbury*, 34, 39; Maser, *Robert Strawbridge*, 19; Schell, "Beginnings," 5-9. Francis Asbury noted in his journal on May 5, 1801, that this society was "the first Society in Maryland and America" (Manning J. Potts et al., eds., *Journal and Letters of Francis Asbury* [Nashville: Abingdon Press; London: Epworth Press, 1958], 2:294). The most conclusive evidence for the priority of the Maryland society, as reported by Schell, is that John England, one of its early members, was a former Quaker whose departure from the Pipe Creek Friends was reported in their June 1766 meeting. This suggests that there was an active Methodist society functioning in the Sam's Creek area of Frederick County, Maryland, by the spring of 1766 (and, in all likelihood, as early as 1763).

17. Wakeley, *Lost Chapters*, 32; Abel Stevens, *The Women of Methodism* (New York: Carlton & Porter, 1866), 183, 178-79.

18. Melinda Hamline, wife of Bishop Leonidas T. Hamline, and Frances E. Willard led the American Methodist Ladies' Centenary Association in this endeavor. In *The Women of Methodism,* Abel Stevens counted Barbara Heck as one of the "three foundresses" of Methodism (along with Susanna Wesley and Selina, Countess of Huntingdon). His volume is still a valuable source of information about early American Methodist women.

19. Stevens, *Women of Methodism*, 181-82. Historians have not always agreed on the details of Barbara Heck's role in early American Methodism. Elizabeth Muir makes the important point that alterations in the Heck legend may well have occurred to fit the changing paradigm of women's appropriate behavior. See Elizabeth Gillan Muir, *Petticoats in the Pulpit: The Story of Early Nineteenth-Century Methodist Women Preachers in Upper Canada* (Toronto: The United Church Publishing House, 1991), 165-78, on "The Legend of Barbara Heck."

20. Wakeley, *Lost Chapters*, 35-36; Stevens, *Women of Methodism*, 185-86. According to Stevens, another group of Germans had arrived in New York from Ireland late in 1765. Only a few of them were Wesleyans, but one of that group was her brother Paul Ruckle. It was apparently these people who were playing cards and

received her rebuke. See also George Coles, *Heroines of Methodism; or, Pen and Ink Sketches of the Mothers and Daughters of the Church* (New York: Carlton & Porter, 1857), 129-32 (on "Mrs. Hick" [*sic*]).

21. Stevens, *Women of Methodism*, 188-91.

22. Ibid., 192-94. Unfortunately, we know less about the wives of the founders of the United Brethren in Christ and the Evangelical Association. What little we do know does not suggest that they exercised leadership roles in the founding of these churches. Philip William Otterbein, a German Reformed pastor, came to this country in 1752, serving churches in Pennsylvania and Maryland before becoming pastor of the German Evangelical Reformed Church in Baltimore (which he served from 1774 to 1813). His wife, Susan LeRoy, from a French Huguenot family, died in 1768 after only six years of marriage. There were apparently no children, and he never remarried. Martin Boehm was a Mennonite preacher born in Lancaster County, Pennsylvania. He married Eve Steiner in 1753 and they had eight children (the youngest of whom, named Henry, became a Methodist). A crucial meeting between Otterbein and Boehm in 1767 was one of the events leading to the rise of the United Brethren as a denomination. The formal organization occurred in 1800. Jacob Albright, founder of the Evangelical Association, was also born in Pennsylvania where he joined the Lutheran Church. In 1758 he married Catherine Cope, a former member of the Reformed Church who joined the Lutheran church with him. Albright began preaching in 1796 and by 1800 had organized three classes calling themselves "Albright's People." The formal organization of the Evangelical Association took place in 1803. The more traditional roles of Eve Boehm and Catherine Albright may have been related to their German cultural background. Their evangelical piety was in many ways similar to that of the early Methodists. See J. Bruce Behney and Paul H. Eller, *The History of the Evangelical United Brethren Church* (Nashville: Abingdon Press, 1979), 31-45, 67-72.

23. Williams, *Garden of American Methodism*, 108-9.

24. Frederick Norwood's account is typical: "He [Asbury] was able to settle in the home of a good Methodist, Judge Thomas White of Kent County, where he remained for the better part of two years from 1778." Frederick A. Norwood, *The Story of American Methodism* (Nashville: Abingdon Press, 1974), 86.

25. Stevens, *Women of Methodism*, 226. See also Williams, *Garden of American Methodism*, 46, 107, 110. Williams confirms that the woman in Peninsula Methodism who came closest to being an exhorter was Mary White (107).

26. Stevens, *Women of Methodism*, 228-29.

27. Ibid., 235-39, 243.

28. Geo. A. Phoebus, comp., *Beams of Light on Early Methodism in America. Chiefly Drawn from the Diary, Letters, Manuscripts, Documents, and Original Tracts of the Rev. Ezekiel Cooper* (New York: Phillips & Hunt, 1887), 116.

29. Williams, *Garden of American Methodism*, 99-100; Phoebus, *Beams of Light*, 116. Francis Asbury also reported that Ennalls had freed his slaves (*Journal and Letters of Francis Asbury* [Nov. 9, 1790], 1:656).

30. Stevens, *Women of Methodism*, 213 (title of chapter).

31. John Ffirth, *The Experience and Gospel Labours of the Rev. Benjamin Abbott* (Philadelphia: Solomon W. Conrad for Ezekiel Cooper, 1809), 91, and 88, reference to "Sister White" as an "Israelite indeed." See also *Sketches of the Life and Travels of Thomas Ware . . . Written by Himself* (New York: T. Mason and G. Lane, 1840), 80. Referring to Methodists who were "wealthy and in the higher circles of life" but

"not ashamed to bear the cross," Ware mentioned in particular Mary White as one of a number of women, "distinguished for piety and zeal, such as I had never before witnessed."

32. Rev. Henry Boehm, *Reminiscences, Historical and Biographical, of Sixty-Four Years in the Ministry,* ed. Rev. Joseph B. Wakeley (New York: Carlton & Porter, 1866), 60-61.

33. Stevens, *Women of Methodism,* 248-52. Stevens tells the story of her accompanying the circuit rider, but it is Muir who uses it to illustrate her claim that "women appear to have been more active than official church records allow." (Muir, *Petticoats in the Pulpit,* 144-45.)

34. Nathan Bangs, *A History of the Methodist Episcopal Church,* 4 vols. (New York: G. Lane and C. B. Tippett, 1845), 1:300-302. This story was also told in the "Religious and Missionary Intelligence" column of the *Methodist Magazine* (New York) 1:12 (Dec. 1818), 474-77.

35. Coles, *Heroines of Methodism,* 136-38, 132.

36. Ibid., 194.

37. Gabriel Disosway, *Our Excellent Women of the Methodist Church in England and America* (New York: J. C. Buttre, 1861), 261-71.

38. Reverend F. A. Mood, *Methodism in Charleston: A Narrative of the Chief Events Relating to the Rise and Progress of the Methodist Episcopal Church in Charleston, S.C.,* ed. Thomas O. Summers (Nashville: A. H. Redford, for the ME Church, South, 1875), 176.

39. Ibid., 190-92. Mood added: "The three last mentioned were all freed by their owners for their faithfulness and virtue" (192). The Reverend William Capers was a native South Carolinian and a strong advocate of the evangelistic "mission to the slaves." He was elected a bishop of the Methodist Episcopal Church, South, at its first General Conference in 1846.

40. Ibid., 194.

41. James B. Finley, *Sketches of Western Methodism* (Cincinnati: R. P. Thompson, 1854), 531 ff. I have used the version in Coles, *Heroines of Methodism,* 320-24. (After recounting this story, Finley commented: "How many would have said, . . . 'How improper! . . . how shocking to delicacy, for women to speak in public, especially in such a mixed assembly!' But we see in this, . . . that God's ways are not as our ways" [Finley, *Sketches,* 535-36].)

42. Disosway, *Our Excellent Women,* 276-80.

43. Douglas Summers Brown, "Elizabeth Henry Campbell Russell: Patroness of Early Methodism in the Highlands of Virginia," *Virginia United Methodist Heritage* 14:2 (Fall 1986): 13-18. See also *A Sketch of Mrs. Elizabeth Russell: Wife of General William Campbell and Sister of Patrick Henry,* by her grandson Thomas L. Preston (Nashville: Publishing House of the ME Church, South, 1888), and Jerry Catron, "Voices," *Virginia United Methodist Heritage* 21:1 (Spring 1995): 6-17.

44. Brown, "Elizabeth Henry Campbell Russell," 16-18. According to Brown, Madam Russell freed outright the one slave she owned, and the six she held by right of dower over her deceased husband's property were freed for the duration of her lifetime.

45. Julia A. Tevis, "Sixty Years in a School-Room," quoted in Preston, *A Sketch of Mrs. Elizabeth Russell,* 42-44.

46. *The Journal of Joseph Pilmore, Methodist Itinerant,* ed. Frederick E. Maser and Howard T. Maag (Philadelphia: Message Publishing Company for the Historical Society of the Philadelphia Annual Conference of the United Methodist Church,

1969), reference to Mrs. Thorn, 131 and 133 n. 11. The Boardman letter, dated Feb. 20 [1772] and in the archives of St. George's Church in Philadelphia, is quoted in Andrews, "Popular Religion," 170.

47. Letter from Mary Evans Thorn Parker to Bishop Coke and Dr. Clarke, 29 July 1813, Archives of St. George's Church, Philadelphia, Pennsylvania.

48. Ibid. Also Andrews, "Popular Religion," 195.

49. Stevens, *Women of Methodism*, 216-17, 218. Also Pilmore, *Journal*, 228 n. 1; Andrews, "Popular Religion," 198.

50. Andrews, "Popular Religion," 197-98.

51. Ibid., 198-200. The Baltimore City Station had 844 members in 1800. Although women made up 63 percent of the members, all thirty of its classes were run by men. The East Baltimore or Fells Point Station (on the harbor) had just 206 members, but two of its eight class leaders in 1800 were women. (On Fells Point see Terry D. Bilhartz, *Urban Religion and the Second Great Awakening: Church and Society in Early National Baltimore* [Rutherford: Fairleigh Dickinson University Press, 1986], 24-25.)

52. Andrews, "Popular Religion," 199-200. See Methodist Episcopal Church, *Doctrines and Discipline*, with Explanatory Notes, 10th ed. (Philadelphia: MEC, 1798), 148: "Through the grace of God our classes form the pillars of our work, and, . . . are in a considerable degree our universities for the ministry." (The same kind of restriction of women's leadership roles occurred in English Methodism in the period of institutional consolidation following John Wesley's death; recall especially the change in sentiment about women's preaching by 1803.)

53. Schell, "Beginnings in Maryland and America," in *Those Incredible Methodists*, 25.

54. Ffirth, *Experience of Benjamin Abbott*, 101-2; "The Journal of Richard What-coat," Jan. 30, 1792–Aug. 25, 1793 (transcribed by Wilbur Wallace, 1940; Garrett-Evangelical Theological School Library), 54-58.

55. John Denig, ed., *Autobiography of the Rev. Samuel Huber, Elder in the Church of the United Brethren in Christ* (Chambersburg, Pa.: M. Kiefer & Co., 1858), 34.

56. Catherine Anne Brekus, " 'Let Your Women Keep Silence in the Churches': Female Preaching and Evangelical Religion in America, 1740–1845" (Ph.D. diss., Yale University, 1993), 53-55. Women's role in the revivals was one of the contested issues in the debate about whether or not the revivals were the work of God. Brekus's evidence for female exhorters is her careful reading of the accounts of New and Old Light ministers as well as revival accounts in contemporary newspapers. Perhaps the best known of these female leaders was Sarah Osborn, who led a religious revival in Newport, Rhode Island, in the 1760s and 1770s. Female exhorters were also permitted among the Separate Baptist Churches of New England and the South. See also Catherine Anne Brekus, *Female Preaching in America: Strangers & Pilgrims, 1740–1845* (Chapel Hill: The University of North Carolina Press, 1998).

57. Andrews, "Popular Religion," 196; Mary Beth Norton, *Liberty's Daughters: The Revolutionary Experience of American Women, 1750–1800* (Boston: Little, Brown and Co., 1980), 128.

58. Andrews, "Popular Religion," 201.

59. Lobody, " 'Lost in the Ocean of Love,' " 124-25.

60. Ibid., 127. See also Lobody, " 'A Wren Just Bursting Its Shell': Catherine Livingston Garrettson's Ministry of Public Domesticity," in Rosemary Skinner Keller,

ed., *Spirituality and Social Responsibility: Vocational Vision of Women in The United Methodist Tradition* (Nashville: Abingdon Press, 1993), 19-38.

61. Stephen Olin, "Life Inexplicable Except as a Probation: A Discourse Delivered in the Methodist Episcopal Church, Rhinebeck, N.Y., July 15, 1849, at the Funeral of Mrs. Catharine [sic] Garrettson" (New York: Lane & Scott, 1851), 40.

62. Lobody, "A Wren Just Bursting Its Shell," 20-21.

63. Ibid., 22-23.

64. Ibid., 24-25.

65. Diane Lobody, "Lost in the Ocean of Love: The Spiritual Writings of Catherine Livingston Garrettson," in *Rethinking Methodist History: A Bicentennial Consultation*, ed. Russell E. Richey and Kenneth E. Rowe (Nashville: Kingswood Books, 1985), 176.

66. Lobody, "A Wren Just Bursting Its Shell," 29.

67. Ibid., 31.

68. Schneider, *The Way of the Cross Leads Home*, 68.

69. Mrs. Elizabeth A. (Lyon) Roe, *Recollections of Frontier Life* (Rockford, Ill.: Gazette Publishing House, 1885; Reprint Edition by Arno Press, 1980).

70. Ibid., 20-21.

71. Ibid., 22, 25-26.

72. Ibid., 26-31.

73. Ibid., 39-48. Lyon gives a lengthy account of this Kentucky camp meeting. She and her mother frequently attended these revival camp meetings, remaining all day on the grounds but boarding with a neighboring widow lady at night. Her other relatives went primarily to "show off" and "make a grand appearance." Her father attended this particular camp meeting because he was a candidate for Congress and "camp-meetings afforded a good opportunity for electioneering." Except for her mother, certainly no one in Elizabeth's family would encourage her to go forward to the altar and pray for salvation.

74. Ibid., 54-55.

75. Ibid., 62, 64.

76. Ibid., 103-6.

77. Ibid., 248.

78. Ibid., 293-94.

79. Schneider, *The Way of the Cross Leads Home*, 69.

80. Roe, *Recollections*, 295.

81. In an unpublished paper, "'. . . many of the poor Africans are obedient to the faith,': Reassessing the African American Presence in Early Methodism in the U.S., 1769-1809," Will Gravely examined this evidence in the journals and letters of early Methodist itinerant preachers. See also his "African Methodisms and the Rise of Black Denominationalism," in Richey, Rowe, and Schmidt, eds., *Perspectives on American Methodism*, 108-26.

82. Richard Boardman, letter to the Reverend J. Wesley, Nov. 4, 1769, in the *Arminian Magazine* (London) 7:3 (Mar. 1784): 163-64.

83. Boardman, letter to the Reverend J. Wesley, Apr. 2, 1771, *Arminian Magazine* 8:2 (Feb. 1785): 113-14.

84. Joseph Pilmore [Pilmoor], letter to the Reverend J. Wesley, May 5, 1770, *Arminian Magazine* 7:4 (Apr. 1784): 222-24.

85. Robert Drew Simpson, ed., *American Methodist Pioneer: The Life and Journals of the Rev. Freeborn Garrettson, 1752–1827* (Rutland, Vt.: Academy Books, 1984), 227.

86. Doris Andrews, "The African Methodists of Philadelphia, 1794–1802," in Richey, Rowe, and Schmidt, eds., *Perspectives on American Methodism*, 145-55.

87. From an unpublished paper by Donald Mathews titled "Francis Asbury in Conference," 20-21.

88. *Journal and Letters of Francis Asbury*, 3:140-41.

89. Ibid., 431.

90. Ibid., 465. The reference to Frank is most likely to Francis Asbury himself.

91. Mathews, "Francis Asbury in Conference," 27-29.

92. See Christine L. Krueger, *The Reader's Repentance: Women Preachers, Women Writers, and Nineteenth-Century Social Discourse* (Chicago: University of Chicago Press, 1992), 50-52.

93. Lobody, " 'A Wren Just Bursting Its Shell,' " 19-20.

Notes to Chapter 3

1. In the Introduction to *The Way of the Cross Leads Home* (Bloomington: Indiana University Press, 1993), A. Gregory Schneider suggested that the forms of social religion in Methodism helped to persuade white middle-class Americans to adopt an evangelical version of Victorian domestic ideology.

2. Nancy F. Cott, *The Bonds of Womanhood; 'Woman's Sphere' in New England, 1780–1835* (New Haven: Yale University Press, 1977), 61; the home was seen as an "oasis" or "sanctuary." In this work Nancy Cott looked at the years before 1830, and at women's personal documents rather than prescriptive literature, in order to explore the relation between change in the circumstances of women's lives and their outlook on their place as women (2-3).

3. Barbara Welter, "The Cult of True Womanhood, 1820–1860," in *Dimity Convictions: The American Woman in the Nineteenth Century* (Athens: Ohio University Press, 1976), 21-41. Welter's analysis was based on prescriptive literature, such as advice books and women's magazines.

4. Ibid., 21-31.

5. Cott, *Bonds of Womanhood*, 119.

6. African Methodists were not unaffected by the ideology of female domesticity. In an unpublished paper entitled " 'Her Children Shall Rise Up and Call Her Blessed': The Use of Rebecca Steward as a Paragon of Female Domesticity," Albert G. Miller demonstrates how the male hierarchy within the African Methodist Episcopal Church began to promote this notion. In 1877 the Reverend Theophilus Gould Steward published a tribute to his recently deceased mother, *Memoirs of Mrs. Rebecca Steward*. These memoirs became a tool for promoting the ideology of female domesticity within the church and attacking two other forces: the growing holiness movement and its attendant women preachers. On the ideology of domesticity in Bishop Daniel Alexander Payne, the dominant figure in the African Methodist Episcopal Church until his death in 1893, see David W. Wills, "Womanhood and Domesticity in the A.M.E. Tradition: The Influence of Daniel Alexander Payne," in Wills and Richard Newman, eds., *Black Apostles at Home and Abroad* (Boston: GK Hall, 1982), 133-46.

7. Both are reprinted in *The American Ideal of the "True Woman" as Reflected in Advice Books to Young Women*, ed., with Intro., Carolyn De Swarte Gifford (New York: Garland Publishing, 1987).

8. The Reverend Daniel Wise, *The Young Lady's Counsellor: or, Outlines and Illus-*

trations of the Sphere, the Duties, and the Dangers of Young Women (New York: Carl-ton & Porter, 1855; Garland Reprint 1987), 88-89.

9. James O. Andrew, *Family Government: A Treatise on Conjugal, Parental, Filial, and Other Duties* (Nashville: E. Stevenson & F. A. Owen, for the Methodist Epis-copal Church, South, 1855). Bishop Andrew was convinced of the importance of "proper family government"; on it, he claimed, depended the "weal or woe of the church and the country" (6).

10. Ibid., 34-35.

11. Ibid., 88, 23-24.

12. Ibid., 25-26, 54, 101, 172, 120.

13. Joanna Bowen Gillespie, "Modesty Canonized: Female Saints in Antebel-lum Methodist Sunday School Literature," in *Historical Reflections/Reflexions His-toriques* 10:2 (Summer 1983): 195-219.

14. Ibid., 195.

15. Ibid., 215, 219. See also Joanna Bowen Gillespie, " 'The Sun in Their Domes-tic System': The Mother in Early Nineteenth-Century Methodist Sunday School Lore," in *Women in New Worlds*, ed. Hilah Thomas and Rosemary Skinner Keller (Nashville: Abingdon Press, 1981), 2:45-59. Many of the early Sunday school materials were by British evangelical writers or heavily dependent on British sources. Although there were some differences (for example, the American fam-ily narratives portrayed "the emerging virtues of ideal American womanhood"), there were also similarities. In both British and American stories, the mother was the dominant figure. (The father was generally absent, according to Gillespie, and the mother's authority in the family was based on her moral superiority.)

16. Joanna Bowen Gillespie, "The Emerging Voice of the Methodist Woman: *The Ladies' Repository*, 1841–61," in Richey, Rowe, and Schmidt, eds., *Perspectives on American Methodism* (Nashville: Kingswood Books, 1993), 248-64.

17. Ibid., 251.

18. Ibid., 251, 254, 164. James L. Leloudis, II, "Subversion of the Feminine Ideal: The *Southern Lady's Companion* and White Male Morality in the Antebellum South, 1847–1854," in *Women in New Worlds*, 2:60-75, describes the publication of this magazine for southern women as a substitute for the *Ladies' Repository* after the for-mation in 1845 of the Methodist Episcopal Church, South. Within five years the *Companion* reached a peak paid circulation of 9,000 and, he estimates, a readership of approximately 25,000 (largely middle-class, white women). He claims that in the *Companion*, white women and ministers criticized white male behavior, espe-cially men's disregard for the burden of women's domestic duties, their drinking and gambling, and their illicit sexual relations with black slave women. "The mag-azine offered white southern men a simple choice. They could abide by their wives' standards of morality and thereby preserve their defense of slavery; or they could persist in ignoring these precepts and risk collapse of that defense through a loss of women's cooperation"(73). Perhaps because this challenge to male behav-ior was too threatening, the *Companion* was replaced in 1854 by a new publication, the *Home Circle*. Leloudis concludes that the real significance of the *Companion* was providing its female readers with a public network of emotional support and friendship that lessened their isolation and encouraged a new assertiveness.

19. Elizabeth Mason North, *Consecrated Talents: or, the Life of Mrs. Mary W. Mason* (New York: Carlton & Lanahan, 1870; Garland Reprint, 1987), 11. This bio-graphical work by Mary Mason's second daughter included extensive quotations from Mason's journal.

20. Ibid., 15-16. This was in 1808–9. Since the first American edition of the *Account of the Experience of Mrs. Hester Ann Rogers* was published in 1804, it is possible that Mary Mason read it and was influenced by it. (Perhaps her uncle John had given her a copy to help in her spiritual development.) Unfortunately I was unable to find direct evidence of this influence.

21. Ibid., 45. Mary Morgan had graduated from the Philadelphia Quakers' Young Ladies Academy in 1808. On her being hired by the Quakers in New York City as a full-time professional schoolteacher, see Marilyn Hilley Pettit, "Women, Sunday Schools, and Politics: Early National New York City, 1797–1827" (Ph.D. diss., New York University, 1991), 158-66.

22. Ibid., 45-46, 49.

23. Ibid., 59-60. The efforts of this society were specifically directed toward assistance to the families of men in the debtors' prison. When the society began to locate and train women to teach weekday school, Mary Morgan was given this important job and spent considerable time traveling to Brooklyn, Long Island, parts of New Jersey, and Westchester County, New York, in connection with it. See Pettit diss., 167-73.

24. Ibid., 67-74, 75-76. In 1812, about a year after her arrival in New York City, Mary Morgan had established a Sunday morning Bible class in her day school room (36-37). What was begun in 1815 came to fruition in 1816 as the New York Sunday School Union. An article by G. P. Disosway in the (New York) *Christian Advocate* confirms Mary Mason's role in the founding of Methodist Sunday schools in New York: "Miss Mary W. Morgan, the present Mrs. Mason, is justly the founder of Methodist Sunday-schools in New York. In 1816 the New York Sunday-School Union was established, . . . Miss Morgan, however, had *privately* commenced the system *four* years before, in 1812, and she conducted her scholars to old John-street Church. . . . Next followed the New York Female Sunday-School Union, and Miss Morgan was the only lady present from our Church at its initiatory proceedings. . . . In November, 1815 . . . Andrew C. Wheeler and Miss Morgan began the *first* regular Methodist Sunday-school in the free school-room then opposite the Forsyth-street Church." When, in 1816, the New York Sunday School Union was organized, "Miss Morgan was the female superintendent for years." G. P. Disosway, "First Methodist S. School in New York," *Christian Advocate* (May 25, 1865), 162.

25. Ibid., 84.

26. Ibid., 87-88.

27. There is some indication that the years immediately prior to his death were troubled ones. The second daughter, Elizabeth, was married in 1842 to Charles Carter North. Creighton Lacy, in his biography of the Norths' third son, Frank Mason North, refers to a "scandal" at the Book Concern, after which Thomas Mason apparently left suddenly in 1840. According to the records of the New York Annual Conference, May 19, 1841, Thomas Mason had been "expelled from the connection" sometime that year. Lacy claims that no public explanation was ever given. See Creighton Lacy, *Frank Mason North* (New York: Abingdon Press, 1967), 21-22. (In his history of the Methodist publishing house, James Penn Pilkington has a similar reference to Thomas Mason, noting his sudden resignation in 1840 and concluding as follows: "When the New York Conference met, Thomas Mason, on stated charges of immorality, was expelled from the church. The particular circumstances of the case remain a mystery." Pilkington, *The Methodist Publishing House: A History* [Nashville: Abingdon Press, 1968], 1:273.)

28. Elaine Magalis, *Conduct Becoming to a Woman: Bolted Doors and Burgeoning Missions* (Cincinnati: Women's Division, Board of Global Ministries, The United Methodist Church, 1973), 15-16.

29. Louise McCoy North, *The Story of the New York Branch of the Woman's Foreign Missionary Society of the Methodist Episcopal Church* (The New York Branch, 1926), 12.

30. Ibid., 18-20. For further consideration of the attitudes of evangelical women toward "heathen women," see chapter 7, on women organized for mission.

31. Ibid., 20-2l.

32. Magalis, *Conduct Becoming*, 17. See also the memorial to "Mrs. Ann Wilkins," *Missionary Advocate* (NY) 13:11 (Feb. 1858): 1, 82-83.

33. McCoy North, *New York Branch*, 15.

34. Ibid., 16, 9. The obituary notice for Ann Wilkins summed up her life in this way: "Few Christians ever endure greater hardships, suffer severer trials, sustain more exhausting labors, or pass through worse perils than did Mrs. Wilkins. Yet she was always divinely supported. Grace was always sufficient for her." *Missionary Advocate* 13:11 (Feb. 1858): 83.

35. Mason North, *Consecrated Talents*, 185, 192-93, 209.

36. Ibid., 241, 193.

37. Ibid., 247, 250, 252, 256, 258, 265, 277.

38. Anne Firor Scott, *The Southern Lady: From Pedestal to Politics, 1830–1930* (Chicago: University of Chicago Press, 1970), x-xi.

39. Welter, "The Cult of True Womanhood," 21.

40. Scott, *Southern Lady*, 17.

41. Perhaps, as Anne F. Scott suggests, these "would-be patriarchs" not only feared insurrection from below, but were also afraid that the women to whom they had granted the custody of conscience and morality might apply that conscience to male behavior (ibid., 18-20).

42. Ibid., 4-5, 9, 44.

43. Elizabeth Fox-Genovese, "Religion in the Lives of Slaveholding Women in the Antebellum South," in *That Gentle Strength: Historical Perspectives on Women in Christianity*, ed. Lynda L. Coon, Katherine J. Haldane, and Elisabeth W. Sommer (Charlottesville: University Press of Virginia, 1990), 207-29. Also Scott, *The Southern Lady*, and Anne Firor Scott, *Making the Invisible Woman Visible* (Urbana: University of Illinois Press, 1984), especially "Women, Religion, and Social Change in the South, 1830–1930," 190-211.

44. The Frances Moore Webb Bumpas Diary, Anne Turberville Beale Davis Diary, and Mary Jeffreys Bethell Diary are all part of the Southern Historical Collection at the University of North Carolina at Chapel Hill. The Ella Gertrude Clanton Thomas Diary is in the Manuscript Department of the Perkins Library at Duke University. The published work is *The Secret Eye: The Journal of Ella Gertrude Clanton Thomas, 1848–1889*, ed. Virginia Ingraham Burr, Intro. by Nell Irvin Painter (Chapel Hill: University of North Carolina Press, 1990).

45. From Frances Moore Bumpas Diary, 12 Mar. 1842, 5 Mar. 1842, 26 June 1842, 24 Apr. 1845. Quoted in Fox-Genovese, "Slaveholding Women," 222-23; Scott, *Southern Lady*, 11, 13. Writing about the burden of being responsible for slaves, Bumpas wrote in 1843: "We contemplate moving to a free state. There we hope to be relieved of many unpleasant things, but particularly of the evils of slavery, for slaves are a continual source of trouble.... They are a source of more trouble to housewives than all other things, vexing them and causing much sin" (Scott, 47).

46. Anne Beale Davis Diary, Oct. 1838, 18 Oct. 1840, quoted in Fox-Genovese, "Slaveholding Women," 216, 222.

47. Mary Jeffreys Bethell Diary, 12 Oct. 1862, 16 Oct. 1856, 3 Dec. 1856, 9 Dec. 1856, quoted in Fox-Genovese, "Slaveholding Women," 215, 223.

48. Both Fox-Genovese (in "Slaveholding Women") and Scott (in *Southern Lady*) make this point; the former on 220-21; the latter on 13.

49. *The Secret Eye*, 2 Feb. 1849, p. 83. Wesleyan was chartered in 1836 as Georgia Female College; a Methodist school, it was the first female college in the nation (82 n.). Nell Irvin Painter says in her Introduction that Gertrude was the first Clanton daughter to go away to school and one of a tiny minority of southern women of her generation with access to higher education (Intro., 4).

50. *The Secret Eye*, 5 Apr. 1851, 10 Apr. 1851, 12 [11] Apr. 1851, 84-87.

51. Ibid., 8 Apr. 1855, 118. She did attend the theater, in spite of the fact that it too was "contrary to the rules of the Methodist church"; she felt very guilty afterward (15 Apr. 1855, 124). Gertrude Clanton had begun keeping a journal on September 29, 1848, and continued it until November 5, 1852. There was a hiatus of about two and a half years after her marriage; she resumed it on April 8, 1855, a few days after her twenty-first birthday.

52. *The Secret Eye*, Painter Intro., 5.

53. *The Secret Eye*, 8 Apr. 1855, 120.

54. Ibid., 10 Apr. 1855, 122.

55. Ibid., 7 Mar. 1852, 100.

56. Ibid., 8 Apr. 1855, 119-20; 1 Jan. 1859, 167.

57. *The Secret Eye*, Painter Intro., 6-7.

58. Ibid., 29-30.

59. *The Secret Eye*, 4 Jul. 1864, 226-27.

60. Ibid., 27 Aug. 1864, 232.

61. Ibid., 8 Oct. 1865, 276-77.

62. Fox-Genovese, "Slaveholding Women," 225.

63. *The Secret Eye*, Painter Intro., 8. For an illustration of Gertrude's perspective see *The Secret Eye*, 31 Dec. 1865, 278: "Sometimes I am inclined to look upon our defeat as a Providential thing and then I grow sceptical and doubt wether [sic] Providence had anything to do with the matter. Slavery had its evils and great ones and for some years I have doubted wether Slavery was right and now I sometimes feel glad that they have been freed and yet I think that it came too suddenly upon them. As it is we live in troublous times."

64. *The Secret Eye*, Painter Intro., 8-9.

65. Ibid., 7 Feb. 1869, 305-6; 9 Jan. 1870, 325.

66. Ibid., 16 Nov. 1879, 386-87. Also Painter Intro., 25.

67. *The Secret Eye*, Epilogue, 447-54.

68. Marilyn Pettit points out that Mary Mason was "unusually active" in the public sphere because of her authority as superintendent of Sunday schools and as principal of various schools. She quotes Quaker patriarch Thomas Eddy who said of Mason at a young age, "I believe she is called to preach the Gospel." North, *Consecrated Talents*, 77. Quoted in Pettit diss., 180.

Notes to Chapter 4

1. Nancy Towle, *Vicissitudes Illustrated, in the Experience of Nancy Towle, in Europe and America*, 2d ed. (Portsmouth, N.H.: John Caldwell, 1833), 22-23.

2. Catherine Anne Brekus, " 'Let Your Women Keep Silence in the Churches': Female Preaching and Evangelical Religion in America, 1740–1845" (Ph.D. diss., Yale University, 1993), 91-92. Another example of a female (nondenominational) itinerant preacher was Dorothy Ripley, who crossed the Atlantic nineteen times between 1825 and 1831. See ibid., 4; also Muir, *Petticoats in the Pulpit* (Toronto: The United Church Publishing House, 1991), 141-44, and Chilcote, *John Wesley and the Women Preachers of Early Methodism* (Metuchen, N.J.: Scarecrow Press, Inc., 1991), 276-78. Brought up in England as a Wesleyan, Ripley left the Methodists because of their opposition to women preachers after 1803. In the U.S., Methodists, Quakers, and Presbyterians invited her to speak to their congregations.

3. Ibid., 103.

4. Ibid., 94. This struggle for official recognition of women preachers by the Methodist denominations in the U.S. was a long one (involving being licensed to preach, being ordained a deacon or elder for ministry in a particular local appointment, and finally being ordained an elder "in full connection," that is, with full clergy rights). This chapter and the two following explore some of the ways women who experienced a call to preach were able to respond to that call. For an account of the struggle for full clergy rights, see chapter 8 and the Epilogue.

5. The shorter version was published in *Sisters of the Spirit: Three Black Women's Autobiographies of the Nineteenth Century,* ed. William L. Andrews (Bloomington: Indiana University Press, 1986). The longer and later version, *Religious Experience and Journal of Mrs. Jarena Lee,* appears in *Spiritual Narratives,* ed. Sue E. Houchins, Schomburg Library of Nineteenth Century Black Women Writers (New York: Oxford University Press, 1988).

6. Nellie Y. McKay, "Nineteenth-Century Black Women's Spiritual Autobiographies: Religious Faith and Self-Empowerment," in Richey, Rowe, and Schmidt, eds., *Perspectives on American Methodism,* 178-91. See also Jean M. Humez, " 'My Spirit Eye': Some Functions of Spiritual Visionary Experience in the Lives of Five Black Women Preachers, 1810-1880," in *Women and the Structure of Society* (from 5th Berkshire Conference; Durham, N.C.: Duke University Press, 1984), 129-43.

7. Lee described her call in this way: "But to my utter surprise there seemed to sound a voice which I thought I distinctly heard, and most certainly understood, which said to me, 'Go preach the Gospel!' I immediately replied aloud, 'No one will believe me.' Again I listened, and again the same voice seemed to say, 'Preach the Gospel; I will put words in your mouth, and will turn your enemies to become your friends.' " *The Life and Religious Experience of Jarena Lee* (1836) in Andrews, ed., *Sisters of the Spirit,* 35.

8. Ibid., 36.

9. Ibid., 44.

10. Ibid., 45-46. Lee does not mention what happened to her other child.

11. Lee, *Religious Experience* (1849), 23.

12. Ibid., 34, 37.

13. Ibid., 42. Paul Chilcote refers to a sermon by John Wesley on "The Ministerial Office" in which he distinguished between the offices of priest and prophet; regarding the latter, Wesley said: "For in this respect God always asserted his *right* to send by whom he *would* send." Quoted in Chilcote, *John Wesley and the Women Preachers,* 81.

14. Ibid., 50-51.

15. Although Lee does not mention Turner by name, she is almost certainly

referring to him as the young man, "professing to be righteous," who in 1831 said he saw in the sky men, marching like armies. "The wickedness of the people," she went on to say, "certainly calls for the lowering Judgments of God to be let loose upon the Nation and Slavery" (ibid., 63). In his "Confessions," Nat Turner described his vision in these words: "And about this time I had a vision—and I saw white spirits and black spirits engaged in battle, and the sun was darkened—the thunder rolled in the Heavens, and blood flowed in streams." See "The Confessions of Nat Turner, the Leader of the Late Insurrection in Southampton, Va., As fully and voluntarily made to Thomas R. Gray" (1831), in Henry Irving Tragle, *The Southampton Slave Revolt of 1831: A Compilation of Source Material* (New York: Vintage Books, 1973), 300-321.

16. Ibid., 72.

17. Ibid., 63, 66, 70-71, 88. See also Jualynne Dodson, "Nineteenth-Century A.M.E. Preaching Women," in Rosemary Skinner Keller and Hilah Thomas, eds., *Women in New Worlds* (Nashville: Abingdon Press, 1981), 2:276-89. The spiritual autobiographies of two other African American women preachers, Mrs. Zilpha Elaw (1846) and Mrs. Julia A. J. Foote (1879), are also included in Andrews, ed., *Sisters of the Spirit.*

18. Lee, *Religious Experience* (1849), 96-97. The last date to which Lee refers is March 31, 1842.

19. Andrews, ed., *Sisters of the Spirit,* 6. According to Dr. Dennis C. Dickerson, historiographer of the AME Church, the grave of Jarena Lee was recently discovered in the graveyard adjacent to Mt. Pisgah AME Church in Lawnside, NJ. A special service and wreath laying was held February 13, 1999. Unfortunately the dates on the headstone are indiscernible; further work is being done to attempt to decipher them.

20. Dodson, "A.M.E. Preaching Women," 278-79.

21. Ibid., 280-81.

22. On June 6, 1809, she wrote in her diary: "I see and lament the condition of poor perishing sinners, my heart is pained for them, . . . and I feel it my duty to tell them of their situation. It is my duty to reprove sin wherever I see it, but the cross is very heavy for a poor young female to take up and bear; therefore I have sometimes tried to get round it by neglecting my duty. But in so doing I pierce myself through with many sorrows." *Diary of Fanny Newell; with a sketch of Her Life, and an Introduction by a Member of the New England Conference of the Methodist Episcopal Church,* 4th ed. (Boston: Charles H. Peirce, 1848), 99.

23. Ibid., 176.

24. Ibid., 198-201.

25. Compare *Memoirs of Fanny Newell; Written by Herself . . . ,* 2d ed., With Corrections and Improvements, published by O. Scott and E. F. Newell (Springfield: Merriam, Little & Co., 1832) with the earlier cited 4th ed., *Diary of Fanny Newell* (1848); note especially the Introduction, 9-16. See also *Life and Observations of Rev. E[benezer] F. Newell* (Worcester, 1847), 138.

26. F. Newell, *Diary of Fanny Newell,* 195-96.

27. Ibid., 207-8.

28. Ibid., 209, 211-12. Because of descriptions like these, I find it difficult to agree with Brekus that Fanny Newell's role was simply that of a minister's wife. See Brekus, "Let Your Women Keep Silence." "Too timid to become a preacher herself, she became the ideal minister's wife, volunteering to visit the sick and comfort the spiritually distressed" (123).

29. Ibid., 219-20. The conclusion to this account explains why she continued to be an exhorter: "My husband preached, and much power attended his word. Near the close, a few fragments fell into my mind, and such a sense of eternity rolled upon me, that I said: O Lord! I will attempt to speak once more, if thou wilt speak through this poor feeble instrument to the awakening of some poor soul. Blessed be God for that peace, that overflowed my heart." The issue is not so much whether particular women *wanted* to preach, but whether or not they felt called by God to take up their cross and preach or exhort in public.

30. We noted earlier (chapter 2) how Catherine Livingston Garrettson's desires to exercise ministerial leadership were revealed in her dreams. (Diane Lobody quoted Elizabeth Janeway's comment that "women explore possibilities in their dreams that they cannot allow themselves to do in the working world." See Lobody, " 'Lost in the Ocean of Love,' " 124.) Regarding dreams and her call to preach, Fanny Newell explained, "That which I cannot comprehend when awake, he [God] revealeth to me when deep sleep locks up the bodily sense" (F. Newell, *Diary*, 94). Compare Jarena Lee: "My mind became so exercised [after hearing her call to preach] that during the night following, I took a text, and preached in my sleep. I thought there stood before me a great multitude, while I expounded to them the things of religion." Two days after this, Lee went to see Richard Allen for the first time. As she approached his house, her courage began to fail her, "so terrible did the cross appear" (Lee, *Life and Religious Experience*, [1836] 35).

31. Lee, *Life and Religious Experience*, 37.

32. F. Newell, *Diary*, 134.

33. Lee, *Religious Experience* (1849), 22.

34. Zilpha Elaw, *Memoirs of the Life, Religious Experience, Ministerial Travels and Labours of Mrs. Zilpha Elaw, An American Female of Colour; Together with Some Account of the Great Revivals in America* in Andrews, ed., *Sisters of the Spirit*, 49-160; quote is on 49.

35. George Brown, *The Lady Preacher: or the Life and Labors of Mrs. Hannah Reeves* . . . (Philadelphia: Daughaday and Becker, 1870; Garland Reprint, 1987).

36. Ibid., 60-61.

37. From 1808 to 1828 there was increasing agitation for reform within episcopal Methodism, especially on the issues of election of presiding elders, conference rights for local preachers, and lay representation. After failing to bring about the desired reforms at the General Conferences of 1820, 1824, and 1828, the reform party (led by Nicholas Snethen and Alexander McCaine) finally moved toward the formation of a separate denomination. The Methodist Protestant Church was formally organized in Baltimore in November 1830. In it the connectional system was preserved (without bishops), laymen gained equal representation in annual and General Conference, but local preachers were denied conference membership. For a brief history of this reform movement, see Frederick A. Norwood, *The Story of American Methodism* (Nashville: Abingdon Press, 1974), 175-84.

38. Brown, *The Lady Preacher*, 100.

39. Quoted in ibid., 116-17.

40. Ibid., 137-38.

41. Ibid., 328-29.

42. Formally organized in 1800, and with roots in both the German Reformed and Mennonite traditions, the United Brethren in Christ had moved west from Pennsylvania into Ohio, Indiana, and Illinois by the 1840s. Among the women

applying to the United Brethren for permission to preach or exhort were Sister S. Copeland (1841) and Sister L. P. Clemens (1843), both of whom applied to the Scioto Annual Conference (Ohio). See J. Bruce Behney and Paul H. Eller, *The History of the Evangelical United Brethren Church* (Nashville: Abingdon Press, 1979) 159-60.

43. Donald K. Gorrell, ed., *"Woman's Rightful Place"* (Dayton, Ohio: United Theological Seminary, 1980), 28-29.

44. *Autobiography of Lydia Sexton* (Dayton, Ohio: United Brethren Publishing House, 1882; Garland Reprint, 1987), 200-202.

45. Ibid., 209.

46. Ibid., 213.

47. Ibid., 214, 217.

48. The license read as follows: "This is to certify that Lydia Sexton is an approved minister of the gospel among us, the United Brethren in Christ. This given by order of the quarterly Illinois Conference, in the year of our Lord, one thousand eight hundred and fifty-one. Josiah Turrell" (ibid., 240).

49. Ibid., 623.

50. Ibid., iii-iv. This is the famous exoduster movement of freedpeople from the South to the West in the late 1870s and early 80s. See "The Exodus" by Methodist Episcopal Bishop Gilbert Haven in Robin W. Winks, *An Autobiography of the Reverend Josiah Henson* (Addison-Wesley Publishing Company, 1969), 188-90. In "The Last Years of Lydia Sexton," Julia Dagenais fills in the years following the *Autobiography*, including reference to Sexton's obituary in the *Seattle Press Times* bearing the headline "Mother Sexton is Dead." See United Theological Seminary's *Telescope-Messenger* 7:2 (Summer 1997): 3-4.

51. F. Newell, *Diary*, 248-49.

NOTES TO CHAPTER 5

1. Leonard I. Sweet, *The Minister's Wife: Her Role in Nineteenth-Century American Evangelicalism* (Philadelphia: Temple University Press, 1983), 3.

2. Ibid., 4-5. For Sweet's discussion of Methodist women see especially 79-86, 117-20, 127-43, and 177-80.

3. Ibid., 3.

4. See also the Introduction to Carolyn De Swarte Gifford, ed., *The Nineteenth-Century American Methodist Itinerant Preacher's Wife* (New York: Garland Publishing, 1987).

5. "Address of the Bishops," in *Journal of the General Conference of the Methodist Episcopal Church* (1844), 158-59; quoted in Sweet, *The Minister's Wife*, 49. ("The admission of married men into the itinerancy, with heavy families, and not infrequently in embarrassed circumstances, and the permanent location of a great number of the families of the preachers, have had a debilitating influence upon the energies of the itinerant system. The number of preachers under these local embarrassments . . . is almost incredible, and constantly increasing.")

6. *Journal and Letters of Francis Asbury* (Nashville: Abingdon Press, 1958), 3:278.

7. Julie Roy Jeffrey, "Ministry Through Marriage," in *Women in New Worlds*, ed. Hilah F. Thomas and Rosemary Skinner Keller (Nashville: Abingdon Press, 1981), 1:143-60.

8. Ibid. Quotes on 143-44.

9. Herrick M. Eaton, *The Itinerant's Wife: Her Qualifications, Duties, Trials, and*

Rewards (New York: Lane & Scott, 1851). It is reprinted in Gifford's volume, along with a useful companion piece, Mary Orne Tucker's *Itinerant Preaching in the Early Days of Methodism, by a Pioneer Preacher's Wife*, ed. by her son, Thomas W. Tucker (Boston: B. B. Russell, 1872). Gifford suggests that the Reverend Eaton and the Tuckers may well have known one another from annual conferences in the 1840s, and that perhaps Mary Orne Tucker's experiences had a part in prompting Eaton to give such a frank account of the trials an itinerant's wife might expect (Gifford introduction).

10. Eaton, *The Itinerant's Wife*, 7-28.
11. Ibid., 68-69.
12. Jeffrey, "Ministry Through Marriage," 147-48.
13. Tucker, *Itinerant Preaching*, 156; also in Gifford Introduction. The dates in the headings here and below are of each woman's active ministry with her husband. They also suggest something of the moving frontier.
14. Tucker, *Itinerant Preaching*, 19-37. It is interesting to note that the date of their marriage was April 25, 1816, a little more than a month after Asbury's death on March 21, 1816.
15. Ibid., 41-42.
16. Ibid., 43-57.
17. Ibid., 59.
18. Ibid., 75-79.
19. Ibid., 91-94.
20. Ibid., 100-101, 107-8.
21. Ibid., 128.
22. Ibid., 152, 157-58.
23. See Theressa Gay, *Life and Letters of Mrs. Jason Lee* (Portland, Oreg.: Metropolitan Press, 1936), and Homer Noley, *First White Frost: Native Americans and United Methodism* (Nashville: Abingdon Press, 1991). Also Nancy Peacocke Fadeley, *Mission to Oregon* (Eugene, Oreg., 1976). The Oregon Mission was inspired by the reported quest of four members of the Flathead tribe for "the white man's book of Heaven." Actually, the Flathead people lived in western Montana. Lee and the others worked with Oregon tribes, possibly the Cayuse and Nez Perce.
24. Jeffrey, "Ministry Through Marriage," 144.
25. Gay, *Life and Letters,* 129.
26. Ibid., 119. Pittman's parents apparently thought the *Life* of Hester Ann Rogers would be an inspiring and comforting traveling companion for their daughter. That Anna Maria's youngest sister was named Hester Ann Rogers Pittman is further evidence of the high regard in which Rogers was held as an exemplar of female piety. (See the letter from Anna Maria to her sister, Hester Ann, April 16, 1838, in ibid., 182-83.)
27. Ibid., 156-57, 158.
28. Ibid., 166.
29. Ibid., 170.
30. Ibid., 171, 173.
31. Ibid., 180.
32. The Great Reinforcement (fifty-two people) sailed from New York on October 9, 1839, stopping in Rio de Janeiro, Brazil, from December 9 to 24, 1839; in Valparaiso, Chile, from February 19 to 23, 1840; and in Honolulu, Hawaii, from April 11 to 28, finally arriving at Fort Vancouver on June 1, 1840. Among them were Henry Bridgman Brewer, a farmer, and his wife, Laura Giddings

Brewer, a teacher, who were assigned to the Dalles Mission Station (under the leadership of the Reverend Daniel Lee), some eighty miles up the Columbia River from Fort Vancouver. See *The Brewer Letters: Transcripts of Letters to Henry and Laura Brewer, Methodist Missionaries to Oregon 1839 to 1848*, ed. John and Charlotte Hook (Commission on Archives and History, Oregon-Idaho Conference of the United Methodist Church, 1994).

33. Gay, *Life and Letters*, 187. Mrs. Pittman, Lee's mother-in-law, had lamented that Lee could not wait to marry again until he had at least seen the grave of his first wife. (Lee's second wife died in March 1842, three weeks after the birth of a daughter.) Lee himself was eventually replaced as the superintendent of the mission. He returned to Canada in ill health and died there in 1845.

34. Quoted in Jeffrey, "Ministry Through Marriage," 145.

35. William Taylor, *California Life Illustrated* (New York: Published for the Author by Carlton & Porter, 1859), 19.

36. Jeffrey, "Ministry Through Marriage," 154.

37. J. C. Simmons, *The History of Southern Methodism on the Pacific Coast* (Nashville: Southern Methodist Publishing House, 1886), 143.

38. Ibid., 144.

39. Ibid., 145-46.

40. Ibid., 152-53. The next day, according to Simmons, the leader's father sent Rebecca Fisher a beautiful piece of Oregon cloth for a cloak, requesting that she accept it as a token of his appreciation for the "timely rebuke" she had given his son.

41. Jeffrey, "Ministry Through Marriage," 145.

42. Simmons, *Southern Methodism on the Pacific Coast*, 28.

43. *Memoirs of Puget Sound, Early Seattle 1853–1856: The Letters of David & Catherine Blaine*, ed. Richard A. Seiber (Fairfield, Wash.: Ye Galleon Press, 1978).

44. Ibid., 87.

45. Ibid., 89.

46. Ibid., 88.

47. Ibid., 137, 139.

48. Ibid., 96-97.

49. Ibid., 15.

50. Frances Potter Peck, *Memoir of Frances Merritt*, with an Introduction by Bishop Henry White Warren (Cincinnati: Cranston & Curts, 1892), 166. In his introduction to her biography, Bishop Warren said of her, "How can a frail woman, hardly able to live herself, become a veritable Atlas, holding up a world of cares for others? She must have reservoirs of strength elsewhere" (8).

51. Ibid., 68.

52. Ibid., 80.

53. Ibid., 84.

54. Ibid., 85. On the Trinidad congregation, see William B. Gravely, " 'Our Church Is Truly the Pioneer Church of the Country': The Expansion of the Colorado Conference, 1863–1883," in *The Methodist, Evangelical, and United Brethren Churches in the Rockies, 1850–1976*, J. Alton Templin, Allen D. Breck, and Martin Rist, ed. (Rocky Mountain Conference of the United Methodist Church, 1977), 71. The members of this congregation were among those who petitioned the 1880 General Conference of the Methodist Episcopal Church to make the language in the *Discipline* gender-inclusive so that women would not be excluded from church offices.

55. Peck, *Memoir*, 108-9.

56. Ibid., 117-18.

57. Ibid., 148.

58. Sherry L. Nanninga, "Laving My Feet in the Waters of Jordan: Frances Merritt, 1839–1891, Life and Struggle of a Methodist Woman in Colorado," from an unpublished student paper for my course on Religious History of American Women, March 1993, 3.

59. Peck, *Memoir*, 133.

60. Ibid., 130-31.

61. Ibid., 144.

62. Ibid., 149.

63. See also Rosa Peffly Motes, "The Pacific Northwest: Changing Role of the Pastor's Wife Since 1840," in *Women in New Worlds*, 2:151.

NOTES TO CHAPTER 6

1. Margaret McFadden, "The Ironies of Pentecost: Phoebe Palmer, World Evangelism, and Female Networks," *Methodist History* 31:2 (Jan. 1993): 63-75.

2. Richard Wheatley, *The Life and Letters of Mrs. Phoebe Palmer* (New York: W. C. Palmer, 1876; Garland Reprint, 1984), 21. For helpful studies of Phoebe Palmer's life and work, see Charles Edward White, *The Beauty of Holiness: Phoebe Palmer as Theologian, Revivalist, Feminist, and Humanitarian* (Grand Rapids, Mich.: Francis Asbury Press of Zondervan Publishing House, 1986), and Harold E. Raser, *Phoebe Palmer: Her Life and Thought*, vol. 22 of *Studies in Women and Religion* (Lewiston, N.Y.: Edwin Mellen Press, 1987).

3. White, *Beauty of Holiness*, 6; Raser, *Phoebe Palmer*, 38-39; Wheatley, *Life and Letters*, 26.

4. White, *Beauty of Holiness*, 7; Wheatley, *Life and Letters*, 26-27; Raser, *Phoebe Palmer*, 40-43.

5. Wheatley, *Life and Letters*, 30-32; White, *Beauty of Holiness*, 9. See also Thomas C. Oden, ed., *Phoebe Palmer: Selected Writings, Sources of American Spirituality Series* (New York: Paulist Press, 1988), 98ff.

6. Raser, *Phoebe Palmer*, 45. Rogers was describing the impact of her meeting with John Fletcher in Leeds, England, on August 24, 1781. See *An Account of the Experience of Hester Ann Rogers* (New York: Carlton & Phillips, 1856), 135-36.

7. Phoebe Palmer led the meeting for thirty-seven years, taking over the leadership from 1840 when the Lankfords moved out of New York City until her death in 1874. After her death her recently widowed sister Sarah became the second Mrs. Walter Palmer and once again led the Tuesday Meeting.

8. Phoebe Palmer, *The Way of Holiness, with Notes by the Way: Being a Narrative of Religious Experience, Resulting from a Determination to Be a Bible Christian* (New York: Piercy and Reed, 1843); reprint edition, *The Devotional Writings of Phoebe Palmer*, "Higher Christian Life" Series (New York: Garland Publishing, Inc., 1985), 125-26. Cf. Wheatley, *Life and Letters*, 36-44. This diary account ends: "Through Thy grace alone I have been enabled to give myself wholly and forever to Thee. Thou hast given Thy Word, assuring me that Thou dost receive. I believe that Word! Alleluia! the Lord God Omnipotent reigneth unrivalled in my heart! . . . O! into what a region of light, glory and purity, was my soul at this moment ushered! I felt that I was but as a drop in the ocean of infinite Love, and Christ was All in All" (43-44).

9. Wheatley, *Life and Letters*, 176.

10. Ibid., 178; Raser, *Phoebe Palmer*, 50. See also Jean Miller Schmidt, "Holiness and Perfection," in Charles H. Lippy and Peter W. Williams, eds., *Encyclopedia of the American Religious Experience*, vol. 2 (New York: Charles Scribner's Sons, 1988), 813-29.

11. Phoebe Palmer, *Promise of the Father; or, A Neglected Specialty of the Last Days* (New York: W. C. Palmer, 1859; Garland Reprint, 1985), 228-34.

12. The Palmers would purchase this journal, now called the *Guide to Holiness*, on their return from Britain in 1863; for the last decade of her life, Phoebe was its editor.

13. *Guide to Christian Perfection* 1:1 (July 1839): 24.

14. Ibid., 1:9 (Mar. 1840): 213.

15. Ibid., 3:1 (July 1841): 8-16. Also 2:12 (June 1841): 274.

16. Ibid., 3:9 (Mar. 1842): 219-22.

17. See Schmidt, "Holiness and Perfection," 815.

18. Theodore Hovet, "Phoebe Palmer's 'Altar Phraseology' and the Spiritual Dimension of Woman's Sphere," *Journal of Religion* 63 (1983): 264-80; quotes on 271-72.

19. Wheatley, *Life and Letters*, 47.

20. See, for example, Anne C. Loveland, "Domesticity and Religion in the Antebellum Period: The Career of Phoebe Palmer," *The Historian* 39 (May 1977): 455-71; quote on 465.

21. Rogers, *Spiritual Letters* (attached to *Account*), 188.

22. Harold E. Raser argues this point in *Phoebe Palmer*; see especially 245-49.

23. Palmer, *The Way of Holiness*, 126.

24. Ibid., 263.

25. In *Phoebe Palmer: Selected Writings*, Thomas Oden suggests that Palmer was the author of this work about the young Mary Yard James. That Mary James herself was the author is clear from *The Life of Mrs. Mary D. James, by her Son* [Joseph H. James], introduction by J. M. Buckley (New York: Palmer & Hughes, 1886), 132-34.

26. James, *Life of Mrs. Mary D. James*, 235.

27. Ibid., 236. A chapter in James's biography is entitled "Pressed by Domestic Cares." In 1846 Mary James had given birth to a daughter, her third child. In a long letter to James (published in 1846 in the *Guide to Holiness*, 9:135-37), Phoebe Palmer had sympathized with her friend, whose new baby kept her from "those outward active services to which you have become accustomed, and in which you . . . have been so much blest in your own soul." Palmer urged her to "exhibit the power of grace to sustain in circumstances where thousands of Christian mothers are placed, and where, alas, too many are prone to let go their hold on the all-sufficiency of grace" (Wheatley, *Life and Letters*, 592-93).

28. James, *Life of Mrs. Mary D. James*, 233, 114.

29. Raser, *Phoebe Palmer*, 58-59, 215; White, *Beauty of Holiness*, 217-27.

30. Raser, *Phoebe Palmer*, 62.

31. Palmer, *Promise of the Father*.

32. The full text of this later work is printed with introduction and notes in Oden, *Selected Writings*, 31-56.

33. White, *Beauty of Holiness*, 102-3.

34. See Nancy A. Hardesty and Adrienne Israel, "Amanda Berry Smith: A 'Downright, Outright Christian,' " in *Spirituality and Social Responsibility: Voca-*

tional Vision of Women in the United Methodist Tradition, ed. Rosemary Skinner Keller (Nashville: Abingdon Press, 1993), 61-79. Also Adrienne M. Israel, *Amanda Berry Smith: From Washerwoman to Evangelist*, Studies in Evangelicalism, No. 16 (Lanham, MD: Scarecrow Press, 1998).

35. *An Autobiography: The Story of the Lord's Dealings with Mrs. Amanda Smith, the Colored Evangelist*, with an introduction by Bishop Thoburn, of India (Chicago: Meyer & Brother, 1893), 23.

36. Hardesty and Israel, "Amanda Berry Smith," 61.

37. Smith, *An Autobiography*, 28.

38. Ibid.

39. Hardesty and Israel, "Amanda Berry Smith," 62.

40. Smith, *An Autobiography*, 42-43.

41. Ibid., 47-49.

42. Ibid., 77-79.

43. Hardesty and Israel, "Amanda Berry Smith," 63.

44. Smith, *An Autobiography*, 147-49.

45. Ibid., 157.

46. Hardesty and Israel, "Amanda Berry Smith," 65.

47. Ibid., 69.

48. Smith, *An Autobiography*, 204.

NOTES TO CHAPTER 7

1. Frances E. Willard, *How to Win: A Book for Girls* (New York: Funk & Wagnalls, 1886), 54-55; reprint edition in *The Ideal of "The New Woman" According to the Woman's Christian Temperance Union*, ed. Carolyn De Swarte Gifford (New York: Garland Publishing, Inc., 1987).

2. Kenneth E. Rowe, "Changing Partners: New Roles for Clergy and Laity in the Victorian Era," from Russell E. Richey, Kenneth E. Rowe, and Jean Miller Schmidt, *The Methodist Experience in America* (Nashville: Abingdon Press, forthcoming).

3. See Rosemary Skinner Keller, "Lay Women in the Protestant Tradition," in Rosemary Radford Ruether and Rosemary Skinner Keller, *The Nineteenth Century*, vol. 1 of *Women and Religion in America* (San Francisco: Harper & Row, 1981), 242-53, and Keller, "Creating a Sphere for Women," in *Women in New Worlds* (Nashville: Abingdon Press, 1981), 1:246-60.

4. Ladies' and Pastors' Christian Union, *First Annual Report, 1869* (Philadelphia: Methodist Episcopal Book Rooms, 1869), 23.

5. Ibid., 8.

6. Ibid., 33. Appeals for the L&PCU regularly noted that more than two-thirds of the church's members were women. The reference to the Gothic chapel describes Methodism's having gone "upscale" from its much more humble origins. By the middle of the nineteenth century Methodists were becoming predominantly middle-class, and more than a few were rich. Bishop Matthew Simpson's *Cyclopedia of Methodism* (New York: Everts & Stewart, 1876) celebrated this dramatic change of Methodism's social location with large numbers of engravings of rich Methodists and handsome churches.

7. Ibid., 35. The earliest call yet discovered (by Kenneth E. Rowe) for deaconesses as an order in the Methodist Episcopal Church was in *Zion's Herald and Wesleyan Journal*, March 17, 1852.

8. Ibid., 38.

9. Mrs. Annie Wittenmyer, *Women's Work for Jesus* (New York: Nelson & Phillips, 1873), 41. Although she did not name the Ladies' and Pastors' Christian Union, her description perfectly fit the new organization.

10. Ibid., 45-47.

11. Ibid., 99.

12. The Reverend I. W. Wiley, "Adaptation of Woman to Home Missionary Work," ibid., 81, 87.

13. MEC, 1872 *Journal* of the General Conference, 392-93. This General Conference played a major role in transforming the structure of the denomination from voluntary societies to mandated boards with regard to its benevolent institutions. Boards of Managers of the various agencies would be elected by the General Conference and program units mandated in local churches. It was no coincidence that the 1872 General Conference was the first to seat lay (male) delegates in the MEC.

14. Members of this committee, announced on May 15, 1872, were: I. W. Wiley, P. Jaques, T. H. Logan, R. L. Waite, W. F. Day, G. B. Jocelyn, J. B. Wakeley, D. A. Whedon, and J. E. Stillman. 1872 *Journal* of the General Conference, 210. (Additional resolutions asking about the propriety of striking male language and inserting the word *persons* in the Discipline so that women could be elected stewards, Sunday school superintendents, and members of the quarterly conferences were generally referred to the committee charged with revising the *Book of Discipline*, called the Committee on Revisals.)

15. Ibid., 392.

16. [Mrs. Susanna M. D. Fry] *Ladies' Repository* 32 (Feb. 1872): 109-12; *Ladies' Repository* 32 (Oct. 1872): 242-45, quote on 245.

17. Paul F. Douglass, *The Story of German Methodism: Biography of an Immigrant Soul* (New York: The Methodist Book Concern, 1939), 139.

18. J. H. Potts, "Ladies' and Pastors' Christian Union," *The Ladies' Repository* (May 1876): 392-96. A young people's catechism at about this time asked, "What are the benevolent societies of the Methodist Episcopal Church?" and included the L&PCU along with the Woman's Foreign Missionary Society in its answer.

19. *Minutes of the 93rd Session of the Philadelphia Annual Conference of the Methodist Episcopal Church* (Philadelphia: Methodist Episcopal Book and Publishing House, 1880), 53. Mauch Chunk is now Jim Thorpe, Pennsylvania.

20. Mary L. Griffith, *Women's Christian Work* (New York: Tract Dept., Phillips & Hunt, n.d.), 3, 5, 7. In 1880 Mary Griffith would address an eloquent appeal for women's rights in the church to the Methodist Episcopal General Conference. (See chapter 8.) She died in 1884 at the age of twenty-nine. "Measured by the standard of years her life was brief; but gauged by the standards of usefulness and activity, it was well filled" (Obituary notice, *Minutes* of the Philadelphia Annual Conference, 1885, 72-73).

21. The "bless and brighten" version is from Willard's annual address at the national convention of the WCTU in St. Louis (*Union Signal*, Oct. 30, 1884, 2). See Carolyn De Swarte Gifford, "Home Protection: The WCTU's Conversion to Woman Suffrage," in Janet Sharistanian, ed., *Gender, Ideology, and Action: Historical Perspectives on Women's Public Lives* (New York: Greenwood Press, 1986), 95-120. See also Gifford, ed., *The Ideal of "The New Woman" According to the Woman's Christian Temperance Union* (New York: Garland Publishing, 1987), Introduction, n.p.: "The 'New Woman' of the WCTU would be a 'True Woman' like her mother and grandmother before her, but her work would be in a far wider sphere than her mother and grandmother had inhabited."

22. For studies of Willard and the WCTU, see Ruth Bordin, *Frances Willard: A Biography* (Chapel Hill: University of North Carolina Press, 1986); Mary Earhart (Dillon), *Frances Willard: From Prayers to Politics* (Chicago: University of Chicago Press, 1944); and Barbara Leslie Epstein, *The Politics of Domesticity: Women, Evangelism, and Temperance in Nineteenth Century America* (Wesleyan University Press, 1981). The definitive interpreter of Frances Willard is now Carolyn De Swarte Gifford. In addition to "Home Protection," see two other foundational articles: " 'For God and Home and Native Land': The WCTU's Image of Woman in the Late Nineteenth Century," in Richey, Rowe, and Schmidt, *Perspectives on American Methodism*, 309-21; and " 'My Own Methodist Hive': Frances Willard's Faith as Disclosed in Her Journal, 1855–1870," in Keller, ed., *Spirituality and Social Responsibility*, 81-97. That Willard's Methodist faith was at the very core of her identity and life's work is persuasively demonstrated in Gifford, ed., *Writing Out My Heart: Selections from the Journal of Frances E. Willard, 1855–96* (Urbana: University of Illinois Press, 1995).

23. Gifford, "Home Protection," 96, 108-13; Gifford, ed., introduction to *Ideal of "The New Woman."*

24. Frances E. Willard, *Do Everything: A Handbook for the World's White Ribboners* (Chicago: The Woman's Temperance Publishing Association, 1895), 173. WCTU women wore as a badge a white ribbon, symbolizing purity, often entwined with a yellow ribbon signifying woman suffrage. Willard explained, "I do not know a White Ribbon woman who is not a Prohibitionist, a Woman-suffragist, a Purity worker, and an earnest sympathizer with the Labor Movement. [W]hoever works for one works for the other," ibid., 45.

25. Ibid., 91, 171.

26. Woman's foreign missionary societies were organized in the United Brethren Church in 1875, the Methodist Episcopal Church, South, in 1878, the Methodist Protestant Church in 1879, and the Evangelical Association in 1883. Separate woman's home missionary societies followed in 1880, MEC; 1886, MECS (expanded in 1890); and 1893, MPC. The (UB) Woman's Missionary Association extended its work to both foreign and home missions. All missionary work in the MECS was reorganized in 1910 into one Board of Missions, with the woman's work directed by the Woman's Missionary Council.

27. Clementina Butler, *Mrs. William Butler: Two Empires and a Kingdom* (New York: Methodist Book Concern, 1929), 107.

28. It is worth noting that most of the founders of these women's missionary societies were married to prominent church leaders. With few exceptions, married women were referred to by their husband's name in the records of these societies. I have used the woman's own name wherever it was possible to discover it.

29. Butler, *Mrs. William Butler*, 108; Louise McCoy North, *The Story of the New York Branch of the Woman's Foreign Missionary Society of the Methodist Episcopal Church* (New York: New York Branch, WFMS, MEC, 1926), 39; Miss Frances J. Baker, *The Story of the Woman's Foreign Missionary Society of the Methodist Episcopal Church, 1869–1895* (Cincinnati: Curts & Jennings, 1898), 22-24.

30. *The Heathen Woman's Friend* (Boston) 1:2 (July 1869): 12. The price of an annual subscription was thirty cents.

31. North, *Story of the N.Y. Branch*, 40; Butler, *Mrs. William Butler*, 109.

32. Mary Isham, *Valorous Ventures, A Record of Sixty and Six Years of the Woman's Foreign Missionary Society, Methodist Episcopal Church* (Boston: WFMS, MEC, 1936), 15-17.

33. Isham, *Valorous Ventures*, 17-18. Isabella Thoburn was a teacher who would go to Lucknow to do educational work with women; Clara Swain was a doctor going to Bareilly as a medical missionary.

34. Baker, *Story of the WFMS*, 25. Since 1867 Gilbert Haven had been editor of *Zion's Herald*, a New England Methodist newspaper. In this post he was well known as a crusader for racial equality and women's rights in both church and society. He would be elected a Methodist Episcopal bishop at his church's General Conference in 1872.

35. Often credited with devising this highly effective organizational pattern, the WCTU actually borrowed it from the earlier WFMS. Patricia Hill recognized the pioneering nature of this structure in "Heathen Women's Friends: The Role of Methodist Episcopal Women in the Women's Foreign Mission Movement, 1869–1915," *Methodist History* 19:3 (April 1981): 146-47. This would remain a hallmark of Methodist women's missionary organizations up to and including United Methodist Women and the Women's Division. See, for example, Theressa Hoover, *With Unveiled Face: Centennial Reflections on Women and Men in the Community of the Church* (New York: Women's Division, General Board of Global Ministries, The United Methodist Church, 1983), 10-11.

36. Butler, *Mrs. William Butler*, 112-15; Isham, *Valorous Ventures*, 22-23.

37. North, *Story of the N.Y. Branch*, 67-71. See also *Heathen Woman's Friend* 2:5 (November 1870): 56-57.

38. Ibid., 95.

39. *Heathen Woman's Friend* 2:2 (August 1870): 20.

40. North, *Story of the N.Y. Branch*, 104-5.

41. Ibid., 99-100.

42. Isham, *Valorous Ventures*, 28.

43. Ibid.

44. From the 50th Annual Report of the Topeka Branch, 1933, 42.

45. The quote about "traveling missionaries" is from an account by Mrs. M. J. Shelley, Treasurer of the Topeka Branch from 1883 to 1890; it appears in a chapter called "Reminiscences" in Baker's *Story of the WFMS*, 56. The tribute is from *Mary Clarke Nind and Her Work*, by Her Children (Chicago, 1906), 193.

46. For the full story of the struggle for laity rights for women, see chapter 10.

47. Joanne E. Carlson Brown, "Jennie Fowler Willing (1834–1916): Methodist Churchwoman and Reformer" (Ph.D. diss., Boston University, 1983), 17, 22, 110. See also Joanne Carlson Brown, "Shared Fire: The Flame Ignited by Jennie Fowler Willing," in *Spirituality and Social Responsibility*, ed. Rosemary Skinner Keller (Nashville: Abingdon Press, 1993), 99-115.

48. Brown, "Shared Fire," 100.

49. Ibid., 101-2. Willing served as one of several vice presidents of the WHMS from 1886 to 1893.

50. Carol Marie Herb, *The Light Along the Way: A Living History Through United Methodist Women's Magazines* (New York: General Board of Ministries, UMC, 1995), viii.

51. *Heathen Woman's Friend* (April 1870): 86.

52. North, *Story of the N.Y. Branch*, 191-93.

53. Ibid., 194; *Heathen Woman's Friend* (January 1874): 781. On "what organizing did for women," see Brown, "Jennie Fowler Willing," 80-82, and Keller, "Creating a Sphere for Women," 251-60. In "Lay Women," 244-46, Keller examined "woman's work for woman" from the perspectives of "the senders," "those who

were sent," and "the receivers." The women missionaries (those who were sent) are discussed later in this chapter.

54. Mrs. T. L. Tomkinson, *Twenty Years' History of the Woman's Home Missionary Society of the Methodist Episcopal Church, 1880–1900*, 2nd ed. (Cincinnati: Woman's Home Missionary Society of the MEC, 1908), 9.

55. Ibid., 22.

56. Ibid., 27.

57. In her address at the third annual meeting of the society in Cleveland in October 1884 (after its official recognition by the MEC General Conference in May), Lucy Webb Hayes insisted that "the claims upon us for Christian civilization" in the home missions field were no less pressing than those of "the heathen of foreign lands." Her major theme could be summed up in one sentence: "We believe that the character of a people depends mainly on its homes." "Addresses by Mrs. Hayes," in *Lucy Webb Hayes: A Memorial Sketch* (Cincinnati: Woman's Home Missionary Society, 1890), 81-84.

58. Ruth Esther Meeker, *Six Decades of Service, 1880–1940: A History of The Woman's Home Missionary Society of the Methodist Episcopal Church* (Cincinnati: Continuing Corporation of The Woman's Home Missionary Society of the Methodist Episcopal Church, 1969), 19, 29. The report of the WHMS to the MEC General Conference in 1896 detailed no fewer than eighteen divisions of the work, including bureaus for immigrants, "Orientals," industrial homes and schools in the South, Alaska, city missions, and a deaconess bureau. "Report of the Woman's Home Missionary Society," *Journal of the General Conference of the Methodist Episcopal Church* (1896), 675-86.

59. See Sara Joyce Myers, "Southern Methodist Women Leaders and Church Missions, 1878–1910" (Ph.D. diss., Emory University, 1990). Myers's dissertation examines the five leaders who established these societies in terms of the categories of "True Womanhood."

60. For more on the lives of Margaret Kelley and Juliana Hayes, see Rev. R. K. Brown, *Life of Mrs. M.L. Kelley* (n.p., 1889), and Sarah Frances Stringfield Butler, *Life, Reminiscences, and Journal, Mrs. Juliana Hayes* (Nashville: Publishing House of the Methodist Episcopal Church, South, 1904). Juliana Hayes, from Font Hill, Virginia, was sixty-five years old when she was appointed president. After her husband's death she moved to Baltimore in 1870. As she traveled through many states alone organizing societies, her attitude was: "This is God's work; it cannot fail" (Butler, *Mrs. Juliana Hayes*, 20).

61. Mrs. F[rank] A. [Sarah Frances Stringfield] Butler, *Mrs. D. H. M'Gavock: Life-Sketch and Thoughts* (Nashville: Publishing House of the Methodist Episcopal Church, South, 1896), 9, 16, 190-91.

62. Butler explained, "The women of the M. E. Church, South, had never before felt that there were any duties for them to perform outside of their own congregations, and indeed many felt that even in this they were venturing beyond the limits of womanly propriety" (Butler, *Mrs. D. H. M'Gavock*, 38).

63. Ibid., 95.

64. Ibid., 96.

65. Ibid., 124-35, 171.

66. Myers, "Southern Methodist Women Leaders," 176-80.

67. These later developments are followed in chapters 9 (deaconesses and training schools) and 10 (laity rights for women).

68. Ethel W. Born, *By My Spirit: The Story of Methodist Protestant Women in Mis-*

sion 1879–1939 (New York: Women's Division, Board of Global Ministries, United Methodist Church, 1990).

69. Ibid., 64.

70. Donald K. Gorrell, " 'A New Impulse': Progress in Lay Leadership and Service by Women of the United Brethren in Christ and the Evangelical Association," in *Women in New Worlds*, 1:233-45. Quote is on 233.

71. *Woman's Evangel* 1:1 (January 1882): 20-21.

72. Ibid., 235.

73. Ibid., 242.

74. See, for example, "Appeal to the Ladies of the Methodist Episcopal Church," *The Heathen Woman's Friend* 1:1 (May 1869): 1-2. Probably the first single woman sent overseas by the Board of Missions of the MEC was Sophronia Farrington, who accompanied two married couples to Liberia in 1834. Although she remained in Liberia after one couple died and the other returned to the United States, she was forced to end her missionary service in early 1835 because of severe illness (Elaine Magalis, *Conduct Becoming to a Woman*, 15). Mrs. Clementina Butler and Mrs. Lois Parker, wives of Methodist missionaries to India, were instrumental in the founding of the WFMS (MEC) in 1869.

75. Carolyn De Swarte Gifford, "Isabella Thoburn (1840–1901)," in *Something More than Human: Biographies of Leaders in American Methodist Higher Education*, ed. Charles E. Cole (Nashville: United Methodist Board of Higher Education and Ministry, 1986), 229-43. See also Earl Kent Brown, "Isabella Thoburn," *Methodist History* 22:4 (July 1984): 207-20. Thoburn's vision for woman's work in India is powerfully expressed in her addresses to the second and third decennial missionary conferences in Calcutta (1882) and Bombay (1893), India. Excerpts from these addresses were published in the *Heathen Woman's Friend*. The quote is from *Report of the Second Decennial Missionary Conference held at Calcutta, 1882-83* (Calcutta: Baptist Mission Press, 1883), 188-95.

76. Laura Haygood came from a prominent Methodist family in Atlanta who were active in Trinity Church. She was president of the home mission society organized there in 1882 to work among the poor. Her brother, Atticus Green Haygood, was a pastor and later bishop of the MECS, an outstanding educator, and a pioneer in improving race relations. He was the author of *Our Brother in Black* (1881). On Laura Haygood see Oswald Eugene Brown and Anna Muse Brown, *Life and Letters of Laura Askew Haygood* (Nashville: Publishing House of the M. E. Church, South, 1904).

77. Adrian A. Bennett, "Doing More Than They Intended: Southern Methodist Women in China, 1878–1898," in *Women in New Worlds*, 2:249-67. See also Jane Hunter, *The Gospel of Gentility: American Women Missionaries in Turn-of-the-Century China* (New Haven: Yale University Press, 1984).

78. Born, *By My Spirit*, 5-13.

79. Helen Griffith, *Dauntless in Mississippi: The Life of Sarah A. Dickey, 1838–1904* (South Hadley, Mass.: Dinosaur Press, 1965). Sarah Dickey was ordained a United Brethren minister by the Miami Annual Conference in 1896.

80. Patricia Hill, "Heathen Women's Friends," 148-49.

81. The following works are important for a consideration of the women's foreign missionary movement in this larger perspective: Joan Jacobs Brumberg, "The Ethnological Mirror: American Evangelical Women and Their Heathen Sisters, 1870–1910," in *Women and the Structure of Society: Selected Research*

from the Fifth Berkshire Conference on the History of Women, ed. Barbara J. Harris and JoAnn K. McNamara (Durham: Duke University Press, 1984), 108-28; Patricia R. Hill, *The World Their Household: The American Woman's Foreign Mission Movement and Cultural Transformation, 1870–1920* (Ann Arbor: University of Michigan Press, 1985); and Jane Hunter, *The Gospel of Gentility: American Women Missionaries in Turn-of-the-Century China.*

82. Susan Hill Lindley, *'You Have Stept Out of Your Place': A History of Women and Religion in America* (Louisville: Westminster John Knox Press, 1996), 88.

83. Ann Taves, "Mothers and Children and the Legacy of Mid-Nineteenth-Century American Christianity," *Journal of Religion* 67 (April 1987): 203-19.

NOTES TO CHAPTER 8

1. *Daily Christian Advocate,* 25 May 1880, 1.

2. *Journal of the General Conference of the Methodist Episcopal Church* (New York: Nelson & Phillips, 1876), 96, 108, 113, 144, 214, 252.

3. D. H. E., "The Woman Question in the Church," *Zion's Herald* 46:47 (November 25, 1869): 554.

4. Mrs. J[ennie] F[owler] Willing, "What Shall American Women Do Next?" *Zion's Herald* 47:21 (May 26, 1870): 242.

5. Ibid.

6. According to John C. Coons, *A Brief History of the Methodist Protestant Church in Indiana* (n.p., 1939), 42, Davison was ordained deacon in 1866 along with her husband and another male candidate. Although the ordination of women was not supported by the 1871 General Conference of the Methodist Protestant Church, she apparently continued to preach until her death in 1877. See also William T. Noll, "Women as Clergy and Laity in the 19th Century Methodist Protestant Church," *Methodist History* 15:2 (Jan. 1977): 110.

7. See John O. Foster, *Life and Labors of Mrs. Maggie Newton Van Cott, the First Lady Licensed to Preach in the Methodist Episcopal Church in the United States* (Cincinnati: Hitchcock and Walden, 1872). According to the preface, Mrs. Van Cott told her experiences to John O. Foster, a member of the Illinois Conference, while she was convalescing during a speaking tour in Illinois. This work was republished in 1876 under a different title, *The Harvest and the Reaper: Reminiscences of Revival Work of Mrs. Maggie N. Van Cott, the First Lady Licensed to Preach in the Methodist Episcopal Church in the United States* (New York: N. Tibbals & Sons, Publishers, 1876). Both editions included an Introduction by Gilbert Haven and an essay on "Woman's Place in the Gospel" by David Sherman.

8. Foster, *Life and Labors,* 67. See also Janet S. Everhart, "Maggie Newton Van Cott: The Methodist Episcopal Church Considers the Question of Women Clergy," in *Women in New Worlds* (Nashville: Abingdon Press, 1982), 2:300-317.

9. Foster, *Life and Labors,* 152-53.

10. When people misunderstood and misrepresented her as a woman preacher, she once prayed to die and be removed from them. However, she heard "a consoling voice whispering in her soul, 'My grace is sufficient' " (Foster, *Life and Labors,* 168).

11. *Autobiography of A[lonzo] C[hurch] Morehouse* (New York: Tibbals Book Company, 1895), 120 (in a chapter entitled "Mrs. Van Cott's Call").

12. Foster, *Life and Labors,* 184.

13. *Morehouse Autobiography,* 123.

14. Ibid., 125; cf. Foster, *Life and Labors,* 206.

15. Foster, *Life and Labors*, 221.
16. Everhart, "Maggie Newton Van Cott," 303-4.
17. *Zion's Herald* 46:42 (21 October 1869): 500.
18. Ibid., 46:43 (28 October 1869): 510.
19. *The Methodist* (New York), 9 April 1870, 1. The article, "from a New-England Correspondent," began: "Probably Mrs. Van Cott never addressed so august or critical an assembly as on Tuesday evening, March 22d. The preachers of the New-England Conference had just arrived, and, in consideration of her rising fame, signal success, and the probability of her being proposed for admission as a probationer to the New-England Conference, they all rushed to Union-street Methodist Episcopal church to hear her."
20. *Zion's Herald* 47:14 (7 April 1870): 167. Haven, editor of *Zion's Herald* from 1867 until his election to the episcopacy of the Methodist Episcopal Church in 1872, was always outspoken on justice issues. He went on to say, "Though the Conference, by a small majority, tabled a resolution in agreement with this act, yet this work of Trinity will abide, and bring forth much fruit, and the almost fifty members that voted in accordance with the action of the Church, will grow to a sweeping majority that will yet by vote praise this Church for its leadership in this Christian work" (ibid).
21. *The Christian Advocate* (New York), 7 April 1870, 106.
22. Ibid., 108.
23. Ibid., 304-5. In his Introduction to *Life and Labors*, Gilbert Haven testified to the authenticity of Van Cott's call to preach and praised her as "the most popular, most laborious, and most successful preacher in the Methodist Episcopal Church" (xxiii). Likewise in his essay "Woman's Place in the Gospel," David Sherman referred to early Methodism's openness to the gifts of women and urged that it remained for his generation of Methodists to "admit her [Van Cott] fully to the privileges of the pulpit." He went on to describe her preaching as "bold, imaginative, electrical," worthy of being compared with (celebrity preacher) Henry Ward Beecher! (xxxviii-xxxix).
24. Hartzell was pastor of Ames Chapel from 1870 to 1873, when he left to become presiding elder of the southern Louisiana district and to found the *Southwestern Christian Advocate*. He was an outspoken advocate of black rights in church and society. He would serve as secretary of the Methodist Freedmen's Aid Society in Cincinnati from 1882 until his election as Methodist Episcopal Bishop for Africa in 1896. See James M. McPherson, *The Abolitionist Legacy: From Reconstruction to the NAACP* (Princeton, N.J.: Princeton University Press, 1975), 229-38, 265-66. Of Maggie Van Cott, Hartzell said: "Mrs. Van Cott as a regularly licensed preacher in the Methodist Episcopal Church is entitled to ordination, and we advocate it, in her particular case. . . . Eligibility to ordination depends on the spiritual power of the candidate to do good" (*Southwestern Christian Advocate*, 26 March 1874, 2, quoted in Everhart, "Maggie Newton Van Cott," 307).
25. Ibid., 308, quoting from the *Minutes of the California Annual Conference* (1874), 21.
26. *Christian Advocate* (New York) 48:38 (18 September 1873): 300. Cf. Everhart, "Maggie Newton Van Cott," 308. Everhart comments in a footnote that some presiding elders were obviously becoming nervous about renewing women's licenses to preach. She claims that Mary Lathrop and Mary McAllister, both of the Albion District, Michigan Conference, had their licenses "held in abeyance" in 1876, and that Jennie Fowler Willing's license, granted in 1873 from the Joliet Dis-

trict of the Rock River Conference and renewed in 1874 and 1875, was not renewed in 1876 (Notes, 409).

27. Janet Everhart claimed at least fourteen on the basis of her own research ("Maggie Newton Van Cott," 309). In her introduction to *The Defense of Women's Rights to Ordination in the Methodist Episcopal Church* (New York: Garland Publishing, 1987), n.p. Carolyn De Swarte Gifford claimed that "over seventy" women received such licenses in the 1870s. Gifford explains: "Two separate committees of the GC ruled along with the bishops of the church that women were ineligible for either clergy or lay rights. The opinion of a minority report submitted to GC stated that it found nothing in the *Discipline* contrary to women being licensed to preach. The issue was not voted on by the GC as a whole at its 1876 quadrennial meeting." While Gifford does not cite a source for her figure of "over seventy" preacher's licenses to women in the 1870s, it may be William T. Noll, "A Welcome in the Ministry: The 1920 and 1924 General Conferences Debate Clergy Rights for Women," *Methodist History* 30:2 (January 1992): 91.

28. In an undated and unpublished statement of Anna Howard Shaw found in her papers at the Radcliffe Library in Cambridge, Massachusetts, Shaw recalled that the bishop of the New England Conference at the time she entered Boston "was very favorable to women and had promised to ordain me, but, unfortunately, he died before I graduated and the new Bishop was bitterly opposed to women ministers." The favorable bishop was almost certainly Bishop Gilbert Haven, who died January 3, 1880. See Anna Howard Shaw, "My Ordination," ed. Nancy N. Bahmueller, *Methodist History* 14:2 (January 1976): 125-31.

29. Anna Howard Shaw, *The Story of a Pioneer* (New York: Harper & Brothers, 1915), 59.

30. Ibid., 65.

31. Shaw recalled, "There was at that time a movement on foot to license women to preach in the Methodist Church, and Dr. Peck was ambitious to be the first presiding elder to have a woman ordained for the Methodist ministry" (*Story of a Pioneer*, 58).

32. Ibid., 83.

33. Ibid., 85-87.

34. Ibid., 108-19.

35. See Kenneth E. Rowe, "Evangelism and Social Reform in the Pastoral Ministry of Anna Oliver, 1868–1886," in *Spirituality and Social Responsibility*, ed. Keller (Nashville: Abingdon Press, 1993), 117-36.

36. Ibid., 117-24.

37. *Boston Globe* (8 June 1876), 2, col. 4; quoted in ibid., 125.

38. Kenneth E. Rowe, "The Ordination of Women: Round One; Anna Oliver and the General Conference of 1880," in Richey, Rowe, and Schmidt, eds., *Perspectives*, 298-308. (Quote is on 299.) On her ministry in Passaic, see also Rowe, "Evangelism and Social Reform," 126-27.

39. Rowe, "The Ordination of Women," 300.

40. Rowe, "Evangelism and Social Reform," 128.

41. Rowe, "The Ordination of Women," 302.

42. Ibid.

43. Shaw, *Story of a Pioneer*, 123-24.

44. As Kenneth Rowe pointed out, there is no evidence to suggest that the pamphlet was read into the Conference record. Only Drew and Garrett reported having copies of this pamphlet. Rowe, "Ordination of Women," n. 21 in *Perspectives*, 565.

45. Pamphlet entitled "Test Case on the Ordination of Women, appealed from the New England Conference to General Conference," Rev. Miss Anna Oliver (1880).

46. This petition was noted, but not published, in the 1880 General Conference *Journal*, 262, 264. It was printed in an appendix to Anna Oliver's "Test Case," and is quoted in Rowe, "Ordination of Women," 304.

47. General Conference *Journal*, 27 May 1880, 353, and in *Daily Christian Advocate*, 22 May 1880, 79, col. 6. Bishop Andrews had ruled as follows: "In my judgment the law of the Church does not authorize the ordination of women; I, therefore, am not at liberty to submit to the vote of the Conference the vote to elect women to orders."

48. Noted in General Conference *Journal*, 25 May 1880, 316; printed in *Daily Christian Advocate*, 26 May 1880, 90.

49. Ibid. The original manuscripts of both these reports are in the General Conference papers at Drew; both are quoted in Rowe, "Ordination of Women," 70-71.

50. See an article by Barbara Campbell in *The Chimes*, a quarterly newsletter of United Methodist Women in the Southern Illinois Conference, Fall (1978), 4. It is based on information gathered from the files of the now defunct *Olney Times*, 11 June 1879; 2 June 1880; 18 August 1880; 25 May 1881. The June 2, 1880, article quoted James M. Buckley in the deliberations of the Itinerancy Committee as follows: "The Rev. Dr. Buckley warned the brethren that if they once opened the doors, the old maids would throng in from all the other denominations, feminine arts would be brought to bear on the Presiding Elders to secure good appointments, scandals would arise, the road to the pulpit would be choked with voluble and emotional women and there would be the mischief to pay generally."

51. Rowe, "Ordination of Women," 71-72; "Evangelism and Social Reform," 128-31. Buckley, as editor of the New York *Christian Advocate*, had said of her in the March 1883 issue (p. 1), "The attempt to force the ordination of women upon the Church by buying a church, and making its re-transfer to our Denomination conditional upon a change without warrant in Scripture, precedent, necessity, or general desire, did not succeed."

52. Elizabeth Cady Stanton et al., *History of Woman Suffrage* (New York: Arno and the New York Times, 1969), 4:206-7; quoted in Rowe, "Evangelism and Social Reform," 131.

53. Shaw, "My Ordination," 125-31; Shaw, *Story of a Pioneer*, 124-30.

54. William T. Noll, " 'You and I Are Partners': A Heritage for Clergy Couples in Nineteenth Century American Methodism," *Methodist History* 26:1 (October 1987): 44-53.

55. *Minutes* of the 25th Session of the Central Illinois Annual Conference of the Church of the United Brethren in Christ (September 11–15, 1889): 5-8, 18-19; also her obituary notice in the *Religious Telescope* (14 October 1944). On United Brethren women and ordination see Jim Will, "The Ordination of Women—The Development in the Church of the United Brethren in Christ," in *"Woman's Rightful Place": Women in United Methodist History*, ed. Donald K. Gorrell (Dayton: United Theological Seminary, 1980), 27-40. The African Methodist Episcopal Zion Church, an independent black Methodist church (1820), ordained Mrs. Julia A. J. Foote a deacon in 1894, and an elder in 1900. For her spiritual autobiography, see Andrews, ed. *Sisters of the Spirit*, 161-234.

56. Carolyn De Swarte Gifford, ed., *The Defense of Women's Rights to Ordination in the Methodist Episcopal Church* (New York: Garland Publishing, 1987), intro. Willard

elaborated eloquently on her point: "We stand once more at the parting of the roads; shall the bold resolute men among our clergy win the day and give ordination to women, or shall women take this matter into their own hands? Fondly do women hope, and earnestly do they pray, that the churches they love may not drive them to this extremity. But if her conservative sons do not yield to the leadings of Providence and the importunities of their more progressive brothers they may be well assured that deliverance shall arise from another place, for the women of this age are surely coming to their kingdom, and humanity is to be comforted out of Zion as one whom his mother comforteth." Frances E. Willard, *Woman in the Pulpit* (Chicago: Woman's Temperance Publication Association, 1889); reprinted in ibid. Quote is on 56-57.

57. Ibid., 172.

58. James M. Buckley, "Letting in the Light," *Christian Advocate* (New York), 2 October 1890, 643-44. It is probably no accident that women were granted preacher's licenses again in the Methodist Episcopal Church in 1920, the same year that the Nineteenth Amendment went into effect, granting women the right to vote. It is also interesting to note that James M. Buckley died on February 8, 1920.

59. The Presbyterians gave full clergy rights to women that same year. The granting of "partial status" is discussed in chapter 12; for the struggle to win full clergy rights in the Methodist Church, see the Epilogue.

Notes to Chapter 9

1. Lucy Rider Meyer, *Deaconesses, Biblical, Early Church, European, American, with the Story of How the Work Began in the Chicago Training School, for City, Home, and Foreign Missions, and the Chicago Deaconess Home*, 3rd ed., rev. and enl. (Cincinnati: Cranston & Stowe, 1889), 94, 100.

2. Isabelle Horton, *High Adventure: [The] Life of Lucy Rider Meyer* (New York: Methodist Book Concern, 1928), 24-25.

3. Mary Agnes Theresa Dougherty, "The Methodist Deaconess, 1885–1918: A Study in Religious Feminism" (Ph.D. diss., University of California Davis, 1979), 34. On the history of the deaconess movement in the broader United Methodist tradition, see also her book, *My Calling to Fulfill: Deaconesses in the United Methodist Tradition* (New York: Women's Division, General Board of Global Ministries, UMC, 1997).

4. Horton, *High Adventure*, 58-63, 73.

5. Ibid., 78.

6. Dougherty, "Methodist Deaconess," 41. Raised among Pennsylvania Quakers, Josiah Shelly Meyer's life had been dedicated to both religion and business. In addition to his work with the YMCA, he attended McCormick Theological Seminary in 1884 and served as student pastor of a mission church. See Horton, *High Adventure*, 88-90.

7. Rider Meyer, *Deaconesses*, 100-104.

8. Ibid., 106-8; Dougherty, "Methodist Deaconess," 42-44. *The Message* displayed the slogan of CTS, "Lo, I have set before thee an open door," and declared the threefold purpose of the School: to give instruction in the Bible, to provide training for "lady missionaries," and to encourage and develop the work of city missions (Horton, *High Adventure*, 120). The title of this publication changed over the years to *The Message and Deaconess World* in 1893, *The Message and Deaconess Advocate* in 1894, and finally *The Deaconess Advocate* in 1903.

9. Rider Meyer, *Deaconesses*, 115-18.

10. Horton, *High Adventure*, 117.

11. Ibid., 122-32, 137.

12. Quoted in Rider Meyer, *Deaconesses*, 148-49.

13. Horton, *High Adventure*, 141-44. (At the time she wrote this announcement Rider Meyer was still in bed after giving birth to a son, Shelly.) Isabella Thoburn was the sister of the Reverend James M. Thoburn, a Methodist Episcopal minister and member of the Pittsburgh Conference, who had served as a missionary to India since 1859. At the 1888 General Conference of the MEC he was elected missionary bishop for southern Asia; he would be an important advocate for the deaconess office in the MEC.

14. *Journal* of the General Conference, MEC (1888), 435.

15. Carolyn De Swarte Gifford, ed., *The American Deaconess Movement in the Early Twentieth Century* (New York: Garland Publishing, 1987), Introduction, n.p.

16. See chapter 10 for a full examination of women's struggle for laity rights in the Methodist family of denominations.

17. Gifford, ed., *American Deaconess Movement*, Intro.

18. Lucy Rider Meyer, "The Mother in the Church," *The Message and Deaconess Advocate* 17:10 (Oct. 1901): 5-6, 11-12.

19. Dougherty, "Methodist Deaconess," 46. See also Horton, *High Adventure*, 154-57.

20. Dougherty, "Methodist Deaconess," 147.

21. Reeves returned to Chicago in 1897 to become superintendent of the Methodist Episcopal Old People's Home there. Still serving in that capacity she celebrated the twenty-fifth anniversary of her work as a deaconess on June 4, 1914. She was widely hailed as the "veteran in deaconess service." See "A Memorial to Isabelle A. Reeves, Superintendent of The Methodist Episcopal Old People's Home, Chicago" (prepared under the direction of The Board of Managers of the Home [1916], 31); *The Deaconess Advocate* (June 1914): 9.

22. Rider Meyer, *Deaconesses*, 210. Bishop Ninde went on to affirm the urgency of "parity" for women—in the churches, schools, and learned professions.

23. Lucy Rider Meyer, "Deaconesses and Their Work," in *Woman in Missions: Papers and Addresses presented at the Woman's Congress of Missions, October 2-4, 1893, in the Hall of Columbus, Chicago* (American Tract Society, 1894), 182-97.

24. Ibid. See also Catherine M. Prelinger and Rosemary S. Keller, "The Function of Female Bonding: The Restored Diaconessate of the Nineteenth Century," in *Women in New Worlds* (Nashville: Abingdon Press, 1982), 2:318-37.

25. Jane M. Bancroft, *Deaconesses in Europe and Their Lessons for America* (New York: Hunt & Eaton, 1889). The motherhouse of the German Lutheran deaconess movement was at Kaiserswerth. Established in 1836 by Lutheran pastor Theodor Fliedner, it became a model for the deaconess movement in a number of American Protestant denominations.

26. Ruth Esther Meeker, *Six Decades of Service, 1880–1940: A History of The Woman's Home Missionary Society of the Methodist Episcopal Church* (Cincinnati: Women's Home Missionary Society, 1969), 91.

27. "Jane Marie Bancroft Robinson," in *Notable American Women: A Biographical Dictionary*, ed. Edward T. James et al. (Cambridge: Belknap Press of Harvard University Press, 1971), 3:183-84.

28. Horton, *High Adventure*, 190.

29. Dougherty, "Methodist Deaconess," 52. Dougherty saw this disagreement

over strategy as similar to that in the woman suffrage movement, which split in 1869 into the National and the American Woman Suffrage Associations.

30. Ibid., 57-60.

31. Ibid., 62. The WHMS claimed priority on the basis of its having appointed a committee in November 1883 to start a training school for mission workers and appropriated a thousand dollars toward the project. Its leaders later asserted that "the connection of Mrs. Lucy Rider Meyer with the Training School in Chicago did not take place until the summer of 1885," nearly two years after their organization had begun to plan for the school. See "The Early History of Deaconess Work and Training Schools for Women in American Methodism, 1883–1885" (Detroit: Hines Press for the Woman's Home Missionary Society, MEC, c. 1912), reprinted in Gifford, ed., *American Deaconess Movement*, 10.

32. Horton, *High Adventure*, 230-31.

33. Rider Meyer suffered a significant loss as a result of this General Conference. When the General Deaconess Board decided that only single women could be licensed as deaconesses, Mrs. Meyer, who had been the first woman to wear the deaconess uniform, could no longer wear it. The personal pain of this loss was clear in her response. On returning to Chicago, Rider Meyer handed her deaconess bonnet to her secretary and said simply, "Take it. I shall never wear it again." According to her biographer, only a very few of her closest friends understood what it had cost her to give it up. Horton, *High Adventure*, 197.

34. Dougherty, "Methodist Deaconess," 67.

35. Ibid., 4. See also her important articles, "The Social Gospel According to Phoebe," in *Women in New Worlds* (Nashville: Abingdon Press, 1981), 1:200-216, and "The Methodist Deaconess: A Case of Religious Feminism," *Methodist History* 21:2 (January 1983): 90-98.

36. Dougherty, "Methodist Deaconess," 4.

37. *Deaconess Advocate* 29:5 (May 1914): 11.

38. Isabelle Horton, *The Burden of the City* (New York: Fleming H. Revell Company, 1904). The book was designed as the basic text for an interdenominational home mission study course. See especially pages 126-28.

39. Ibid.

40. Grace Scribner and then, after she was killed in 1922 by a hit-and-run driver, Winifred Chappell served as joint editor with Harry F. Ward of the *Social Service Bulletin* of MFSS.

41. Virginia Lieson Brereton, "Preparing Women for the Lord's Work," in *Women in New Worlds*, 1:178-99.

42. Mabel K. Howell, "The Service Motive" (manuscript, Scarritt College, n.d.), 35; quoted in Brereton, "Preparing Women for the Lord's Work," 186.

43. Brereton, "Preparing Women for the Lord's Work," 187.

44. Noreen Dunn Tatum, *A Crown of Service: A Story of Woman's Work in the Methodist Episcopal Church, South, from 1878–1940* (Nashville: Parthenon Press, 1960), 325.

45. Quoted in ibid., 326.

46. Ibid., 328-31.

47. Dougherty, "Methodist Deaconess," 82.

48. Ibid., 88, 91.

49. Ibid., 117, 120.

50. Ibid., 122.

51. Ibid., 125-34; Lucy Rider Meyer was quoted from the *Deaconess Advocate* (May 1905): 9.

52. *Deaconess Advocate* (April 1914): 3.

53. William E. Blackstone, who became treasurer of CTS in 1885, taught a class on foreign missions for a number of years, and served as a trustee until 1904, was also one of the early leaders of the Fundamentalist movement during and after World War I. A biblical literalist, he particularly objected to Rider Meyer's views on the Bible. See Dougherty, "Methodist Deaconess," 175-78.

54. Ibid., 195.

Notes to Chapter 10

1. Carolyn De Swarte Gifford, ed., *The Debate in the Methodist Episcopal Church Over Laity Rights for Women* (New York: Garland Publishing, 1987), intro.

2. See his biography by George Preston Mains, *James Monroe Buckley* (New York: Methodist Book Concern, 1917).

3. *The Encyclopedia of World Methodism*, ed. Nolan B. Harmon (Nashville: United Methodist Publishing House, 1974), 1:349.

4. Mains, *James Monroe Buckley*, 127.

5. Ibid., 137.

6. Lay delegates were admitted only after a long and bitter battle. After the exodus of the Methodist Protestants in 1830, the reform movement was nurtured for more than twenty years by the Reverend George Crooks of Philadelphia. In the 1860s Crooks moved to New York where he founded and edited an independent Methodist newspaper (*The Methodist*) to advocate lay rights. At the 1852 General Conference of the MEC, a special Committee on Lay Delegation had concluded that the laity already had ample opportunities to serve their church and that most of them opposed such a change. The committee's report was overwhelmingly adopted. By the 1860 General Conference, opinion in the church was beginning to change. The question of lay delegation was referred to a churchwide vote of both clergy and "laymen" (only male church members over age twenty-one), in which the proposed plan was defeated. A lay rights convention held concurrently with the 1864 General Conference maintained that the referendum was in no way decisive. By the time of the 1868 General Conference the demand of the laity for representation had become "irresistible." See Kenneth E. Rowe, "Power to the People: George Richard Crooks, *The Methodist*, and Lay Representation in the Methodist Episcopal Church," *Methodist History* 13:3 (April 1975): 145-76.

7. Dr. David Sherman in the Appendix to Alpha J. Kynett, *Our Laity: and Their Equal Rights Without Distinction of Sex* (Cincinnati: Cranston and Curts, 1896), 39-40; reprinted in Gifford, ed., *The Debate in the Methodist Episcopal Church Over Laity Rights for Women*. According to both Sherman and Kynett, the motion to amend carried by a vote of 142 to 70.

8. Kynett, *Our Laity*, 7.

9. Gifford's Introduction is helpful in clarifying this point in *The Debate in the Methodist Episcopal Church Over Laity Rights for Women*.

10. See, for example, Dr. David H. Moore, "The Question of Intention," in the Appendix to Kynett, *Our Laity*, 33-36.

11. Kynett, *Our Laity*, 8-9.

12. "The General Conference has submitted the decision of the question of Lay Representation in our Church to a vote of all the members thereof, of either sex,

above the age of twenty-one years. By this, we, as well as our fathers, husbands, brothers, and sons, have been made interested parties."

13. *The Methodist* (New York), 5 June 1869, 183. It was generally agreed that the women's vote had helped appreciably to secure lay representation.

14. Quoted in Kynett, *Our Laity*, 18.

15. Gifford, Introduction, *The Debate in the Methodist Episcopal Church Over Laity Rights for Women*.

16. For Nind's account of the efforts to elect Newman and herself, see "Elected to the ME General Conference," in *Mary Clarke Nind and Her Work* by Her Children (Chicago: Published for the Woman's Foreign Missionary Society by J. Newton Nind, 1906), 41-49.

17. "For the first time in our history several 'elect ladies' appear, regularly certified from Electoral Conferences, as lay delegates to this body. . . . If women were included in the original constitutional provision for lay delegates they are here by constitutional right. If they were not so included it is beyond the power of this body to give them membership lawfully except by the formal amendment of the Constitution, which cannot be effected without the consent of the Annual Conferences" (Address of the Bishops, *Journal* of the General Conference, [1888], 51).

18. Gifford, Introduction, *Debate*.

19. *Journal* of the General Conference (1888), 462.

20. The vote was "ayes, ministerial, 159; lay, 78; noes, ministerial, 122; lay, 76; a total of ayes, 237; noes, 198." *Mary Clarke Nind*, 47; *Journal* of the General Conference (1888), 104-6.

21. *Mary Clarke Nind*, 46.

22. Ibid.

23. Ibid., 47.

24. Frances E. Willard, *Glimpses of Fifty Years: The Autobiography of An American Woman* (Chicago: Woman's Temperance Publication Association, 1889), 615-21. (Quote is on 621.) The level of her pain and disappointment was, however, clear in the lines preceding these: "But when I read that the lay delegates gave a majority against the admission of women, and remembered that the vote of women, as they well knew, at the time of the debate on the eligibility of the laity to the General Conference, had forced open its doors to the laymen who now deliberately voted to exclude women, I had no more spirit in me. Once more it was a case of 'Thou, too, Brutus!'"

25. Gifford, Introduction, *Debate*.

26. [James M. Buckley,] " 'The Rights' of Women and Others," in *"Because They Are Women" and Other Editorials From "The Christian Advocate" on The Admission of Women to the General Conference* (New York: Hunt and Eaton, 1891), 5; reprinted in Gifford, *The Debate in the Methodist Episcopal Church Over Laity Rights for Women*.

27. Gifford, Introduction, *Debate*. Gifford explained that, at the time Buckley wrote, the number of delegates to General Conference was based in part on proportional representation, according to the numbers of church members in each annual conference. Although there were two (male) lay delegates representing each annual conference, the (also male) clergy delegates were chosen on a proportional basis.

28. Buckley, "Letting in the Light," and "Because They Are Women," in *"Because They Are Women,"* 25-26, and Reverend G[eorge] W. Hughey, *The Admission of Women to the General Conference* (Chicago: Press of WTPA, 1891), 100; both works reprinted in Gifford, *The Debate in the Methodist Episcopal Church Over Laity Rights for Women*.

29. The only restriction indicated in the 1872 *Discipline* regarding lay delegation was that "no layman shall be chosen a delegate either to the Electoral Conference or to the General Conference" who was not at least twenty-five years old, or had not been a member of the Church in full connection for five consecutive years preceding the election (1872 *Discipline*, [part I, chap. 1, par. 62] cited in Kynett, *Our Laity*, 6).

30. Kynett, *Our Laity*, 24.

31. Ibid., 10.

32. Ibid., 32. As David H. Moore had explained in the Introduction, the Ohio Lay Electoral Conference had chosen Mrs. Jane Field Bashford as a lay delegate, and the Foochow Lay Electoral Conference had sent Miss Lydia A. Trimble.

33. David H. Moore, Introduction, 2-3.

34. Gifford, Introduction, *Debate*. See also Karen Heetderks Strong, "Ecclesiastical Suffrage: The First Women Participants at General Conference in the Antecedents of the United Methodist Church," *Methodist History*, 25:1 (October 1986): 30-31. I compared Strong's list with those in the *Journal* of the General Conference of the MEC (1904): 25-33, 56-71.

35. William T. Noll, "Laity Rights and Leadership: Winning Them for Women in the Methodist Protestant Church, 1860–1900," in *Women in New Worlds*, ed. Hilah F. Thomas and Rosemary Skinner Keller (Nashville: Abingdon Press, 1981), 1:220-21.

36. Ibid., 226.

37. Ibid. Additional information on Eugenia St. John was given in the *Methodist Protestant* 62:21 (May 25, 1892): 1. While living in Illinois she had married Charles H. St. John, an MEC minister, and had been asked by the church to fill his pulpit for two months when he was required to take a leave due to ill health. Since her own ordination in 1889 she had been engaged primarily in evangelistic work in Kansas City. She was described as "a lady of middle age, prepossessing appearance, with an attractive manner and pleasant voice. She is thoroughly versed in the legal and ecclesiastical features of her case, and fully prepared to defend her position if necessary."

38. Ibid., 227-30. Noll refers to D. S. Stephens's account of the General Conference in the *Methodist Recorder*, 1892, and attendant articles in that journal both preceding and following the General Conference. See especially Eugenia F. St. John, "A Symposium: Some Women on the Woman Question," *Methodist Recorder*, May 14, 1892, 189.

39. Ibid., 230-31.

40. Heetderks Strong, "Ecclesiastical Suffrage," 29-30.

41. *Religious Telescope* 59:20 (May 17, 1893): 308.

42. Ibid., 59:22 (May 31, 1893): 338.

43. Heetderks Strong, "Ecclesiastical Suffrage," 31.

44. As described in chapter 7, a Woman's Missionary Society (later the WFMS) had been organized in 1878, and what would become the WHMS began in 1886.

45. Virginia Shadron, "The Laity Rights Movement, 1906–1918: Woman's Suffrage in the Methodist Episcopal Church, South," in *Women in New Worlds*, 1:263.

46. Ibid., 264-65.

47. Ibid., 266-68. For the full text of Bennett's speech, see *Daily Christian Advocate*, MECS 20 May 1910, 117-18.

48. Shadron, "Laity Rights Movement," 268-71.

49. Ibid., 271-72.

50. Ibid., 272-74.
51. Ibid., 274.
52. Heetderks Strong, "Ecclesiastical Suffrage," 32.
53. See J[ames] M. Buckley, "What Methodism Owes to Women," *Centennial Methodist Conference Proceedings*, ed. Henry K. Carroll et al. (New York: Phillips & Hunt, 1885), 303-16.

Notes to Chapter 11

1. In 1984–85 the General Commission on Archives and History of The United Methodist Church sponsored a series of consultations with historians and leaders of its Native American, Hispanic, Asian American, and African American communities to encourage and support the recovery of their histories. The four resulting racial-ethnic history volumes, published by the Abingdon Press in 1991, are an important contribution to the history of United Methodism in America. They are disappointing, however, in their coverage of the history of women in these communities; much more remains to be done to recover the history of women of color in the Methodist tradition. See Homer Noley, *First White Frost: Native Americans and United Methodism*; Justo L. González, ed., *Each in Our Own Tongue: A History of Hispanic United Methodism*; Artemio R. Guillermo, ed., *Churches Aflame: Asian Americans and United Methodism*; Grant S. Shockley, ed., *Heritage and Hope: The African American Presence in United Methodism*.

2. Letter of JW to Francis Asbury, 1787, John Telford, ed., *The Letters of the Rev. John Wesley, A.M.* (London: Epworth Press, 1931), 8:24-25. "How many millions of them have already died in their sins! Will neither God nor man have compassion upon these outcasts of men? Undoubtedly with man it is impossible to help them. But is it too hard for God?"

3. Wade Crawford Barclay, *History of Methodist Missions, Part One: Early American Methodism, 1769–1844* (New York: Board of Missions and Church Extension of The Methodist Church, 1949–50), 1:203-5; Homer Noley, *First White Frost: Native Americans and United Methodism* (Nashville: Abingdon Press, 1991), 88. Noley referred to the Wyandott Mission as "a model for the times in which it flourished." Ibid., 91.

4. Barclay, *History of Methodist Missions*, 2:113.

5. Bruce David Forbes, "'And Obey God, Etc.': Methodism and American Indians," in *Perspectives on American Methodism: Interpretive Essays*, ed. Richey, Rowe, and Schmidt (Nashville: Kingswood Books, 1993), 209-27.

6. *Eighth Annual Report of the Missionary Society of the Methodist Episcopal Church, 1826–27*; cited in Barclay, *History of Methodist Missions* 2:125.

7. Forbes, "'And Obey God, Etc.,'" 212.

8. From a handwritten note on a photograph of Mother Solomon in the Women's History files, United Methodist Archives and History Center, Drew University.

9. Pamphlet on the Wyandott Mission ("The first Methodist Mission in America," designated a Historical Shrine in 1960), 1989.

10. Apparently there was no Methodist mission at this time among the Seminole people.

11. Barclay, *History of Methodist Missions*, 2:128.

12. William G. McLoughlin, *Cherokees and Missionaries: 1789–1839* (New Haven: Yale University Press, 1984), 291-92.

13. Barclay, *History of Methodist Missions*, 2:130-34.

14. Ibid., 134-38.

15. Ibid., 139-43. Also Walter N. Vernon, "Indian Methodists in South Central States," in *One in the Lord: A History of Ethnic Minorities in the South Central Jurisdiction of The United Methodist Church*, ed. Walter N. Vernon (Bethany, Okla.: Cowan Printing and Litho., 1977), 3-5.

16. Noley, *First White Frost*, 149; Forbes, " 'And Obey God, Etc.,' " 214.

17. Barclay, *History of Methodist Missions*, 2:146.

18. Noley, *First White Frost*, 109; Barclay, *History of Methodist Missions* 2:148.

19. Noley, *First White Frost*, 106.

20. Forbes, " 'And Obey God, Etc.,'" 216.

21. Barclay, *History of Methodist Missions*, 2:200, 204. The immediate impetus was a letter published in the N.Y. *Christian Advocate* (March 1, 1833) recounting the visit to St. Louis of four Flathead Indians purportedly in search of "the white man's Book of Heaven" (ibid., 205).

22. Ibid., 212.

23. Ibid., 210-17; Noley, *First White Frost*, 141. Oregon State Representative and historian Nancie Peacocke Fadeley detailed the accomplishments and struggles of the Oregon Mission from 1833 until its termination in 1847 in "Mission to Oregon" (booklet published on the occasion of the first meeting in Oregon of the General Conference of the United Methodist Church, 1976). Anna Pittman Lee is one of the Methodist women whose religious vocation as wives of itinerant preachers is explored in chapter 5 of this book. The Indians with whom Lee and the others worked in Oregon were probably Cayuse and Nez Perce.

24. Noley, *First White Frost*, 151-53.

25. Barclay, *History of Methodist Missions*, 2:171-79, 195.

26. Ibid., 2:262-63.

27. George E. Tinker, *Missionary Conquest: The Gospel and Native American Cultural Genocide* (Minneapolis: Fortress Press, 1993). See especially chapter 1: "Missionary Intentions, Missionary Violence," 1-20.

28. Noley, *First White Frost*, 160-64.

29. Ibid., 171.

30. Forbes, " 'And Obey God, Etc.,' " 225-27.

31. *Woman's Home Missions* [MEC] 6:12 (Dec. 1889): 180.

32. Frederick A. Norwood, "American Indian Women: The Rise of Methodist Women's Work, 1850–1939," in *Women in New Worlds*, 2:176-95. See also Sidney H. Babcock and John Y. Bryce, *History of Methodism in Oklahoma* (n.p., 1937), 274-76; Walter N. Vernon, "Indian Methodists in South Central States," in *One in the Lord*, ed. Walter N. Vernon (Oklahoma City: South Central Jurisdiction Commission on Archives and History, 1977), 9-10.

33. *Woman's Missionary Advocate* (January 1895): 207.

34. Ibid., (July 1896): 18.

35. Ibid., 17.

36. Ibid., (November 1895): 140.

37. *Woman's Home Missions* (September 1938): 5; (October 1938): 4; recounting the history of the first decade of the WHMS. With the reunion in 1939 of the two Methodist Episcopal churches (north and south) and the Methodist Protestant Church, all of the women's missionary organizations would be merged into one Woman's Division of Christian Service of the Board of Missions of The Methodist Church.

38. Ibid., 6:11 (November 1889): 169-70.

39. Ibid., 6:2 (February 1889): 19-21.

40. Ibid., 6:9 (September 1889): 131-32; 6:10 (Oct. 1889): 148.

41. Norwood, "American Indian Women," 183.

42. Ibid., 193.

43. *Our Brother in Red*, 7 (April 6, 1889): 6; cited in Norwood, "American Indian Women," 186.

44. Norwood, "American Indian Women," 193.

45. Walter N. Vernon, "Indian Methodists in South Central States," 29-30.

46. Ibid., 30. It did not, however, have the status of an annual conference.

47. Norwood, "American Indian Women," 193-94.

48. Ibid., 194.

49. Ibid., 194. See also excerpts from Kay Parker's 1983 interview with Reverend Hazel Botone in Ruether and Keller, eds., *Women and Religion in America*, 3:52-53, 60, 71-75; and *1966 Journal* of the Oklahoma Indian Mission, The Methodist Church, 13; *1968 Journal* of the Oklahoma Indian Mission, The United Methodist Church, 21.

50. Justo L. González, ed., *Each in Our Own Tongue: A History of Hispanic United Methodism* (Nashville: Abingdon Press, 1991), 19-30.

51. Alfredo Náñez, "Methodism Among the Spanish-Speaking People in Texas and New Mexico, in *One in the Lord*, ed. Vernon, 50-94. Quote is on 50.

52. Joel N. Martínez, "The South Central Jurisdiction," in *Each in Our Own Tongue*, 41.

53. Ibid., 42; also Náñez, "Methodism Among the Spanish-Speaking People," 54-56.

54. Alfredo Náñez, "Methodism Among the Spanish-Speaking People," 58-59.

55. Ibid., 61; also Noreen Dunn Tatum, *A Crown of Service: A Story of Woman's Work in the Methodist Episcopal Church, South, from 1878–1940* (Nashville: Parthenon Press, 1960), 164-67.

56. Alfredo Náñez, "Methodism Among the Spanish-Speaking People in Texas and New Mexico," 62-69; Tatum, *A Crown of Service*, 232-33.

57. Clotilde Falcón Náñez, "Hispanic Clergy Wives," in *Women in New Worlds*, 1:161-77.

58. Ibid., 166-67.

59. Ibid., 168-69.

60. Ibid., 169-70.

61. Minerva N. Garza, "The Influence of Methodism on Hispanic Women," *Methodist History* 34:2 (January 1996): 78-89.

62. Clotilde Falcón Náñez, "Hispanic Clergy Wives," 170.

63. Martínez, "South Central Jurisdiction," 51.

64. Alfredo Náñez, "Methodism Among the Spanish-Speaking People," 74-76.

65. Mrs. Thomas [Emily J.] Harwood, "Field and Work of the New Mexico Spanish Methodist Episcopal Mission" (from *Gospel in All Lands*, July 22, 1901), in Harriet S. Kellogg, *Life of Mrs. Emily J. Harwood* (Albuquerque: El Abogado Press, 1903), 330-43.

66. Alfredo Náñez, "Methodism Among the Spanish-Speaking People," 76-77.

67. Ibid., 80-81.

68. Clotilde F. Náñez, "Hispanic Clergy Wives," 170-72.

69. Martínez, "South Central Jurisdiction," 54; *They Went Out Not Knowing: 100 Women in Mission* (Women's Division, General Board of Global Ministries, The United Methodist Church, 1986), 15.

70. Robert H. Terry, "The McCurdy Mission School Story," *Methodist History* 25:2 (January 1987): 111-26.

71. Félix Gutiérrez, "The Western Jurisdiction," in Gonzalez, *Each in Our Own Tongue*, 70.

72. Ibid., 77-83.

73. Gildo Sánchez, "Puerto Rico," in González, *Each in Our Own Tongue*, 131-51.

74. Ruth Esther Meeker, *Six Decades of Service, 1880–1940: A History of the Woman's Home Missionary Society of the Methodist Episcopal Church* (Cincinnati: Women's Home Missionary Society, 1969), 304-9.

75. Sánchez, "Puerto Rico," 141, 150.

76. Alfredo Cotto-Thorner, "The Northeastern Jurisdiction," in González, *Each in Our Own Tongue*, 106-10.

77. Tatum, *A Crown of Service*, 189-95.

78. Humberto Carrazana, "The Southeastern Jurisdiction," in *Each in Our Own Tongue*, 92-105.

79. June Shimokawa, "Asian American Women in the United Methodist Church," in *Response: United Methodist Women* (Jan. 1978): 16-19, 47.

80. Ronald Takaki, *Strangers from a Different Shore: A History of Asian Americans* (New York: Penguin Books, 1989), 7-14.

81. Ibid., 31-42; Shimokawa, "Asian American Women," 17.

82. Takaki, *Strangers from a Different Shore: A History of Asian Americans*, 15, 385-405; Shimokawa, "Asian American Women," 18. At its third annual meeting in 1942 the Woman's Division of Christian Service adopted a resolution deploring the relocation of Japanese Americans. The women expressed their heartfelt sympathy with all evacuees, reiterated their confidence in the loyalty of citizens of Japanese ancestry, and summoned the whole church to "unceasing efforts" to overcome racial discrimination toward Asian Americans. "We hope," they said, "for the repeal of the Oriental Exclusion Act, for the full protection of civil rights, and the natural return to free American life of all persons now affected by emergency war measures" (*Journal of the Third Annual Meeting of the Woman's Division of Christian Service of the Board of Missions and Church Extension of The Methodist Church*, Cleveland, Ohio [29 Nov.- 4 Dec. 1942]: 37-38).

83. Takaki, *Strangers from a Different Shore: A History of Asian Americans*, 53-57.

84. Ibid., 57-62.

85. Otis Gibson, *The Chinese in America* (Cincinnati: Hitchcock & Walden, 1877), 176.

86. Wilbur W. Y. Choy, "Strangers Called to Mission: History of Chinese American United Methodist Churches," in *Churches Aflame: Asian Americans and United Methodism*, ed. Artemio R. Guillermo (Nashville: Abingdon Press, 1991), 68.

87. Ibid.

88. Ibid., 69.

89. Ibid., 70, 74-76.

90. Gibson, *Chinese in America*, 201.

91. Choy, "Strangers Called to Mission," 71.

92. Gibson, *Chinese in America*, 194-95.

93. Ibid., 72.

94. Peggy Pascoe, *Relations of Rescue: The Search for Female Moral Authority in the American West, 1874–1939* (New York: Oxford University Press, 1990), 6, 52-55, 85.

95. Meeker, *Six Decades of Service*, 285-87; Stella Wyatt Brummitt, *Looking Backward; Thinking Forward: The Jubilee History of the Woman's Home Missionary Society*

of the Methodist Episcopal Church (Cincinnati: The Woman's Home Missionary Society, 1930), 98.

96. Lester E. Suzuki, "Persecution, Alienation, and Resurrection: History of Japanese Methodist Churches," in Guillermo, ed., *Churches Aflame*, 113-34. Quote is on 114.

97. Ibid., 114-15.

98. Ibid., 115-17.

99. Ibid., 119.

100. Ibid., 122.

101. Ibid., 126.

102. Meeker, *Six Decades*, 286.

103. Key Ray Chong and Myong Gul Son, "Trials and Triumphs: History of Korean United Methodist Churches," in *Churches Aflame*, 47-64.

104. Ibid., 50.

105. Ibid., 52.

106. Alice Chai, "Korean Women in Hawaii, 1903–1945," in *Women in New Worlds*, 1:328-44.

107. Ibid., 331-32.

108. Ibid., 333.

109. Ibid., 333-35.

110. Ibid., 336-42, 344.

111. Ibid., 342.

112. Chong and Son, "Trials and Triumphs," 52-56.

113. Ai Ra Kim, *Women Struggling for a New Life* (New York: SUNY Press, 1996), 34.

114. Kim, *Women Struggling*, 51; Chai, "Korean Women in Hawaii," 330.

115. Artemio Guillermo, "Gathering of the Scattered: History of Filipino American United Methodist Churches," in *Churches Aflame*, 91-112. Quote is on 92.

116. Ibid., 93-94.

117. Ibid., 95-97.

118. Pascoe, *Relations of Rescue*, 115, 172.

NOTES TO CHAPTER 12

1. Sara M. Evans, *Born for Liberty: A History of Women in America* (New York: The Free Press, 1989), 147-48, 172.

2. Ibid., 128, 160.

3. Ibid., 160-66, 172-73, 195. In terms of visibility, the high point was probably the suffrage parade of some five thousand women in the nation's capital the day before Woodrow Wilson's presidential inauguration in 1913. During these years women achieved significant gains in new legislation for working women and children, including the creation of a Federal Children's Bureau in 1912. Evans suggests, however, that the struggle for suffrage allowed a broad coalition of women that could not hold together around any other issue.

4. Ann Fagan, *This Is Our Song: Employed Women in the United Methodist Tradition* (New York: Women's Division, General Board of Global Ministries, UMC, 1986), 34.

5. Ibid., 36, 43.

6. *Forty-second Annual Report of The Woman's Home Missionary Society of the Methodist Episcopal Church For the Year 1922–23*, 267. Quoted in ibid., 45.

7. Ibid., 46-47.

8. Ibid., 44, 67-72.

9. Ibid. See also Florence L. Norwood, "The Wesleyan Service Guild," in *Sourcebook of American Methodism,* ed. Frederick A. Norwood (Nashville: Abingdon Press, 1982), 567-70.

10. William T. Noll, "A Welcome in the Ministry: The 1920 and 1924 General Conferences Debate Clergy Rights for Women," *Methodist History* 30:2 (January 1992): 91-99. Quote is on 92-93. Southard wrote a compelling article on "Woman and the Ministry" that was published in *The Methodist Review,* November-December 1919 (and also printed separately). Noting that it had been forty years since Anna Howard Shaw was refused the right to preach in the Methodist Episcopal Church, Southard refuted the arguments that had been used to keep women out of the ministry. With reference to the final objection she concluded: "This whole argument from nature loses much of its weight when we remember that it is the same time-worn word of woman's sphere that so long deprived her of educational opportunity and political justice. . . . Shall the Church cling to this argument when in all other fields it has been cast aside as obsolete?"

11. "How the Licensing of Women to Preach Came to Pass," the (NY) *Christian Advocate,* 28 October 1920, 1436-37.

12. *Journal* of the General Conference, (1920), 517. Forty-one of the 425 lay delegates to the 1920 General Conference were women. *The Christian Advocate* ran both pictures and brief biographical descriptions of these "Women in the General Conference of 1920" (29 April): 578-79, 590-92, and (13 May): 663. Five of the women were African Americans, two from the Washington Conference, one from Upper Mississippi, one from South Carolina, and one from Texas. The disciplinary change read simply: "The provisions of para. 219-226 include women, except in so far as these provisions apply to candidates for the traveling ministry and for Deacon's and Elder's orders" (1920 *Discipline,* footnote to chapter 1, 167).

13. *The Christian Advocate,* 3 June 1920, 763; 17 June 1920, 835.

14. See "The Chief," the obituary notice for Dr. James M. Buckley, *The Christian Advocate,* 19 February 1920, 243-46. Also George Preston Mains, *James Monroe Buckley* (New York: Methodist Book Concern, 1917).

15. *The Christian Advocate,* 10 April 1924, 454-55.

16. Noll, "A Welcome in the Ministry," 98-99; *Daily Christian Advocate,* 9 May 1924, 208 and 10 May 1924, 233 (summary of proceedings on May 8-9); *Journal of the GC,* 1924, 1697-98 (commission report). Before the annual conferences met in spring of 1927, eighty-one women had been ordained local deacons and sixteen of them had gone on after two years to be ordained local elder. See Elizabeth Wilson, ed., *The Relative Place of Women in the Church in the United States* (New York: n.p., 1927), 56-57.

17. Alice G. Knotts, *Fellowship of Love: Methodist Women Changing American Racial Attitudes, 1920–1968* (Nashville: Kingswood Books, 1996), 42-43; John Patrick McDowell, *The Social Gospel in the South: The Woman's Home Mission Movement in the Methodist Episcopal Church, South, 1886–1939* (Baton Rouge: Louisiana State University Press, 1982), 84-87. Black Methodists of the MECS organized the Colored Methodist Episcopal Church in 1870.

18. Wilma Dykeman and James Stokely, *Seeds of Southern Change: The Life of Will Alexander* (Chicago: University of Chicago Press, 1962), 85. The CIC itself neither advocated racial equality nor challenged segregation. It was an attempt to bring together whites and middle-class blacks to work on solutions to some of the

South's most pressing racial problems. It actually took over a year before the CIC itself had black members!

19. Quoted in Jacquelyn Dowd Hall, *Revolt Against Chivalry: Jessie Daniel Ames and the Women's Campaign Against Lynching* (New York: Columbia University Press, 1979), 89.

20. Ibid.

21. Dykeman and Stokely, *Seeds of Southern Change*, 92.

22. Quoted in Hall, *Revolt Against Chivalry*, 93-94.

23. Dykeman and Stokely, *Seeds of Southern Change*, 85.

24. McDowell, *The Social Gospel in the South*, 91-92.

25. Hall, *Revolt Against Chivalry*, 96. See also Paula Giddings, *When and Where I Enter: The Impact of Black Women on Race and Sex in America* (New York: Bantam Books, 1984), 175-76.

26. Knotts, *Fellowship of Love*, 55, 81.

27. *The Interracial Front* (Atlanta: CIC, 1933), pamphlet pp. 10-11. Quoted in Arnold M. Shankman, "Civil Rights, 1920–1970: Three Southern Methodist Women," in *Women in New Worlds*, 2:222-23.

28. *Twenty-seventh Annual Report of the Woman's Missionary Council* (1936–37): 140. Louise Young, professor of sociology at Scarritt College and chair of the Committee on Interracial Cooperation of the WMC, led this study group. "Of all the white groups in the MEC and MECS speaking on the subject of unification," Alice Knotts claimed, "the WMC most nearly reflected the views of the African American Methodists." (Knotts *Fellowship of Love*, 86.)

Notes to the Epilogue

1. *Journal of the Uniting Conference of The Methodist Church* (1939): 382. See also Alice Knotts, "The Debates Over Race and Women's Ordination in the 1939 Methodist Merger," *Methodist History* 29:1 (October 1990): 42-43.

2. "News of the World Parish," *Christian Advocate*, 24 May 1956, 663.

3. *Discipline* of The Methodist Church (1956), par. 303, 115.

4. *Christian Advocate*, 24 May 1956, 663. The next issue (May 31, 1956), explained that the new legislation would open the way for "many of the church's 300 or so women ministers" to become members of annual conferences (694).

5. *Daily Christian Advocate*, 7 May 1956, 534.

6. Maud Keister Jensen, interview by Naomi Kooker, 1984, United Methodist Women's Oral History Project, General Commission on Archives and History, UMC. On the Korean Methodist Church, see J. S. Ryang, "How Two Methodisms Unite," *Missionary Voice* (Oct. 1931): 13-15, 50.

7. *Christian Advocate*, 7 June 1956, 726; 14 June 1956, 759. These dates have been confirmed by consulting the 1956 *Journal* of each annual conference. The North Dakota Conference voted unanimously in special Executive Session to receive Miss Grace Huck on trial into the conference. She was introduced to the conference by Dr. James S. Chubb, "long a champion" of full clergy rights for women; the conference believed her to be "the first woman to be received into full connection in The Methodist Church of the United States" (*Journal* of the North Dakota Conference of The Methodist Church, 21–25 May 1956, 12). See also Grace E. Huck, "I Was Not Disobedient to the Heavenly Vision," 1997 Convocation of the North Central Jurisdiction, Commission on Archives and History, July 7–10, 1997.

8. *Christian Advocate,* 14 June 1956, 762.

9. Ibid., 21 June 1956, 795. The name of Mrs. Hill's mother was not given.

10. List from 1956 *Christian Advocate,* supplemented by annual conference journals. The other women received on trial that year were: May 27, Ellen Maria Studley (Northern Indiana); June 5, Myrtle S. Speer (Missouri); June 10, Helena L. Champlin (Genesee), Ruth M. Ellis (Newark), Mary MacNicholl (Minnesota), Nancy J. Nichols (Iowa-Des Moines); June 16, Marion Kline (Detroit); June 17, Frances Bigelow and Margaret E. Scheve (Colorado), Jessie O. Todd, Mary Louise Long, and Eva Maxwell (California-Nevada); June 22, Ellen Rose (Montana), and June 29, Sally [Sallie?] A. Crenshaw and Nora E. Young (East Tennessee). Of the two women who were the exceptions, Emma P. Hill became a member in full connection of the Washington Conference in 1959. Myrtle Speer apparently did not become a member in full connection of the Missouri Conference.

11. James E. Will, "The Ordination of Women—The Development in the Church of the United Brethren in Christ," in *"Women's Rightful Place": Women in United Methodist History,* ed. Donald K. Gorrell (Dayton, Ohio: United Theological Seminary, 1980), 33; J. Bruce Behney and Paul H. Eller, *The History of the Evangelical United Brethren Church* (Nashville: Abingdon Press, 1979), 360-61. Behney and Eller noted that there had been several "isolated instances" where women were ordained in the EUB Church, but that they "neither provoked any recorded objections nor inspired any generally accepted practice."

12. Jonathan Cooney, "Maintaining the Tradition: Women Elders and the Ordination of Women in the Evangelical United Brethren Church," *Methodist History* 27:4 (October 1988): 25-35. (In the EUB Church there was just one order of ordained ministry, that of elder, in contrast with the two-step deacon-elder process of the Methodist tradition.)

13. Noreen Dunn Tatum, *A Crown of Service* (Nashville: Parthenon Press, 1960), 396-97. See also Ruth Esther Meeker, *Six Decades of Service* (WHMS, MEC, 1969), 87.

14. Evelyn Riley Nicholson papers, archives of Garrett-Evangelical Theological Seminary, Evanston, Illinois.

15. Tatum, *Crown of Service,* 397; Meeker, *Six Decades,* 88.

16. The others were the Division of Foreign Missions, Division of Home Missions and Church Extension, and a joint Division on Education and Cultivation. See Thelma Stevens, *Legacy for the Future* (Women's Division, Board of Global Ministry, UMC, 1978), 18-23.

17. *Woman's Missionary Friend* and *Woman's Home Missions* (MEC), *Missionary Record* (MPC), and *The Bulletin* (local church/community); also *Woman's Missionary Advocate* and *Our Homes* (former magazines of MECS; merged with *World Outlook* in 1910).

18. Stevens, *Legacy for the Future,* 18.

19. Alice G. Knotts, *Fellowship of Love: Methodist Women Changing American Racial Attitudes, 1920–1968* (Nashville: Kingswood Books, 1996).

20. Ibid., 18.

21. Ibid., 22.

22. Ibid., 22-23.

23. Between 1864 and 1939, twenty-five black annual conferences were organized in the Methodist Episcopal Church. They were: Delaware, Washington, Mississippi Mission, South Carolina, Tennessee, Texas, Central Alabama, Mississippi, Louisiana, North Carolina, Lexington, Florida, West Texas, Savannah, Lit-

tle Rock, East Tennessee, Central Missouri, Upper Mississippi, Atlanta, Mobile, Okaneb, Lincoln, South Florida, Southwest, Central West. From Albea Godbold, "Table of Methodist Annual Conferences (USA)," *Methodist History* 8 (January 1969): 25-64, quoted in Grant S. Shockley, ed., *Heritage and Hope: The African American Presence in United Methodism* (Nashville: Abingdon Press, 1991), 310-11.

24. Task Group on the History of the Central Jurisdiction Women's Organization, *To a Higher Glory: The Growth and Development of Black Women Organized for Mission in The Methodist Church, 1940–1968* (Women's Division of the Board of Global Ministries, UMC, n.d.), 14-18.

25. Ibid., 23-24.

26. There would be four presidents of the Central Jurisdiction WSCS: Margaret Bowen (New Orleans), 1940–48; Ruth Carter (New Orleans), 1948–60; Anita Fields (Kentucky), 1960–64; and Mary Drake (Tennessee), 1964–68. Ibid., 57.

27. *To a Higher Glory*, 27. See also Clarence G. Newsome, "Mary McLeod Bethune and the Methodist Episcopal Church North: In But Out," in *This Far By Faith: Readings in African–American Women's Religious Biography*, ed. Judith Weisenfeld and Richard Newman (New York: Routledge,1995), 124-39.

28. Ibid., 31-32.

29. Ibid., 32-33.

30. Ibid., 33.

31. Ibid., 42.

32. *To a Higher Glory*, 73.

33. Ibid., 74. See also Knotts, *Fellowship of Love*, 111. Peggy Billings, one of five leaders of CSR profiled by Knotts, noted the courageous public stands in race relations taken by Mrs. Arrington, whose husband was lieutenant governor of Mississippi.

34. Helena Huntington Smith, "Mrs. Tilly's Crusade," *Collier's*, 30 Dec. 1950, 29, 66-67 (reprinted in the *Negro Digest* [July 1951]: 3-11); Dorothy Tilly, "The Fellowship of the Concerned," *The Woman's Press* (February 1950): 8-9, 19; Ruth H. Collins, "We Are the Inheritors," *Response* (July-August 1971): 30-32.

35. *To a Higher Glory*, 80.

36. Ibid., 86.

37. Theressa Hoover, *With Unveiled Face: Centennial Reflections on Women and Men in the Community of the Church* (New York: Women's Division, General Board of Global Ministries, UMC, 1983), 28-29.

38. Ibid., 26-27.

39. Ibid., 27.

40. Ibid., 30-31.

41. Ibid., 31.

42. Ibid., 33.

43. Ibid., 40-44.

44. Ibid., 36-39.

NOTES TO THE CONCLUSION

1. Ann Braude, "Women's History *Is* American Religious History," in *Retelling U.S. Religious History*, ed. Thomas A. Tweed (Berkeley: University of California Press, 1997), 87-107.

2. Ibid., 100.

3. Ibid., 101.

4. See Bernice Johnson Reagon's introduction to "I Remember, I Believe" from the Sweet Honey in the Rock CD entitled *Sacred Ground*: "It almost seemed to be saying that practicing history could be the basis of believing. If I hold within myself the memory of the journey of my people, if I know that I am evidence of the success of that journey, then I can believe that I too will be able to move through the challenges I face on the path I walk with my life."

SELECTED BIBLIOGRAPHY

PRIMARY SOURCES
Published Sources: Memoirs, Journals, Letters

Anonymous [British Methodist Minister]. *The Life of Faith Exemplified; or Extracts from the Journal of Mrs. Hester Ann Rogers*. New York: Carlton & Porter, 1861.

Asbury, Francis. *Journal and Letters of Francis Asbury*. 3 vols. Nashville: Abingdon Press, 1958.

Bahmueller, Nancy N. "My Ordination: Anna Howard Shaw." *Methodist History* 14, no. 2 (1976): 125.

Boehm, Rev. Henry. *Reminiscences, Historical and Biographical, of Sixty-Four Years in the Ministry*. Edited by Rev. Joseph B. Wakeley. New York: Carlton & Porter, 1866.

Brown, George. *The Lady Preacher: or the Life and Labors of Mrs. Hannah Reeves . . .* Philadelphia: Daughaday and Becker, 1870. Reprint, New York: Garland, 1987.

Brown, Oswald Eugene, and Anna Muse Brown. *Life and Letters of Laura Askew Haygood*. Nashville: Publishing House of the M.E. Church, South, 1904. Reprint, New York: Garland, 1987.

Burr, Virginia Ingraham, ed. *The Secret Eye: The Journal of Ella Gertrude Clanton Thomas, 1848-1889*. Introduction by Nell Irvin Painter. Chapel Hill: University of North Carolina Press, 1990.

Butler, Clementina. *Mrs. William Butler: Two Empires and a Kingdom*. New York: Methodist Book Concern, 1929.

Butler, Mrs. F[rank] A. [Sarah Frances Stringfield]. *Mrs. D. H. M'Gavock: Life-Sketch and Thoughts*. Nashville: Publishing House of the Methodist Episcopal Church, South, 1896.

Butler, Sara Frances Stringfield. *Life, Reminiscences, and Journal, Mrs. Juliana Hayes*. Nashville: Publishing House of the Methodist Episcopal Church, South, 1904.

Coles, Rev. George, ed. *Memoir of Miss Catharine Reynolds, of Poughkeepsie, New York: With Selections from Her Diary and Letters*. New York: Published for the Proprietors, at the Methodist Book Room, 1844.

Denig, John, ed. *Autobiography of the Rev. Samuel Huber, Elder in the Church of the United Brethren in Christ*. Chambersburg, Pa.: M. Kiefer & Co., 1858.

Elaw, Zilpha. *Memoirs of the Life, Religious Experience, Ministerial Travels and Labours of Mrs. Zilpha Elaw, An American Female of Color*. In *Sisters of the Spirit:*

Three Black Women's Autobiographies of the Nineteenth Century, edited by William L. Andrews, 49-160. Bloomington: Indiana University Press, 1986.

Ffirth, John. *The Experience and Gospel Labours of the Rev. Benjamin Abbott.* Philadelphia: Solomon W. Conrad for Ezekiel Cooper, 1809.

Foster, John O. *Life and Labors of Mrs. Maggie Newton Van Cott, the First Lady Licensed to Preach in the Methodist Episcopal Church in the United States.* Cincinnati: Hitchcock and Walden, 1872.

Gay, Theressa. *Life and Letters of Mrs. Jason Lee.* Portland, Oreg.: Metropolitan Press, Publishers, 1936.

Gifford, Carolyn De Swarte. *Writing Out My Heart: Selections from the Journal of Frances E. Willard, 1855-96.* Urbana: University of Illinois Press, 1995.

Hook, John, and Charlotte Hook, eds. *The Brewer Letters: Transcripts of Letters to Henry and Laura Brewer, Methodist Missionaries to Oregon 1839 to 1848.* Commission on Archives and History, Oregon-Idaho Conference of the United Methodist Church, 1994.

Lee, Jarena. *The Life and Religious Experience of Jarena Lee* (1836). In *Sisters of the Spirit,* ed. William L. Andrews, 25-48.

———. *Religious Experience and Journal of Mrs. Jarena Lee* (1849). In *Spiritual Narratives,* edited by Sue E. Houchins. Schomburg Library of Nineteenth Century Black Women Writers. New York: Oxford University Press, 1988.

Maser, Frederick E., and Howard T. Maag, eds. *The Journal of Joseph Pilmore, Methodist Itinerant.* Philadelphia: Message Publishing Co. for the Historical Society of the Philadelphia Annual Conference of the United Methodist Church, 1969.

Maser, Frederick E. *Robert Strawbridge: First American Methodist Circuit Rider.* Rutland, Vt.: Strawbridge Shrine Association, Inc., in cooperation with Academy Books, 1983.

Merritt, Rev. T[imothy]. *Memoir, Diary, and Letters of Miss Hannah Syng Bunting, of Philadelphia, Who Departed This Life May 25, 1832, in the Thirty-First Year of Her Age.* 2 vols. New York: T. Mason and G. Lane, for the Sunday School Union of the Methodist Episcopal Church, 1837.

Morehouse, A. C. *Autobiography of A[lonzo] C[hurch] Morehouse.* New York: Tibbals Book Company, 1895.

Newell, Fanny. *Memoirs of Fanny Newell; Written by Herself . . .* 2nd ed. Springfield: Merriam, Little & Co. [O. Scott and E. F. Newell], 1832.

———. *Diary of Fanny Newell; with a sketch of Her Life, and an Introduction by a Member of the New England Conference of the Methodist Episcopal Church.* 4th ed. Boston: Charles H. Peirce, 1848.

Newell, Rev. E. F. *Life and Observations of Rev. E[benezer] F. Newell.* Worcester, 1847.

Nind, Mary Clarke's Children. *Mary Clarke Nind and Her Work.* Chicago: Published for the Woman's Foreign Missionary Society by J. Newton Nind, 1906.

North, Elizabeth Mason. *Consecrated Talents: or, The Life of Mrs. Mary W. Mason.* New York: Carlton & Lanahan, 1870. Reprint, New York: Garland, 1987.

Olin, Stephen. *Life Inexplicable Except as a Probation: A Discourse Delivered in the Methodist Episcopal Church, Rhinebeck, N.Y., July 15, 1849, at the Funeral of Mrs. Catharine [sic] Garrettson.* New York: Lane & Scott, 1851.

Peck, Frances Potter [with an introduction by Bishop Henry White Warren]. *Memoir of Frances Merritt.* Cincinnati: Cranston & Curts, 1892.

Phoebus, Geo. A., and comp. *Beams of Light on Early Methodism in America. Chiefly*

Drawn from the Diary, Letters, Manuscripts, Documents, and Original Tracts of the Rev. Ezekiel Cooper. New York: Phillips & Hunt, 1887.

Potts, J. Manning, et al., eds. *Journal and Letters of Francis Asbury.* Vol. 3: The Letters. London and Nashville: Epworth Press and Abingdon Press, 1958.

Roe, Mrs. Elizabeth A. [Lyon]. *Recollections of Frontier Life.* Rockford, Ill: Gazette Publishing House, 1885; Arno Press Reprint, 1980.

Rogers, Hester Ann Roe. *Account of the Experience of Mrs. Hester Ann Rogers.* New York: John C. Totten, for the Methodist Episcopal Church, 1804.

———. *The Life of Faith Exemplified; Or, Extracts from the Journal of Mrs. Hester Ann Rogers.* New York: Carlton & Porter, 1861.

Seiber, Richard A., ed. *Memoirs of Puget Sound, Early Seattle 1853-1856: The Letters of David & Catherine Blaine.* Fairfield, Wash.: Ye Galleon Press, 1978.

Sexton, Lydia. *Autobiography of Lydia Sexton.* Dayton, Ohio: United Brethren Publishing House, 1882. Reprint, New York: Garland, 1987.

Shaw, Anna Howard. *The Story of a Pioneer.* New York: Harper & Brothers, 1915.

Simpson, Robert Drew, ed. *American Methodist Pioneer: The Life and Journals of the Rev. Freeborn Garrettson, 1752-1827.* Rutland, Vt.: Academy Books, 1984.

Smith, Amanda Berry. *An Autobiography: The Story of the Lord's Dealings with Mrs. Amanda Smith, the Colored Evangelist.* Chicago: Meyer & Brother, 1893.

Summers, Thomas A., ed. *Life and Correspondence of Mrs. Hester Ann Rogers.* Nashville: E. Stevenson & F. A. Owen, 1854.

Towle, Nancy. *Vicissitudes Illustrated, in the Experience of Nancy Towle, in Europe and America.* 2nd ed. Portsmouth, N.H.: John Caldwell, 1833.

Tucker, Mary Orne. *Itinerant Preaching in the Early Days of Methodism, by a Pioneer Preacher's Wife.* Edited by Thomas W. Tucker. Boston: B. B. Russell, 1872.

Ware, Thomas. *Sketches of the Life and Travels of Thomas Ware . . . Written by Himself.* New York: T. Mason and G. Lane, 1840.

Wesley, John. *The Letters of the Rev. John Wesley.* Edited by John Telford. 8 vols. London: Epworth Press, 1931.

Wheatley, Richard. *The Life and Letters of Mrs. Phoebe Palmer.* New York: W. C. Palmer, 1876. Reprint, New York: Garland, 1987.

Published Sources: Periodicals

Arminian Magazine (London), 1784.

Christian Advocate (New York), 1870-1890, 1920.

Deaconess Advocate (Chicago), 1914.

Guide to Christian Perfection (Boston), 1839-1842.

Heathen Woman's Friend (Boston, MEC), 1869-1874.

Ladies' Repository (Cincinnati), 1872-1877.

Methodist Magazine (New York), 1818-1828.

Religious Telescope (Dayton, UB), 1844, 1893.

Woman's Evangel (Dayton, UB), 1882.

Woman's Home Missions (MEC), 1889, 1938.

Woman's Missionary Advocate (Nashville, MECS), 1895-1896.

Zion's Herald (Boston), 1867-1872.

Published Sources: Books, Pamphlets, Minutes

Andrew, James O. *Family Government: A Treatise on Conjugal, Parental, Filial, and Other Duties*. Nashville: E. Stevenson & F. A. Owen, for the Methodist Episcopal Church, South, 1855.

Bancroft, Jane M. *Deaconesses in Europe and Their Lessons for America*. New York: Hunt & Eaton, 1889.

Bangs, Nathan. *A History of the Methodist Episcopal Church*. 4 vols. Vol. 1. New York: G. Lane and C. B. Tippett, 1845.

Eaton, Herrick M. *The Itinerant's Wife: Her Qualifications, Duties, Trials, and Rewards*. New York: Lane & Scott, 1851.

Finley, James B. *Sketches of Western Methodism*. Cincinnati: R. P. Thompson, 1854.

Gifford, Carolyn De Swarte, ed. *The American Ideal of the "True Woman" as Reflected in Advice Books to Young Women*. New York: Garland Publishing, Inc., 1987.

———. *The Nineteenth-Century American Methodist Itinerant Preacher's Wife*. New York: Garland Publishing, Inc., 1987.

———. *The Ideal of "The New Woman" According to the Woman's Christian Temperance Union*. New York: Garland Publishing, Inc., 1987.

———. *The American Deaconess Movement in the Early Twentieth Century*. New York: Garland Publishing, 1987.

———. *The Debate in the Methodist Episcopal Church Over Laity Rights for Women*. New York: Garland Publishing, Inc., 1987.

Griffith, Mary L. *Women's Christian Work*. New York: Tract Dept., Phillips & Hunt, n.d.

Horton, Isabelle. *High Adventure: [The] Life of Lucy Rider Meyer*. New York: Methodist Book Concern, 1928.

Hughey, Rev. G. W. *The Admission of Women to the General Conference*. Chicago: Press of W.T.P.A., 1891.

James, Joseph H. *The Life of Mrs. Mary D. James, by her Son*. New York: Palmer & Hughes, 1886.

Journal of the General Conference of the Methodist Episcopal Church. 1872, 1876, 1880, 1884, 1888, 1892, 1896, 1900, 1904, 1920, 1924.

Journal of the General Conference of The Methodist Church, 1956.

Kynett, Alpha J. *Our Laity: and Their Equal Rights Without Distinction of Sex*. Cincinnati: Cranston and Curts, 1896.

Ladies' and Pastors' Christian Union. *First Annual Report, 1869*. Philadelphia: Methodist Episcopal Book Room, 1869.

Lednum, John. *A History of the Rise of Methodism in America*. Philadelphia: John Lednum, 1859.

Meyer, Lucy Rider. *Deaconesses, Biblical, Early Church, European, American, with the Story of How the Work Began in the Chicago Training School, for City, Home, and Foreign Missions, and the Chicago Deaconess Home*. 3rd rev. and enl. ed. Cincinnati: Cranston & Stowe, 1889.

———. "Deaconesses and Their Work." In *Woman in Missions: Papers and Addresses Presented at the Woman's Congress of Missions, Oct. 2-4, 1893*, 182-97. New York: American Tract Society, 1894.

Mood, Rev. F. A. In *Methodism in Charleston: A Narrative of the Chief Events Relating to the Rise and Progress of the Methodist Episcopal Church in Charleston, S.C.*, edited by Thomas O. Summers. Nashville: A. H. Redford, for the M.E. Church, South, 1875.

Oden, Thomas C., ed. *Phoebe Palmer: Selected Writings, Sources of American Spiritu-ality*. New York: Paulist Press, 1988.

Oliver, Rev. Miss Anna. "Test Case on the Ordination of Women, appealed from the New England Conference to General Conference." 1880.

Palmer, Phoebe. *The Way of Holiness, with Notes by the Way: Being a Narrative of Reli-gious Experience, Resulting from a Determination to Be a Bible Christian*. New York: Piercy and Reed, 1843.

———. *Promise of the Father; or, A Neglected Specialty of the Last Days*. New York: W. C. Palmer, 1859. Reprint, New York: Garland, 1985.

———. *The Devotional Writings of Phoebe Palmer, Higher Christian Life*. New York: Garland Publishing, Inc., 1985.

Rowe, Elizabeth Singer. *Devout Exercises of the Heart in Meditation and Soliloquy, Praise and Prayer*. London: Isaac Watts, 1737.

Sweet, William Warren. *Religion on the American Frontier: 1783-1840*. Vol. 4, *The Methodists*. Chicago: University of Chicago Press, 1946.

Wesley, John. "A Plain Account of Genuine Christianity." In *John Wesley*, edited by Albert Outler, 181-96. New York: Oxford University Press, 1964.

Wesley, John. *The Works of John Wesley: Bicentennial Edition*. Vols. 1-4: *Sermons*, edited by Albert C. Outler. Nashville: Abingdon Press, 1984-1987.

Willard, Frances E. *Woman in the Pulpit*. Chicago: Woman's Temperance Publica-tion Association, 1889.

———. *How to Win: A Book for Girls*. New York: Funk & Wagnalls, 1886. Reprinted in *The Ideal of "The New Woman" According to the Woman's Christian Temperance Union*, edited by Carolyn De Swarte Gifford. New York: Garland Publishing, 1987.

Wise, Rev. Daniel. *The Young Lady's Counsellor: or, Outlines and Illustrations of the Sphere, the Duties, and the Dangers of Young Women*. New York: Carlton & Porter, 1855. Reprint, Garland, 1987.

Wittenmyer, Annie. *Women's Work for Jesus*. New York: Nelson & Phillips, 1873.

Secondary Sources
Dissertations

Andrews, Doris E. "Popular Religion and the Revolution in the Middle Atlantic Ports: The Rise of the Methodists, 1770-1800." Ph.D., University of Pennsylva-nia, 1986.

Brekus, Catherine Anne. "'Let Your Women Keep Silence in the Churches': Female Preaching and Evangelical Religion in America, 1740-1845." Ph.D., Yale University, 1993.

Brown, Joanne E. Carlson. "Jennie Fowler Willing (1834-1916): Methodist Church-woman and Reformer." Ph.D., Boston University, 1983.

Dougherty, Mary Agnes Theresa. "The Methodist Deaconess, 1885-1918: A Study in Religious Feminism." Ph.D., University of California Davis, 1979.

Graham, E. Dorothy. "Chosen By God: The Female Itinerants of Early Primitive Methodism." Ph.D., University of Birmingham, 1986.

Lobody, Diane. "Lost in the Ocean of Love: The Mystical Writings of Catherine Livingston Garrettson." Ph.D., Drew University, 1990.

Myers, Sara Joyce. "Southern Methodist Women Leaders and Church Missions, 1878-1910." Ph.D., Emory University, 1990.

Schantz, Mark. "Piety in Providence: The Class Dimensions of Religious Experience in Providence, Rhode Island, 1790-1860." Ph.D., Emory University, 1991.

Wigger, John H. "Taking Heaven by Storm: Methodism and the Popularization of American Christianity, 1770-1820." Ph.D., University of Notre Dame, 1994.

Unpublished Papers

Brekus, Catherine A. "Female Evangelism in the Early Methodist Movement, 1784-1845."

Gravely, Will B. " '. . . many of the poor Affricans are obedient to the faith': Reassessing the African-American Presence in Early Methodism in the U.S., 1769-1809."

Long, Kathryn. "The Way of Holiness and the Gospel of Gentility: Phoebe Palmer, Methodism, and the Refinement of America."

Mathews, Donald G. "Francis Asbury in Conference."

Nanninga, Sherry L. "Laving My Feet in the Waters of Jordan: Frances Merritt, 1839-1891, Life and Struggle of a Methodist Woman in Colorado."

Published Works

Andrews, Dee E. "Religion and Social Change: The Rise of the Methodists." In *Shaping a National Culture: The Philadelphia Experience, 1750-1800,* edited by Catherine E. Hutchins. Winterthur, Del.: Winterthur Museum, 1994.

Andrews, Doris. "The African Methodists of Philadelphia, 1794-1802." In *Perspectives on American Methodism: Interpretive Essays,* edited by Russell E. Richey, Kenneth E. Rowe, and Jean Miller Schmidt, 145-55. Nashville: Kingswood Books, 1993.

Babcock, Sidney Henry, and John Y. Bryce. *History of Methodism in Oklahoma: Story of the Indian Mission Annual Conference of the Methodist Episcopal Church, South.* Oklahoma City: Times Journal Publishing Company, 1937.

Bacon, Margaret Hope. *Mothers of Feminism: The Story of Quaker Women in America.* San Francisco: Harper & Row, 1986.

Baker, Miss Frances J. *The Story of the Woman's Foreign Missionary Society of the Methodist Episcopal Church, 1869-1895.* Cincinnati: Curts & Jennings, 1898.

Baker, Frank. *From Wesley to Asbury: Studies in Early American Methodism.* Durham, N.C.: Duke University Press, 1976.

————. "Susanna Wesley: Puritan, Parent, Pastor, Protagonist, Pattern." In *Women in New Worlds: Historical Perspectives on the Wesleyan Tradition,* edited by Rosemary Skinner Keller, Louise L. Queen, and Hilah H. Thomas, 2:112-31. Nashville: Abingdon Press, 1982.

Barclay, Wade Crawford. *History of Methodist Missions.* 4 vols. New York: Board of Missions, The Methodist Church, 1949-1957.

Behney, J. Bruce, and Paul H. Eller. *The History of the Evangelical United Brethren Church.* Nashville: Abingdon Press, 1979.

Bilhartz, Terry D. *Urban Religion and the Second Great Awakening: Church and Society in Early National Baltimore.* Rutherford: Fairleigh Dickinson University Press, 1986.

Blauvelt, Martha Tomhave. "Women and Revivalism." In *Women and Religion in America,* edited by Rosemary Radford Ruether and Rosemary Skinner Keller. Vol. 1, *The Nineteenth Century,* 1-9. San Francisco: Harper & Row, 1981.

Bordin, Ruth. *Frances Willard: A Biography.* Chapel Hill: University of North Carolina Press, 1986.

Born, Ethel W. *By My Spirit: The Story of Methodist Protestant Women in Mission 1879-1939.* New York: Women's Division, Board of Global Ministries, United Methodist Church, 1990.

Boyd, Lois A., and R. Douglas Brackenridge. *Presbyterian Women in America: Two Centuries of a Quest for Status.* Westport, Conn.: Greenwood Press, 1983.

Braude, Ann. "Women's History *Is* American Religious History." In *Retelling U.S. Religious History,* edited by Thomas A. Tweed, 87-107. Berkeley: University of California Press, 1997.

Brereton, Virginia Lieson. "Preparing Women for the Lord's Work." In *Women in New Worlds,* ed. Keller, Thomas, and Queen, 1:178-99.

———. *From Sin to Salvation: Stories of Women's Conversions, 1800 to the Present.* Bloomington: Indiana University Press, 1991.

Brown, Earl Kent. *Women of Mr. Wesley's Methodism.* Vol. 11, *Studies in Women and Religion.* New York: The Edwin Mellen Press, 1983.

Brown, Joanne Carlson. "Shared Fire: The Flame Ignited by Jennie Fowler Willing." In *Spirituality and Social Responsibility: Vocational Vision of Women in the United Methodist Tradition,* edited by Rosemary Skinner Keller, 99-115. Nashville: Abingdon Press, 1993.

Brumberg, Joan Jacobs. "The Ethnological Mirror: American Evangelical Women and Their Heathen Sisters, 1870-1910." In *Women and the Structure of Society: Selected Research from the Fifth Berkshire Conference on the History of Women,* edited by Barbara J. Harris and JoAnn K. McNamara, 103-28. Durham: Duke University Press, 1984.

Chai, Alice. "Korean Women in Hawaii, 1903-1945." *Women in New Worlds.* ed. Keller, Thomas, and Queen, 1:328-44.

Chilcote, Paul Wesley. *John Wesley and the Women Preachers of Early Methodism.* Metuchen, N.J.: Scarecrow Press, Inc., 1991.

———. "John Wesley as Revealed by the Journal of Hester Ann Rogers, July 1775-October 1784." *Methodist History* 20:3 (April 1982): 111-23.

———. *She Offered Them Christ: The Legacy of Women Preachers in Early Methodism.* Nashville: Abingdon Press, 1993.

Coles, George. *Heroines of Methodism; or, Pen and Ink Sketches of the Mothers and Daughters of the Church.* New York: Carlton & Porter, 1857.

Cooney, Jonathan. "Maintaining the Tradition: Women Elders and the Ordination of Women in the Evangelical United Brethren Church." *Methodist History* 27, no. 4 (1988): 25-35.

Cott, Nancy F. *The Bonds of Womanhood; "Woman's Sphere" in New England, 1780-1835.* New Haven: Yale University Press, 1977.

DeBerg, Betty A. *Ungodly Women: Gender and the First Wave of American Fundamentalism.* Minneapolis: Fortress Press, 1990.

Disosway, Gabriel. *Our Excellent Women of the Methodist Church in England and America.* New York: J. C. Buttre, 1861.

Dodson, Jualynne, "Nineteenth-Century A.M.E. Preaching Women." In *Women in New Worlds,* ed. Keller, Thomas, and Queen, 1:276-89.

Donovan, Mary Sudman. *A Different Call: Women's Ministries in the Episcopal Church, 1850-1920.* Wilton, Conn.: Morehouse-Barlow, 1986.

Douglass, Paul F. *The Story of German Methodism: Biography of an Immigrant Soul.* New York: The Methodist Book Concern, 1939.

Earhart, Mary (Dillon). *Frances Willard: From Prayers to Politics.* Chicago: University of Chicago Press, 1944.

Evans, Sara M. *Born for Liberty: A History of Women in America.* New York: The Free Press, 1989.

Everhart, Janet S. "Maggie Newton Van Cott: The Methodist Episcopal Church Considers the Question of Women Clergy." *Women in New Worlds,* ed. Keller, Thomas, and Queen, 2:300-17.

Fadeley, Nancy Peacocke. *Mission to Oregon.* Eugene, Oreg., 1976.

Fagan, Ann. *This Is Our Song: Employed Women in the United Methodist Tradition.* New York: Women's Division, General Board of Global Ministries, United Methodist Church, 1986.

Forbes, Bruce David. "'And Obey God, Etc.': Methodism and American Indians." In *Perspectives,* ed. Richey, Rowe, and Schmidt, 209-27.

Fox-Genovese, Elizabeth. "Two Steps Forward, One Step Back: New Questions and Old Models in the Religious History of American Women." *Journal of the American Academy of Religion* 53, no. 3 (1985): 465-471.

———. "Religion in the Lives of Slaveholding Women in the Antebellum South." In *That Gentle Strength: Historical Perspectives on Women in Christianity,* edited by Lynda L. Coon, Katherine J. Haldane, and Elisabeth W. Sommer, 207-29. Charlottesville: University Press of Virginia, 1990.

Garza, Minerva N. "The Influence of Methodism on Hispanic Women." *Methodist History* 34, no. 2 (1996): 78-89.

Gifford, Carolyn De Swarte. "Home Protection: The WCTU's Conversion to Woman Suffrage." In *Gender, Ideology, and Action: Historical Perspectives on Women's Public Lives,* edited by Janet Sharistanian, 95-120. New York: Greenwood Press, 1986.

———. *The Defense of Women's Rights to Ordination in the Methodist Episcopal Church.* New York: Garland Publishing, Inc., 1987.

———. " 'For God and Home and Native Land': The W.C.T.U.'s Image of Woman in the Late Nineteenth Century." In *Perspectives,* ed. Richey, Rowe, and Schmidt, 309-21.

———. " 'My Own Methodist Hive': Frances Willard's Faith as Disclosed in Her Journal, 1855-1870." In *Spirituality and Social Responsibility,* ed. Keller, 81-97.

Gillespie, Joanna Bowen. "Angel's Food: A Case of Fasting in Eighteenth-Century England." In *Disorderly Eaters: Texts in Self-Empowerment,* edited by Lilian R. Furst and Peter W. Graham. University Park, Pa.: Pennsylvania State University Press, 1992.

———. "Modesty Canonized: Female Saints in Antebellum Methodist Sunday School Literature." *Historical Reflections/Réflexions Historiques* 10, no. 2 (1983): 195-219.

———. " 'The Clear Leadings of Providence': Pious Memoirs and the Problems of Self-Realization for Women in the Early Nineteenth Century." *Journal of the Early Republic* 5 (1985): 197-221.

————. "The Emerging Voice of the Methodist Woman: *The Ladies' Repository,* 1841-61." In *Perspectives,* ed. Richey, Rowe, and Schmidt, 248-64.

————. "'The Sun in Their Domestic System': The Mother in Early Nineteenth-Century Methodist Sunday School Lore." In *Women in New Worlds,* ed. Keller, Thomas, and Queen, 2:45-59.

Gonzalez, Justo L., ed. *Each in Our Own Tongue: A History of Hispanic United Methodism.* Nashville: Abingdon Press, 1991.

Gorrell, Donald K., ed. *Woman's Rightful Place.* Dayton, Ohio: United Theological Seminary, 1980.

————. "'A New Impulse': Progress in Lay Leadership and Service by Women of the United Brethren in Christ and the Evangelical Association." In *Women in New Worlds,* ed. Keller, Thomas, and Queen, 1:233-45.

Gravely, Will B. "African Methodism and the Rise of Black Denominationalism." In *Perspectives,* ed. Richey, Rowe, and Schmidt, 108-26.

Griffith, Helen. *Dauntless in Mississippi: The Life of Sarah A. Dickey, 1838-1904.* South Hadley, Mass.: Dinosaur Press, 1966.

Guillermo, Artemio, ed. *Churches Aflame: Asian Americans and United Methodism.* Nashville: Abingdon Press, 1991.

Hardesty, Nancy A., and Adrienne Israel. "Amanda Berry Smith: A 'Downright, Outright Christian'." In *Spirituality and Social Responsibility,* ed. Keller, 61-79.

Heitzenrater, Richard P. "The Meditative Piety of the Oxford Methodists." In *Mirror and Memory: Reflections on Early Methodism,* edited by Richard P. Heitzenrater, 78-105. Nashville: Kingswood Books, 1989.

Herb, Carol Marie. *The Light Along the Way: A Living History Through United Methodist Women's Magazines.* Women's Division, General Board of Global Ministries, United Methodist Church, 1995.

Hill, Patricia. "Heathen Women's Friends: The Role of Methodist Episcopal Women in the Women's Foreign Mission Movement, 1869-1915." *Methodist History* 19, no. 3 (1981): 146-47.

————. *The World Their Household: The American Woman's Foreign Mission Movement and Cultural Transformation, 1870-1920.* Ann Arbor: University of Michigan Press, 1985.

Hoover, Theressa. *With Unveiled Face: Centennial Reflections on Women and Men in the Community of the Church.* New York: Women's Division, General Board of Global Ministries, The United Methodist Church, 1983.

Hovet, Theodore. "Phoebe Palmer's 'Altar Phraseology' and the Spiritual Dimension of Women's Sphere." *Journal of Religion* 63 (1983): 264-80.

Humez, Jean M. "'My Spirit Eye': Some Functions of Spiritual and Visionary Experience in the Lives of Five Black Women Preachers, 1810-1880." In *Women and the Structure of Society [from 5th Berkshire Conference],* 129-43. Durham, N.C.: Duke University Press, 1984.

Hunter, Jane. *The Gospel of Gentility: American Women Missionaries in Turn-of-the-Century China.* New Haven: Yale University Press, 1984.

Isaac, Rhys. *The Transformation of Virginia, 1740-1790.* Williamsburg, Va.: The Institute of Early American History and Culture, 1982.

Isham, Mary. *Valorous Ventures, A Record of Sixty and Six Years of the Woman's Foreign Missionary Society, Methodist Episcopal Church.* Boston: WFMS, MEC, 1936.

"Jane Marie Bancroft Robinson." In *Notable American Women: A Biographical Dic-*

tionary, edited by Edward T. James et al., 183-84. Cambridge: Belknap Press of Harvard University Press, 1971.

Jeffrey, Julie Roy. "Ministry Through Marriage." In *Women in New Worlds,* ed. Keller, Thomas, and Queen, 1:143-60.

Jewett, Robert. "Corinthians." In *Encyclopedia of Early Christianity,* edited by Everett Ferguson, 234-36. New York: Garland Publishing, 1990.

Keller, Rosemary Skinner. "Creating a Sphere for Women: the Methodist Episcopal Church, 1869-1906." In *Women in New Worlds,* ed. Keller, Thomas, and Queen, 1:246-60.

Keller, Rosemary Skinner, ed. *Spirituality and Social Responsibility: Vocational Vision of Women in The United Methodist Tradition.* Nashville: Abingdon Press, 1993.

Keller, Rosemary Skinner, Hilah F. Thomas, and Louise L. Queen, eds. *Women in New Worlds: Historical Perspectives on the Wesleyan Tradition.* 2 vols. Nashville: Abingdon Press, 1981-82.

Knotts, Alice G. *Fellowship of Love: Methodist Women Changing American Racial Attitudes, 1920-1968.* Nashville: Kingswood Books, 1996.

Krueger, Christine L. *The Reader's Repentance: Women Preachers, Women Writers, and Nineteenth-Century Social Discourse.* Chicago: University of Chicago Press, 1992.

Lacy, Creighton. *Frank Mason North.* New York: Abingdon Press, 1967.

Lagerquist, L. DeAne. *From Our Mother's Arms: A History of Women in the American Lutheran Church.* Minneapolis: Augsburg Publishing, 1987.

Leloudis, James L. II. "Subversion of the Feminine Ideal: The *Southern Lady's Companion* and White Male Morality in the Antebellum South, 1847-1854." In *Women in New Worlds,* ed. Keller, Thomas, and Queen, 2:60-75.

Lindley, Susan Hill. *'You Have Stept Out of Your Place': A History of Women and Religion in America.* Louisville: Westminster John Knox Press, 1996.

Lobody, Diane. "Lost in the Ocean of Love: The Spiritual Writings of Catherine Livingston Garrettson." In *Rethinking Methodist History: A Bicentennial Consultation,* edited by Russell E. Richey and Kenneth E. Rowe, 175-84. Nashville: Kingswood Books, 1985.

———. " 'A Wren Just Bursting Its Shell': Catherine Livingston Garrettson's Ministry of Public Domesticity." In *Spirituality and Social Responsibility,* ed. Keller, 19-38.

———. "'That Language Might Be Given Me': Women's Experience in Early Methodism." In *Perspectives,* ed. Richey, Rowe, and Schmidt, 127-44.

Loveland, Anne C. "Domesticity and Religion in the Antebellum Period: The Career of Phoebe Palmer." *The Historian* 39 (1977): 455-71.

Lyerly, Cynthia Lynn. "Religion, Gender, and Identity: Black Methodist Women in a Slave Society, 1770–1810." In *Discovering the Women in Slavery: Emancipating Perspectives on the American Past,* edited by Patricia Morton. Athens: University of Georgia Press, 1996.

MacHaffie, Barbara J. *Her Story: Women in Christian Tradition.* Philadelphia: Fortress Press, 1986.

Magalis, Elaine. *Conduct Becoming to a Woman: Bolted Doors and Burgeoning Missions.* Cincinnati: Women's Division, Board of Global Ministries, The United Methodist Church, 1973.

Mains, George Preston. *James Monroe Buckley.* New York: Methodist Book Concern, 1917.

Mathews, Donald G. *Religion in the Old South.* Chicago: University of Chicago Press, 1977.

———. "Evangelical America—The Methodist Ideology." In *Perspectives,* ed. Richey, Rowe, and Schmidt, 17-30.

McClain, William B. *Black People in the Methodist Church: Whither Thou Goest?* Cambridge, Mass: Schenkman Publ. Co., 1984.

McFadden, Margaret. "The Ironies of Pentecost: Phoebe Palmer, World Evangelism, and Female Networks." *Methodist History* 31, no. 2 (1993): 63-75.

McKay, Nellie Y. "Nineteenth-Century Black Women's Spiritual Autobiographies: Religious Faith and Self-Empowerment." In *Perspectives,* ed. Richey, Rowe, and Schmidt, 178-91.

Meeker, Ruth Esther. *Six Decades of Service, 1880–1940: A History of the Woman's Home Missionary Society of the Methodist Episcopal Church.* Cincinnati: Women's Home Missionary Society, 1969.

Mitchell, Norma Taylor. "From Social to Radical Feminism: A Survey of Emerging Diversity in Methodist Women's Organizations, 1869–1974." *Methodist History* 13 (1975): 21-44.

Motes, Rosa Peffly. "The Pacific Northwest: Changing Role of the Pastor's Wife Since 1840." In *Women in New Worlds,* ed. Keller, Thomas, and Queen, 2:148-61.

Muir, Elizabeth Gillan. "The Legend of Barbara Heck." In *Petticoats in the Pulpit: The Story of Early Nineteenth-Century Methodist Women Preachers in Upper Canada,* edited by Elizabeth Gillan Muir, 165-78. Toronto: The United Church Publishing House, 1991.

Náñez, Alfredo. "The Transition from Anglo to Mexican-American Leadership in the Rio Grande Conference." *Methodist History* 16, no. 2 (1978): 67-74.

Náñez, Clotilde Falcón. "Hispanic Clergy Wives." In *Women in New Worlds,* ed. Keller, Thomas, and Queen, 1:161-77.

Noley, Homer. *First White Frost: Native Americans and United Methodism.* Nashville: Abingdon Press, 1991.

Noll, William T. "Laity Rights and Leadership: Winning Them for Women in the Methodist Protestant Church, 1860–1900." In *Women in New Worlds,* ed. Keller, Thomas, and Queen, 1:219-32.

———. "Women as Clergy and Laity in the 19th Century Methodist Protestant Church." *Methodist History* 15, no. 2 (1977): 107-21.

———. "A Welcome in the Ministry: The 1920 and 1924 General Conferences Debate Clergy Rights for Women." *Methodist History* 30, no. 2 (1992): 91-99.

North, Louise McCoy. *The Story of the New York Branch of the Woman's Foreign Missionary Society of the Methodist Episcopal Church.* New York: New York Branch, WFMS, MEC, 1926.

Norton, Mary Beth. *Liberty's Daughters: The Revolutionary Experience of American Women, 1750–1800.* Boston: Little, Brown and Co., 1980.

Norwood, Frederick A. *The Story of American Methodism.* Nashville: Abingdon Press, 1974.

———. "American Indian Women: The Rise of Methodist Women's Work, 1850–1939." In *Women in New Worlds,* ed. Keller, Thomas, and Queen, 2:176-95.

Pascoe, Peggy. *Relations of Rescue: The Search for Female Moral Authority in the American West, 1874–1939.* New York: Oxford University Press, 1990.

Pilkington, James Penn. *The Methodist Publishing House: A History.* Vol. 1. Nashville: Abingdon Press, 1968.

Prelinger, Catherine M., ed. *Episcopal Women: Gender, Spirituality and Commitment in an American Mainline Denomination.* New York: Oxford University Press, 1992.

Raser, Harold E. *Phoebe Palmer: Her Life and Thought.* Vol. 22, *Studies in Women and Religion.* Lewiston, N.Y.: Edwin Mellen Press, 1987.

Richardson, Harry V. *Dark Salvation: The Story of Methodism as It Developed Among Blacks in America.* New York: Doubleday, 1976.

Richey, Russell E. *Early American Methodism.* Bloomington: Indiana University Press, 1991.

Richey, Russell E., Kenneth E. Rowe, and Jean Miller Schmidt, eds. *Perspectives on American Methodism: Interpretive Essays.* Nashville: Kingswood Books, 1993.

Rowe, Kenneth E. "The Ordination of Women: Round One; Anna Oliver and the General Conference of 1880." *Methodist History* 12 (1974): 60-72.

———. "Power to the People: George Richard Crooks, *The Methodist,* and Lay Representation in the Methodist Episcopal Church." *Methodist History* 13, no. 3 (1975): 145-76.

———. "Evangelism and Social Reform in the Pastoral Ministry of Anna Oliver, 1868–1868." In *Spirituality and Social Responsibility,* ed. Keller, 117-36.

Ruether, Rosemary Radford, and Rosemary Skinner Keller, eds. *In Our Own Voices: Four Centuries of American Women's Religious Writing.* New York: HarperCollins, 1995.

Ruether, Rosemary Radford, and Rosemary Skinner Keller, eds. *Women and Religion in America.* Vol. 1, *The Nineteenth Century.* San Francisco: Harper & Row, Publishers, 1981.

Schell, Edwin. "Beginnings in Maryland and America." In *Those Incredible Methodists: A History of the Baltimore Conference of The United Methodist Church,* edited by Gordon Pratt Baker. Baltimore: Commission on Archives and History, The Baltimore Conference, 1972.

Schmidt, Jean Miller. "Holiness and Perfection." In *Encyclopedia of the American Religious Experience,* edited by Charles H. Lippy and Peter W. Williams. New York: Charles Scribner's Sons, 1988.

———. "Reexamining the Public/Private Split: Reforming the Continent and Spreading Scriptural Holiness." In *Perspectives,* ed. Richey, Rowe, and Schmidt, 228-47.

———. "Denominational History When Gender Is the Focus: Women in American Methodism." In *Reimagining Denominationalism: Interpretive Essays,* edited by Robert Bruce Mullin and Russell E. Richey. New York: Oxford University Press, 1994.

Schneider, A. Gregory. "The Ritual of Happy Dying Among Early American Methodists." *Church History* 56:3 (Sept. 1987): 348-63.

———. *The Way of the Cross Leads Home: The Domestication of American Methodism.* Bloomington: Indiana University Press, 1993.

Scott, Anne Firor. *The Southern Lady: From Pedestal to Politics, 1830–1930.* Chicago: University of Chicago Press, 1970.

———. *Making the Invisible Woman Visible.* Urbana: University of Illinois Press, 1984.

Shadron, Virginia. "The Laity Rights Movement, 1906–1918: Woman's Suffrage in the Methodist Episcopal Church, South." In *Women in New Worlds,* ed. Keller, Thomas, and Queen, 1:261-75.

Shankman, Arnold M. "Civil Rights, 1920-1970: Three Southern Methodist Women." In *Women in New Worlds,* ed. Keller, Thomas, and Queen, 2:211-33.

Shimokawa, June. "Asian American Women in The United Methodist Church." *Response: United Methodist Women* (Jan. 1978): 16-19, 47.

Shockley, Grant S., ed. *Heritage and Hope: The African American Presence in United Methodism.* Nashville: Abingdon Press, 1991.

Simmons, J. C. *The History of Southern Methodism on the Pacific Coast.* Nashville: Southern Methodist Publishing House, 1886.

Simpson, Bishop Matthew. *Cyclopedia of Methodism.* New York: Everts & Stewart, 1876.

Smith-Rosenberg, Carroll. "The Female World of Love and Ritual: Relations Between Women in Nineteenth-Century America." In *Disorderly Conduct: Visions of Gender in Victorian America.* New York: Alfred A. Knopf, 1985.

Stevens, Abel. *The Women of Methodism.* New York: Carlton & Porter, 1866.

Strong, Karen Heetderks. "Ecclesiastical Suffrage: The First Women Participants at General Conference in the Antecedents of the United Methodist Church." *Methodist History* 25, no. 1 (1986): 30-31.

Sweet, Leonard I. *The Minister's Wife: Her Role in Nineteenth-Century American Evangelicalism.* Philadelphia: Temple University Press, 1983.

Takaki, Ronald. *Strangers from a Different Shore: A History of Asian Americans.* New York: Penguin Books, 1989.

———. *A Different Mirror: A History of Multicultural America.* Boston: Little, Brown & Co., 1993.

Task Group on the History of the Central Jurisdiction Women's Organization. *To a Higher Glory: The Growth and Development of Black Women Organized for Mission in The Methodist Church, 1940–1968.* Women's Division of the Board of Global Ministries, United Methodist Church, n.d.

Tatum, Noreen Dunn. *A Crown of Service: A Story of Woman's Work in the Methodist Episcopal Church, South, from 1878–1940.* Nashville: Parthenon Press, 1960.

Taves, Ann. "Mothers and Children and the Legacy of Mid-Nineteenth-Century American Christianity." *Journal of Religion* 67 (1987): 203-19.

Terry, Robert H. "The McCurdy Mission School Story." *Methodist History* 25, no. 2 (1987): 111-26.

They Went Out Not Knowing: An Encyclopedia of 100 Women in Mission. Women's Division, General Board of Global Ministries, United Methodist Church, 1986.

Tomkinson, Mrs. T. L. *Twenty Years' History of the Woman's Home Missionary Society of the Methodist Episcopal Church, 1880–1900.* 2nd ed. Cincinnati: Woman's Home Missionary Society of the MEC, 1908.

Valenze, Deborah M. *Prophetic Sons and Daughters: Female Preaching and Popular Religion in Industrial England.* Princeton: Princeton University Press, 1985.

Vernon, Walter N., ed. *One in the Lord: A History of Ethnic Minorities in the South Central Jurisdiction, The United Methodist Church.* Bethany, Okla.: Cowan Printing & Litho., 1977.

Wakeley, Joseph B. *Lost Chapters Recovered from the Early History of American Methodism.* New York: Carlton & Porter, 1858.

Watson, David Lowes. *The Early Methodist Class Meeting: Its Origins and Significance.* Nashville: Discipleship Resources, 1987.

———. "Methodist Spirituality." In *Protestant Spiritual Traditions,* edited by Frank C. Senn. New York: Paulist Press, 1986.

Welter, Barbara. "The Cult of True Womanhood, 1820–1860." In *Divinity Convictions: The American Woman in the Nineteenth Century.* Athens: Ohio University Press, 1976.

White, Charles Edward. *The Beauty of Holiness: Phoebe Palmer as Theologian, Revivalist, Feminist, and Humanitarian.* Grand Rapids, Mich.: Francis Asbury

Press, of Zondervan Publishing House, 1986.

Will, James E. "The Ordination of Women—The Development in the Church of the United Brethren in Christ." In *"Woman's Rightful Place": Women in United Methodist History*, edited by Donald K. Gorrell, 27-40. Dayton: United Theological Seminary, 1980.

Williams, William H. *The Garden of American Methodism: The Delmarva Peninsula, 1769–1820*. Wilmington, Del.: Scholarly Resources, Inc., 1984.

Wills, David W. "Womanhood and Domesticity in the A.M.E. Tradition: The Influence of Daniel Alexander Payne." In *Black Apostles at Home and Abroad*, edited by David W. Wills and Richard Newman, 133-46. Boston: G. K. Hall, 1982.

INDEX